Minerva Series

MINERVA SERIES OF STUDENTS' HANDBOOKS
No. 24

General Editor

BRIAN CHAPMAN

Professor of Government
University of Manchester

INTERNATIONAL ECONOMICS
a general textbook

International Economics

a general textbook

BY

SIDNEY J. WELLS
Late Professor of Economics in the University of Salford

REVISED BY

E. W. BRASSLOFF
Senior Lecturer in Economics at the University of Salford

London
GEORGE ALLEN & UNWIN LTD
RUSKIN HOUSE · MUSEUM STREET

FIRST PUBLISHED IN 1969

Second Impression 1970
Third Impression 1971
Revised Edition 1973
Second Impression 1974

© *George Allen & Unwin Ltd* 1969, 1973
ISBN 0 04 330224 6 Paperback

PRINTED IN GREAT BRITAIN

in 10 *on* 11 *pt Times*

BY LOWE AND BRYDONE (PRINTERS) LTD
THETFORD, NORFOLK

PREFACE AND ACKNOWLEDGEMENTS

This book aims at meeting the oft-repeated demand by teachers and students for a modern textbook to cover the elements of modern international economics at a level appropriate to a second or third year undergraduate course, in which the student might or might not wish to specialize intensively in international economics. My object is to produce a book containing the body of knowledge with which every aspiring graduate in economics ought to be familiar, and which will at the same time provide a groundwork text upon which those who wish to specialize in international economics at postgraduate level might be able to build. For the benefit of the latter, I have indicated throughout the text the lines along which the advanced student should develop his more specialized reading—although I hope that *all* students will refuse to be content with reading this one book.

I also have in mind that a large number of intelligent people, whether university students or not, are seriously interested in a wide range of problems in international economics. In my work as an occasional extra-mural lecturer I have been most impressed by the keen desire of many people in all walks of life to become more fully acquainted with problems of the world economy. Accordingly I have tried to write this book in such a way that intelligent laymen, who have little grounding in formal economic analysis, will find their way about it without undue difficulty.

In writing a textbook it is difficult to make full acknowledgement to all the people who have played a part, directly or otherwise, in its writing. As an economist who has always been especially interested in international economic problems, I owe a debt to a large number of scholars who have influenced my thinking; notably Professors James Meade and Harry Johnson, and Dr W. M. Corden. On particular points I have tried to make full acknowledgement in text and footnotes; if there has been any omission, I trust the oversight will be forgiven. I feel that it is also appropriate to place on record the enormous debt (intellectual and personal), which I owe to Professor James Meade. My debt to James Meade as a scholar should be apparent from the following pages. My debt to him as a teacher and one-time supervisor is even more profound.

Part of the pleasure I have derived from writing this book has been due to the help received from a large number of people. Indeed it has seemed at times a truly co-operative endeavour. I am especially grateful to those who read through and commented upon the first draft, either in whole or in part. I would like to record my thanks to my colleagues at the University of Salford, Dr Wolfgang Brassloff and Mr Peter

Lomas. With Dr Brassloff I spent many hours discussing the basic framework of the book, as well as the final draft. For penetrating criticism on content I am especially indebted to Dr W. M. Corden, Nuffield Reader in International Economics at the University of Oxford, Mr Dudley Peake of the University College of North Wales, Bangor, Professor D. J. Coppock of the University of Manchester, and Mr David Robertson of the University of Reading. I also showed the draft to one of my ex-students at Salford, Miss Margaret Smith. As representing the consumer interest, Margaret Smith's comments were invaluable and, I hope, have made the book a little more acceptable to the undergraduate reader. My Secretary Miss Margaret Parker has typed and retyped seemingly endless drafts with fortitude and patience; in the closing stages of the work she has been helped by Miss Pauline Bolger of Salford University and also by Mrs Callaghan and Mrs Parker. I am grateful to Mr Reginald Oliver, who prepared the diagrams for the press. As with every piece of work I have attempted I owe a great debt to my wife, Margaret, and family who not only helped in drawing up the tables and checking facts and figures, but also provided the encouragement which every writer requires. Finally, I must thank Mr Charles A. Furth, of Allen and Unwin, who not only suggested that I should write this book but who has been a model of patience and kindliness in seeing this work completed.

SIDNEY WELLS

University of Salford
November 1968

PREFACE TO THE REVISED EDITION

With the untimely death of Sidney Wells, it has become my sad privilege to prepare this new edition. The structure of the book remains unchanged. Apart from minor corrections in the text, alterations and additions (which have been kept to a minimum) are of three kinds: reference to new analytical work done since the first edition, and to new policy problems, and updating of statistical material.

The following policy chapters have undergone the most radical changes: Chapter 11, where the recently introduced method of presenting UK balance of payments accounts in an analytically more meaningful way is discussed in the light of the 1960–71 data; Chapters 17 to 19, covering the world monetary scene, and the role of the dollar—and of sterling—as international currencies; Chapters 22 and 23, where further developments in existing integration projects are examined, including the advance to economic and monetary union in the European communities; finally, Chapter 24, dealing with the problems of underdeveloped countries as manifested in the second UN development decade and at the third UNCTAD.

I have to thank the reviewers of the book whose kind comments and criticisms have greatly assisted in the preparation of a new edition, Mr J. R. C. Lecomber of Bristol University for many extremely helpful suggestions and my friends, Professor W. R. Cook of Laurentian University and Mr N. Peera of Salford University, who have read the manuscript and offered most useful advice. My wife Audrey has helped enormously. I should also like to thank Mr Charles A. Furth of Allen and Unwin for his great patience in awaiting the new manuscript.

E.W.B.

University of Salford
December 1972

CONTENTS

CHAPTER I

WHY INTERNATIONAL ECONOMICS?

1. A CHALLENGING SUBJECT

Why do we need textbooks on international economics? What indeed differentiates economic transactions between countries from those that take place within a country? Are economic principles relating to the international economy different from those appropriate to a single country? What is special about international economics to justify separate textbooks, courses, and, in some places of learning, separate examination papers?

In many ways it is neither necessary nor desirable for the student to make a hard and fast distinction in his mind between problems in general economics and those in international economics. Indeed, the greater the number of links that he can find between general economic theory and the special field of international economics, the better will he understand the latter. My hope is that as he (or she) works through this book the reader will constantly relate what he learns to the broad body of general economic theory with which he is already familiar—or becoming familiar.

Professor Haberler[1] introduces his 1961 *Survey of International Trade Theory* by reminding his readers of the wisdom of not drawing too sharp a dichotomy between 'general' and 'international' economics:

'Strictly speaking, it is neither possible nor essential to draw a sharp distinction between the problems of foreign and domestic trade.[2] If we examine the alleged peculiarities of foreign trade, we find that we are dealing with differences in degree rather than with such basic differences of a qualitative nature as would warrant sharp theoretical divisions.'

There are nevertheless several reasons for the development of a distinctive branch of economics dealing with problems of the international economy. Some of these reasons are practical, some pedagogic.

[1] G. Haberler, 'A Survey of International Trade Theory', *Special Papers in International Economics*, no. 1, July 1961, International Finance Section, Princeton University, 1967.

[2] 'In terms of the labor theory of value, however, it is necessary to make such a distinction inasmuch as the prerequisites of this theory, occupational and geographical mobility, clearly do not exist at the international levels' (footnote in the original).

Perhaps the most obvious justification for a separate study arises from the barriers between countries which prevent the completely free movement of goods, persons and capital. These barriers may be political, social or linguistic, as well as economic. Barriers which are primarily economic take the form of customs duties, direct trade restrictions or exchange controls. Sometimes the impediments are more subtle, taking the form of elaborate customs procedures, packing requirements, health regulations and 'mixing' regulations which require the use of a given minimum quantity of a domestically produced raw material in conjunction with an imported product. Such trade barriers are rarely important enough to impede the flow of trade *within* a country; but to the extent that they are important *between* countries they give rise to a number of problems which form part of the study of international economics.

The existence of such barriers permits a country's wages and incomes structure to be different from what it would be in their absence. As we shall see later (Chapters 7 and 8) a system of import controls sometimes allows a Government to pursue internal economic policies which would be impossible or difficult in a regime of free trade as we expect to find to be present in the various regions of a single country.

The nineteenth-century classical writers in the Ricardian tradition believed that the immobility of factors of production between countries, as contrasted with their mobility within a country was the most important distinguishing feature of international trade. Although the Ricardian view is now outmoded and it is widely realized that factors do move extensively between countries (and sometimes sluggishly within a country), it still remains true that restrictions, legal or otherwise, on inter-country factor movements are much more widespread and the prevalence of these restrictions has important economic consequences.

Another justification for a special book on international economics is the differences between countries in their currency systems. Now the mere existence of different currencies is in itself of minor significance. For example, if the value of one currency in terms of another is rigidly fixed and a citizen of one country can freely convert his currency into that of any other country, the fact that one country uses pounds while another some other currency matters little. But in the real world differences in currencies often reflect more fundamental differences in economic systems and policies. In the world in which we live, the value of one currency in terms of another does change; in some cases frequently, in others only at rare intervals. Every time a change takes place, or indeed looks as if it *might* take place, a number of economic (and sometimes political) problems arise. Neither are all currencies equally acceptable; some are widely used in international trade; others are virtually inconvertible into any other currency. This consideration itself gives rise to a further set of economic problems.

Another factor—perhaps the most significant one which distinguishes international from internal economic transactions—is that, at any point in time, overall economic conditions and policies are likely to differ much more markedly between countries than within a country. Demand may be high in Britain, where incomes are rising rapidly: as the result Britons are likely to purchase more goods from France—or perhaps take more and longer holidays in that country. British residents accordingly lose foreign exchange; their holdings of French francs will decline (or their debts to French residents rise). Britain therefore, has a balance of payments deficit with France and some means must be found of correcting the deficit. The very choice of policies to correct balance of payments· disequilibrium itself gives rise to a host of problems. Should a country in deficit try to improve its balance of payments by internal deflation, by devaluation or by imposing some direct restriction on imports or currency movements? Now such questions do not arise within a country. The residents of a *region* might very well 'import' more from other regions than they 'export' to them, but no balance of payments problem would become apparent. This is because all regions use the same currency, and since they share a common banking system, the outflow of funds from the deficit to the surplus region takes the form of a transfer of balances between banks of the same country, or even between branches of the same bank. Accordingly there is little danger of a region losing all its means of payments; the fact that capital moves between regions is a source of stability. But even within a country, factors are not fully mobile and the economy of a deficit region will tend to contraction and unemployment and to re-establishment of equilibrium at a lower level of economic activity. While a country can deal with a disequilibrium by means of various policies—including exchange rate alterations—*vis-à-vis* other countries, no such alternative policies—*vis-à-vis* other parts of the country—are available to regions in disequilibrium.

Finally, if two or more regions form part of the same country it is likely that similar broad economic policies will be followed in all areas; the central Government is unlikely to follow a policy of expansion involving low interest rates and budget deficits in one region while pursuing a policy of contraction in another. However, this is not to deny that in recent years there has been a tendency for Governments to discriminate between regions in the execution of their economic policies.

For example, during the 1960s the UK Government tried (but not very successfully) to modify the harshness of some of its deflationary measures in areas of relatively high unemployment when it seemed such measures would have a particularly harmful local effect. A domestic policy differentiated in this way constitutes a regional balance of payments policy pursued not *by* a region, which has no sovereign decision-making powers, but *for* the region by a central Government. This brings us to the vital feature distinguishing international from internal transactions: the existence of national policy centres, sovereign both in respect of the regions of the country and in respect of other countries, and the consequences of its existence. It is also true that as a result of the establishment of customs unions and free trade areas there has recently been a tendency for Governments to *surrender*, and as a result of increasing trade interdependence and capital integration to *lose*, some sovereignty in the pursuit of domestic economic policies. Insofar as this happens, a national economy acquires the features of a regional economy. The growing constraints on national balance of payments policies demand growing supra-national regional policies if national disequilibria are to be avoided: in the last resort a unified market and a unified currency require a unified regional as well as general economic policy. For the time being, differences in economic policy are likely to be much more marked between countries than within a country. In the economic relations between countries these differences themselves create problems which may conveniently be studied under the heading of international economics.

The significance of policy differences should not be exaggerated. But as we shall see later (especially in Chapters 20 and 21), divergences in their internal policies often create difficulties for countries' balances of payments.

Geographical considerations also give rise to a number of special economic problems best dealt with under the umbrella of international trade theory. Countries differ in size and resource endowment. They often have their own transport systems with differences in transport tariffs and freight regulations.

So far, the reasons I have given for a separate study of international economic problems have been general ones. But the serious student should find that the specialized study of International Economics sheds a great deal of light on other aspects of his work. After all, many advances in general economic analysis had their origin in the study of specifically international economic problems. Many great economists have devoted time and energy to this particular field, and if they seem to have left us with more problems than they have solved, this itself makes the study the more exciting and challenging. Furthermore International Economics is an enquiry into ever changing facts and events. The student who perseveres with this difficult but stimulating branch of economics will know that he is not only following in a great intellectual tradition, but is trying to understand some of the most complex economic problems facing modern man.

2. ABOUT THIS BOOK

Some Important Distinctions

It has sometimes been the practice of writers of textbooks to divide their books into two parts, one concerned with Theory and another with the Application of Theory to Current Problems. Pedagogically such a practice is now little in vogue. Most teachers and students find that the understanding of economic analysis is made easier and enriched by relating theory step-by-step to the real world, while various 'applied' problems can be tackled more intelligently and satisfyingly if the student is continually relating problems arising in the real world to the theory he has learned. Accordingly, in this book I have tried to illustrate theory by application to concrete problems, while in the discussion of current economic problems I have endeavoured to suggest the kind of analytical tools the economist will want to use. Clearly there are some chapters where the emphasis is on theory rather than application but I would plead with the serious student throughout the book continually to ask the question, 'How does this piece of theory fit in with the real world?'—or in the case of a practical problem, to ask, 'What piece of economic analysis will help me in understanding or solving this problem?'

Whilst most teachers have abandoned the hard and fast distinction between Theory and Application, there is a growing realization of the distinction between what we call 'positive' or 'objective' economics on the one hand and 'normative' economics on the other. Positive economics deals with the world as it is; we are concerned not so much with policy recommendations describing the world *as it ought to be* as with the present reality of what *is*. In his excellent textbook *Introduction to Positive Economics*,[1] Professor Richard Lipsey has expressed the difference as follows:

'It is possible to classify statements into positive statements or normative statements. Positive statements concern what *is, was or will be* and normative statements concern what *ought to be*. Positive statements,

---

[1] Weidenfeld and Nicholson, London, 2nd edition, 1966, p. 4.'

assertions or theories may be simple or they may be very complex, but they are basically about what *is* the case. *Thus disagreements over positive statements are appropriately settled by an appeal to the facts.* Normative statements concern what ought to be. They are thus inextricably bound up with our whole philosophical, cultural and religious position; they depend upon our judgements about what is good and what is bad. We say that normative statements depend upon our value judgements. Disagreements may arise over normative statements because different individuals have different ideas of what is good and bad and thus of what constitutes the good life. *Disagreements over normative statements cannot be settled merely by an appeal to facts.*'

Historically, specialists in International Economics have dealt with problems in both their positive and normative aspects; sometimes without too careful a distinction between the two. For example, as we shall see later (p. 28) there has been much confusion as to whether Ricardo, in his formal statement of the principle of comparative costs, was setting out the causes of the pattern of International Trade, or trying to prove that free trade was better than protection! The former is the positive or objective approach; the latter the normative interpretation.

In the study of international economic problems it is particularly difficult to separate the 'normative' from the 'positive' aspect of many problems. As Professor Haberler wrote:

'Pre-classical writers, particularly the Mercantilists, were strongly policy oriented. Classical theory not only serves to explain the trade taking place but at the same time also provided the economic justification for free trade ideas. The "newer" neo-classical theory also generally leaned towards the free trade side, but as time went on, more and more exceptions to the free trade rules were recognized so that by now, for many theorists the position of rules and exceptions seems to be reversed.'

Haberler goes on to stress the difficulty in separating theory and policy recommendation, but argues that one need not shy away from the application of theory to problems of economic policy as long as the nature of value judgements is recognized. Accordingly, at each stage in his study, the student should be clear in his own mind whether he is dealing with problems in their positive or normative aspects. For example in an examination of the effects of devaluation, the factors influencing the elasticity of demand for a devaluing country's exports may be determined by an examination of the facts as they are known— to this extent the student is dealing with a problem in positive economics.

If, however, he goes on to say that he feels that as a matter of practical politics devaluation at a given time is the best available remedy for a balance of payments deficit, he is then making a value judgement. He has moved out of the field of positive into normative economics. The student should accustom himself to the mental discipline of continually asking whether a statement can be supported by an appeal to ascertainable facts or whether a value judgement is being made.

From the time of Marshall, it has been customary to distinguish between the 'pure' and the 'monetary' branches of International Trade Theory. As an expository device this distinction has much to commend it; for it helps the student to relate his work in International Trade to other fields of economics. Pure theory is concerned with real as opposed to monetary magnitudes, its subject matter being the theory of value or price in its international context. Much tariff theory and such questions as the determination of the pattern of international trade and the terms of trade, fall within its purview. International monetary economics, on the other hand, is concerned with general monetary and employment theory in an international setting; it deals with such problems as balance of payments equilibria, exchange rates, the transmission of business fluctuations between countries, and the international implications of domestic economic growth. The whole field of monetary international economics has in recent years been fairly intensively worked over and a number of exciting changes have occurred in the approach to problems in this area.

The Plan

Our study starts with a discussion of one of the fundamental problems in the Pure Theory of International Trade; namely the question of what determines the pattern of International Trade: why should a country export x or import y rather than export y and import x? Closely linked with this question (indeed in the classical tradition, inextricably entwined with it) is the normative question of the advantage which a country derives from International Trade: is it better for a country to export x and import y rather than to try to be self-sufficient in both x and y? These matters are the subject of Chapters 2 and 3 of this book. In Chapter 4 we see what economists have had to say about the terms of trade between countries, and discuss the various methods used to measure changes in these terms. The student is then asked to examine the nature of free trade and protection—matters dealt with in Chapters 5 and 6. Arguments for interference with free trade are advanced in Chapter 7 and 8. Chapter 9 deals with the vexed question of the freedom of factor movements: if trade in commodities is quite free, is it necessary also to ensure the free movement of capital and labour? Chapter 10 deals with a branch of international trade theory which is very young indeed; the relationship between economic growth and trade.

In Chapter 11 we move into the field of international monetary economics, discussing the problem of drawing up a country's balance of payments statement. In Chater 12 we examine the effect of income changes in one country upon its balance of trade and the economies of its trading partners. In the following Chapters, 13, 14 and 15, we examine the implications of the different international monetary regimes. Chapter 16 deals with the important question of the relationship between internal and external equilibrium and the appropriate policies for securing both objectives. Chapters 17 and 18 are concerned with the development of the International Monetary Fund system, and recent suggestions for its reform, while Chapter 19 deals with the special problem of the UK and sterling. In Chapters 20 to 23 we examine some problems of economic integration; in these chapters we make an assessment of some post-war attempts at integration. Finally in Chapter 24 there is an examination of perhaps the most intractable world economic problem in recent years, namely the special problems of the developing countries.

It is hoped that the reader who perseveres through this book will feel at the end that, although he has learnt something, he has still a vast amount more to learn. At best a textbook should be like an iceberg, showing but a fraction of the vast bulk of material which makes up the whole study. If, after working through it, the student comes to regard this book as an introduction to an exciting field of economic science, and feels moved to acquaint himself at first hand with some of the more detailed and more distinguished texts, then its writing will be abundantly worthwhile.

CHAPTER 2

COMPARATIVE COSTS:
SOME PAGES OF HISTORY

It is perhaps more true of international trade theory than any other branch of economics than an appreciation of past theory is necessary for a full understanding of present approaches. Accordingly, in this chapter we see how modern comparative cost theory has evolved from the (sometimes crude) theories of the past.[1] Most students find that time spent on the development of ideas helps them to understand more fully the complexities of modern trade theory.

1. MERCANTILISM

The Balance of Trade

Until the end of the eighteenth century, most statesmen believed in what came to be known as the mercantilist approach to trade. Mercantilism took many forms, but essentially it was a belief that national power depended upon national economic wealth. Wealth was at this time equated with possession of the precious metals, and a nation aspiring to greatness would try to amass as large as possible a stock of gold and silver. Since a country's stock of bullion increased when exports exceeded imports, a corollary of mercantilism was the attempt to build up a surplus of exports over imports. This excess was accordingly referred to by the mercantilists as a favourable balance of trade—a term which Viner tells us was first used in 1767.[2] Little account was taken of the fact that it was impossible for all countries simultaneously

---

[1] The best and most scholarly study of the evolution of international trade theory to the 1930s is to be found in Jacob Viner's *Studies in the Theory of International Trade*, London, G. Allen and Unwin, 1937. The story is brought up to date in two excellent Special Papers published by the International Finance Section of Princetown University, the first by Gottfried Haberler (*Special Papers*, no. 1, July 1961), 'A Survey of International Trade Theory'; the second by W. M. Corden (*Special Papers*, no. 7, March 1965), 'Recent Developments in the Theory of International Trade'. Many of the issues raised in this chapter are discussed at length by Richard E. Caves, *Trade and Economic Structure*, University of Harvard Press, 1963; and by M. O. Clement, R. L. Pfister, and K. J. Rothwell, *Theoretical Issues in International Economics*, London, Constable & Co., 1967.

[2] Although 'balance in our favour' had been used much earlier—by John Cary in 1695. J. Viner, cited above, p. 10.

to achieve a 'favourable' balance of trade.[1] To those accepting mercantilist principles, trade was a means of national political aggrandize-
ment; its object was power rather than plenty. Mercantilist ideas were
never universally accepted, and economic policy measures associated
with them were often enforced only half-heartedly. But, until well into
the eighteenth century, they were the ideas which influenced the
attitudes of most statesmen and economists towards overseas trade.

Hume and Adam Smith

Growing criticism of mercantilist doctrine, was sharpened in the
middle eighteenth century by David Hume, who, in his *Political
Discourses*, in 1752 argued that the conscious pursuit of a favourable
balance of trade was not only foolish, but was certain to fail. Hume
argued that if a country's exports increased more than its imports, the
resulting inflow of gold would itself automatically lead to an increase
in domestic money supply; in accordance with the Quantity Theory of
Money, a raising of domestic prices would follow.[2] On the other hand,
abroad, the outflow of gold to the surplus country and the consequent
reduction in money supply would cause a fall in prices. The raising of
the surplus country's domestic prices and the lowering of the deficit
country's prices would tend to bring about a fall in the surplus country's
exports and an increase in its imports—thus automatically correcting
the original imbalance. Thus Hume claimed to show that given a free
market in bullion, and internal price flexibility, any attempt by a
country to build up a long-term favourable balance of trade was

[1] It should be remembered that the accumulation of bullion was but one aspect—
and not necessarily the most important aspect—of mercantilism. The essence of the
system was the creation of a 'balanced' economy which, it was believed, could
guarantee independence. The broader objectives of mercantilism are fully examined
by E. Lipson, *The Growth of English Society*, London, A. C. Black Ltd, 1949.

A wide variety of measures was adopted to secure a 'favourable' trade balance;
these included tariffs and prohibitions on imports, the encouragement of domestic
production and export by subsidies, and restrictions on the outflow of precious
metals. Other, less direct, devices were Navigation Laws encouraging the transport
of goods in ships owned or manned by nationals of the home country. In addition
there were often controls on the economic policies of colonial territories. See Lipson,
quoted above, pp. 142 ff.

[2] As Viner points out, Hume was by no means the first writer to show an understanding of the self-regulating mechanism of the balance of trade. 'But he stated the
theory with a degree of clarity, ability of exposition, and emphasis of importance . . .
which most of these early writers did not even distantly approach.' Viner, cited
above, p. 84.

One obvious deficiency in Hume's analysis was his uncritical acceptance of a
crude Quantity Theory of Money.

fore-doomed to failure. Mercantilist policies carried the seeds of their own destruction.

Hume's approach to the effect of gold movements upon prices and the balance of trade was naïve in the extreme, but to mercantilist contempories his conclusions were a searching challenge. An even more significant challenge was to come in 1776, with the publication of Adam Smith's *Wealth of Nations*.[1] Smith applied his famous principle of Division of Labour to specialization among countries. He was critical of all measures preventing specialization, arguing that just as attempts at self-sufficiency by individuals or households resulted in a loss of the advantages of specialization, so also did such attempts among countries. Adam Smith argued that so far from creating wealth and adding to national prosperity, policies for self-sufficiency resulted in a net reduction in prosperity and human welfare. Having demonstrated the advantages of specialization within a country, he went on to show how similar gains could be derived from division of labour among nations.

'It is the maxim of every prudent master of a family, never to attempt to make at home what it will cost him more to make than buy. The tailor does not attempt to make his own shoes, but buys them from the shoemaker. The shoemaker does not attempt to make his own clothes but employs a tailor. The farmer attempts to make neither the one nor the other, but employs those different artificers. All of them find it for their interest to employ their whole industry in a way in which they have some advantage over their neighbours, and to purchase with a part of its produce, or what is the same thing, with the price of part of it, whatever else they have occasion for. What is prudence in the conduct of every private family, can scarce be folly in that of a great kingdom. If a foreign country can supply us with a commodity cheaper than we ourselves can make it, better buy off them with some part of the produce of own industry, employed in a way we have some advantage.'[2]

The corollary of Smith's reasoning was that impediments to free trade were undesirable and should be abolished. However, he accepted that in a world of established trading restrictions it was sometimes necessary to move with some caution towards free trade—he conceded, for example, that where large numbers of workers were engaged in a heavily protected industry 'humanity may in this case, require that freedom of trade should be restored only by slow gradations.'[3] But of

[1] Adam Smith, *An Inquiry into the Nature and Causes of the Wealth of Nations*, London, 1776. Page references to E. Cannan edition, 1937.

[2] Ibid. pp. 423.

[3] Ibid. p. 435. Smith accepted also that foreign trade restrictions might be necessary for defence, and for this reason he felt unable to condemn the Navigation Acts.

the advantages of free trade as a general rule he was in no doubt. Hume and Smith between them provided the intellectual justification for those anxious to see greater freedom of trade between nations. But this did not mean that victory for free trade was secured, either in the realm of ideas or in practical policy-making. Such a victory has indeed never been fully achieved; but from the end of the eighteenth century advocates of free trade were equipped with a set of logical and intellectually respectable arguments with which to argue their case. It is important to realize the limitation of Adam Smith's free trade argument. He demonstrated that two countries would gain from specialization when one was more efficient than another at producing product x but less efficient than its partner at producing y. But it was left to a later writer, Ricardo, to show that there might be a gain even when one country was better than its partner at producing *both* products. This was the famous principle of comparative cost advantage.

2. COMPARATIVE COSTS

Ricardo

Many students find the principle of comparative costs difficult. Usually, the difficulty disappears when they remember that the principle is a general one which applies to individuals as well as to nations. A barrister might be a better gardener than the man he employs to grow his fruit and vegetables. But if his superiority over his gardener is more marked in law than in gardening, it pays him to concentrate on law, leaving the cultivation of the garden to an employed worker. Since his time and energy are limited he cannot become a professional in both spheres—although of course he might be a keen spare-time gardener. It is better for him to concentrate on his professional efforts in law, where his advantage is greater.

David Ricardo in his *Principles of Political Economy* (1817) was the first writer systematically to apply this principle of comparative advantage or comparative costs to trade between countries.[1] In doing so, Ricardo made a substantial advance from Adam Smith's position. Whereas Smith showed that trade between two countries was profitable

---

[1] See P. Sraffa (ed.), *The Works and Correspondence of David Ricardo*, Cambridge University Press, 1951, vol. 1, *On the Principles of Political Economy and Taxation*, Chapter VII.

Other writers before Ricardo had realized the principle of comparative cost advantage. But, to quote Marshall, it was Ricardo who 'built a number of fragmentary truths into coherent doctrine'. For a full discussion of this question see Jacob Viner, cited above, p. 441.

if each had an *absolute* advantage over the other in the production of a commodity, Ricardo showed that gain was also possible in cases where one country had an absolute advantage over the other in the production of *both* commodities, but where its advantage was greater in one commodity than in the other.

Ricardo illustrated the principle of comparative cost by his famous example of trade between Portugal and England. He assumed that Portuguese labour was more efficient than English labour at producing both wine and cloth; but the gap in efficiency was wider in wine-making than in cloth-making. To produce a given quantity of cloth in England required 100 men working for one year while a given quantity of wine would require the labour of 120 men. The production of the same quantities of cloth and wine in Portugal would require a year's labour from 90 and 80 men respectively. Now England could either make a given quantity of wine, or could obtain this quantity in exchange for cloth. Ricardo showed that it was better to follow the latter course. One hundred Englishmen would in one year produce enough cloth to exchange for the amount of wine it would take 120 of them to produce at home. Similarly, in Portugal, 80 men could produce enough wine to exchange a quantity of cloth which would require 90 men's labour at home. As Ricardo himself expressed the principle:

'Though she (i.e. Portugal) could make the cloth with the labour of 90 men, she would import it from a country where it required the labour of 100 men to produce it, because it would be advantageous to her rather to employ her capital in the production of wine, for which she would obtain more cloth from England, than she could produce by diverting a portion of her capital from the cultivation of vines to the manufactures of cloth.'[1]

Ricardo did not discuss the actual ratio at which wine and cloth would exchange (this was a matter to be taken up later by J. S. Mill),[2] but he did demonstrate that both countries would gain from trade so long as England could obtain more wine from Portugal than could be produced at home employing 120 men for one year and provided Portugal could obtain from England more cloth than could be produced at home with the labour of 90 men.

The situation as outlined by Ricardo could not exist within a single country, for if one region in a country were more efficient than another in making both wine and cloth, labour and capital would move into the favoured region, all production ultimately being concentrated there. But

[1] P. Sraffa, *The Works and Correspondence of David Ricardo*, cited above, p. 136.
[2] See Chapter 4, below.

since he assumed factors are not mobile between countries, differences in costs can persist. Accordingly, Ricardo's analysis rested upon the relative immobility of factors of production between countries and their relative mobility within a country. Labour and capital might move freely between, say, the manufacturing and agricultural sectors within a country but could not move easily from one country to another.

Before examining some of the criticisms levied against Ricardo, it is worth reminding ourselves what he and his successors were trying to do. The principle of comparative costs as it evolved over the nineteenth century was made to serve two distinct but interrelated purposes. Firstly comparative cost theory is used to explain the *pattern* of international trade; in this sense it may be regarded as an attempt to isolate those influences determining the course of international trade. It tries to answer such questions as 'why does country A export *x*, while country B exports *y*?' In the original Ricardian example, the most important factor affecting the pattern of international trade was the difference in labour time costs. This is the 'explanatory' or 'positive' interpretation of Ricardian comparative cost theory. On the other hand, the doctrine has been used as a 'proof' of the *advantage* of free trade. This is comparative cost theory used in its 'normative' or 'welfare' sense. It is not clear in which sense Ricardo himself used the approach, and his interpreters in the nineteenth century oscillated between the 'positive' (i.e. the pattern-explaining) approach, and the 'normative' (i.e. the proposition that trade is beneficial) approach.[1] The comparative cost approach has perhaps stood the test of time rather as a welfare justification of the advantage of free trade than as an explanation of why trade takes place; illustrations similar to Ricardo's wine and cloth example are used even today as 'proof' of the advantages of free trade.

Although Ricardo's method of approach has now been superseded both as a demonstration of the advantages of free trade and as an explanation of trade patterns, to assert that it has been replaced by other, more modern approaches implies no belittlement of his intellectual achievement. Ricardo was a pioneer, and as with all pioneers in the realm of human thought, his ideas have been modified,—in some respects almost out of all recognition—by his successors. It is to an examination of these modifications that we must now turn.

Ricardo couched his doctrine in labour time costs, but he did not

[1] Professor Bhagwati, in his 'The Pure Theory of International Trade: A Survey', *Economic Journal*, March 1964, argues that although Ricardian theory can be construed in either of the two ways, there is good evidence that Ricardo himself regarded the theory as primarily a demonstration of the *advantages* of free trade. This implies that Ricardo believed that he had developed a 'normative' theory.

imply that these were the only costs of production. Neither did he accept without reservation that the amount of *time* devoted to producing a commodity always reflected the amount of 'real' effort put into its production. But, as stated by Ricardo, the doctrine assumed that, in general, prices in international trade corresponded to relative labour time costs. Thus England concentrated on producing cloth rather than wine because of difference in labour *time*.

Senior and Mill

Ricardo's emphasis upon labour time costs invited—and certainly attracted—criticism. Only a few years after the publication of Ricardo's *Principles*, another classical writer, Naussau Senior, pointed out that it was misleading to explain trade primarily in terms of labour time, since money cost differentials might reflect productivity differentials rather than differences in the length of labour time required to produce a commodity. Senior drew attention to the very obvious fact that trade takes place because of differences in goods prices. These prices reflect labour costs expressed in money rather than in labour *time*. Labour cost differences are in turn influenced by differences in productivity. Accordingly, Senior fixed attention on labour productivity rather than on the relative amount of labour time devoted to producing various products.

Senior argued that the 'diligence and skill' with which English labour was applied enabled 'one English labourer' to make in a year the equivalent of what eight workers might produce elsewhere. He not only lifted comparative cost doctrine out of the narrow confines of a labour time theory; he also emphasized the importance of money wage-rates, in determining international trade patterns.[1] Of course Ricardo himself had realized that the immediate cause of international trade was to be found in differences in goods prices, but he assumed that in general such differences reflected labour-time costs. Ricardo would have said that, if the labour-time cost of producing x was 10 per cent higher than that of producing y, the export price of commodity x would be 10 per cent higher than that of commodity y. Senior, by directing attention to the importance of money costs and productivity differences, emphasized that there might be cases in which exports did *not* accurately reflect labour time cost differences.

A similar criticism of Ricardo was advanced by J. S. Mill,[2] who argued that since special factors might depress wages in certain

---

[1] N. W. Senior, *Three Lectures on the Cost of Obtaining Money*, 1830.
[2] J. S. Mill, *Principles of Political Economy*, ed. Ashley, 1920, pp. 680–687.

industries (for example, slavery in the cotton states of the U.S.A.), but not in other industries in the same country, the products of those industries whose wages were 'artificially' low might sell at relatively low prices. These low prices would not, however, reflect relatively low real labour costs, but merely the fact that workers in the industries concerned were receiving artificially low wages. In other words, the relatively low export prices of cotton from Georgia would not reflect Georgia's real comparative cost advantage in producing cotton, so much as the fact that a high proportion of plantation labour received artificially depressed wages. In such a case the pattern of trade would not reflect real labour cost ratios. Indeed, it is conceivable that if slavery had been abolished, and a truly free labour market established, Georgia might have had a comparative cost advantage in some commodity other than cotton. Like Senior before him, Mill believed that such cases were exceptional.

Some twenty years after the publication of Mill's book, however, J. E. Cairnes[1] made a more fundamental attack on Ricardo. Cairnes suggested that so far from being exceptional, cases where relative money wage costs failed to reflect relative real labour costs were the rule rather than the exception. He believed that this situation was a result of the lack of mobility between different wage earning groups in a country: internal immobility enabled one group of workers to enjoy more or less permanently a level of remuneration which did not accurately reflect any real advantage which they had over their fellow countrymen in other sectors of the economy. Within a country there existed non-competing labour groups.

Few, if any, of Ricardo's followers believed that labour costs were the only costs entering into production; they rather used the term 'labour cost' as a kind of shorthand to cover all 'real costs'.[2] For example, they were not unduly worried by differences in capital costs between countries, believing that capital was really a form of 'stored-up' labour, and that in any case it was so evenly employed in the traded goods sector that this constant proportion could be neglected. Accordingly, in the classical statement, comparatively little attention was paid to the significance of capital in trade theory.

However, a number of writers substituted for Ricardo's 'labour' cost various other real cost measures. Marshall, for example, endeavoured to include capital and other production costs along with labour costs by his use of the concept of a 'representative bundle' of a nation's

---

[1] J. E. Cairnes, *Some Leading Principles of Political Economy Newly Expounded*, 1874, pp. 66–68.
[2] On this see Viner, cited above, pp. 489 ff.

factors of production,[1] while, earlier, Bastable had used the idea of a 'unit of productive power' consisting of 'a given amount of labour working with an average amount of capital'.[2] All these were attempts to develop a more realistic measure of costs than one which took account only of Ricardo's labour time costs. But they had in common the notion that differences in comparative *real costs* determined comparative advantage. Classical writers in general tried to show that international trade reduced the *real cost* of obtaining a given level of income, whether this real cost were measured in terms of labour hours or in some more sophisticated cost unit. A country had a comparative advantage in producing *x* rather than *y* because the real cost (or the effort, or the relative 'disutility') in making *x* was less than in making *y*.

Taussig

Although each made a valuable contribution to theory, neither Senior, Mill, nor Cairnes attempted a full examination or reformulation of Ricardo's doctrine. This was left to Taussig who, in 1927, published what was up to that time perhaps the most systematic analysis of the doctrine of comparative costs, as developed by Ricardo and the English classical writers. Ricardo's ideas stood up rather well to Taussig's scrutiny. Indeed, Taussig's work may be regarded as in many respects almost a twentieth-century *apologia* for Ricardo's labour cost doctrine.[3]

Taussig paid very careful attention to the role in international specialization of factors other than labour costs—in particular he examined the part played by the relative cost of capital, namely relative interest rates. He also examined in some detail the significance of the non-competing groups discussed by Mill and Cairnes. Taussig carried out a fairly full study of the importance of capital as a determinant of comparative cost advantage. He concluded that his analysis provided a qualified justification for the emphasis placed by Ricardo upon *labour* as opposed to other costs. Taussig pointed out that if one country has a substantially higher interest rate structure than its trading partners, this does not by itself affect the pattern of comparative costs. The high rate of interest, provided it applies to all fields of production equally, simply results in higher absolute costs in the country concerned. Comparative costs are in no way affected. But a rate of interest higher in one country than in another does affect the conditions for trade when the amount of capital used in production is greater in one commodity

[1] A. Marshall, *Money, Credit and Commerce*, London, 1923, Appendix J.
[2] C. Bastable, *The Theory of International Trade*, p. 24.
[3] F. W. Taussig, *International Trade*, 1927.

than in another. The higher rate of interest bears more heavily on those commodities embodying much capital, making them relatively more expensive in the country with the higher rate of interest. Thus interest rate differences can cause the pattern of international trade to diverge from what it would be if determined only by labour costs, or if interest rates between countries were equal. But this divergence occurs only if the higher rate of interest affects a commodity more in country A than in country B, and if conditions of production in the two countries are such that more capital is required in, say, clock making in country A than in country B. Taussig believed that even in this special case any influence of interest rate differentials upon production costs was limited, since as between the industrialized countries of Western Europe interest differentials were small, and it was in trade between such countries that comparative as opposed to absolute cost differences were important.

Taussig also took up the question of Cairnes' 'non-competing groups'. Taussig did not deny the existence of such groups; the absence of mobility between town and country might perpetuate a situation where workers engaged in say wheat growing might be paid less than those in factories. Accordingly, wheat might be cheap as compared with linen, although an equal amount of real effort had gone into producing both commodities. But Taussig argued that the existence of non-competing groups within a country could affect international trade only so far as the situation was peculiar to that country. If, in the United States, wheat growers' wages were depressed to the same extent *vis-à-vis* linen producers' as those of wheat growers in Germany *vis-à-vis* linen producers in that country, then (to quote Taussig) 'trade takes place exactly as if it were governed by the strict and simple principle of comparative costs'.[1] When what he described as the 'hierarchy' of these non-competing groups is on similar lines in each country, trade opportunities would be exactly as if prices within each country were governed by labour costs alone. He believed that throughout the relatively developed countries these hierarchies are arranged in approximately the same order. Thus both on the score of capital charges and of non-competing groups, Taussig believed there to be little justification for departing from the basic argument of Ricardian doctrine, namely that countries would gain from trade if there existed differences in comparative labour costs.

The criticisms of classical comparative cost doctrine examined by Taussig were not the only ones raised during the nineteenth and early

[1] F. W. Taussig, *International Trade*, 1927, p. 48.

twentieth centuries. A number of writers attacked the classical position on the grounds that it presupposed a two country two commodity world. Others lamented the absence of any discussion of transport costs. The assumption of Ricardo and his followers that costs were constant was also called into question. A number of writers in the classical tradition tried to accommodate comparative cost theory to the real world situation where more than two commodities normally exchange between two countries. Perhaps the best known and most useful contribution in this field was that of von Mangoldt,[1] summarized and developed in English by Edgeworth.[2] The Mangoldt-Edgeworth approach admits that in a many-commodity world, a knowledge of real costs alone is insufficient to show which commodities will be imported and which exported by any given country. In order to determine the pattern of import export trade, one needs to know the relative money wage rates in the two countries. If this ratio were to change—if for example, wages rose more in country A than in country B, then certain goods which had been exported by A may no longer be exportable; they might even become imports.

Transport Costs

An obvious omission in our discussion so far is the absence of any consideration of transport costs. Early international trade theory paid very little attention to transport costs, an omission which applied also to much other economic analysis. The existence of transport costs may well effect the profitability and pattern of international trade. If the cost of transporting a product from country A to country B is greater than the difference in domestic prices of the product in the two countries then some trade which would have taken place in the absence of transport costs will no longer occur.[3]

[1] H. von Mangoldt. *Grundriss der Volkswirthschaftslehre*, 2nd edition, 1871. The whole question is fully examined by Jacob Viner, *Studies in the Theory of International Trade*, cited above, pp. 453–462.

[2] F. Y. Edgeworth, *Papers Relating to Political Economy*, vol. ii, 1925. Edgeworth explained this with the aid of a simple diagram, showing that as money costs in country A rose relative to those in B, certain products, instead of being exported by A, become exports of B. The diagram is produced by Viner, cited above, p. 459.

[3] The theory of transport costs and location has now become a specialized study. The reader anxious to pursue the subject further is referred to W. Isard, *Location and Space Economy*, New York, John Wiley and Sons, 1956. There is a useful summary of some of the literature in C. P. Kindelberger, *International Economics*, R. D. Irwin, Homewood, Illinois, pp. 101 ff. There is also a valuable study on the role of transport costs in intra-European trade by W. Beckerman 'Distance and the Pattern of Intra-European Trade', *Review of Economics and Statistics*, February 1956.

Varying Costs

Classical theory has also been criticized for its assumption of constant costs. It is arguable that if a country has a comparative cost advantage in an industry subject to increasing costs but a disadvantage in a decreasing costs industry it may not be desirable to specialize in the former. The more sophisticated criticism along these lines is that of F. D. Graham.[1]

Graham assumes that country A initially has a comparative advantage in watch-making, country B in wheat growing. Suppose that in both countries, watch making is subject to decreasing costs, and wheat growing to increasing costs; then as country A expands its output of watches, its watch-making industry will enjoy increasing economies of scale, while, as wheat output decreases, its wheat producers benefit from falling unit costs. Its gain from the transfer of resources is a clear one. But in the case of country B, the expansion of its wheat production involves higher costs whilst the contraction of watch making results in increasing costs. Thus in country B the productivity of labour will fall in both industries. Graham's analysis may be criticized at many points, but perhaps the most fundamental weakness of his exposition is his treatment of decreasing costs. As Knight has shown, Graham failed to distinguish between the significance of internal and external economies.[2]

Let us briefly consider Knight's objections to Graham's thesis. If we assume first that the economies are internal to the watch-making firms in the two countries there will be a tendency towards monopoly in this industry—since the larger the firm the greater the internal economies of scale. Ultimately, one firm will produce all the watches. But even if we assume that this position is not reached, and competition is still effective, there will be no movement of productive factors from watch making to wheat growing in country B, unless the gain from the additional output of wheat is at least equal to the loss in income resulting from the reduction in output of watches. In the case of internal economies there can be no transfer of resources unless transfer results in an increase in marginal product. Thus it is inconceivable that any transfer from watch making to wheat growing will occur if a loss in the value of the product results. No producer of watches will switch to wheat production unless he gains thereby.

[1] F. D. Graham, 'Some Aspects of Protection further Considered', *Quarterly Journal of Economics*, vol. xxxvii, 1923, pp. 199–216.

[2] F. H. Knight. 'Some Fallacies in the Interpretation of Social Cost', *Quarterly Journal of Economics*, vol. xxxviii, 1924, pp. 592–604. There is also a useful criticism of Graham's analysis by Viner in his *Studies in the Theory of International Trade*. A further set of criticisms has been advanced by R. E. Caves, *Trade and Economic Structure*, Harvard University Press, 1963.

If, however, the economies and diseconomies are external to the firm, then the individual producer, in determining his output, will not be influenced by the effect of changes in *his* output upon unit costs. Thus a number of watch making firms might contract their output in switching over to wheat production, but since all the diseconomies of a smaller output are *external* to the individual firms, they will not prevent any single firm from contracting. Whereas in the case of internal diseconomies each firm (or the monopoly firm) could detect higher marginal costs as it varied its own output, such a change in costs would not be apparent in the case of external economies. Accordingly, the switch from decreasing-cost watch making to increasing-cost wheat growing *could* occur. But as Viner points out there is only a very limited field for the practical application of this particular case.

Firstly, many external economies are a function of the world, not of a national industry. Thus, if the reduction in size of a national watch-making industry is matched by an expansion of this industry in another country, then such economies, as the industries in both countries derive from being part of the world industry, would in no way be reduced. Such advantages as a national watch-making industry derives from being part of a large world-wide industry would remain although it had itself contracted.

Secondly, if the external economies enjoyed by a firm are national, but also entirely pecuniary—that is to say if they rest on the fact a firm can obtain its domestic supplies relatively cheaply simply because it is a member of a large industry, then although the expansion of the industry results in lower money costs to the firm, e.g. cheaper purchase of raw materials, these advantages are purely pecuniary, accruing to the firm, not the nation. The disappearance of such economies, while unfortunate for the firm, would in no way diminish the welfare of the country as a whole. Accordingly, Viner argues that the only conceivable case where Graham's argument is justified and increasing and decreasing returns invalidate comparative cost theory, is (a) where economies are external to a firm, and (b) where these external economies depend upon the size of the national, as against the world industry, and (c) where they are technological rather than pecuniary.

Graham's argument is of course very relevant to the whole question of protection. Graham himself argued that it might be necessary to give protection to an industry, operating under decreasing costs, even if such an industry had a permanent comparative cost disadvantage. As we shall see in Chapter 7, there are powerful arguments for the adoption of protection by a country anxious to implement a development programme, and part of this justification rests upon the achievement of scale economies in industry. But as it stands, Graham's argument is hardly a strong justification for protection.

One of the neatest attempts to incorporate increasing costs into traditional trade theory is that of Sir Roy Harrod, who by means of very simple tables shows that as trade takes place, the fact of increasing and/or decreasing costs might well erode the initial advantages of differing comparative costs.[1] Harrod assumes that one country has initially a comparative cost advantage in producing wheat, while another has a comparative cost advantage in coal production. If we assume that both products are subject to increasing cost, then as the country which has a comparative cost advantage in coal production increases its coal output but decreases its output of wheat, its unit cost of coal production will rise while its unit cost of wheat production will fall. Conversely, the unit cost of production of producing coal abroad will rise, while the unit cost of producing wheat abroad will fall. We can conceive of trade taking place until a situation is reached when the ratio of the cost of producing wheat to that of producing coal at home is equal to this ratio abroad. At this point there will be no gain from further trade, although *both* countries are producing some coal and some wheat. Clearly the greater the initial disparity in cost ratios as between the two countries, the larger the volume of *profitable* trade.

As regard the possibility of decreasing costs, Harrod points out that it is conceivable that, if economies of scale are sufficiently great, one of the countries will produce enough of its export commodity (say coal) to enable it to purchase all the imports of wheat it requires, before trade has reached the point where internal cost ratios in the two countries are equalized. But of course, in this situation, where production of wheat has been abandoned by one country, there is in a sense no 'cost ratio', in that country. The country does not produce the commodity and hence the question of different comparative cost ratios does not arise. Sir Roy Harrod's stimulating book first appeared just at the time when quite fundamental changes were taking place in attitudes towards the real cost theory of international trade. It is to some of these changes that we turn in the following chapter.

SHORT GUIDE TO THE LITERATURE

The fullest discussion of the classical approach to international economics is in J. Viner's detailed work *Studies in the Theory of International Trade*, London, Allen and Unwin, 1937. The student interested

[1] R. F. Harrod, *International Economics*, Cambridge University Press, 1960, reprint.

in the history of economic thought will wish to follow up the footnote references in Viner as well as those in this chapter. A very useful book, which summarizes clearly the development of classical trade theory, is S. E. Harris' *International and Interregional Economics*, New York, McGraw-Hill, 1957 (especially Chapters 1–7).

CHAPTER 3

COMPARATIVE COSTS: SOME MODERN VIEWS

1. OPPORTUNITY COST

In the 1930s, fundamental changes were occurring in attitudes towards the real cost theory of international trade. One of the most significant developments was the appearance in 1933 of Professor Gottfried Haberler's *Theory of International Trade*.[1] This book, still widely read and quoted, is a most distinguished study, and includes a careful analysis of many aspects of trade theory. Haberler himself was sympathetic to the classical tradition (and a stalwart advocate of free trade), but in his book pleaded for a restatement of international trade theory in terms of opportunity rather than real cost. He argued that as opportunity cost had taken the place of real cost theorizing in general economic analysis; so should opportunity cost be applied also to international trade theory. Since the modern approach to trade theory is based on opportunity cost the student should make sure that he grasps this method of analysis—and the very simple geometry that goes with it.

With a given factor endowment, a country can produce various combinations of commodities. Let us follow Haberler by assuming that a country possesses only two factors of production, labour and capital. With these factors it can produce two commodities, wheat and cloth. At one extreme the country can produce all wheat and no cloth; at the other it can produce all cloth and no wheat. Or it can produce some of each commodity. In either case what we call a country's production possibilities are limited by its factor endowments. The greater the quantity of wheat that is produced, the less cloth will be manufactured and *vice-versa*.

Some Geometry

In figure 1 the amount of wheat that can be produced in country A is shown on the horizontal axis, and quantities of cloth on the vertical axis. When all factors are fully employed, country A can produce either OW units of wheat, or OC units of cloth. By producing less

[1] *The Theory of International Trade with its Applications to Commercial Policy*, London, W. Hodge and Co., 1936, translated from the German.

wheat it can increase output of cloth. Thus, if only OW_1 of wheat is produced, OC_1 of cloth may be obtained. Alternatively the combination OW_2 plus OC_2 is possible. Accordingly, in order to produce the extra quantity C_1C_2 of cloth, the quantity W_1W_2 of wheat must be foregone. Since we have drawn the curve pp concave towards the origin, to obtain a given increment in cloth output increasing amounts of wheat must be surrendered. If the amount of wheat required to be given up to obtain a given quantity of cloth were constant, whatever the quantity, pp would be a straight line.

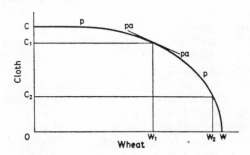

FIGURE 1. Production Possibility Curve.

If the marginal cost of producing more wheat in terms of cloth were decreasing, the slope would be convex towards the origin; increasing quantities of cloth would then be obtainable for given reductions in wheat output.

If one or other factor is specific to production of a given commodity the substitution of one type of product for another will not easily be achieved; the curve will have a marked 'bulge'. If it is quite impossible to transfer a factor of production between cloth output and that of wheat, the curve pp would be inverted 'L' shape. In practice the production frontier would shrink to a single point. This curve, whatever its shape, is referred to in various ways; Haberler himself christened it the substitution curve. Samuelson later used the term production possibility curve, while Lerner described it as the production indifference curve. It is often known also as the transformation function. In this book I generally use the term 'production frontier'; since this gives the idea that the curve shows the maximum possible output of a commodity with a given factor endowment. It is the frontier, beyond which production cannot be carried unless there is some increase in factor supplies or improvement in factor utilization. Whatever description we choose, the curve shows us the 'cost' of getting a little more wheat in terms of cloth, or *vice-versa*. The reader will of course note that we are not measuring the cost of producing wheat, in terms of labour, or 'bundles' of factors, or indeed in terms of any 'real' cost, but in the amount of cloth foregone in order to produce one more unit of wheat. This is of course the opportunity cost concept, so familiar in general economic analysis.

Now let us suppose that we have a closed economy, and one where no market imperfections exist. Price ratios reflect marginal cost ratios. In this case, the price of wheat in terms of cloth reflects the marginal rate of substitution of the one for the other in production, or, to use slightly different terminology, marginal rates of transformation. If this were not so, there would be an incentive for producers to switch from, say, growing wheat to producing cloth in order to take advantage of the relatively favourable price ratio. Now the actual amounts of wheat and cloth produced will clearly depend upon both the shape of production frontier and demand conditions. It is conceivable that the marginal rate of substitution in consumption of cloth in terms of wheat is such that the price of wheat in terms of cloth would be relatively low. On the other hand, the reverse could be the case. We can show the price ratio between wheat and cloth by means of a *price line*. In figure 1 this is depicted by the line pa. It is clear that production will take place at the point where the line pa is tangential to the production frontier pp. At no other point would the marginal rate of substitution of wheat in terms of cloth in consumption be equal to the marginal rate of transformation in production.

Our model relates to the absence of market imperfections, this term being regarded as a kind of shorthand for those elements in the market which cause price ratios to diverge from marginal transformation ratios. The most obvious of these is the absence of perfect competition between sellers; another is the presence of Government or other institutional intervention in the market by the granting of subsidies or by indirect taxation. If, for example, the Government imposes a purchase tax on the consumption of cloth but not on wheat, the price ratio between cloth and wheat will diverge from the marginal rate of transformation between the products.

Let us now suppose that, like country A, country B can produce either cloth or wheat; in figure 2 the concave curve represents the marginal rate of transformation of cloth in terms of wheat. Inspection shows that the curve pp_1 is parallel to the curve pp_2 in figure 2, but that at all points, country B can produce more of both products than A. Thus country B has an absolute cost advantage over country A in both products. But because the gradients are identical in both countries, the marginal rates of transformation and hence the price ratios in the two countries are also identical. In other words, country A can get its cloth as cheaply by domestic production as by employing factors of production to produce wheat, and exporting the wheat in exchange for cloth. There is no advantage in trade taking place—unless of course the pattern of demand is different in the two countries, in which case there can still be gain from trade.

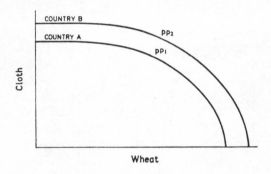

FIGURE 2. Production Possibility Curves for Countries A and B.

It is, however, likely that the production possibility frontier in B has a different shape from its counterpart in A. If so, then in the absence of market imperfections, the price ratios in the two countries will also differ. If these price ratios are different, countries gain from trading one with the other. Accordingly it is vital for the student to understand that the advantage of trade depends upon the *shapes* of the production possibility curves being different, not upon whether or not they are in identical positions in regard to the origin.

Figure 3 depicts the case where the production possibility frontier of country B differs in shape from that of A. From this it is clear that in country B, as contrasted with country A, conditions favour the production of cloth rather than wheat. At the point where the price ratio between cloth and wheat lies, a considerable amount of cloth has to be given up in order to produce a little more wheat.

Now the apparatus developed by Haberler enables us to show what happens when trade takes place. In figure 3 we depict B's production possibility frontier in the case where the marginal ratio of transformation differs from that in A. The price ratios between wheat and cloth also differ between the two countries. In figure 3 the slopes of the tangents NTA and NTB representing the price ratios between the two products before trade in countries A and B respectively, clearly differ. Since wheat is relatively cheap in terms of cloth in country A, country B will gain by purchasing wheat from A, exporting some of its relatively cheap cloth in exchange. Country A will gain by producing more wheat and less cloth. Country B will produce more cloth and less wheat, while country A will produce less cloth and more wheat. Since the countries

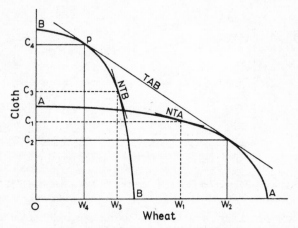

FIGURE 3. The Gains from Specialization.

are now freely trading together, however, there can be only one price ratio between wheat and cloth, which is determined by the interaction of demand and supply in both countries together. This ratio we can represent by the line TAB, depicting the ratio of exchange after trade between A and B has been opened up. Each country now produces quantities of wheat and cloth until the respective marginal rates of transformation of wheat in terms of cloth are exactly equal to the new price ratio.

Country A will contract output of cloth in which it is relatively inefficient from OC_1 to OC_2, but will expand output of wheat from OW_1 to OW_2. Country B on the other hand, will contract output of wheat in which it is relatively inefficient from OW_3 to OW_4, but will expand output of cloth from OC_3 to OC_4. Country A now produces OW_2 of wheat, but exports W_4W_2, leaving OW_4 for domestic consumption. Country B imports W_4W_2 wheat from A, but itself produces only OW_4, making its total consumption equal to OW_2. Country A on the other hand, has curtailed its production of cloth to OC_2, but imports C_2C_4 from country B. Its total consumption is therefore OC_4. Country B exports C_2C_4 of cloth, but retains OC_2 for domestic consumption. From country A's viewpoint, more cloth is obtained for every unit of wheat surrendered than was the case before trade; the slope of TAB is greater than NTA. For country B, more wheat is obtained for every unit of cloth surrendered than before trade; the slope of TAB is less steep than NTB.[1]

Neither country is entirely specialized, but at the point at which trade settles, there is no gain from additional trade and specialization. Residents in each country obtain goods in the production of which their country is relatively inferior at prices lower than if no trade (or less trade) took place. It is in fact true that although residents in country A can consume more cloth than before trade (OC_4 as against OC_2), they nevertheless have less wheat than before trade (OW_4 as against OW_1). In view of their decreased consumption of wheat after trade can we be sure that as a community they are in fact better off? Does the increased consumption of cloth more than compensate for the decreased consumption of wheat? Modern welfare economics suggests that the post-trade position is better than the pre-trade position if those individuals who gain in welfare as the result of the change can fully compensate those who suffer, and still be better off. This is an application of the compensation principle, which is of course an important tool in general welfare economics.

2. THE HECKSCHER-OHLIN APPROACH

Haberler's approach to international trade theory lifts it out of a real cost strait-jacket in which it had been held for so many generations. It demonstrates that where production possibilities differ countries will gain from freer trade. But it does not take us very far along the road towards explaining *why* production possibilities differ between countries. Why does the production possibility curve in country B differ from that of country A? Such an explanation was in fact provided by Bertil Ohlin in 1935.[2] Ohlin based his analysis on a hitherto little-read work of

[1] Only exceptionally will one line TAB, the line representing the new price, be tangential to the post-trade output positions of both country A and country B as in this example. In most cases, two lines parallel to each other will represent the new international price ratio.

[2] B. Ohlin, *Interregional and International Trade*, Harvard University Press, 1935.

one of his mentors, the Swedish economist Eli Heckscher.[1] Heckscher emphasized the differences in factor endowments of countries as a pre-requisite for profitable international trade. His article (in Swedish), appeared just after the end of the First World War and was little read outside his own country; it certainly failed to receive the attention it deserved. Ohlin, however, developed Heckscher's ideas into a fuller explanation of the pattern of international trade.

Factor Endowments

According to Ohlin, trade between nations is profitable when it enables them to take advantage of their differing *factor endowments*. In a country relatively rich in natural resources, for example land, but with a small labour force, land-intensive products are relatively cheap, whilst labour intensive products are relatively dear. Such a country will tend to export products with a relatively high 'land' content for example, arable crops, importing those with a relatively high labour content, eg. manufactures. Unlike Ricardian comparative cost doctrine, Ohlin's approach takes account of a multiplicity of factors. It also differs from the traditional English classical approach in emphasizing differences in relative quantities of factors rather than differences in relative qualities. Ohlin holds that the most important *raison d'être* of international trade is the differing endowments of regions or countries with the various factors of production. He accepts, however, that even if two countries are equally endowed, opportunities for profitable trade might still exist since differences in factor prices (and hence in export product prices) could arise from differences in demand patterns between the two countries. These demand patterns could be dissimilar as the result of different patterns of income distribution, or differences in tastes and institutional arrangements. Dissimilar domestic demand conditions in prospective trading countries might offset differences in factor endowments.[2] Accordingly, a country might be relatively rich in a certain type of labour, but if internal demand for the products of that labour is sufficiently great, the advantage might be fully offset.

In this connection it is important to note the distinction between relative abundance of a factor in the sense of physical quantity and of cheapness. In the latter sense, the price of a factor depends upon demand as well as supply; the influence of demand may well outweigh

[1] Eli Heckscher, 'The Effect of Foreign Trade on the Distribution of Income', *Ekonomisk Tidskrift*, vol. xxi, 1919, reprinted in *Readings in the Theory of International Trade*, Allen and Unwin.

[2] This and related points are examined by R. E. Caves in *Trade and Economic Structure*, Harvard University Press, 1963, pp. 28 ff.

that of supply. Accordingly it is possible for a country to be physically well endowed with say, capital, but for domestic demand conditions for capital intensive goods to be such that the price of capital is relatively high; so that exports are labour rather than capital intensive. A further complication arises from the fact that it is sometimes technically possible to substitute one factor for another at the margin if relative factor prices change. When factor-substitution is feasible, a rise in, say, wage rates might cause hitherto labour intensive goods to become capital-intensive ones. We have an instance of what is known as factor intensity reversal.[1]

Ohlin's book is a long one; it is rich in empirical studies and illustrations supporting the central thesis that the explanation for a given trade pattern lies in differences in factor endowments. But the contribution of Ohlin and Heckscher to international trade theory does not end there, for what has become known as the Heckscher—Ohlin approach (H-O for short) has led to notable advances in a wider field of trade theory.

Trade and Income Distribution

In his book Ohlin presented a somewhat static theory,[2] but it is a short step from arguing that the trade pattern is a function of factor endowments to a realization that these endowments are themselves affected by trade. Accordingly one of the most fruitful results of the H-O approach is an awareness of the relationship between trade and domestic economic structure. In particular it raises directly the question of the impact of trade upon income distribution within a country. Heckscher argued that free trade tends to equalize the relative returns to factors of production among trading nations. Thus if Australia is well endowed with land and relatively poorly endowed with labour, while the opposite is true of Britain, Australian wheat will be relatively cheap and Australian manufactures relatively dear. British wheat, on the other hand, will be relatively dear and British manufactures relatively cheap. Australia then exports wheat to Britain in exchange for manufactures. But the additional demand for Australian wheat results in a raising of the returns to land in Australia—and hence an increase

---

[1] There is a substantial literature on factor-intensity reversals; much of it suggests that the phenomenon is sufficiently frequent to be empirically important. The question has been investigated by B. S. Minhas, *An International Comparison of Factor Costs and Factor Use*, Amsterdam, North Holland Publishing Co., 1963.

[2] It should be noted, however, that Ohlin accepted that the supply of factors 'may sometimes more adequately be described as the result of trade than its cause', p. 67. The question is also discussed by Caves, cited above, pp. 102 ff.

in rents, while the decline in demand for British wheat causes rents in Britain to fall. On the other hand, wages in British manufacturing industries rise, since British factories are supplying the Australian markets as well as the domestic one, while in Australian manufacturing industry wages fall, since manufactures are being supplied from Britain. Accordingly, there is a tendency for free trade to force down British rents but raise Australian rents, and to force down Australian wages but raise British wages. There is a tendency towards international equalization both of rents and wage rates. Free trade thus results in some income redistribution. In our example, the redistribution favours wage earners to the detriment of land-owners in Britain, but in Australia land owners gain at the expense of industrial workers.[1]

If in trading countries, the relative returns to factors of production are changed in the way outlined above, free trade has an effect on relative factor prices similar to an international movement of the factors themselves. Thus relative wage rates in Britain can be raised either by an increase in the demand for those British products with a high labour content, or by a movement of labour away from Britain to a country where it is relatively less abundant. Free trade thus becomes a substitute for the movement of factors. Economists have argued as to whether free trade is a partial or complete substitute for factor mobility. Ohlin himself was careful to argue that free trade would not completely equalize factor prices between the trading countries; in other words, free trade was only a partial substitute for the free movement of factors. We shall, however, take up this question in Chapter 9 where we examine more fully the relationship between trade and factor movements.

In certain respects, the Heckscher-Ohlin doctrine fits neatly into the story of the development of pure trade theory. It takes us one stage further back from the Haberler approach by explaining what lies behind comparative cost differences. On the other hand, as an explanation of trade patterns there are important differences between the Heckscher-Ohlin view and traditional comparative cost doctrine. The classical position assumes that difference in productivity of one factor—namely labour—is the main explanation of differences in trade patterns. The Heckscher-Ohlin model on the other hand assumes a multiplicity of factors. Secondly, traditional comparative cost theory emphasizes differences in relative factor inputs as between countries; for example in one country *more* labour is required to secure a given output of a

---

[1] The relevance of this analysis to the argument for protection as a means of income redistribution is examined in Chapter 8.

commodity than in another country. Country A produces cotton goods with less labour in relation to other factors than country B. Implicit in this approach is the idea that a different amount of labour in association with other factors is required in one country than in another, or to use a slightly more technical expression, *production functions* differ between countries. Ohlin, on the other hand, assumes that as between countries production functions are identical. To produce a given commodity, the same combination of factors is required in country A as in country B. The advantage which one country has over another is in its relatively abundant endowment of a particular factor or factors. As we shall see below (p. 52) there is some doubt, as to whether production functions are identical between countries. In fact, the two approaches rest on not only different, but mutually exclusive assumptions.[1]

3. TESTING THE THEORIES

MacDougall and Comparative Costs

Both the classical comparative cost doctrine of the earlier writers and the factor proportions theory of Ohlin have been subject to testing in the last twenty years. In 1951 Sir Donald MacDougall tested classical comparative theory by examining labour productivity in those industries where one of the trading countries appeared to have a comparative cost advantage as shown by its export performance.[2] MacDougall tried to determine whether a country's exports tended to be concentrated in those industries where labour productivity was above average. His starting point was the fact that before the Second World War, the United States weekly wage in manufacturing was about twice as high as that of the United Kingdom. In some industries US output per worker was more than twice as great as that of the United Kingdom; in others it was less. MacDougall tried to see whether products of the former industries, that is those where US labour appeared to have a comparative cost advantage, were those where the US was more successful than the UK in the export market. Similarly, he asked whether the UK had an advantage in exports where its labour productivity was more than half that of the United States.

[1] See J. Bhagwati, 'The Pure Theory of International Trade' in *International Trade Theory in a Developing World*, ed. Harrod and Hague.

[2] G. D. A. MacDougall, 'British and American Exports; A Study suggested by the Theory of Comparative Costs', *Economic Journal*, part I, December 1951, part II, September 1952.

MacDougall found that the UK did in fact appear to be more successful in those products where its labour productivity disadvantage was
least marked. For the year 1937, in each of the twenty-four industries
which he examined US output per worker was higher than in the UK,
but in twelve industries it was more than twice as high. In these twelve
industries, there were seven cases where US exports were larger than
those of the UK, in five cases they were smaller. But in all the twelve
cases where US output per head was not more than double that of the
UK, exports from the latter country were larger than from the US.
MacDougall's results seemed to justify the classical emphasis upon
relative labour productivity in determining the pattern of trade flows.
On the other hand some of his results invited further discussion and
some cases are difficult to explain. There are, for example, instances
where in the US productivity just offsets the high wage level, but so far
from equalling UK exports those from the United States appeared to be
only about 40 per cent as large. MacDougall suggests that Commonwealth preference might be one explanation for differences of this kind.
In fact there are many factors which might account for this situation;
for example differences in the import content of the two countries'
exports.[1]

A more fundamental difficulty in the technique used by MacDougall
arises from the possibility of differences in inter-industry wage leveis
distorting output ratios. Thus it could be that although the US had a
comparative cost advantage in particular industries owing to relatively
high labour productivity, this advantage is offset by the fact that money
wages in such industries are higher than the average. This could arise
from the existence of non-competing groups of labour, a matter dealt
with half a century ago by Taussig.[2]

Later Studies

A recent test of comparative cost theory was carried out by Professor
Bela Balassa, who examined productivity in the UK and the US in
twenty-eight industries. The industries he analysed covered about
42 per cent of manufacturing output in each country. Balassa found a
high correlation between productivity and export performance in
third country markets,[3] not only were productivity ratios in particular
industries not always offset by money wage differences but differences

[1] Richard E. Caves, *Trade and Economic Structure, Models and Methods*, Cambridge, Massachusetts, Harvard University Press, 1963, p. 269.

[2] See above, p. 32.

[3] B. Balassa, 'An Empirical Demonstration of Classical Comparative Cost Theory',
Review of Economics and Statistics, August 1963.

in capital cost per unit appeared also to have little influence upon exports. Balassa's results tend to bear out Taussig's conclusion that neither wage differences resulting from non-competing groups within a country or differences in capital costs are as important as productivity differences in determining the pattern of trade.

Further verification of Taussig's contention that, although non-competing groups exist in many countries, the structure of these is roughly the same in all industrial countries, (see p. 32) is shown by the work of I. B. Kravis.[1] According to Kravis, US and Japanese data suggest that the ranking of industries by hourly earnings of workers in different countries are almost identical. He also notes the tendency of competition in the labour market to bring about a clustering of wages 'around the national average afforded by the nation's general level of productivity'. Thus the research of MacDougall and Kravis provides some evidence that differences in labour productivity are important, perhaps the most important influence affecting the pattern of international trade. To this extent the assertions of traditional labour comparative cost theory are confirmed.

Testing the H–O Approach: Leontief

How has the Heckscher–Ohlin factor endowment theory stood up to the test of empirical analysis? The Heckscher–Ohlin analysis leads us to believe that a country exports products embodying relatively intensive inputs of factors abundant in that country, while importing products containing substantial inputs of factors with which it is less well endowed. Thus if a country is well endowed with capital, but poorly endowed with labour, one would expect its exports to be capital intensive while its imports are labour intensive. An early test of this was made by MacDougall in the course of the 1951 study referred to above. He tried to discover whether US exports were relatively more capital intensive than those of the UK. MacDougall's criterion for capital intensiveness was the amount of horse-power used in the various industries. His results showed that the UK did *not* have a relatively smaller, and the United States a relatively larger share in the market in capital intensive commodities. To this extent his conclusions shed some doubt on the validity of the H–O approach. A much fuller study of the question was however made by Wassily Leontief in 1954.[2]

[1] I. B. Kravis, 'Availability and other influences on the Commodity Composition of Trade', *Journal of Political Economy*, April 1956.
[2] W. W. Leontief, 'Domestic Production and Foreign Trade; the American Capital Position re-examined', *Proceedings of the American Philosophical Society*, September 1953. Leontief's paper was printed in *Economia Internazionale*, 1954.

Leontief computed the direct and indirect capital and labour required to produce a given value of output in a number of US industries. He then assumed that the United States transfers the factors of production, formerly engaged in export industries to import replacement. If the United States is relatively more capital intensive than her trading partners, one would expect the contraction in export industries to release relatively more capital and relatively less labour than the import replacement industries absorb. The ratio of capital to labour would be lower in the import-replacement industries than in the export industries. Leontief's results, however, showed quite clearly that the ratio of capital to labour is higher in the import replacement industries than in the export industries. Accordingly, Leontief concludes that 'American participation in the international division of labour is based on its specialization in labour intensive rather than capital intensive lines of production. In other words this country resorts to foreign trade in order to economize its capital and dispose of its surplus labour, rather than *vice-versa*.'[1]

What has become known as Leontief's paradox has called forth a substantial literature of its own. Clearly there was something to explain in Leontief's somewhat astonishing results and writers in international trade theory have had a most exciting time analysing the paradox. Leontief himself tried to explain it by suggesting that the US was not in fact relatively better supplied with capital than other nations, if one took into account the superior physical effectiveness of American labour. He suggested that one American worker is perhaps as effective as three foreign workers; if true this would imply that America was not in fact poorly endowed with labour. Although in the US, the working population might appear to be numerically small in relation to the capital stock, the quality of the labour is such that the *effective* supply is relatively great. Another line of criticism was developed by Buchanan, who claimed that Leontief's contribution neglected the role of natural resources which were very important in determining trade patterns.[2] In a study of US natural resources, Jaroslav Vanek has shown that the United States is relatively under-supplied with these.[3] Since capital and natural resources are complementary in many fields of production Vanek suggests that although capital is relatively abundant in the US, it may be less effective in terms of production because

---

[1] Leontief, cited above, p. 25, 1954.

[2] N. S. Buchanan, 'Lines on the Leontief Paradox', *Economia Internazionale*, November 1955.

[3] J. Vanek, 'The Natural Resource Content of United States Foreign Trade 1870–1955', *Harvard Economic Studies*, 1963.

capital inputs require substantial amounts of scarce natural resources. Accordingly the US may not be able to make full use of its capital.

A number of commentators have criticized the Leontief paradox on statistical and methodological grounds. Swerling argued that the inclusion of certain industries with low capital labour ratios excessively influenced Leontief's results.[1] In response to such criticism Leontief reworked his sums by taking a much wider coverage of the United States industries but the results were very similar to those of the original study.[2] Romney Robinson has suggested that demand conditions within a country might be so biased towards consumption of a product embodying a relatively abundant factor of production that its relative abundance is neutralized by a high level of domestic demand. Likewise a country well endowed with capital may import the capital intensive commodity if it has reached the level of real income at which its income-elasticity of demand for such goods is high. Similarly a labour endowed country may export a capital-intensive product if its income level at the margin is such that it chooses to use the labour-intensive product at home.[3] As regards the first point, Professor A. J. Brown has however shown the American consumption patterns do not appear to be biased towards capital-intensive goods; rather the reverse.[4] W. P. Travis has suggested that tariffs often distort the pattern of trade which would reflect relative factor endowments. He argues thet Leontief's results are seriously affected by the US and foreign tariffs. Factor endowment cannot be expected to determine trade patterns in a tariff-ridden world.[5]

A widely discussed criticism of Leontief is that of Professor P. T. Ellsworth.[6] Ellsworth's central criticism is that the capital intensity of United States import replacement industries is irrelevant to the comparison. What is really required is a comparison of the capital intensity of US exports with the capital intensity in the countries which produce

[1] B. C. Swerling, 'Capital Shortage and Labour Surplus in the United States', *Review of Economics and Statistics*, August 1954.

[2] W. W. Leontief, 'Factor proportions and the structure of American Trade: Further Theoretical and Empirical Analysis', *Review of Economics and Statistics*, November 1956.

[3] Romney Robinson, 'Factor Proportions and Comparative Advantage', *Quarterly Journal of Economics*, vol. lxx, May 1956, pp. 169–192. Reprinted in R. E. Caves and H. G. Johnson *Readings in International Economics*, American Economic Association, London, Allen and Unwin, 1968.

[4] A. J. Brown, 'Professor Leontief and the Pattern of World Trade', *Yorkshire Bulletin of Economic and Social Research*, November 1957.

[5] W. P. Travis, *The Theory of Trade and Protection*, 1964.

[6] P. T. Ellsworth, 'The Structure of American Foreign Trade. A New View Examined', Review of Economics and Statistics, August 1954.

US imports. Since America is a capital rich country, and employs capital intensive production methods import replacements would naturally use relatively more capital to produce similar goods than the countries supplying them to the US. It is not surprising that to make in America goods normally imported from other countries would require a higher capital to labour ratio than is typically found in American export industries. Leontief considers import replacements in terms of American productive practice. What he really ought to do is to see whether goods imported into America are capital or labour intensive *in the countries of origin.*

A cornerstone of Professor Ellsworth's criticism is that *production functions,* that is ways of producing goods, are not identical as between countries. Rice can be produced in Burma with abundant labour and little capital, or it can be produced as in the southern USA, with little labour and abundant capital. Ohlin assumed that production functions were similar the world over, and Leontief tacitly also assumed this in his analysis. In fact goods which the US makes *and* imports, e.g. cotton textiles, may be capital intensive in the US but labour intensive in their countries of origin. The assumption of identical production functions no longer holds. It is along these lines that much of the 'explaining' of the Leontief paradox has taken place.

Other Evidence

The Leontief approach as a test of the factor endowment theory has been applied to a number of other countries. One of these is Bharadwaj's study on India.[1] Bharadwaj shows that India's exports to the US turn out to be capital intensive while its imports from the United States are labour intensive! This rather surprising result appears to refute the Heckscher-Ohlin analysis. But here again it is possible that production methods differ widely as between the US and India. Other studies are those of Stolper and Roskamp for East Germany,[2] Tatemoto and Ichimura for Japan[3] and Wahl for Canada.[4] In the case of the Stolper

[1] R. Bharadwaj, *Structural Basis of India's Foreign Trade* (Series in Monetary and International Economics, no. 6), University of Bombay, 1961, and 'Factor Proportions and the Structure of Indo-US Trade', *Indian Economic Journal* vol. 10, October 1962.

[2] W. Stolper and K. Roskamp, 'Input-Output Table for East Germany with Applications to Foreign Trade', *Bulletin of Oxford University Institute of Statistics,* vol. 23, no. 4, November 1961.

[3] M. Tatemoto and S. Ichimura, 'Factor Proportions and Foreign Trade: The Case of Japan', *Review of Economics and Statistics,* vol. 41, November 1959.

[4] D. F. Wahl, 'Capital and Labour Requirements for Canada's Foreign Trade', *Canadian Journal of Economics and Political Science,* vol. 27, August 1961.

and Roskamps study of East German trade for 1956 they find that exports are capital intensive while imports are labour intensive; this would be in line with the Ohlin–Heckscher approach since three-quarters of East German trade is with the Communist block, of which East Germany is one of the most highly industrialized members.

The Tatemoto and Ichimura study of the foreign trade of Japan with the world as a whole suggests that her exports are capital, and imports labour, intensive—a surprising result from Ohlin theorizing. But as the authors of this study point out, some three quarters of Japan's exports go to less developed countries, which are relatively *less* well endowed with capital than Japan. In trade with the United States, Tatemoto and Ichimura found imports from the United States to have a higher capital labour ratio than Japanese exports to the United States, a result in line with the Ohlin theory. Thus disaggregation suggests that in the case of Japan, as with East Germany, there is a correspondence between export patterns and factor endowment. On the other hand, Wahl found that for Canada, exports are capital intensive and imports labour intensive. Since the bulk of Canadian trade is with the United States, this result seems to refute the Ohlin-Heckscher approach. Clearly much more research remains to be done in this very intricate field; so far we really know very little about the precise relationship between any country's pattern of trade and its factor endowment.

4. SOME LATER IDEAS

The trade theory which we have outlined, from Ricardo to Ohlin has much to commend it. Intellectually, it must be regarded as a remarkable achievement; provided its simplifying assumptions are always recognized, the theory can help us to understand and solve many practical problems. Even when its highly limiting assumptions prevent a detailed application to a real world problem, the theory can often be of great value in clarifying and isolating the important issues.[1] But in spite of its immense value, the pure theory of comparative costs, how-ever expressed, has in recent years attracted criticism from a number of quarters.

Several modern writers have been concerned at the seeming inability of traditional doctrine to explain satisfactorily the pattern of interna-tional trade in manufactured goods. The H-O approach emphasizes differences in factor endowments as a cause of trade between nations.

[1] On this subject I can do no better than refer the reader to Dr Corden's *Recent Developments in the Theory of International Trade*, cited above, pp. 30 ff.

But the overwhelming proportion of trade in manufactures takes place between countries of *similar* economic structure. Factor endowments of the countries of the European Economic Community and the UK do not differ substantially; yet a substantial and growing volume of trade takes place between these countries. One of the most interesting criticisms of the H–O approach as applied to trade in manufactures is by S. Linder,[1] who argues that so far from being explicable by *differences* in factor endowments, trade in manufactures is explained by *similarity* in demand patterns. In contrast to much earlier theorizing, the Linder approach emphasizes the role of demand conditions in making trade worthwhile. A country is normally able to export a sophisticated manufactured good to another country only if it has a buoyant home market for the product. The more similar the market conditions are in the two countries, especially in regard to income levels, the greater the prospect of successful export performance in any given product. Accordingly it would seem that two conditions are necessary for the trade to take place. Firstly, economies of scale in the home market must be such as to enable a country to manufacture a product sufficiently cheaply for it to be competitive in export markets. Secondly, general economic conditions in those export markets must be rather similar to those in the domestic market. These conditions are, of course, satisfied over a wide range of products in the modern western world.

In an interesting article in 1961, Michael Posner sets out to explain some of the causes of the pattern of trade in manufactured goods between advanced countries.[2] Why does country A, whose economy is very similar to that of country B, export commodity x to B and import commodity y from B? If economic conditions are similar in the two countries there seems no reason why this particular pattern of trade takes place. Why does A export x, and not y? Posner argues that a substantial volume of trade is caused simply because technical changes and developments happen in A rather than B. An invention occurs in country A: for a period A has a comparative cost advantage over B in this particular product. The advantage last until either a similar cost reducing invention is made in B, or until A's innovating firm sells its patent to B. By the end of this period, A's initial advantage will have disappeared. Clearly, in such a case we have a phenomenon which as Posner himself expresses it 'does not come neatly under the umbrella of traditional analysis'.

A rather different criticism of the Heckscher–Ohlin approach comes

[1] S. B. Linder, *An Essay on Trade and Transformation*, New York, J. Wiley, 1961.
[2] M. V. Posner, 'International Trade and Technical Change', *Oxford Economic Papers*, vol. 13, October 1961.

from Kravis, who argues that the determinant of trade pattern is 'availability' or supply elasticity within trading countries rather than their relative factor endowments.[1] Kravis also argues that in the real world the volume and pattern of trade depends much more upon various controls and interventions, e.g. domestic agricultural support programmes, than on relative factor endowments. It should be obvious to the student that there can be no simple explanation for the pattern of trade between any particular group of countries at any given point of time. The Heckscher–Ohlin factor endowments approach helps us in our search for explanations, but it needs to be modified in the light of some of the considerations stressed by the later writers.

SHORT GUIDE TO THE LITERATURE

There is a voluminous literature on the subject matter of this chapter, and the student is referred not only to the footnotes of this chapter but also to the useful bibliographies in W. M. Corden, 'Recent Developments in the Theory of International Trade', *Special Papers in International Economics*, no. 7, Princeton University, March 1965, in G. Haberler, 'A Survey of International Trade Theory', *Special Papers in International Economics*, no. 1, Princeton University, 1961 and J. Bhagwati, 'The Pure Theory of International Trade', *Economic Journal* vol. lxxiv, no. 293, March 1964, pp. 1–84. All three of these studies should be regarded as 'musts' by the keen student. It is quite impossible to list here all the important books and articles—Professor Bhagwati's bibliography contains 142 items. But especially worthy of note are (a) R. E. Caves' *Trade and Economic Structure*, Cambridge, Mass., Harvard University Press, 1960, which covers much of the ground of this chapter, (b) G. Haberler, 'Some Problems in the Pure Theory of International Trade', *Economic Journal*, vol. lx, no. 238, June 1950, pp. 223–240, reprinted in *Readings in International Economics*, ed. R. E. Caves and H. G. Johnson, London, Allen and Unwin, 1968 and (c) Romney Robinson, 'Factor Proportions and Comparative Advantage', *Quarterly Journal of Economics*, vol. lxx, no. 2, May 1966, pp. 169–192, reprinted in *Readings in International Economics* cited above.

[1] I. B. Kravis, 'Availability and other Influences on the Commodity Composition of Trade', *Journal of Political Economy*, vol. 64, April 1965, pp. 143–155.

CHAPTER 4

THE TERMS OF TRADE

1. THE EARLY APPROACH

We saw in Chapters 2 and 3 that the principle of comparative costs shows that there is a gain from trade if the ratio of domestic costs as it would be under self sufficiency diverges from the ratio at which goods are exchanged internationally. Ricardo himself paid little attention to the question of how much gain accrues from trade, or how gain is divided between the trading partners. In his illustration, trade takes place between England and Portugal at a point when the gain appears to be divided almost equally between the countries; there is, however, no evidence that he believed that this would always be the case. He might equally well have framed his example to give the greater part of the gain to one or other of the countries. It was left to J. S. Mill[1] to examine in some detail this question of the division of gains from trade.

Ricardo showed that comparative cost ratios determine the limits between which goods might profitably be exchanged. No country would surrender a given quantity of commodity x in exchange for y, unless the amount of y obtained is at least as great as the amount which could be produced at home as an alternative to producing the given quantity of x. Similarly, the trading partner country would not surrender a given quantity of y, unless the amount of x obtainable by trade was at least as great as the amount which could be produced at home as the alternative to y. Thus comparative costs set the outer limits between which trade takes place. But within these limits the actual ratio at which the exchange takes place depends upon the demand of the two countries for each others products, or what we call reciprocal demand. Accordingly, if the citizens of country A are desperately anxious to buy a good y from country B, but the citizens of country B are for some reason less anxious to buy good x from country A, then the greater part of the gain from trade accrues to country B. The ratio at which the goods exchange, that is the 'terms of trade' are more favourable to B than to A.

J. S. Mill

Mill illustrates what he calls the Equation of International Demand by assuming that Germany and England each produce both cloth and

[1] J. S. Mill, *Principles of Political Economy*, London, 1848.

linen. In England the real cost of producing 10 yards of cloth is equivalent to the real cost of producing 15 yards of linen, while in Germany
10 yards of cloth cost as much to produce, in real terms, as 20 yards of
linen. England therefore concentrates on cloth, Germany on linen
production. The ratio at which exchange takes place lies between the
limits 10 yards of cloth = 15 yards of linen, and 10 yards of cloth =
20 yards of linen. In his example, Mill assumes domestic demand
conditions in the trading countries to be such that 10 yards of cloth =
17 yards of linen, showing that England gains rather less than Germany
from the trade.

Mill goes on to analyse the consequences of an improvement in the
technique of German linen production, which has the effect of reducing
the cost of producing linen in that country by one third. In Germany
linen is now more plentiful, and a greater quantity of linen than hitherto
exchanges against ten yards of cloth. The terms on which linen will
exchange against cloth have become 'less favourable' to linen. The
extent to which the ratio of international exchange of one commodity
in terms of the other changes, depends not only on the relative abundance of linen in Germany, but also the reaction of English purchasers
to the reduction of its price in terms of cloth. In other words, it will
depend upon the elasticity of demand in England for linen in terms of
cloth. If this elasticity is low, that is, if Englishmen are reluctant to give
up more cloth in order to obtain a little more linen, English consumers
will purchase relatively little additional linen, in spite of its cheapness.

As Mill himself expressed the position: 'When two countries trade
together in two commodities, the exchange value of these commodities
relatively to each other will adjust itself to the inclinations and circumstances of the consumers on both sides, . . . in such manner that the
quantities required by each country, of the articles which it imports
from its neighbour, shall be exactly sufficient to pay for one another.'[1]

Mill linked the concept of the ratio of exchange with comparative
cost doctrine, laying the foundation for much of the subsequent work
of Marshall and others. Mill showed the importance of demand conditions in determining the terms of trade between countries. He did not
pay the same attention, however, to the question of supply. This was
left to Marshall, who argued that the terms of trade of a country are
influenced not only by demand, but also by the ability of a country to
adjust supplies of its own products to the demands of foreign markets.[2]
It was in order to draw out the importance of both demand and supply

[1] J. S. Mill, cited above (Ashley edition), p. 587.
[2] Alfred Marshall, *Money Credit and Commerce*, London 1923.

elasticities that Marshall developed the device of the 'offer curve'. Since these curves are used in the discussion of a number of problems in the theory of international trade the student should familiarize himself with their meaning.

Marshall's Offer Curves

In figure 4 following Marshall, we assume that there are two countries; England, producing only E goods, and Germany, producing only G goods. The curve e_1 represents the number of bales of 'E' goods

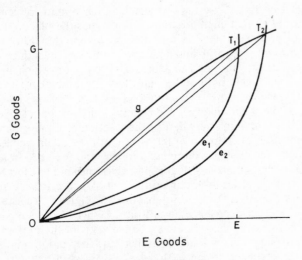

FIGURE 4. Marshall's Offer Curves.

which England will give up for various quantities of 'G' goods at various prices represented by radials from the origin. Clearly the magnitude of this quantity will be determined by conditions of both demand and supply. Likewise in the case of Germany, the curve g, represents the number of bales of 'G' goods which Germany will give up for various quantities of 'E' goods. Where the curves intersect (T_1), relative prices (represented by the slope of OT_1) are such that the offers of the two countries match. At these prices, British exporters wish to sell the same number of 'E' bales (OE) that German importers wish to buy, while British importers wish to buy the same number of 'G' bales (OG) that German exporters wish to sell. This is thus a point of equilibrium. A change in the conditions of supply in England might cause a change in the shape of England's offer curve. England might now be prepared to trade more 'E' goods than hitherto in order to obtain a given quantity of 'G' goods. We have depicted England's new offer curve as the curve e_2, which intersects Germany's offer curve at T_2.

2. MEASURING CHANGES IN THE TERMS OF TRADE

Barter Terms of Trade

In Mill's time, statistical techniques were still in their infancy and it was some years before an accurate measurement of changes in a country's terms of trade was possible. Today we measure changes in the barter or commodity terms of trade over a period by comparing changes in a country's import prices with changes in its export prices. A reduction in import prices means that a country can obtain a larger volume of imports than hitherto in exchange for a given quantity of exports. We measure such an improvement by an increase in T_a where T_a stands for a country A's barter terms of trade and where

$$T_a = \frac{P_{x_1}}{P_{x_0}} \div \frac{P_{m_1}}{P_{m_0}} \quad \text{or} \quad \frac{P_x}{P_m}$$

P_{x_0} = The average price of exports at the base date

P_{x_1} = The average price of exports at a subsequent date

P_{m_0} = The average price of imports at the base date

P_{m_1} = The average price of imports at the subsequent date

P_x = Export price index

P_m = Import price index

If, over the period, export prices rise more than import prices, then taking the ratio of export prices to import prices at the base date as 100, the index will show a value greater than 100. The change in the index can be expressed either as the ratio of the export price index to the import price index, or as the ratio of the import price index to the export price index. It does not much matter which ratio is adopted, so long as the method is clearly stated. In this chapter we have used the ratio of the export price index to that of the import price index; accordingly, a greater rise in export prices as compared with import prices shows itself as a rise in the terms of trade index. This is sometimes referred to as an 'improvement' in the terms of trade, but as we shall see below, terminology of this kind should be treated with extreme caution.

While a change in the barter terms of trade is clearly of significance to a country's external position, measurement presents certain difficulties. In the first place, there is the usual index number problem of choosing an appropriate base year. For a change to be meaningful a reasonable time should elapse between the base date and the date in question. But if this period is too long a country's export or import

TABLE 1. CHANGES IN COMMODITY TERMS OF TRADE OF THE UNITED KINGDOM[1]
1961 = 100

	Import prices	Export prices	Terms of trade
1962	99	101	102
1964	107	106	99
1966	109	113	104
1967	109	114	105
1968	121	123	102
1970	132	136	104
1971	137	150	109

[1] Export value index divided by import value index. For method of calculation of indices see *Board of Trade Journal*, September 13, 1963.

SOURCE: *Monthly Digest of Statistics*.

pattern is likely to have altered so much as to make the comparison irrelevant. There seems to be very little point, for example, in trying to measure the change in the UK terms of trade between 1913 and the present. There is also the obvious difficulty of building quality changes into the index. This consideration is relevant in estimating the changes in the terms of trade of agricultural producing countries *vis-à-vis* industrial ones. Although the quality content of grains and most foodstuffs has probably altered little over the last twenty-five years, that of many industrial goods has improved immensely. Thus although the primary producing countries perhaps get a smaller volume of imported manufactures in exchange for a given quantity of foodstuffs exports than twenty or fifty years ago, the quality of the manufactures is undoubtedly greatly improved.

Since most students find a concept easier to comprehend when clothed in the flesh and blood of actual examples, changes in the terms of trade of the UK for recent years are set below in Table 1, compiled from the *Monthly Digest of Statistics* and for the developed and less developed countries in Table 2.

Table 1 shows that between 1961 and 1971, prices of UK imports rose by 37 per cent whereas prices of UK exports rose by 50 per cent.

This means that in order to obtain a given volume of imports, fewer goods were required to be exported in 1971 than in 1961. The 'barter' or 'commodity' terms of trade had 'improved'.

Table 2 shows that between 1953 and 1969, the terms of trade of the

TABLE 2. COMMODITY TERMS OF TRADE OF DEVELOPED AND LESS DEVELOPED COUNTRIES [1]

1958 = 100

	Developed areas [2]	Less developed areas
1953	97	110
1956	96	112
1960	99	103
1961	100	100
1962	100	98
1963	100	100
1964	100	100
1965	100	99
1966	100	100
1967	100	99
1968	100	99
1969	100	100
1970	102	101
1971	101	101

[1] Unit value index of exports as percentage of unit value index of imports.
[2] North America, Western Europe, Australia, New Zealand, South Africa, Japan.

SOURCE: UN *Monthly Bulletin of Statistics*, October 1972.

developed countries as a group improved by 3 points, whereas for the less developed countries there was a deterioration of 10 points. The fluctuations were especially marked in the case of the African countries, whose economies are of course particularly dependent upon prices of primary products. The decline in the purchasing power of exports from less developed countries, especially in the late 1950s has had serious consequences for their economies, a matter which we shall take up in Chapter 24. At this point it is perhaps worth warning students of the dangers of using aggregates too casually in interpreting data such as that shown in Table 2. While there is little doubt that for less developed countries as a group, the terms of trade deteriorated in the 1950s, it by no means follows that this deterioration applied equally to each and every commodity and country. For example, between 1953 and 1963, the world price of the beverages coffee, tea and cocoa fell by over 25 per cent, while the price of fats, oils and oilseeds declined by only 10 per cent. The price index of minerals showed a change of less than one percentage point over this period.[1]

There is, however, a less obvious objection to the uncritical use of the index. Although it is generally assumed that an 'improvement' has taken place in a country's terms of trade when its export prices rise in relation to the price it pays for imports, a distinction should be made between a relative rise in export prices due to a change in demand conditions abroad for a country's products and one due to rising domestic costs. Only the former represents a genuine 'improvement' in a country's external position. Mill himself realized this distinction, and in his illustration of trade between England and Germany avoided arguing that the 'unfavourable' movement in Germany's terms of trade due to improved production techniques in linen manufacture would be harmful to that country. Mill pointed out that the fall in German export prices might have been due to cost reductions in Germany. Accordingly one should distinguish between a 'deterioration' in a country's terms of trade due to cost reductions, and one due to a fall in overseas demand for its products. One way round the difficulty is to take account in the index not only of changes in export and import prices, but also of productivity changes. Thus a reduction in export prices due to an improvement in efficiency reflects itself in the index differently from a reduction resulting from declining foreign demand. Such an index is the factoral terms of trade.[2]

Factoral Terms of Trade

Marshall used this concept in developing his offer curves technique. His representative bales of 'E' and 'G' goods traded between England and Germany are such that each contains the product of a constant input of resources.[3] If England gives up more 'E' goods in exchange for a given quantity of 'G' goods than hitherto, this is really saying that more of England's resources are being devoted to obtaining a given volume of imports. There is thus a real deterioration in the external position of the UK. The factoral terms of trade index shows us whether increased resources have to be used to obtain a given volume of imports. It can be calculated by multiplying the barter terms of trade index by

[1] See UN *Monthly Bulletin of Statistics*, especially the November issue of each year.

[2] This and other indices discussed below are examined at length by G. Meier, *International Trade and Development*, Harper and Row, 1963.

[3] Although Marshall himself used offer curves to demonstrate changes in the double factoral terms of trade, the analysis is equally applicable to the simpler case of showing changes in the barter terms of trade.

an index of productivity changes in export industries, and can be expressed as:

$$Sa = T_a \cdot Z_a$$

When S_a = Country A's single factoral terms of trade

T_a = Country A's barter terms of trade

Z_a = Index of productivity in A's export industries

If a country's export industries become more efficient, its factoral terms of trade might improve, although it suffers a deterioration in its barter terms of trade.

In measuring changes in the terms of trade, we might wish to be concerned not only with productivity changes in the country whose terms of trade we are measuring but also with productivity changes in other trading partner countries. Thus if account is taken not only of changes in productivity in a country's export industries, but also of changes in the export industries of countries supplying its imports, we have a yet more refined measure. This time we take account not only of the real effort put into Country A's exports, but also of the real effort put into Country A's imports by the supplying countries. The index measuring this is the double factoral terms of trade.

$$D_a = T_a \cdot \frac{Z_a}{Z_b}$$

Where D_a = Country A's double factoral terms of trade

T_a = Country A's barter terms of trade

Z_a = Index of productivity in A's export industries

Z_b = Index of productivity in supplying countries' export industries

In practice, an index of the double factoral terms of trade is almost impossible to calculate since it involves measuring and comparing productivity changes in the export industries of a large number of countries. Moreover even if it were possible to produce, such an index would be of less value as a guide to policy making than the simple factoral index. After all, the citizens of a country are interested in the total volume of goods they can obtain from a given real effort, not in the relative efficiency or otherwise of other countries. The single factoral terms of trade index focuses attention on something which is susceptible to policy—namely domestic efficiency. Adjusting for productivity changes in other countries is only likely to obscure its message.

In no country do the official statistics provide a measure of changes in even the single factoral terms of trade, but in 1954 the late Professor Ely Devons made some estimates of changes in the UK single factoral terms of trade between 1948 and 1953.[1] Devons made this calculation by weighting the index of the commodity terms of trade by the increase in productivity of British export industries. Over the period the barter terms of trade 'deteriorated' by about 1 per cent while the export productivity index rose by 15 per cent. Thus the single factoral terms of trade improved by 12 per cent.

The barter terms of trade index is concerned only with unit values; it tells us nothing about quantities of goods traded. If, for example, domestic inflation causes export prices to rise, and if foreign price elasticity of demand is more than zero, the volume of goods exported will decrease. But this will not be reflected in the index. Accordingly, a country might find that the apparent 'improvement' in its barter terms of trade results in a deterioration in its trade balance. Taussig[2] suggested avoiding this difficulty by using what he christened the *gross* barter terms of trade. This index is simply the change over a period in the ratio of physical imports to physical exports. A change in the gross barter terms of trade facing country A can be measured as follows:

$$G_a = \frac{Q_b}{Q_a}$$

where G_a = Country A's gross barter terms of trade

Q_a = The volume of country A's exports

Q_b = The volume of country A's imports

The higher the ratio, the greater the 'improvement' in a country's gross barter terms of trade, for it means that a bigger volume of imports can be obtained from the same volume of exports.

This concept has been criticized, for although it takes account of quantities of goods moving from one country to another, these may include unilateral transfers. We cannot distinguish between the various types of unilateral transaction lumped together in the index; thus a transfer of goods associated with the export of capital is treated in the same way as the payment of a tribute by a defeated nation at the end of a war. In both cases the gross barter terms of trade of the country exporting the goods appear to improve, but only in the former case is the 'improvement' an indication of strength rather than of weakness.

[1] E. Devons, 'Statistics of the United Kingdom Terms of Trade', *Manchester School*, September 1954.

[2] F. W. Taussig, *International Trade*, p. 113.

As Haberler remarks, 'it will not do to lump together in one category these different kinds of payments'.[1]

Income Terms of Trade

A more recent approach to the terms of trade question is that of Dorrance, who uses the concept of the 'income terms of trade'. This index, which takes account of the volume of exports of a country as well as its export and import prices,[2] is designed to show changes in a country's capacity to import in exchange for exports. It accordingly takes into account changes in export and import prices (the barter terms of trade) and the *volume* of exports.

A change in the income terms of trade of country A is measured as follows:

$$I_a = T_a Q_a$$

where I_a = Country A's income terms of trade

T_a = Country A's net barter terms of trade

Q_a = Country A's export volume index

The index is accordingly calculated by dividing the index of the value of exports by an index of the price of imports.[3] A rise in the value of the index of the income terms of trade indicates that a country can obtain a larger volume of imports than before from the sale of exports. Its capacity to import has increased. A country's income terms of trade can improve while its barter terms of trade deteriorate, for with constant import prices, a fall in export prices might be accompanied by an increase in export sales such that the total value of exports rises.

This index does not measure in any meaningful sense the 'gains' from trade. An improvement in the index may simply mean that more exports are being surrendered than hitherto, and it should never be forgotten that exports embody real resources which can be used to improve domestic living standards. Neither does the index tell us whether a country's total capacity to import, based on all its foreign exchange receipts, has increased. It merely tell us what is happening to its export-based import capacity. If a 'deterioration' in the income terms of trade is accompanied by a substantial inflow of foreign capital

[1] G. Haberler, *The Theory of International Trade*, cited above, pp. 163–165.

[2] G. S. Dorrance, 'The Income Terms of Trade', *The Review of Economic Studies*, vol. xvi, 1948–9.

[3] A. H. Imlah also uses this index labelling it the 'Export Gain from Trade Index'. See his 'Terms of Trade of the United Kingdom', *Journal of Economic History*, November 1950.

or an improvement in invisible earnings, a country's import capacity has increased, in spite of the movement in the index.

In his article, Dorrance shows that in 1930–8, the net barter terms of trade of the UK rose from 100 to 108, while the income terms of trade dropped from 100 to 98. The divergence between the two indices was especially marked between 1930 and 1931, when the net barter terms of trade moved from 100 to 110, but the income terms of trade index fell to 84! Clearly, the UK barter terms of trade had 'improved' between the two years, but export volume had sagged so much that the export-based import capacity of the UK actually deteriorated.

Our discussion of the various terms of trade indices is by no means exhaustive,[1] and doubtless as the years pass other concepts will be added to those already existing. The indices we have mentioned are sometimes useful in shedding light on a particular country's economic problem; they are at least useful aids in clarifying the forces affecting the gain a country derives from trade. The reader will realize that some methods of measurement are more appropriate than others for a particular purpose. If, for example, we wish to assess the impact of changing commodity prices upon the ability of a less developed country to carry out an import programme, then Dorrance's income terms of trade approach seems sensible. This index tells us whether, say, a fall in the prices of such a country's exports results in a sufficient increase in export volume to offset the deterioration in the commodity terms of trade. But whatever index of the terms of trade is used, its message must be interpreted with caution, and with due allowance for the special circumstances of any given situation.

SHORT GUIDE TO THE LITERATURE

By far the fullest treatment of the development of terms of trade theory is in J. Viner, *Studies in the Theory of International Trade*, Allen and Unwin, 1937. There is a more up-to-date treatment in Gerald M. Meier, *International Trade and Development*, Harper and Row, 1963. Meier's Chapter 3 is excellent. There is also a highly readable summary of the different concepts of the terms of trade in G. Haberler, 'A Survey of International Trade Theory', *Special Papers in International*

---

[1] Viner, in his historical study, devotes a number of pages to a discussion of what is perhaps an even more fundamental (but certainly also more elusive) concept of the terms of trade, namely the utility index. This incorporates changes in the disutility of producing a unit of exports and changes in the relative satisfactions yielded by imports and the domestic products foregone as the result of export production. See J. Viner, *Studies in the Theory of International Trade*, cited above, pp. 559 ff.

Economics, no. 1, July 1961, Princeton University. A modern 'classic' in terms of trade analysis is C. P. Kindleberger, *The Terms of Trade: A European Case Study*, New York, 1956.

As mentioned in the text there is a substantial literature on the terms of trade facing less developed countries. It is usefully summarized in Gerald M. Meier, *International Trade and Development*, Harper and Row, 1963, p. 197. Professor Meier himself takes a somewhat sceptical view of the idea that there is a long-term tendency for the terms of trade of less developed countries to deteriorate (see Chapter 3 of his book). Among other books and articles dealing with this subject the following are noteworthy: R. Prebisch, 'The Economic Development of Latin America and Its Principal Problems', *Economic Bulletin for Latin America*, February 1962; W. A. Lewis, 'World Production, Prices and Trade', 1870–1960, *Manchester School*, May 1952; G. Haberler, 'Terms of Trade and Economic Development', in H. S. Ellis ed., *Economic Development for Latin America*, New York, 1961, pp. 275–297; J. Bhagwati, 'A Sceptical Note on the Adverse Secular Trend in the Terms of Trade of Underdeveloped Countries', *Pakistan Economic Journal*, December 1960.

See also Short Guide to the Literature for Chapter 8.

CHAPTER 5

IMPLICATIONS OF FREE TRADE

Chapter 2 dealt at some length with the classical approach to the theory of international trade. Inspiring the arguments of the classical writers was the belief that free trade might generally be expected to secure the highest possible degree of economic welfare. In the present chapter, we examine the implications of this proposition; noting first the conditions which must be satisfied if free trade is to result in maximum economic welfare. In Chapter 6 we examine some of the devices by which there is deliberate interference with this free trade pattern. Some of the arguments for interference with free trade advanced by protectionists and others are examined in Chapters 7 and 8.

1. THE ADVANTAGES OF FREE TRADE RESTATED[1]

Free traders stress the advantage of free trade as a means of securing both the maximum possible economic output and the best possible allocation of goods for the consumer. These are gains resulting from a re-allocation of factors of production or of consumption goods, along the lines discussed in Chapter 3. There are in addition what we might call efficiency gains resulting from a more efficient utilization of factors within a firm or industry, e.g. competition from abroad might encourage or compel businessmen to sacrifice leisure in order to increase efficiency; it might force them to consider seriously 'organization and method' in their businesses. In short, foreign competition might provide a 'salutary jolt' which raises the level of national output per head.[2] In terms of our diagrams in Chapter 3, free trade might cause an outward movement of the production frontier. In this chapter, however, we are concerned primarily with the re-allocative advantages of free trade. These gains take two forms; first there is a gain from increased output; second, there is a gain from an improved consumption pattern. We shall first consider free trade as a means of securing the maximization of output.

[1] This section follows the argument developed by Professor Meade in *Trade and Welfare*. Oxford University Press, 1955, Chapters II and III.
[2] The 'salutary jolt' argument is one of the most frequently advanced economic argument for the UK joining the EEC. It is examined further in Chapter 20.

Free Trade and Output Maximization

Let us assume that Britain has a comparative cost advantage in producing cars while Denmark has a comparative advantage in producing butter. In Britain more sacrifice in terms of alternatives foregone is required to produce a given amount of butter than in Denmark. If prices in Britain and in Denmark reflect relative internal production costs, then in Britain, cars will be relatively cheap and butter relatively dear whilst in Denmark, cars will be relatively dear and butter relatively cheap. Now if trade is opened up, in the absence of transport costs, Britain can gain by concentrating more of its resources on car production; and importing part at least of its butter requirements from Denmark; Denmark can gain by concentrating on butter production and importing cars from Britain. The shift of resources in Britain from butter into car production and in the reverse direction in Denmark results in an increased total output of both cars and butter. But since Danish residents will buy British cars only if they are cheaper than Danish ones, while British residents will buy Danish butter only if it is cheaper than British butter, this desirable result will come about only if comparative cost advantage is reflected in the price ratios of these products. Accordingly, if Britain has a comparative cost advantage in producing cars, but the Government levies an export duty on them, or in some other way artificially raises the price of British cars on the world market, some or all of the advantage of international division of labour is lost.

In welfare economics we are concerned with marginal social costs rather than with marginal private costs. In a free enterprise economy, however, production decisions are normally taken in the light of private costs. These private costs might well diverge from social costs. A firm producing motor cars might cause considerable congestion on the roads in its vicinity. Dairy farming, on the other hand, might produce social economies accruing to the community as well as to an individual producer. The assurance of a constant supply of milk in time of war, as the result of the existence of prosperous dairy industry, is a social benefit not necessarily reflected in the present price received by the dairy farmer. The private marginal cost ratio between cars and dairy products will not, however, take into account any of the social economies of dairy farming.

There are a number of other reasons why, in the real world, marginal cost ratios diverge from marginal price ratios and hence prevent free trade from leading automatically to output maximization. Firstly, a producers' monopoly in one industry might cause the price of the product of that industry to be higher than if monopoly were absent.

For example, a Government selling monopoly might establish prices which fail to reflect marginal costs. Secondly, a production subsidy on some products but not on others could cause price ratios to diverge from cost ratios. Thirdly, differential rates of internal taxation might bring about a divergence between price and cost ratios. Other conditions making possible this divergence include lack of market information, the possibility of external economies or diseconomies and price or wage rigidities. If one or more of the distortions we have listed is present, price ratios will not accurately reflect marginal cost ratios. There will be a distortion of trade. We can express the optimum position as follows:

In each country,

$$\frac{\text{the price of cars}}{\text{the price of butter}} = \frac{\text{the marginal social cost of producing cars}}{\text{the marginal social cost of producing butter}}$$

It is by no means easy to identify, let alone neutralize, distortions in the market created in the ways we have outlined. However, in so far as the authorities successfully offset some of these distortions by taxation and other measures, they are not interfering with the 'free' operation of market forces, but rather restoring the market situation to what it would have been in the absence of distortions. Professor Meade describes policy measures which aim to restore the true *laissez-faire* position as constituting a policy of *'modified laissez-faire'*. Whether the restoration of mere *laissez-faire* is an adequate policy objective in this context is another matter, for if *laissez-faire* leads to monopoly— as it might—the result could be a less than optimum one. Perhaps the creation of an 'ideal' trade position sometimes requires more than simply the creation of *laissez-faire*.

Free Trade and the Optimization of Consumption

Much of the classical literature was concerned with free trade as a means of obtaining maximum output. But in the absence of market distortions, it secures also the optimization of consumption. In our previous example of trade between Britain and Denmark, Britain was well endowed with the factors necessary for producing cars relatively cheaply. In the absence of trade, we should expect British residents to be faced with a relative abundance of cars and a relative scarcity of butter; the opposite will be the case in Denmark. In this situation Britons would be prepared to give up rather more cars in order to get additional supplies of butter than would Danish consumers. To British consumers the marginal utility of butter is higher in terms of cars than to Danish consumers. Accordingly, the price of cars as compared with the price of butter will be lower in Britain than in Denmark.

If trade between the two countries is now opened up, Danish residents take advantage of the relative cheapness of British cars, while British residents purchase the relatively cheap Danish butter. Now British residents gain, since the marginal utility of butter in terms of cars to them is high, and trade enables them to obtain butter on more favourable terms. Danish consumers also gain since in their case the marginal utility of cars in relation to that of butter is high. The flow of cars from Britain and of butter from Denmark enables consumers in both countries to improve their consumption patterns; both sets of consumers are able to optimize their consumption. It should be noted that this improvement in consumption occurs irrespective of any change in output in either country. No movement of factors from one industry to the other need occur, yet free trade enables residents in both countries to obtain greater satisfaction from the spending of a given income. But, as in the case of output maximization, the advantage from free trade to consumers will occur only if in each country, price ratios accurately reflect marginal utility ratios; that is if in both countries

$$\frac{\text{the price of cars}}{\text{the price of butter}} = \frac{\text{the marginal utility of cars}}{\text{the marginal utility of butter}}$$

Divergences between marginal utility and price ratios can occur if market conditions are imperfect, or if the Government creates a distortion by subsidizing or taxing one group of products. If this happens, then trade does not necessarily create optional conditions of consumption. As in the case of output maximization, some Government intervention might be necessary in order to bring about the 'modified *laissez-faire* solution.

The reader should be wary to distinguish carefully between Government intervention necessary to eliminate distortions and thus secure the advantages of free trade, and deliberate interference with free trade by means of protectionist policies. The former intervention establishes the situation which would exist if there were no distortions, the latter aims at changing this situation.

In the optimum situation, then, the domestic rate of substitution between two products in consumption will equal both the domestic rate of transformation and the price ratio. We can use the geometry introduced in Chapter 3 to illustrate this situation. In figure 3, AA represents A's production possibility frontier for wheat in terms of cloth, and the line TAB the *international* exchange ratio between these products. In the absence of foreign trade, domestic production takes place at the point where NTA is a tangent to the curve AA. But given trade, consumers in country A are able to move along the line TAB. If they move to a point which is above and to the right of the point of tangency of NTA with the production frontier AA, they are clearly better off as the result of trade. They can consume more wheat *and* more cloth. But if consumption is to the left of this point, say at p, then it can be argued that consumers in country A as a group would be better off as a group if those who were adversely affected by the change could compensate those whose welfare had diminished, and still remain better off than before the change. Economists are, however, accustomed to analyse this question of changing welfare by means of the community indifference curve. They constructed it by combining the indifference curves of individual members of the community.

The Community Indifference Curve

This very useful tool of the community map[1] was developed by Leontief,[2] Kaldor[3] and Scitovsky.[4] Kaldor defines the community consumption indifference curve as 'the locus of points representing a constant real income for the community as a whole'. In figure 5, CIC is the indifference curve for citizens of country E. The total satisfaction yielded to the community at point A is equal to that at point B. The community is indifferent as to whether it consumes OE 'G' goods + OP 'E' goods or OV 'G' goods + OW 'E' goods—although of course some citizens might prefer combination A to combination B. To the community as a whole, however, any combination of goods represented along CIC_2 is preferable to any combination along CIC_1. Some interests might object to a change in the assortment of goods represented by a change from one position to another, but since the total quantity of goods is greater, those who gain can compensate those who lose, while still remaining better off than before the imposition of the tariff.

[1] Edgeworth made use of community indifference curves in 1894, in his 'Pure Theory of International Trade', *Econpmic Journal*, vol. 4, 1894, reprinted in F. Y. Edgeworth, *Papers Relating to Political Economy*, London, 1925, vol. ii.

[2] Wassily W. Leontief, 'The Use of Indifference Curves in the Analysis of Foreign Trade', *Quarterly Journal of Economics*, vol. xlvii, May 1933, reprinted in *Readings in the Theory of International Trade*, American Economic Association, London, Allen and Unwin, 1950.

[3] N. Kaldor, 'A Note on Tariffs and the Terms of Trade', *Economica*, November 1940.

[4] T. de Scitovsky, 'A Reconsideration of the Theory of Tariffs,' *Review of Economic Studies*. 1942, reprinted in *Readings in the Theory of International Trade*, cited above.

The use of the community indifference curve has been criticized. For example Scitovsky showed that community indifference curves might cut one another between the relevant points. This is because the shape of the curve is partly determined by the distribution of income within the country imposing the tariff; if income changes follow the imposition (or increase or removal) of a tariff then the original community indifference curve must be replaced by a new one. Before a tax is imposed one set of indifference curves is relevant, but after its imposition another. In such a case there could be more than one point

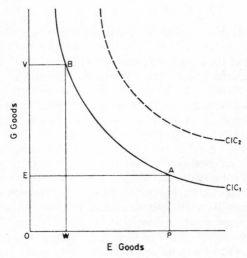

FIGURE 5. A Community Indifference Curve.

where the foreigner's offer curve is tangential to the indifference curves of the country imposing the duty, and therefore more than one optimum rate of duty. We cannot say that situation B after the imposition of the duty is better or worse than A, before its imposition. In spite of reservations, economists make frequent use of the community indifference curve, using certain simplifying assumptions, and the student should be familiar with it. It can be used *legitimately*, for instance, if constant income distribution or insignificant income changes can be assumed.

In the ideal and utopian situation, the domestic marginal rate of transformation = the domestic marginal rate of substitution = the foreign trade price ratio. As we have seen, however, in the real world these equalities are unlikely to be achieved. One or other of the distortions we have mentioned might supervene. This could be monopoly or oligopoly, price or wage rigidity, lack of information, external economies or diseconomies or a divergence between social and private costs. For example, the production possibility frontier as determined by social marginal costs might dictate concentration on, say cars, but if the gap between marginal and social costs is sufficiently[1] great, a country might find itself importing cars and exporting butter, since private marginal cost ratios dictate price ratios and it is these rather than social costs which determine trade patterns.

2. THE THEORY OF THE SECOND BEST

An important development in economics since the Second World War is an awareness of the problem of what is called 'the second best'. The general theory of the second best has in fact largely been developed in the context of international trade. Essentially, the theory is quite simple, but is of considerable importance in a number of areas of trade theory. Basically, it starts from the premise that in what we might call a utopian economic world there are no distortions whatever to mar perfect competition. Price ratios between products reflect marginal social cost and marginal rates of substitution in consumption. Output is maximized and consumption optimized. If this Utopian world is marred by one solitary distortion—say a producers' monopoly of one product—then the elimination of this distortion represents a clear gain. But suppose there are several distortions. Is it still true that the elimination of one of these will be a clear gain?

Let us suppose that there are several producers' monopolies, each controlling output of a product which is a reasonable substitute for products of the other monopolists. In some cases the producers' organization is more successful in obtaining monopoly profit than in others; that is to say, the divergence between market price and marginal cost in the case of producer A is greater than in the case of producer B. Now suppose that, in an oligopolistic market situation, oligopoly B is forced out of business. Are we nearer to, or further away from, conditions of Utopian efficiency? It is not difficult to see that if, as is likely to be the case, B's market is taken over by producer A, a greater proportion of sales than before is taking place under conditions where the gap between price and marginal cost is relatively wide. The limited

[1] Some diagrammatic examples of this kind of situation are given by Haberler in 'Some Problems in the Pure Theory of International Trade', *Economic Journal*, vol. lx, June 1950, pp. 223–240, reprinted in *Readings in International Economics*, ed. R. E. Caves and H. G. Johnson, cited above.

amount of freer competition has paradoxically caused a net decrease in the overall amount of competition in the economy as a whole. Of course, in this situation the wisest course would have been the removal of *all* oligopoly; this would have secured the conditions of Utopian efficiency. But given that such a Utopian policy was impossible the 'second best' solution was clearly not the removal of B's relatively mild oligopoly.[1]

Second best situations fall into two categories, those caused by behavioural constraints, e.g. an unwillingness of businessmen to maximize profits or workers to obtain the maximum return for the labour, and those created by environmental constraints, e.g. taxes, subsidies, restrictions on output, monopoly, distortionary wage differentials, increasing returns to scale and external gains or losses in production and consumption.[2]

The theory of the second best is especially applicable to tariff theory. If a group of countries impose tariff restrictions on their mutual trade but two of them decide to remove the tariff on their trade with one another, it is by no means certain that there will be a net welfare gain. For the removal of the tariff on imports from one trading partner is likely to cause a diversion of imports from third countries (against whose products the tariff still applies), to the country with which trade is now free. If the latter country is a relatively high cost producer while the country which previously supplied the exports is a relatively low cost producer the net effect of 'freer trade' might well be a diversion of output from low to high cost sources! Again, the paradox applies. The removal of one market distortion while others are left intact, results in a net diminution of economic welfare. The theory of the second best is of importance over a wide range of economic problems. It is especially relevant to some of the problems of economic integration and we shall accordingly encounter it again in Chapter 20.

The reader who has carefully worked through this Chapter may well feel that since we obviously live in a world of distortions, where the second-best solution seems to be the rule rather than the exception, there is little point in concerning himself unduly with the economic implications or advantages of a free trade world. To this there are two answers. Firstly, even if conditions appropriate to free trade are never

---

[1] Professor Meade deals systematically with a number of problems in the theory of the second best in *Trade and Welfare*, cited above. A rather more general statement of the theory is by R. G. Lipsey and K. Lancaster in 'The General Theory of the Second Best', *Review of Economic Studies*, vol. 24, 1956-7.

[2] There is a useful classification of second-best situations in J. Bhagwati, 'The Pure Theory of International Trade', *Economic Journal*, March 1964, p. 56.

met with in practice, there is much to be said analytically for setting the free trade case up as an ideal. It is much easier to build a single model and then to note deviations from it than to list an infinite number of cases where the free trade case is not applicable and then to generalize from these diverse situations. Secondly, on the question of 'ideal' policy, the damage done to the free trade argument by the many qualifications we have introduced in this Chapter should not be exaggerated. A given market imperfection may be temporary. It may not necessarily always weaken rather than strengthen the case for free trade. Moreover, the administrative cost (including economic inefficiencies) resulting from the imposition of a set of restrictions might be more damaging than the initial distortion.

As Haberler expresses the position:
'But these imperfections may just as well be such as to strengthen the economic case for free trade. A mere enumeration of possible imperfections and deviations from the ideal case does not prove more than the possibility that certain controls might be beneficial (provided of course that they are efficiently administered—which amounts to assuming quite a lot). In order to prove that the restriction of international trade (rather than the opposite) is justified, it is necessary to show that these imperfections are persistent (in other words that there is not even a tendency for the ideal situation to work itself out) and that they persistently operate in such a direction.as to weaken (rather than to strengthen) the case for free trade.'[1]

SHORT GUIDE TO THE LITERATURE

The two volumes which cover the ground of this chapter are Professor J. E. Meade's *The Theory of International Economic Policy*, vol. ii— *Trade and Welfare*, published under the auspices of the Royal Institute of International Affairs by the Oxford University Press, London, 1955 and *Problems of Economic Union*, London, Allen and Unwin Ltd., 1953. The principle of the 'Second Best' is set out in R. G. Lipsey and K. Lancaster, 'The General Theory of the Second Best', *Review of Economic Studies*, vol. 24, 1956–7. The whole subject matter of this chapter is closely related both to tariff theory and custom union theory and the student is referred to the Short Guides to the Literature following Chapters 6, 7 and 8.

[1] G. Haberler, 'Some Problems in the Pure Theory of International Trade', *Economic Journal*, vol. lx, June 1950, pp. 223–240, reproduced in Caves and Johnson, *Readings in International Economics*, cited above.

CHAPTER 6

METHODS OF PROTECTION

Before examining the arguments advanced by protectionists, we shall consider the implications of various methods of interfering with free trade. A country may protect its industry in several ways. Apart from tariffs, quantitative and exchange controls, protection can be given by less obvious means such as a state trading monopoly, the requirement that a given proportion of home consumption be met from domestic production, discriminatory transport rates, health regulations and customs procedures which discriminate against foreigners. But measures which discriminate in favour of some section of the domestic population, agricultural support schemes for instance, can also act as protective devices. Trade organizations have identified several hundred different rules, regulations and general policies that give rise to discrimination in international trade, whether this is their primary purpose or merely a side effect. With the growing role of Government in the economy and with the lowering of traditional tariffs, these 'non-tariff barriers' are now recognized as a prime obstacle to trade liberalization.

In this chapter we shall deal only with the tariff, quantitative trade controls, and exchange controls. The reader who has worked through the chapter should then be able to apply what he has learned to the special problems arising from alternative methods of protection. We are not concerned so much with the question of whether a tariff or other trade impediment is or is not 'harmful'; our attention is here confined to how these measures operate.

1. THE TARIFF

Effects of a Tariff

The tariff is still the most common form of protection. The adoption of a tariff does not necessarily mean the abrogation of the price system, for unless a tariff is prohibitive, it can be climbed over, and a country with a sufficiently low cost structure might well be able to sell its product over the tariff wall. In this respect a tariff differs from a quantitative contròl restricting imports irrespective of cost considerations. A tariff can be *specific* or *ad valorem*. A specific duty is based upon the quantity of a product imported and is expressed as so much duty per lb. or per some other quantity unit. An *ad valorem* duty is based upon value; it is expressed as so much per cent of the value of a given import. The tariffs of most countries are generally *ad valorem* ones, although a large number of specific rates still exist, especially on food products. The protective effect of a specific duty becomes eroded with inflation, while from this point of view an *ad valorem* rate remains constant.

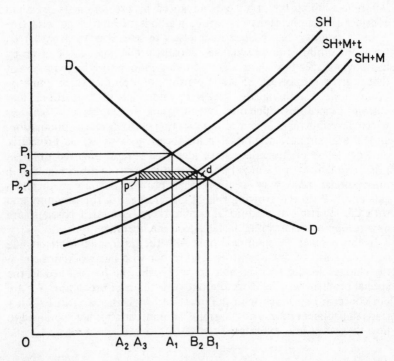

FIGURE 6. Effect of an import duty on Price, Domestic Output and Government Revenue.

We can assess the effect of a tariff by looking at the consequences of a duty upon a particular product (the partial equilibrium approach) or by examining the effect of a general duty on all (or almost all) a country's imports (the general equilibrium approach). For the moment we shall concern ourselves only with the effects of a duty upon a particular product, postponing a discussion of the effect of a general tariff until we consider the terms of trade argument for a tariff in Chapter 8.

Let us suppose that the UK produces cars, the relevant demand and supply curves being shown in figure 6. D is the demand curve and SH the home supply curve. In the absence of imports the equilibrium price is P_1. If imports are permitted, demand will remain constant but there is a new supply curve (SH + M) which shows the quantity produced at home plus the quantity imported at various prices. The new equilibrium price is at P_2. At this price domestic supply is OA_2 and imports A_2B_1. The total quantity consumed is OB_1. Now suppose the country imposes an import duty. The new combined home and import supply curve will be (SH + M + t) with the new price at P_3. This new price will be higher than the pre-duty price, although not as high as P_1, where there were no imports at all. The extent of the price increase will of course depend upon the elasticities of demand and supply. The less elastic demand in the UK, the greater the price increase following the imposition of the duty. The greater the foreign elasticity of supply the smaller the price increase. If foreign suppliers react to the tariff by selling less in the UK, this will help maintain their price in the UK market. If, on the other hand, supply in the exporting country is completely inelastic, there would be no price increase in the UK import market. The whole burden of the duty would be born by the supplying country. The primary effect of a tariff is a price one, but the price change also triggers off other changes. In figure 6 the increase in price from OP_2 to OP_3 causes domestic output to increase from OA_2 to OA_3 and imports to fall from A_2B_1 to A_3B_2. Total consumption falls from OB_1 to OB_2. There is also a revenue effect since the government will collect the duty equivalent to the shaded area (the duty multiplied by the number of units imported). The revenue affect of a tariff is particularly important in some developing countries. Indeed the importance of a tariff as a means of government revenue has been one of the reasons why some countries in West and Central Africa are reluctant to enter into customs union arrangements.

There is also a redistributive effect since domestic producers of the protected goods gain at the expense of those who consume the imported product. In figure 6 the protective effect of the tariff is shown by the area of the triangle p, while the consumption effect is shown by d. The area of the triangle p depends upon the height of the tariff and the increase in domestic output—this latter depending upon the shape of the domestic supply curve. The area of the triangle d, which represents the loss to consumers caused by the tariff, depends upon the extent to which import supplies are reduced (OB_1, minus OB_2) and the rise in price following the imposition of the duty (OP_3 minus OP_2). It thus gives a measure of consumers' loss following the imposition of the duty.

Accordingly, in welfare terms we may measure the economic loss resulting from the tariff by adding together the areas 'p' and 'd', the former measuring a production loss, the latter a consumption loss.[1]

Nominal and Effective Tariffs

How far is it possible to measure the protective effect of a tariff? A bare survey of the height of various duties imposed by a country is unlikely to give us a true picture of the degree of protection afforded by the tariff unless we know something about the conditions under which domestic production takes place, and about the height of the duty on raw material inputs. In recent years there has been a growing awareness among economists of the distinction between *nominal* and what have come to be known as effective tariff rates. The *effective* tariff rate tries to measure the extent to which a domestic manufacturer can increase his processing costs as compared with a foreign competitor without exceeding the price of the imported product.[2] Accordingly it concentrates upon the relationship between the tariff and the 'value added' by processing rather than upon the selling price.

It is clear that the protective effect of a tariff on domestic manufacturing is larger the lower the import duty on the raw materials used in its manufacture. Other things being equal, the closer the two rates of duty are, the smaller the difference between nominal and effective protection enjoyed. The other factor which must be taken into account is the value of imported material content. If this is very considerable in relation to total output, that is, if the *value added* is relatively small, the greater will be the ratio of a given rate of duty to value added. We can generalize by stating that the higher the proportion of value added to output, and the smaller the difference between the final nominal duty and the duty on raw material, the lower the degree of protection on the final product. This can be expressed as a simple formula.

$$e = \frac{n - mi}{v}$$

[1] This diagrammatic apparatus is discussed fully in C. P. Kindleberger, *International Economics*, Homewood, Illinois, R. D. Irwin, Inc., pp. 106 ff.
[2] One of the fullest expositions of the significance of effective tariff rates is by W. M. Corden, 'The Structure of a Tariff System and the Effective Protective Rate', *Journal of Political Economy*, vol. lxxiv, June 1966, and 'The Effective Protective Rate, the Uniform Tariff Equivalent, and the Average Tariff', *Economic Record*, vol. 42, June 1966, pp. 200–216. See also H. G. Grubel and H. G. Johnson, 'Nominal Tariffs, Indirect Taxes and Effective Rates of Protection: The Common Market Countries 1959', *The Economic Journal*, December 1967; and T. S. Barker and S. S. Han, 'Effective Rates of Protection for United Kingdom Production', *The Economic Journal*, June 1971.

where e = effective rate of duty

   n = nominal rate of duty on final product

   m = nominal rate of duty on material input

   i = coefficient of material input

   v = proportion of final output accounted for by value added.

Let us suppose the nominal duty on raw steel imports is 5 per cent and that raw steel accounts for 80 per cent of manufacturing costs of finished steel, upon which the nominal duty is 10 per cent. How much 'protection' does the 10 per cent duty give to the domestic steel processing industry? In terms of our formulas $n = 10$ per cent, $m = 5$ per cent, $i = 80$ per cent, $v = 20$ per cent. Then $e = 30$ per cent. Thus the effective rate of duty on steel processing is three times higher than the nominal rate on finished steel suggests. The high value in our example is of course the result of a relatively high import content. The proportion of domestic value added to final price is accordingly relatively low.

Economists have for long been aware of the importance of processing costs in determining the effectiveness of a tariff, but only in recent years have they made quantitative assessments of differences between nominal and effective rates of duty. One of the most significant contributions in this respect is that of Professor Bela Balassa of Yale University who has calculated nominal and effective rates for thirty-six groups of manufactured products for the USA, the UK the EEC, Sweden and Japan.[1]

In order to calculate effective rates of tariff it is necessary to know nominal rates and also inputs of raw materials. Balassa's work shows that the measure of protection afforded to domestic industries is substantially larger than nominal rates suggest for all the countries analysed. In some products the effective rate appears to be twice as high as the nominal rate. In only a few it is lower; in such cases the protective effect of the duty on the manufactured product is more than offset by high duties on the material inputs. Balassa's researches also suggest that the tariff structures of the United States and Sweden are more protective relative to those of the UK, the EEC and Japan than nominal rates of duty suggest. This approach to tariff analysis suggests that in industrial countries tariffs are a more potent source of protection than is generally realized. The distorting effect of the tariff on the

[1] Bela Balassa, 'Tariff Protection in Industrial Countries: An Evaluation', *Journal of Political Economy*, vol. lxiii, December 1965. Professor H. G. Johnson has also dealt with this subject in a valuable and highly readable article 'Trade Preferences and Developing Countries', *Lloyds Bank Review*, April 1966, and in his more demanding but also rewarding *Aspects of the Theory of Tariffs*, Allen and Unwin, 1971.

pattern of production and on the structure of economy is therefore likely to be considerable. Professor Johnson has shown that the gap between effective and nominal tariffs is particularly wide in the case of those products of especial interest to developing countries; the reduction or removal of tariffs on these products is accordingly likely to lead to a considerable change in the allocation of resources. This gives added significance to the system of generalized preferences on manufactures now operated by most industrial countries in favour of less developed countries.[1]

One feature of the tariff system of most industrialized countries is the degree of escalation in their tariffs. Raw materials usually enter free of duty or at very low rates of duty, semi-processed goods at higher rates; fully manufactured goods are usually subject to the highest rates of all. Such products accordingly enjoy relatively high effective rates of protection, and this undoubtedly discourages less developed countries from expanding their processing and manufacturing industries.

Serious difficulties arise in attempting to 'measure' the overall height of a country's tariff and in comparing the height of a tariff between countries, whether in terms of nominal or effective tariff rates. Broadly speaking, most people know what they mean when they say that Sweden's tariff is low, while that of Portugal is high. If one sets down the relative heights of tariffs on a long list of products, side by side for the two countries, Swedish tariffs will generally be lower than those of Portugal. But there is no widely accepted method for measuring and comparing these heights. Apart from difficulties in regard to nomenclature there is the problem of whether to use a weighted or an unweighted average for comparing tariff levels. If the former procedure is used, no account is taken of cases when the tariff is so prohibitively high that imports of such goods are zero. On the other hand, if unweighted rates are used, duties on goods of little importance in a country's trade count as much as those which are major imports.

Duties may be weighted by imports or by the value of domestic production of various commodities to which the tariff rates apply. Thus if a duty of 10 per cent is applied to imports of commodity x, output of which in the importing country is ten times as great as of commodity y, upon imports of which the same duty is levied, ten times as much weight should be given to the duty on x as to the duty on y. This method is useful in that it takes account of tariffs to the extent of which there is domestic production but eliminates from the calculation duties on products not directly competitive with home produced goods.

[1] These generalized preferences are discussed in Chapter 24.

On the other hand, it is a calculation difficult to make accurately since production and tariff classifications seldom coincide.

Whatever the difficulties of measurement, it is certain that there have been substantial ebbs and flows in tariff protection over the last hundred years.[1] A century ago, it looked as if the nations of western Europe at least would be knit together into one rapidly growing free trade community. This· was the vision of liberals like Cobden to whom the free trade movement was nothing less than a crusade. But this dream of the 1860s was not to be fulfilled. By the end of the following decade, Germany had become protectionist, as had France, smarting under the effects of defeat in the Franco-Prussian war and the need to make reparations payments. As protection took hold in France and Russia, the tariff was raised even higher in the USA, which had been strongly protectionist since the early nineteenth century. In spite of the fair trade campaigns of Chamberlain and others, successive British Governments remained loyal to free trade principles until well after the start of the First World War. The first inroads were made in the free trade policy when the McKenna duties of 33½ per cent were imposed on a wide range of imports including vehicles, clocks, watches and some scientific instruments. Protection continued after the war, being consolidated in the Safeguarding of Industry Act of 1921, which gave protection to 'key' industries. In the 1920s the British tariff continued moderately protective, but was much less high than that of the US. At this time both Britain and the US tended to eschew direct controls, although they were widely employed in Europe. The big step towards high protection was taken by most countries in the early 1930s following the onset of the Great Depression. Although there were a number of tariff modifications in the later thirties, the Second World War broke upon a highly protectionist world. In post-war years there has been a general move towards tariff reductions.

The GATT

The GATT since its inception in 1947, has worked for the progressive removal of tariffs between its Contracting Parties, as adherents to the General Agreement are called. During the Second World War a great deal of thought was given to the question of establishing a Charter upon which nations should base their post-war commercial policies. In spite of the very great intellectual effort put into elaborating what became

[1] There is an outline of tariff systems as they have developed in the modern world in W. M. Corden's contribution to the *International Encyclopedia of the Social Sciences*, 'Tariffs and Protectionism', I have also given a very potted history of changes in the UK tariff in my Institute of Economic Affairs Research Monograph, *The Shape of Britain's Tariff*, London, 1968.

known as the Havana Charter, the Charter failed to be ratified by the US. By 1950 it became clear that there would be no comprehensive arrangements for international co-operation in commercial matters— as, for example, had been secured by the IMF in the monetary field.[1] But even while discussions on the Havana Charter were still in progress, some countries, including the USA and Britain, resolved to work immediately for a measure of trade liberalization. Accordingly, twenty-three countries decided in 1947 to negotiate mutual tariff reductions and in this way gave birth to the GATT.

The core of the GATT is an undertaking by the Contracting Parties to engage in mutual tariff reductions, and to extend to all other Contracting Parties any reductions made in favour of a participating country. There is also provision for the 'binding' of tariffs; that is in negotiation a member might undertake not to raise certain tariffs. Since the essence of the GATT is non-discrimination and reciprocity, the Contracting Parties undertook not to extend new *preferences*, although existing preferential arrangements, e.g. British Commonwealth Preferences, were allowed to continue. Customs Unions and Free Trade Areas are permitted, provided they satisfy certain requirements.[2]

Much of the work of the GATT has taken the form of tariff reducing negotiations, the first of which took place in 1947. The most recent 'round' of negotiations, the Kennedy Round, was completed in 1967.[3] Years of talks brought substantial cuts which were implemented in five annual instalments and reduced the industrial tariffs of nearly forty countries by about a third. The average US tariff is now 9% (14% pre-Kennedy), that of the EEC 8·4% (13·1%), of the UK 10·2% (16·3%), and of Japan 10% (18·3%). It is suggested that the tariff cuts have helped to open up major world markets and have contributed to a rate of growth of world trade that over the period 1967–70 was nearly twice as high as in the period 1964–7, accelerating in value from 7·5% to 13% annually and in volume from 6% to 10·5%. The annual growth in the value of world output had remained unchanged at 5·5%.[4]

[1] The reasons for the failure of the US to ratify the Havana Charter were several and cannot be discussed briefly. Various interests in the US raised objections. The whole question is examined by W. A. Brown Jnr., *The United States and the Restoration of World Trade*, Brookings Institution, Washington D.C., 1950, pp. 362–365, and W. Diebold Jnr, *The End of the ITO*, Princeton Essays in International Finance No. 16, October 1952.

[2] This latter question is taken up again in Chapter 20.

[3] President Kennedy had inspired the Trade Expansion Act of 1962 which gave the US Administration considerable leeway in negotiating tariff cuts 'across the board' rather than by the traditional commodity-by-commodity procedure.

[4] GATT Press Release, December 28, 1971.

Unfortunately, the GATT has not been at all successful in securing a reduction in the level of agricultural protection among the Contracting Parties. Neither has it fully satisfied the aspirations of the less developed countries—partly on account of its seeming impotence in face of protective farm policies in western industrialized countries.

Although the Contracting Parties to the GATT have from time to time expressed considerable concern at the special trade problems of less developed countries and have indeed carried out several surveys of these problems,[1] the less developed countries as a group have frequently shown impatience at the lack of progress in the GATT in solving their problems. Their doubt about the usefulness of the GATT as an instrument for furthering their interests was one of the main reasons for the calling of a special UN Conference on Trade and Development, UNCTAD, in 1964—an exercise repeated in 1968 and 1972.[2]

2. QUANTITATIVE RESTRICTIONS

Although tariffs are serious impediments to free trade, some other forms of restriction, namely quantitative restrictions and exchange controls have over the last thirty or forty years probably been even more significant. It is to these direct controls that we now turn.

Quantitative controls, usually taking the form of quota restrictions, place a limit on the importation of a particular product or group of products in a given period of time. Quotas restrict imports either by value or by quantity. In terms of foreign exchange savings, limitation by value will be the most predictable in its consequences. In operating a quota system the authorities may distribute licences either on the basis of 'first come first served' or according to previous import requirements.

In so far as they reduce the supply of imports relative to domestic demand, quantitative restrictions tend to raise domestic prices, creating a gap between the selling price and the price received by the exporter. Unless the exporter succeeds in raising his prices, a profit will accordingly accrue to the importer. Thus, whereas in the case of a tariff, there is a revenue gain to the Government, when quantitative restrictions are imposed, the gains arising from the imposition of quantitative

---

[1] Notably *Report by a Panel of Experts: Trends in International Trade*, GATT, Geneva 1958. Following this Report the GATT established three standing Committees to make recommendations on some of the urgent problems of the international economy, as part of its Action Programme. There is a useful short study of the GATT in Virginia L. Gailbraith, *World Trade in Transition*, Washington D.C., Public Affairs Press, 1965.

[2] See Chapter 24.

restrictions are likely to go to either the exporter or the importer. A Government can, of course, skim off this revenue by means of a fee on all import licences; or it can auction import licences.

Origins

In modern times quantitative restrictions originated during the First World War. After some easement of controls in the years immediately after the armistice, they were stiffened in the early 1920s, spreading fairly rapidly in Western Europe and elsewhere. There were several reasons for the persistence of trade restrictions at this time. A number of countries had built up additional industrial capacity during the war; protection offered a fairly easy way of continuing to employ this capacity. In other cases the motive was the serious balance of payments disequilibrium affecting many countries. For countries suffering balance of payments difficulties trade controls appeared more effective than a tariff, which is often uncertain in its impact on the balance of trade and not easily adjustable in accordance with a country's changing external position. Post-1918 Germany was in an especially difficult position, since, although forced to make very substantial reparation payments, the German Government was forbidden to raise the tariff. Trade controls were adopted even by certain strong currency countries, notably Switzerland, as a defence against the dumping of exports by countries with relatively weak balances of payments.

During the early 1930s, trade controls were immensely strengthened, and indeed introduced by countries which had hitherto refrained from adopting them. Countries dependent upon food exports were particularly affected by the violence and persistence of the fall in commodity prices in and after 1929. They could ill afford to wait for the slow operation of the tariff to protect their rapidly dwindling reserves. Not all trading countries adopted quantitative trade restrictions; some used alternative devices to protect their balances of payments and maintain domestic employment. The United States, for example, avoided quotas except in very few cases, but in 1931 and 1932 imposed an exceptionally high tariff.

Post-1945 Experience

Quantitative restrictions became stricter during the Second World War and continued in the early post-war years. In the case of a large number of countries (again with the notable exception of the United States) quantitative restrictions, sometimes in association with exchange controls, took the place of tariff protection. It was only in 1950 that the OEEC countries of Western Europe launched the Code of

Liberalization, the object of which was the dismantling of trade controls by the establishment of liberalization targets, first for intra-European trade and later for trade with North America.[1]

Countries participating in the OEEC undertook to free from controls by certain dates a given proportion of their 1948 level of private trade. In spite of some setbacks in 1951 and 1952 (largely caused by UK and French balance of payments difficulties), by the middle of the 1950s quantitative restrictions were of declining significance in the trade of the Western World. Since that period quantitative restrictions have been retained by two types of countries; by less developed countries wishing to foster infant industries and to encourage import substitution, and by high income countries anxious to protect industries—notably textiles—subject to international competition from low cost imports.

The GATT has been primarily concerned with the reduction of tariffs rather than the elimination of quantitative restrictions. The Agreement does, however, specifically permit Contracting Parties to impose trade controls, (a) in the case of balance of payments difficulties, and (b) where a Government regards the restrictions as necessary to implement domestic agricultural support policies. A Contracting Party restricting imports for balance of payments reasons undertakes to relax restrictions as its external position improves. To the free trader, quantitative controls are more obnoxious than tariffs. They cannot normally be circumvented by price or cost reductions; and they are often more discriminatory than tariffs. When the authorities operate any licensing system there is the danger of special favours to particular interests. Nevertheless in spite of the strictures of free traders, trade controls appear a more or less permanent element of the post-war world economy and are unlikely to disappear in the foreseeable future. In fact, a particularly disturbing form of quantitative restrictions appears to be gaining ground. It is the practice of asking countries to limit their exports 'voluntarily'. This has been used widely by industrial countries against low-cost manufactures from some developing countries but also, for example, by the US against steel imports from Western Europe and Japan.

3. EXCHANGE CONTROLS

Like quantitative trade restrictions, exchange controls are more certain than tariffs in their impact upon a country's balance of payments. They have the additional advantage of controlling invisible

[1] The OEEC was formed to administer American aid and to further economic co-operation among the countries of Western Europe. Its role in the post-war world is discussed more fully in Chapter 22.

transactions and capital movements as well as visible trade. As compared with trade controls there is also a difference of administration. Whereas the latter are usually operated by a Trade Ministry through the usual customs offices, exchange controls are normally operated by the Central Bank, working through the commercial banks. There is often—but not always—a limited degree of discretion delegated to the individual banks which has no counterpart in the case of quantitative trade restrictions.

Modus Operandi

Although there were some half-hearted attempts at exchange control during the First World War, exchange controls as practised today were adopted outside the USSR on a significant scale only in the 1930s. First imposed in 1930, they spread rapidly through Central Europe. Apart from a pause in 1935 and 1936, they became progressively more restrictive until the outbreak of the Second World War. Exchange controls systems were—and still are—particularly common in many Latin American countries.

In the inter-war years, exchange controls were introduced in Central Europe as a means of checking the outflow of foreign capital. Many countries had been borrowing heavily at short term; in the financial panics of 1930 and 1931, these foreign-owned funds were called home on an unprecedented scale.[1] The outright prohibition of capital repatriation seemed to be the only way to stem this enormous outflow. Although exchange controls were imposed primarily to check capital outflow, it soon became obvious that controls would have to be exercised also over current payments and receipts if capital movements were to be effectively controlled.

In practice it is difficult to distinguish between payments arising from capital and those arising from current transactions. An exporter anxious to export capital (or indeed merely willing to be party to a transfer of capital to a forbidden centre), can undervalue his exports in making his return to his exchange control authorities, leaving a proportion of the foreign exchange proceeds from their sale in the country of destination. On the other hand, an importer can allege to the authorities that his purchases are costing more foreign exchange than is really the case, the balance of what he pays to the seller over and above an agreed price being held on the importer's account (or that of his nominee) in the foreign centre. In either case capital has been exported. Controls must also be

[1] Finance Ministers found that exchange controls served a variety of purposes. In Germany they became an instrument of the Nazi rearmament policy, by limiting foreign exchange outgoings on so-called luxuries.

exercised over tourist expenditure, otherwise capital outflow might take the form of the export of bank notes. Indeed to make control of capital absolutely water-tight it might be necessary to exercise postal censorship. Even so, it is extremely difficult for the authorities to be certain that they have effectively stopped all clandestine export of capital.

Not only is it difficult to maintain close control over capital movements without at the same time controlling also current account transactions; the very attempt to exercise control can have an adverse effect upon confidence. It then becomes necessary to tighten the controls even further. Accordingly controls tend to become steadily more far-reaching, in order to plug successive exchange leaks. Something of this kind undoubtedly happened in Nazi Germany, where extremely harsh penalties were imposed upon those convicted of evading exchange controls.

An exchange control system involves rationing of foreign exchange either by price or by allocation procedures. The arrangements may or may not involve deliberate discrimination as between types of transaction or geographical areas. If foreign exchange is rationed not by price, but by some system of administrative allocation, it can be allotted like an import quota, on a discretionary basis or simply on the basis of first come, first served. The discretionary system has obvious advantages, not least of flexibility, but is open to abuse where the administration lacks integrity or efficiency. On the other hand an allocation on the basis of 'first come first served' can be equally arbitrary. A common practice is to base allocations on the applicants' previous exchange requirements. This has the disadvantage of undue rigidity: it discriminates not only against new firms, but also those which by cost reduction have become more efficient since the base period. These objections apply equally to quantitative trade controls.

Rationing by Price

The authorities might eschew the quantitative method of rationing and fix buying and selling prices at a level such that demand for foreign exchange is brought into equilibrium with available supply. This is rationing by price. There are, of course, numerous variants of this method. For example it might be possible for the authorities to charge one rate for buying and one for selling. A whole series of buying and selling rates could be laid down so that some transactions are encouraged while others are discouraged. This is the system of multiple exchange rates. One rate might apply to visible, another to invisible transactions. Used in this way an exchange control system can become a means for influencing the pattern of economic growth. Since the Second World War, developing countries have often so ordered their exchange rates as to encourage the growth of certain industries at the expense of other sectors whose development they do not wish to encourage.

A system of multiple exchange rates is possible only if foreign exchange markets can be divided into fairly water-tight compartments. The authorities must be certain that foreign currencies purchased relatively cheaply for the purpose of importing necessary raw materials are not resold to potential buyers of luxury imports. Multiple exchange rates are likely to commend themselves to the authorities when demand and supply elasticities for the goods or services which it imports or exports respectively differ either as between types of transaction or types of goods. For example, in the case of an essential raw material, the foreign elasticity of demand for which is relatively low, a country

TABLE 3. COLOMBIA

TABLE OF EXCHANGE RATES

(as at December 31, 1965)

(pesos per us dollar)

Buying	Selling
7.67[1] (Fixed rate) Exchange sales by petroleum companies for exploration and exploitation	
8.50 (Fixed rate) Exports of coffee	
9.00 (Preferential Market rate) Exports of manufactured products with an import component exceeding 50 per cent paid for at the preferential rate.	9.00[1,2] (Preferential market rate) Certain imports. Certain payments by the National Government. Certain students' expenses.
	10.83[1] (Preferential rate plus 10 per cent remittance Tax[3]) Principal and interest on official external debt registered before June 17, 1957. Repatriation of and service on foreign capital registered before that date.

TABLE 3—*continued*

Buying	Selling
13.50 (Intermediate market rate) All other exports except those of crude oil by foreign-owned petroleum companies.[4] Capital inflow electing intermediate market registration. Exchange receipts of local authorities and public agencies, including those from foreign loans.	13.50[1,2] (Intermediate market rate) Other imports. Eighty per cent of import freight payments on merchandise transported by conference ships. Service on new foreign debt. Service on old foreign debt registered under special provisions. Repatriation and profits on new foreign capital electing intermediate market registration.
18.27 (Free market rate) Invisibles. Other capital.	18.29 (Free market rate) Other invisibles and capital.

SOURCE: IMF Annual Report on Exchange Controls, 1966, p. 145.

[1] The banks may charge a commission of not more than Col. $0.05 per US $1.
[2] Certain commodities require an import license when imported at the preferential rate but are liberalized when imported at the immediate market rate.
[3] The remittance tax is payable in US dollars purchased in the free market.
[4] These need not be surrendered.

will find it in its interest to overvalue its currency in regard to exports of such a product. On the other hand, if a country is trying to diversify its economy, and wishes to encourage exports of manufactured goods, for which the foreign price elasticity of demand is relatively high, it is worth fixing a more favourable rate of exchange for these exports.[1] A multiple exchange rate system, carefully devised and efficiently enforced can enable a country to get—temporarily at least—the best of all worlds, as regards its balance of payments and development policies.

Multiple exchange rate policies have been widely adopted since the war. They were widespread in Europe in the early post-war years and still operate in many countries of South America, Africa and Asia.

[1] The attitude of the IMF towards multiple currency practices is discussed in Chapter 17.

Some countries have special foreign exchange markets for capital and other 'invisible' transactions. Rates in these markets are often left free to fluctuate; in this way the sometimes volatile inflow and outflow of capital can take place without disturbing the fixed rates at which trading transactions take place.

Some idea of the complexity of multiple exchange rates can be obtained from Table 3, taken from the IMF 1966 *Annual Report on Exchange Controls*. This Table shows the rates in force in Colombia at the end of 1965. There were two markets, an official one and a free market. The free market rate was allowed to fluctuate, but in the official market there were several rates. For those wishing to sell pesos, the least favourable rate was that relating to sales by foreign owned petroleum companies. This rate was 7.67 pesos = $1 US. Exporters of coffee received a slightly more favourable rate (8.50 pesos); exporters of manufactures with a high import content received 9.00 pesos per dollar. Other exporters received 13.50 pesos. At the same time, in the free market where transactions relating to invisibles and certain capital items took place, the rate was 18.27 pesos to the dollar. There was an equally complex gradation on the import side. In the case of many products, the importer would have to surrender 13.50 pesos per US dollar, while for certain favoured goods only 9.00 pesos were required.

4. DISCRIMINATION

Where multiple exchange rates are in force there is a clear case of discrimination. But almost any form of trade or exchange control involves some degree of discrimination, even if the discrimination is not deliberate but only incidental to some other policy objective.

When the size of an import or foreign exchange quota depends upon the recipients' previous imports there is discrimination against new importing firms, or new foreign sources of supply. Firms (either at home or abroad), whose costs have fallen to such an extent that they might reasonably have expected to attract to themselves a larger share of the market in the absence of controls, are penalized. Similarly, the authorities might pride themselves that although they distinguish between 'necessary' and 'luxury' imports or even between different types of transactions, they do not discriminate between countries. In practice discrimination on the basis of type of transaction often involves country discrimination and *vice versa*. For example the limitation of tourist expenditure in non-sterling countries by UK residents affects France and Switzerland more than Argentina and Chile, since few Britons in fact wish to spend their holidays in Latin America.

In the early post-war years of inconvertible currencies there was a great deal of controversy as to the advisability of a country in serious balance of payments difficulties, vis-à-vis a particular country or currency area, imposing discriminatory exchange controls on transactions with that country or area while allowing relative freedom in regard to transactions with other countries. This is a matter too complex to be analysed in full here, and the student who wishes to examine the matter further should consult one of the specialist works. The idea that direct controls should be discriminatory was developed by Professor Ragnar Frisch in 1947 and 1948.[1]

Given that exchange controls exist it is arguable that it is better for a deficit country to employ them in a discriminatory manner, so that the impact falls upon surplus countries than that controls should be applied without discrimination to all its trading partners. If a deficit country tries to restore balance of payments equilibrium by non-discriminatory restrictions on exports of countries, some of which are in deficit and others in surplus, the deficit countries will be driven more deeply into deficit while countries which were either in approximate balance or had small surpluses will find themselves moving into deficit. They in turn will feel justified in imposing import controls, again with adverse effects on a wide circle of countries. In fact, taken to their logical conclusion non-discriminatory controls would multiply until only one country was left not applying restrictions! Accordingly, it is better for deficit countries as a group to discriminate in favour of one another by imposing restrictions most heavily against 'strong' balance of payments countries.[2]

Early discussion of this question was largely in terms of balance of payments effects of discrimination. The question was whether restrictions applied in a discriminatory manner would restore balance of payments equilibrium with the minimum reduction in the total volume of trade. Largely due to the work of Fleming and Meade, however, the analysis has been carried forward in welfare terms. The question now becomes 'what is the most effective way of using direct controls for balance of payments purposes in order to secure the minimum reduction in the total volume of world trade after taking into account the contribution

[1] R. Frisch, 'On the Need for Forecasting a Multilateral Balance of Payments', American Economic Review, xxxvii, September 1947, and 'The Problems of Multi-compensatory Trade', Review of Economics and Statistics, November 1948.

[2] The point is made by J. Marcus Fleming, 'On Making the Best of Balance of Payments Restriction on Imports', Economic Journal, vol. lxi, March 1951 (reprinted in Caves and Johnson, Readings in International Economics, Allen and Unwin, 1968), and by J. E. Meade in The Theory of International Economic Policy, vol. 1. The Balance of Payments, chapters XXVIII to XXXI.

of each unit of trade to economic welfare?' A loss of £1 million of trade to country A might have more adverse welfare consequences than a similar loss to country B.

In his *Trade and Welfare*, Professor Meade has dealt very thoroughly with welfare aspects of discrimination, using the device of apportioning 'welfare weights' to the trade of various participating countries, and taking into account, also, differences in supply elasticities. Meade evolves four 'rules' which should be followed if a group of countries is to secure the 'ideal' pattern of trade controls. It is impossible here to do more than simply draw attention to the approach.[1] Meade uses the concept of the protective incidence of an import restriction to draw up various rules which should be followed if the optimum welfare position is to be achieved by countries imposing trade controls. For example, if two countries are restricting imports from each other, they should simultaneously relax their import restrictions on each others' products until one of them has completely removed its restrictions on imports from the other; if there are three countries, they should all relax their restrictions from each other simultaneously (in such a way that each country's balance of payments remains in equilibrium) until one of the countries has completely removed its restrictions on imports from the other two. Meade's rules imply that countries should arrange themselves in a kind of hierarchy in order of balance of payments strength, such that a weaker country is restricting imports from a stronger, and the restrictions which the weakest country imposes on imports from the strongest has a protective incidence equal to the sum of the protective incidences of the restrictions which the weakest country imposes on the intermediate country and which the intermediate country imposes on the strongest country. But it is impossible to do justice to the Fleming-Meade approach without making this chapter inordinately long and the keen student is strongly advised to consult the original sources.

SHORT GUIDE TO THE LITERATURE

An outline of many issues discussed in this chapter is in W. M. Corden, 'The Structure of a Tariff System and the Effective Protection Rate', *Journal of Political Economy*, vol. 74, no. 3, 1966. The question of effective v. nominal tariff rates is also dealt with by Bela Balassa,

---

[1] The argument is set out in *The Theory of International Economic Policy*, vol. ii. *Trade and Welfare*, Royal Institute of International Affairs, Chapter XXXIV. In this Chapter Meade acknowledges his substantial debt to Marcus Fleming, cited above.

'Tariff Protection in Industrial Countries, An Evaluation', *Journal of Political Economy*, vol. lxxiii, December 1965, reprinted in Caves and Johnson, cited above.

On the historical side of tariff building I recommended Dr Corden's contribution to the *Encyclopedia of the Social Sciences*. I have also outlined the development of the British tariff in my *The Shape of the British Tariff*, Institute of Economic Affairs Research Monograph, London 1968. This also contains a bibliography and a list of UK, USA and EEC tariff rates. Developments in the GATT are recorded in *Basic Instruments and Select Documents*, a series of collections of important decisions and records of the GATT and its Committees.

CHAPTER 7

ARGUMENTS FOR PROTECTION: A

In spite of the intellectual case for free trade, much of the history of trade between countries consists of attempts to impose barriers of the kind we have outlined in the previous chapter on the free movement of goods (and capital) between nations. Some arguments for protection are non-economic. For example, the establishment of domestic aircraft manufacturing in a small or medium-sized country is often supported by political rather than economic arguments. Undoubtedly there are many cases of this kind where political considerations must be given due weight but the economic cost should always be balanced against the political benefits of a project involving protection. It is the duty of the economist to draw attention to this cost, even if on balance he and his fellow citizens are convinced that political arguments justify the protection.

1. SPURIOUS ARGUMENTS

We shall not delay long on some arguments for protection which although allegedly economic, are obviously spurious. These, castigated by Haberler as 'untenable',[1] can be disposed of fairly quickly. Among such arguments is the plea that international trade is 'fair' only if the domestic tariff offsets low costs enjoyed by foreign producers. If this were taken to its logical conclusion all international trade arising from cost differentials would cease.[2]

Almost equally untenable, but to many people emotionally attractive, is the idea that it is immoral for a country like Britain to import the products of 'cheap labour' countries, not because this trade is injurious to British interests but because it is harmful to foreign labour. This line of reasoning argues that it is morally wrong for British consumers to encourage the growth of 'sweated' labour industries in overseas countries. Of course the fallacy of this argument is that low-wage workers in foreign countries would be even poorer if importing countries refused to buy their products. Presumably advocates of the argument would be happier if the 'sweated' workers of low-cost countries had no work at all. If abnormally high profits are being made out of sweated

---

[1] See G. Haberler, *The Theory of International Trade*, cited above.

[2] Absurd though this argument seems, it provided part of the justification for the revision of the United States tariff of 1924.

labour abroad, there might theoretically be a case for international action among importing countries to insist on reasonable working conditions by refusing to buy the products of sweated labour unless conditions were improved. This boycott could, however, be successful only in certain rarely attainable circumstances, and may be forgotten as a practical policy. In any case, a collective boycott is by no means the same as the unilateral imposition of a tariff or other restriction by a high-income importing countries. In practice, of course, arguments about sweated labour conditions abroad are often closely intertwined with special pleading for domestic industries.[1]

It is extremely misleading to make money wage comparisons between countries without taking into account also differences in labour productivity. Thus the GATT has estimated that, in 1964, Italian productivity per worker in cotton yarn manufacture was one quarter of that of the USA. In India, productivity was only 17 per cent of the USA.[2] It has been calculated that in India, 10·68 operatives are required to look after 1,000 spindles to produce a given grade of cotton yarn at a total cost of £133 10s 0d, while in Western Europe only 1·8 workers would be required at a total cost of £67 10s 0d. At the weaving stage, seventy Indian operatives are needed to attend 100 looms. In Europe, only fifteen are required.[3] Furthermore, in some sectors of production it is misleading to compare only direct labour costs. There are few products where other costs can be neglected. For example, according to the GATT study referred to above, in Hong Kong the direct labour element in yarn production accounts for less than 10 per cent of the cost of the final product. The same study estimates that if 100 yards of Hong Kong grey fabric sells for $14 the direct labour cost in weaving could be as little as $1.4.

Although many employees in low wage countries may be working in bad conditions for poor pay, this is not universally true. Often workers in the export sector enjoy conditions more favourable than in factories catering for the home market. For example, in the late 1950s well over

---

[1] See for example, the complaints in the 1950's of British M.P.s for the cotton areas of Lancashire, about the conditions and long hours of work in the Hong Kong textile industry. This was claimed as one reason why the British Government should restrict imports of cotton goods from the colony.

[2] GATT *Cotton Textiles*, Geneva 1966, p. 67. The reader should treat estimates of this kind with caution, for as the authors of the GATT study remark, there are likely to be important differences as between countries in the type of product (in this case yarn). There is also inevitably some lack of comparability between national productivity data.

[3] Information from *Cotton Textiles Export Promotion Council of India*.

two-thirds of all Japanese exports were produced in factories employing over 500 workers. In these larger firms wages were relatively high and working conditions good. In fact wages in enterprises employing a thousand or more workers were twice as high as in those where less than fifty were employed. It is the products of these relatively high wage, high productivity units, which compete most successfully in the US and West European markets.[1]

2. WHO GAINS FROM PROTECTION?

Although some of the weakest arguments for protection are those most frequently invoked, often because of their strong emotional appeal, there are nevertheless some acceptable arguments for protection; in the remainder of this and in the following chapter we set out some of these 'more tenable' arguments. Among those to be taken seriously are those concerned with the fostering of infant industries, with encouraging growth in less developed countries, improving a country's terms of trade, securing a redistribution of income within a country, maintaining full employment and safeguarding a country's balance of payments. At the outset, however, we must be quite clear as to *who* is alleged to gain from a tariff.[2]

The essence of the case for free trade is that it raises economic welfare for the world as a whole. It does not follow that each and every nation will be better off. But the gains of one country will outweigh the losses of another so that the former will be able to compensate the latter for any losses resulting from free trade, and still be better off. This is the compensation principle with which students should now be familiar. The free trade argument does not deny that a single country or group of countries might improve its own economic position by means of a tariff, but it does deny that (with the possible exception of the infant industry case) the world as a whole can be made a better place as the result of a tariff.

Almost the only tariff argument that substantially modifies this case is the infant industry one, which claims that in certain circumstances only by a tariff can an optimum international allocation of resources

[1] I have discussed this question at some length in *British Export Performance*, Cambridge University Press, 1964, pp. 85 ff.

[2] For the remainder of this chapter, the word 'tariff' is used as a short-hand for all measures which directly distort trade, e.g. quantitative restrictions, exchange controls, subsidies on exports and mixing regulations. The reader should continually ask himself what modifications are required in the argument in these special cases.

be secured. The argument is that in a free trade situation a country may never have a chance to develop the production and export of certain products in which it has a potential comparative cost advantage, because established foreign producers have an early start. Thus the infant industry argument claims that *in the long run*, the world as a whole will benefit fom a temporary tariff. This cannot be said of another 'respectable' argument for protection, namely the terms-of-trade one which claims that, by imposing a tariff, a *country* might improve its own welfare position. Free traders insist that although the imposing country gains an advantage, *the world as a whole* is worse off as the result of such a tariff.

In like case, the argument that certain groups in a country might improve their welfare position *vis-a-vis* other groups in the same country (the redistribution of income argument) does not suggest that the tariff-imposing country as a whole would be better off than under free trade. Only certain groups within the country improve their position. Accordingly, when faced by tariff arguments, the student should be very careful to distinguish between gains alleged to accrue to the world, to the tariff imposing country, and to a sectional interest in the country.

3. THE INFANT INDUSTRY ARGUMENT

Among free traders the infant industry argument has traditionally been regarded as one of the most acceptable (or least reprehensible) justifications for interference with free trade. The basis of the argument is that a country might have a potential comparative cost advantage in the development of a certain industry, but simply because of an earlier start the industry has been developed in another country to a point where it would be impossible for a newly established industry to compete with it. In this situation a tariff might be necessary to make possible the establishment of the industry in the country where it has the potential cost advantage. In such a case a refusal to grant protection is tantamount to neglecting the potential advantage of an international division of labour based on comparative cost differences.[1]

There are various reasons why in the absence of a tariff, a new industry in which a country has a potential (but not present) cost advantage would never be established. In the first place scale economies might

[1] The infant industry argument was formulated in the United States (where it had considerable influence on commercial policy) by Alexander Hamilton in his *Report on Manufactures 1790*. It was further developed in Germany (where again it proved highly acceptable as a policy justification) by Friedrich List in his *National System of Political Economy*, 1841.

be impossible while the home market is supplied from abroad. Secondly, a country might possess a labour force potentially superior to that of another country in a particular occupation, but several years of the learning process might be required for potential skill to become actual skill. In such a case a tariff provides a period of protection in which these skills can be developed. Thirdly, if the protected industry is sufficiently large, economies external to firms might be reaped. For example, when a country's engineering industry is of a sufficient size, it becomes worthwhile establishing technological colleges and research centres. These institutions produce a feed-back leading to further economies for the engineering industry.

Fourthly, a tariff might assist industries other than those directly protected. If protection results in expansion of domestic industry, which in turn leads to a lowering of costs and prices, firms in industries using the products of the protected industry also gain. For example, if steel prices fall as the result of scale economies consequent upon infant industry protection, all firms using domestic steel benefit. Of course the steel using firms gain only if protection offered by the tariff eventually results in domestic steel prices becoming lower than prices of similar imported steels. Moreover, even if the price of home produced steel ultimately falls below that of the imports, there may well be a protracted period during which the domestic steel industry is incurring high costs of growth, or during which the (usually expensive) learning process is taking place. During these years, costs in the steel-using industries are likely to be higher than before the imposition of the tariff. Something of this kind has in fact occurred in India, whose motor and other industries have been forced to use high cost domestic steel. Nevertheless, if a country really has a potential comparative cost advantage in steel making, the tariff will result ultimately not only in cheaper steel but also in a lowering of costs in all steel-using industries At this stage, the 'infant industry' argument merges into the 'infant country' argument for protection, a question which we take up below (p. 102).

The theoretical validity of the infant industry argument has hardly been challenged, being accepted by such free traders as J. S. Mill, Marshall, Pigou and Taussig, all of whom, however, insist that the protection must be carefully justified by reference to the facts of a particular case. Free traders stress that it is generally difficult to identify in advance industries in which a country has a potential comparative advantage. There is also the danger that tariff protection, once granted, becomes difficult to remove. Who is to decide, and by what criteria, when an industry can stand on its own feet? For these reasons, free trade economists are reluctant to approve tariff building on infant industry grounds.

There is, however, an even more fundamental question upon which the infant industry argument, as frequently advocated, should be challenged. Often it is argued that since an industry might make substantial losses for a period of years while it is establishing itself and before it begins to yield a profit, the community should support it during its loss-making infancy. Now if this is the only reason for protecting an infant, it is not a very strong one, for *if* the industry is expected eventually to make a profit unaided, there is no real reason why it should be subsidized by the State. For the loss-making infancy period may be regarded as simply an investment towards a more profitable future. If profits are likely, private enterprise ought to be able to find the finance to carry the industry forward through its early years in the fairly certain knowledge that the fruits of the investment will be reaped when profits begin to come in. Accordingly, there seems little justification for aiding an infant industry by means of protection if the only beneficiary is the industry itself. The real argument for infant industry protection is different from this. It is the argument that if, as the result of infant industry growing, other firms, or the community at large gain, then it is reasonable for the community to pay a price in terms of protection in order to see the infant to maturity. Thus the infant industry argument becomes an argument for protecting a firm or industry from which *external* economies might be expected as time passes.[1]

We can perhaps summarize the criteria that must be satisfied if the infant industry argument for protection is valid by stressing three considerations. Firstly, economies resulting from protection must be external to the firm. Secondly, there must be some dynamic element in the model, that is to say the competitive position of an industry must be expected to change over time, following the granting of protection. Finally, the present cost of protection must not exceed the size of future gains. Clearly it is not always easy, in a particular case, to know whether these criteria are likely to be satisfied.

We have seen that external economies might accrue over a fairly wide field when, as the result of a tariff a country reaps the full benefit of its potential comparative cost advantage in a certain product. The gain might be even greater when not merely one industry but a group of industries are protected. Protection might be the means by which a relatively underdeveloped, non-industrial country reaches a point of

---

[1] This is lucidly discussed by J. E. Meade in Chapter XVI of *Trade and Welfare*. Professor Meade examines the infant industry argument for protection under the heading of 'The Structural Argument for Trade Control'.

relatively rapid economic growth. This is to some extent what happened in Germany and in the United States in the latter part of the nineteenth century. Accordingly, while free trade is probably the optimum policy for highly industrialized countries, there are strong arguments for an interference with free trade in the case of less developed ones. It is to these arguments that we now turn.

4. PROTECTION AND LESS DEVELOPED COUNTRIES

The Infant Country

The infant industry argument, properly understood, is one of the most powerful of all arguments for protection. It is perhaps even stronger, when applied not merely to one industry or group of related industries, but to a whole sector of a country's economy, when that country is at an early stage of development. Almost by definition, a less developed country is unlikely to be reaping the full gains from its potential comparative cost advantage. If a country does not exploit to the full its comparative cost advantage, not only the country but the world as a whole is a poorer place. The argument runs that in the case of such a country present cost ratios might dictate that it should concentrate upon primary production but these cost ratios are not necessarily what they would be if the country had reached a higher level cf development. Accordingly the case for protection as applied to a less developed country does not deny the validity of the principle of comparative costs. It rather argues that a better distribution of world output and resources might eventually be secured if the country is given the opportunity to develop industries in which it has a potential—but not yet an actual—comparative cost advantage.

We have seen that protection might enable an infant industry not only to reap internal and external economies of scale, but also to gain advantage from the training up of a skilled labour force. When a range of industries is protected the gain is likely to be even greater. The forward and backward linkage effects, that is, effects on using and supplying industries will be even stronger. There are also likely to be powerful 'lateral' or horizontal effects. These occur when the growth of an industry increases the demand for complementary products. For example, the development of a domestic bicycle manufacturing industry is likely to encourage also the growth of firms making small dynamos, plastic saddle bags, or waterproof cycling capes.

Protective policies are often adopted in a developing country to support a general programme of industrialization. Indeed, the desire to industrialize is the most obvious *raison d'être* for the protectionist policies of less developed countries. In such countries, the argument for protection is especially strong when development plans impose a short or medium-term burden on their balances of payments. In order to appreciate the argument for protection as seen by less developed countries, it is necessary to understand some of the reasons why they are so anxious to industrialize. Accordingly, the next few pages are in a sense a digression from our main theme, but nonetheless seem to be necessary if the student is fully to appreciate attitudes towards protection in such countries.

Industrialization

There are a number of reasons why less developed countries wish to industrialize. Firstly their economies are heavily dependent upon production and export of primary products, often exporting an extremely narrow range of these goods.[1] Such dependence can have serious economic consequences. In the first place, as every novice in economics knows, prices of many primary products fluctuate much more than those of manufactured goods. These price fluctuations cause marked variations, not only in the incomes of individual producers in such countries, but also in the countries' export receipts. Thus both cyclical fluctuations and swings in the balances of payments of primary producing countries tend to be more marked than in manufacturing countries.[2] A widening of the base of the economies of primary producing countries is accordingly likely to make for greater internal and external stability.

Closely linked with the 'vulnerability' argument is the one associated with the deterioration in the terms of trade of developing countries. As *per capita* world incomes rise, a declining proportion is devoted to food and certain other raw materials. Accordingly, it is alleged, countries which depend heavily upon foodstuffs exports face a long-term deterioration in their terms of trade. By creating a demand for industrial products, protection will diversify the economies of such countries helping

[1] See Chapter 24 below for examples of this dependence.

[2] Such fluctuations have indirect repercussions on manufacturing countries *via* the foreign trade multiplier. A fall in incomes in primary producing countries will reduce their capacity to import thus affecting countries which supply their markets. This question is discussed in some detail in Chapter 12.

The argument that a narrow range of export products itself necessarily leads to export instability and that fluctuations in prices of primary product exports lead to instability in domestic prices, national incomes and growth rates has received a salutary jolt at the hands of Professor A. I. MacBean, who in a recent study has examined the common assumptions about price instability of primary product exports I. A. MacBean, 'Export Instability and Economic Development', *University of Glasgow Social and Economic Studies* No. 9, London, Allen and Unwin, 1966.

rescue them from the consequences of the deterioration in their terms of trade.[1]

As we shall see in Chapter 24, there is evidence that the trade of less developed countries has grown more slowly than that of developed countries. For the less developed countries, it is no longer true that foreign trade is 'an engine of growth'. Technological developments (notably the growth of synthetics), changes in consumer taste, and restrictive policies in regard to imports of goods which the less developed countries can produce most efficiently have encouraged their concentration on import substitution rather than export promotion. This emphasis on import replacement may be a temporary phenomenon; there are signs that the Indian authorities, for example, are now passing from a period when the stress was entirely on import substitution to one where increasing attention is paid to export promotion.[2] But for many decades yet developing countries are likely to have a strong incentive to insulate themselves from the ups and downs of world trade.

A more fundamental argument for the fostering of domestic manufacturing industry in less developed countries arises from the belief that, since incomes per head are generally higher in manufacturing industry than in agriculture, a transfer of labour from the agricultural to the industrial sector is one way to raise average living standards, by raising the proportion of the population engaged in manufacturing. This argument was developed systematically by Mihail Manoilesco in 1931[3]. Manoilesco's main thesis was that since marginal productivity of labour is low in agriculture, compared with other branches of the economy, a transfer of labour from agriculture to these other branches

---

[1] Statements regarding the long-term deterioration in the terms of trade of primary producing countries should be treated with some reserve. As in all index number problems, much depends upon the choice of a base-date. Secondly, there are wide variations in price movements as between different commodities. It is misleading to lump all primary products together or to generalize from primary producing countries as a whole to the experience of one particular country. These difficulties are fully discussed in G. M. Meier, *International Trade and Development*, New York, Harper and Row, 1964, Chapter 7.

[2] There was little discussion of external problems in the First Indian Five Year Plan, 1950/1 to 1955/6: the Second Plan showed a greater awareness of the external repercussions of development, but the primary need was believed to be an inflow of foreign capital and import substitution. Exports were barely mentioned. Only in the Fourth Plan Period, 1965/6 to 1970/1, was there a full realization of the need for India deliberately to promote exports. I have discussed this question at greater length in a contribution to *The Crisis in Indian Planning*, ed. P. Streeten and M. Lipton, Oxford University Press, for the Royal Institute of International Affairs, 1968.

[3] *The Theory of Protection and International Trade*, London, 1931.

would raise the marginal productivity in agriculture and hence average productivity in the economy as a whole. For many people this argument is reinforced by the belief that industrialization has important economic and social by-products. Industrial development imposes certain economic and social changes—for example, habits of regular and punctual work—which are likely to spill over to influence the whole of national life. There is also much to be said for the amenities of town life, with all the incentives towards a higher living standard that urbanization involves. The social advantages of living in towns might be disputed, but there can be no doubt that, in a less developed country, urban dwellers are more likely than their peasant compatriots to be susceptible to new ideas, to desire new and more varied patterns of consumption, and to be influenced by the prospect of attaining higher living standards.

Viner and others have vigorously denied that a switch from agriculture to manufacturing necessarily involves a raising of *per capita* incomes. In their eyes, agriculture does not necessarily spell poverty and industrialization prosperity. Of course they accept that many agricultural countries are poor and many industrial ones rich—although the examples of New Zealand, Australia, and Denmark, should belie such generalizations.[1] But Viner questions the assumption that dependence upon agriculture *causes* poverty and the development of industry *causes* prosperity. He argues that in many cases agricultural countries are poor not because they have failed to industrialize, but simply because they are backward. 'The misallocation of resources as between agriculture and manufactures is probably rarely a major cause of poverty. . . . The real problem in poor countries is not agriculture as such, or the absence of manufactures as such, but poverty and backwardness, poor agriculture, or poor agriculture and poor manufacturing—The remedy is to remove the basic causes of the poverty and backwardness.'[2]

Viner insists that for many countries the most promising field for rapid economic development is in agriculture rather than industry; in his view the measures needed are those which promote health, education,

[1] The difference in *per capita* incomes may be due to the large size of families in the farming community or the inadequacy of money income measure as a true indication of real income in a less developed countries. There is what Viner calls 'a concealed rural income in occupacy of farm houses' and the virtually automatic provision of many services which would have to be paid for in cash by the urban dwellers. These matters are discussed by Viner in *International Trade and Economic Development*, Oxford, Clarendon Press, 1953, pp. 47 ff.

[2] Ibid. p. 52.

transportation facilities and cheap rural credit. He does not deny that as such a country develops there will be a steady increase in the proportion of the labour force engaged in secondary and tertiary employment—one of the distinguishing features of a country whose living standards are rapidly rising. But the rise of employment in these sectors is the consequence, not the cause of, the improvements in the economy.

The Underemployment Argument

An aspect of the industrialization argument, which has received considerable attention in recent years, is underemployment in agriculture. While Manoilesco maintained that the marginal productivity of labour in agriculture was low, modern writers have gone further, suggesting that in the case of some countries, it might even be zero. In other words, the degree of underemployment in agriculture in certain countries is such that a part of the labour force could be removed from the farms without any fall in total agricultural output. Indeed owing to present rural overcrowding output might actually rise (in which case marginal productivity is negative!) This is the concept of underemployment or 'disguised' unemployment, developed by Professor Arthur Lewis.[1]

Underemployment in agriculture is often said to be associated with fixed technical coefficients of production. Thus it is claimed that a certain number of workers are required to work a given piece of land, and beyond a certain point, the addition of marginal units of labour to given quantities of land and other factors results in no increase in aggregate output—perhaps even a decrease. This is more likely to be true of subsistence peasant family agriculture than of plantation crops, for in the former case the peasant is not only likely to be ignorant of cost considerations; he will almost certainly be expected to provide employment for the extended family—for whom few opportunities for outside employment exist. Overcrowding on the land can lead to the destruction of soil fertility by excessive cropping. The problem is especially serious where the growth of population leads to a fragmentation of holdings.[2]

It should be noted that such 'underemployed' agricultural workers are not necessary idling; they could in fact be using up a great deal of

[1] W. A. Lewis, *The Theory of Economic Growth*, Allen and Unwin, London 1955, and more briefly in 'Economic Development with Unlimited Supplies of Labour', Manchester School, May 1954.

[2] The whole question is discussed by W. A. Lewis in *The Theory of Economic Growth*, cited above, p. 327.

physical energy. They are only underemployed in the sense that they are relatively unproductive. Neither is it necessarily true that they require fewer calories of food intake than if they were employed in factories. Accordingly, Lewis and others argue that the transfer of such labour to the towns would neither diminish the output of agriculture nor increase aggregate demand for food.[1] Hence a tariff might improve the allocation of resources.

The underemployment argument for a tariff has been criticized, notably by Haberler, Viner and Meier.[2] Firstly, they argue that technical production co-efficients are less rigid than proponents of the transfer of workers assume. Viner, for example, finds it 'impossible to conceive' of a farm on which some addition to the crop might not be secured by using additional labour in 'more careful selection and planting of the seed', or 'more intensive cultivation of the crop'.[3] By the same token there would be some decrease in absolute farm output if some workers were to leave agriculture. Secondly, where a labour market exists it is difficult to see why any cultivator should engage labour, the marginal product of which he knows to be less than its marginal cost (i.e. the wage rate). Of course he might continue to employ workers who do not justify their wages, through sheer ignorance. In subsistence cultivation the likelihood of workers not 'earning their keep' is of course much greater, although given some mobility of labour it seems likely that even in this case in the long run there will be a movement out of the subsistence sector.

From this brief outline of some of the issues involved in economic development of poor countries[4] the student will appreciate some of the complexities of the questions raised by protection in such countries. Today few economists would argue that developing countries should never foster development by means of protection. But protective policies should be undertaken only after careful consideration of their implications. A general blanket protection granted to any and every

---

[1] Jacob Viner, however, makes the point that there is invariably some loss in the transportation of food from country to town, as the result of deterioration, and spillage. See also G. Meier in *Leading Issues in Development Economics*, Oxford University Press, 1964, p. 81.

[2] The criticisms of these three economists are set out in G. Meier, *Leading Issues in Development Economics*, cited above.

[3] Ibid. p. 80.

[4] In a textbook on International Economics it is clearly impossible to give to the broader questions of development the attention which they deserve. The student is strongly urged to read more of this exciting subject in one of the texts referred to in this chapter. I would also like to commend Professor Hla Myint's simply written but scholarly paperback *The Economics of Developing Countries*, London, Hutchinson University Press, 1967.

industry might well involve such a country in high and quite unnecessary costs.

SHORT GUIDE TO THE LITERATURE

One of the ablest expositions of the free trade case is still Haberler's distinguished text *Theory of International Trade With its Applications to Commercial Policy*, New York, 1950. In this book Haberler deals *seriatim* with many of the arguments but forward by protectionists. The classics on the infant industry arguments are referred to in footnotes to this chapter. Meade's *Trade and Welfare*, Chapter XVI, recasts the traditional infant industry argument in terms of the structural argument. There is a large and rapidly growing literature on the special arguments for trade controls advanced by less developed countries. Perhaps two of the most significant contributions are those of Professor Hla Myint, 'The "Classical Theory" of International Trade and the Underdeveloped Countries', *Economic Journal*, vol. lxviii, No. 270, June 1958, pp. 317–337, reprinted in *Readings in International Economics*, ed. R. E. Caves and H. G. Johnson, London, Allen and Unwin, 1968; and Gunnar Myrdal's book *An International Economy, Problems and Prospects*, London, Routledge and Kegan Paul, 1956.

The controversial question of the extent to which industrialization in the less developed countries should be encouraged by tariff or other means is examined from several points of view in G. M. Meier, *Leading Issues in Development Economics, Selected Materials and Commentary*, New York, Oxford University Press, 1964. Professor Meier has compiled a selection of extracts from the writings of a large number of authorities and the student can hardly do better than refer to this book as an introduction to the field. Also strongly recommended to the student who wants a lucidly written short introduction is H. Myint, *The Economics of the Developing Countries*, London, Hutchinson University Library, 1967.

CHAPTER 8

ARGUMENTS FOR PROTECTION: B

1. THE TERMS OF TRADE ARGUMENT

The English classical economists were aware that a suitable tariff might have a favourable effect upon the terms of trade of the country imposing the duty. Mill, Marshall, Edgeworth, and Taussig realized that a country could gain at the expense of its neighbours in this way. Although both Marshall and Edgeworth doubted whether a government could in practice be trusted to impose a sufficiently moderate rate of tax, they accepted that in theory at any rate, a given tariff, if it were a 'suitable' one, might make a country better off than under free trade. Now as we have seen, the essence of the classical position was not that free trade would make each and every country better off, but would increase the welfare of the world as a whole. Free trade would not increase everybody's welfare, but would produce a situation in which no country could be made better off without at the same time another country being made worse off. Free traders certainly never asserted that a tariff could not improve the terms of trade. Those who read this in their arguments are going further than the classical writers intended.[1] They are being more royalist than the king.

Affinity with Imperfect Competition

In the 1930s there was a revival of interest in the whole question of tariff theory. A body of literature grew up, emphasizing that a country *could* often improve its position by exploiting its trading partners. In general the tendency of writers in this stream of thought—Kaldor, Samuelson, Lerner and Scitovsky, was to demonstrate the close affinity between tariff theory and monopoly theory. Just as in conditions of imperfect competition, one producer might increase his profit by exerting his monopoly influence on price, so might a country gain in some circumstances by raising its export prices. A tariff imposing country might 'exploit' its trading partners in the same way that a monopolist 'exploits' consumers. Some tariff protagonists go even further, arguing that, since we cannot measure in quantitative terms the gain of one country against the losses of another, there is not even a presumption that trade barriers always reduce welfare for the world as a

---

[1] Although it is worth noting that the nineteenth-century free trade campaign was largely based on the idea that a country could *not* improve its lot by means of protection.

whole. Thus if a poor country improves its terms of trade at the expense of its wealthier trading partners, it is arguable that protection has enabled the world as a whole to raise its level of real welfare.

Offer Curve Analysis

The proposition that a country might improve its terms of trade by means of a suitable tariff is usually discussed with the aid of Marshallian offer curves,[1] already referred to in Chapter 4 where we discussed the

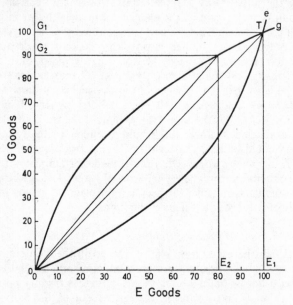

FIGURE 7. Effect of an Import Duty on Barter Terms of Trade.

terms of trade. We have used this device again in figure 7. Following Marshall, we assume two countries, England and Germany, producing respectively 'E' goods and 'G' goods. The curve 'e', known as England's offer curve, shows how many 'E' goods English residents will surrender in order to obtain a given quantity of 'G' goods. Similarly, Germany's offer curve 'g' shows how many 'G' goods German residents are prepared to surrender in exchange for a given quantity of 'E' goods. The point where the two countries' offer curves intersect is the equilibrium one at which exchange takes place. The rate at which 'E' goods are traded against 'G' goods is equivalent to the slope of OT.

[1] Explained in *Money, Credit and Commerce*, cited above.

We can use this apparatus to show what happens when one of the countries, let us say England, imposes an import duty. It is obvious from the shape of the offer curves that Germany would in fact be prepared to trade OG_2 'G' goods for only OE_2 'E' goods. In other words if the supply of 'E' goods traded were reduced by 20 per cent the

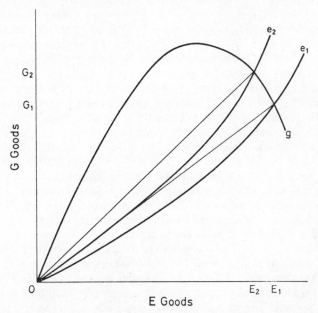

FIGURE 8. Effects of a Tariff on Terms of Trade when Offer Curve is Falling.

supply of 'G' goods offered in exchange would be reduced by only about 10 per cent. The English traders would get more 'G' goods in return for a given quantity of 'E' goods; the barter terms of trade moving in favour of England (see p. 59). Now the reduction in the volume of 'E' goods traded in exchange for 'G' goods can be brought about by (a) an export duty in England, (b) an import duty in England, (c) the establishment of a State-trading monopoly in England.[1] The effectiveness of these policies in improving England's terms of trade

[1] For a proof that an export duty in England would have exactly the same effect on England's terms of trade as an import duty, see A. P. Lerner 'The Symmetry Between Import and Export Taxes', *Economica*, vol. iii, August 1936, reproduced in R. E. Caves and H. G. Johnson, *Readings in International Economics*, Allen and Unwin, 1968.

will depend upon the shape of the 'G' curve—that is, upon reciprocal elasticity of demand for 'E' goods in Germany in terms of 'G' goods.

If the German offer curve is horizontal between the relevant points, then as England restricts its exports, the *same* quantity of imports from Germany is obtainable. German demand for 'E' goods is of unit elasticity. If the German offer curve is downward sloping between the relevant points, Germany would actually surrender *more* 'G' goods in exchange for OE_2 'E' goods than for OE_1 'E' goods. This situation is depicted in figure 8. It shows that England could actually obtain *more* German goods by restricting export of her products. In such a case, Germans are so desperately anxious to obtain England's exports that they are prepared actually to expand their exports in order to obtain the diminished volume of 'E' goods. This situation is perhaps unusual— Marshall described a falling offer curve as an 'exceptional' one, but it serves to illustrate the importance of the elasticities in determining the gains or otherwise from imposing a tariff. In fact, the reciprocal demand abroad for a country's products is usually fairly elastic, for the proportion of a given product supplied to the world market by one country is small—except perhaps in the case of some primary products; even in such cases substitutes are often available. Accordingly the g curve is likely to be rising, and some decrease in the quantity of imports obtainable is likely if exports are restricted.

Now free traders, while accepting the logic of the argument thus far, might point out that undesirable consequences might follow the improvement in England's terms of trade. Firstly, Germany might retaliate; secondly, although some improvement in England's terms of trade is possible, the diminished volume of trade might mean a smaller measure of real welfare. Let us take the second point first. It is clear that only if Germany's elasticity of demand for 'E' goods is less than unity, will a duty result in an increase in the quantity available for home consumption in England of *both* imports and exportables. As we have seen this will be the case only when the German offer curve is falling. If the foreign offer is horizontal over the relevant portion, that is the elasticity of German demand for 'E' goods is unity, then the quantity of exportables available for consumption in England will increase, although the volume of imports remains unchanged. In both cases, English consumers have at least as many of both 'E' goods and 'G' goods available for consumption as they had before. There is accordingly no question of a diminution of the real economic welfare of English consumers. But if the German reciprocal demand curve is sloping upwards, that is if demand for 'E' goods in terms of 'G' goods is elastic, the volume of 'G' goods available for consumption in England will have decreased—although the volume of exportables available has increased. Consumers are presented with a different assortment of goods after the imposition of the duty. Can we assume that in terms of real welfare they have gained?

We need to compare the degree of satisfaction enjoyed by a community after the imposition of a tariff with the degree of satisfaction before the change. The obvious tool of analysis for this purpose is the community indifference map, discussed in Chapter 5.

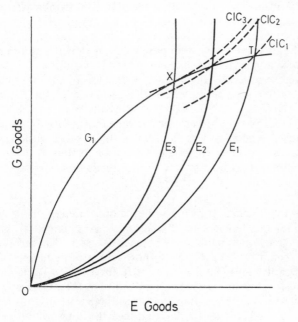

FIGURE 9. Effect of Tariff on Community Indifference Curves.[1]

Kaldor argued quite simply that if the effect of a given commercial policy is to bring a country's consumers on to a higher indifference curve, then there is a clear gain to the country as a whole. Let us see how this looks in diagrammatic form. In figure 9 we superimpose the family of community indifference curves CIC for English citizens on the offer curves. It is clear that if we go on increasing the duty imposed by

[1] Trade increases the supply of 'G' goods but decreases the supply of 'E' goods. This is why the indifference curves slope from north-east to south-west.

England, the 'E' offer curve is pushed further and further along 'G' towards the origin. For a time—up to the point marked X on our diagram—English residents move on to a higher indifference curve. The real welfare of English consumers as a whole increases, since CIC_3 is higher than either CIC_1 or CIC_2. Beyond X, however, welfare decreases, for further increase in the tariff will push English consumers on to a lower indifference curve than they are on at X. The point X, where an English indifference curve is tangential to Germany's offer curve is the point where the tariff is at the optimum. This is where English residents are in the best position compatible with demand conditions for their products in Germany. Accordingly, unless the foreign demand is infinitely elastic—and in the real world this is un-likely—the residents of a tariff imposing country might well move on to a higher consumption indifference curve than is possible under free trade.

Although, as we saw in Chapter 5, the use of the community in-difference curve can be criticized, the general effect of the work of Leontief, Kaldor and Scitovsky confirms the view that a tariff im-proves a country's position if the foreigner's elasticity of demand for the country's product is less than unity. In the real world, countries are generally unwilling to let themselves be exploited and the tariff raising country must be prepared to face retaliation.

Retaliation

In figure 10 England, by imposing a duty, moves on to a higher consumption indifferences curve Ce_2. Trade takes place at T_2. Germany has been forced on to a lower indifference curve Cg_2. The terms of trade are represented by OT_2. Germany now retaliates by herself imposing an import duty, thus distorting her offer curve to G_2. Trade now takes place at OT_3—less favourable to England than OT_2. Germany is on a higher indifference curve; England on a lower one. It is now open to England to retaliate; as battle continues the total volume of trade decreases—T approaches the origin. The more heavily Germany taxes trade—the nearer T is to O—the more difficult it becomes for England to levy a duty which will bring trade to a point at which OG is tangential to a relatively high 'E' indifference curve. In figure 10 if no further taxes are imposed, trade will take place at T_4.

It should be clear that the extent to which a country can improve its term of trade as the result of a tariff will depend upon relative demand and supply elasticities at home and abroad. A country which is a sub-stantial world importer of a particular commodity will, in general, be in a better position to 'make the foreigner pay' than one which imports only a small quantity of a given product. Similarly, a country which is a major world supplier of a group of products will be better able to improve its position as the result of an export tax than one which is merely one of a large number of producers.

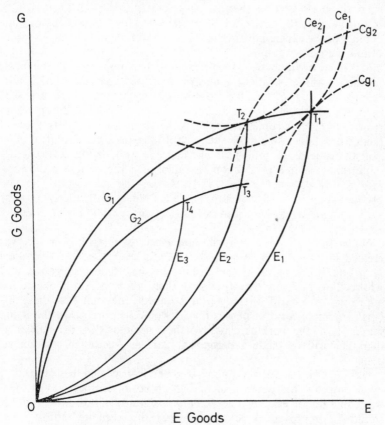

FIGURE 10. Effect of Retaliation on Community Indifference Curves.

The general conclusion we must draw is that a suitable duty—or retaliation—can often improve a country's welfare position. This contradicts Beveridge's claim in 1931[1]—that retaliation can never improve a country's welfare position.

[1] The case for unilateral free trade was argued by Beveridge in *Tariffs: The Case Examined*, ed. W. Beveridge, London, Longmans, 1931. The work remains a classic in free trade theory and is still worth reading. Other contributors included Benham, Bowley, Hicks, Plant and Robbins.

2. PROTECTION AND THE DISTRIBUTION OF INCOME

We have seen that theoretically it is possible for a country to improve its position *vis-à-vis* another by means of a carefully designed tariff. Is it also possible for protection to benefit one group of persons within a country at the expense of another? If so a tariff might become an engine of income redistribution.

It is fairly obvious that if the protection of an industry—say the textile industry—which is labour intensive, increases the output of textiles relative to that of other products—say foodstuffs which are land intensive, there will be an aggregate increase in demand for labour relative to land. Incomes of textile workers will rise relative to those of landowners. Let us suppose that a tariff increases the output of good x at the expense of good y. If one factor of production plays a more important part in a production of x than of y, the change in the composition of national income will increase the proportion of total product accruing to that factor. There is nothing particularly novel or surprising in this concept. Indeed, as long ago as 1906 Pigou explicitly stated what would happen.[1]

Wider interest in the redistribution aspect of a tariff, however, was created by the *Report of a Committee of Enquiry into the Australian Tariff*, published in 1929. The authors of this Report suggested that whilst they believed that the Australian terms of trade would be improved by a tariff on industrial products, they felt that the principal argument for a tariff was that it would help maintain the living standards of the working class. On these grounds they recommended that the tariff be made a permanent part of Australian commercial policy.

Although in the 1930s economists generally accepted that protection might improve the position of one group *vis-à-vis* other groups there was some doubt whether the *absolute* position of the protected group would be improved. Viner argued that the absolute returns to a protected factor would be unlikely to increase as the result of protection. Although the relative income of a factor might be raised, there would not necessarily be an increase in its *real* income; since total real national income would be less under protection than under free trade, a tariff might simply result in labour securing a larger *share* of a smaller national cake. Accordingly if it was desired to improve the economic lot of one group in a community relative to another, it

---

[1]. A. C. Pigou, *Protective and Preferential Import Duties*, 1906, p. 58.

would be better to do so by direct income redistribution through internal taxation.

The Stolper–Samuelson Approach

In 1941 Stolper and Samuelson showed in an important article[1] that, given certain restrictive assumptions, a tariff might improve not only the comparative, but also the absolute real income of a given factor of production; or more generally that a tariff will benefit a country's relatively scarce factor of production and cause the real income of the abundant factor to fall.

Let us suppose that in the case of Australia where wheat is relatively land intensive and where textiles are relatively labour intensive, textiles are protected. The output of textiles will then rise relative to that of wheat, and since textiles are labour intensive, there will be an increase in the demand for labour. Given internal factor mobility both capital and labour will move into textiles, but since textiles are more labour than capital intensive, the movement of labour will be greater than capital. The wheat growing industry will lose both capital and labour but especially labour. Now the raising of the proportion of land to labour in wheat growing will clearly raise the marginal product of labour. Thus the marginal product of labour in *both* wheat growing and textiles has increased, and as far as wage rates may be assumed to reflect marginal productivity, it is reasonable to assume that wages in both sectors have increased.

3. THE FULL-EMPLOYMENT ARGUMENT

Protective policies are often invoked as a means to cure unemployment. When large numbers are unemployed the imposition of a tariff or some other system of protection is extremely tempting. Indeed in the 1930s, the existence of large scale unemployment was in many countries the most frequently used argument for protection. There is little doubt that in the short run, a tariff can provide a higher level of domestic employment. Protection brings about some switch in demand from imports and towards home-trade products. It is difficult to envisage such a switch taking place without some of the slack being taken up in the domestic economy, particularly if there is a strong multiplier effect. But this is a short-term view. In the first place, it assumes that the foreign repercussions are negligible. In fact a reduction in supplying countries'

[1] Wolfgang F. Stolper and Paul A. Samuelson, 'Protection and Real Wages', *Review of Economic Studies*, 1941, reprinted in the *American Economic Association Readings in the Theory of International Trade*, Allen and Unwin, 1950.

exports resulting from the tariff will cause a fall in these countries' domestic incomes which in turn brings about some reduction in their imports.[1] If the tariff imposing country exports to these countries there will be a drop in its exports, and hence a fall in employment in its export industries. Thus the imposition of a tariff in a given country might well redound to the disadvantage of its export industries—even in the absence of deliberate retaliation. In the real world, however, deliberate relatiatory policies are likely—particularly if protection is introduced in time of general recession. There is then a danger that a round of beggar-my-neighbour tariff building will follow, as indeed occurred in the 1930s.

Apart from foreign repercussions, it is important to know whether the unemployment which it is hoped to alleviate is the kind which can be appropriately reduced by domestic protection. Unemployment might be structural; that is due to internal technological changes. The appropriate remedy in this case is certainly not a tariff, which although temporarily creating more jobs, does so only at the cost of slowing down economic progress. The correct policy in such a situation is a sensible overall economic development policy providing alternative employment and training facilities for workers displaced by technical change.[2] Special regional arrangements may be necessary.

Keynes and Protection

In spite of the limited nature of the argument for protection as a means of countering domestic unemployment, it was the one most frequently advanced in favour of the British tariff in the 1930s. Indeed, before Britain left the gold standard, Keynes himself used a somewhat sophisticated version of the employment argument. In common with most economists of the Cambridge school, Keynes had been brought up a free trader. It was he who in 1923 asked, somewhat rhetorically, 'Is there anything a tariff can do, which an earthquake cannot do better ?[3]

[1] The fall in imports into a country resulting from a given change in national income is known as a country's marginal propensity to import, a concept discussed more fully in Chapter 12.

[2] As we shall see in Chapter 22 such a policy was envisaged in the European Coal and Steel Community to assist those workers made redundant in the coal and steel industries of the community as the result of free trade, or (after 1960) as the result of long term structural changes in these industries.

[3] 'Free Trade and Unemployment', *Nation and Athenaeum*, November 24, 1923. In the same article Keynes wrote 'The protectionist has to prove, not merely that he has made work, but that he has increased the national income. Imports are receipts; and exports are payments. How, as a nation, can we better ourselves by diminishing our receipts?'

But in 1930, in his *Treatise on Money*, Keynes was considering a tariff as a means of attaining a higher level of employment than would have been possible under free trade.[1] Keynes made his suggestion of a 15 per cent duty on all manufactured and semi-manufactured goods with a 5 per cent duty on foodstuffs and certain raw materials, in a popular article in the *New Statesman and Nation*, in the spring of 1931.[2] His conversion to protection as the proper policy for Britain had also become clear in his contribution to the work of the Macmillan Committee, of which he was a member.[3]

At that time, Keynes was a aware of the difficulty for Britain of implementing a full employment policy without taking steps to safeguard the gold reserves. In the context of a fixed exchange rate, a domestic financial policy sufficiently expansionist to make a substantial inroad into unemployment would have weakened Britain's external position. Keynes argued that in this situation the correct policy was domestic expansion accompanied by devaluation. But since at that time the Government appeared determined at all costs to maintain the exchange rate, the necessary degree of domestic expansion would only be feasible if it took place behind a tariff wall. Hence Keynes advocated a tariff, not as the best possible policy but as one which would be preferable to allowing the economy to stagnate. It was a second best remedy.[4] Behind the moderate tariff wall, policies for full employment could be adopted without fear of serious external repercussions. Such a tariff would not harm Britain's trading partners, but merely offset the external consequences of internal expansion, by making sure that expansion would not result in a substantial *increase* in imports. There was no question of deliberately reducing imports as the result of the measures Keynes advocated. Accordingly Keynes denied that the tariff involved a beggar-my-neighbour policy. Indeed, if Britain's trading partners agreed to adopt expansionist policies, the need for a tariff would disappear. But since this seemed unlikely, the tariff was the only way

---

[1] J. M. Keynes, *A Treatise on Money*, London, Macmillan, vol. i, pp. 131–132 and pp. 326–363; vol. ii, pp. 184–189.

[2] 'Proposals for a Revenue Tariff', *New Statesman and Nation*, London, March 7, 1931.

[3] Keynes' view on protection is set out in Addendum I of the *Report of Committee on Finance and Industry* (Macmillan Report), London, HMSO, 1931.

[4] As soon as Britain went off the gold standard Keynes wrote a letter to *The Times* (September 29, 1931) withdrawing his proposal for a tariff. But Keynes was never again the convinced free trader that he had been in earlier years. His somewhat individual approach to the tariff controversy in the 1930s is described in Sir Roy Harrod's *Life of John Maynard Keynes*, London, Macmillan, 1952, especially pp. 424 ff.

in which the correct internal policy could be followed without damage to the balance of payments.[1]

Thus the employment argument as developed by Keynes was in a sense one resting upon a particular set of circumstances and was not intended to be a general justification for protection. Keynes believed that the best way to secure full employment was by appropriate domestic economic policies. If external factors made the implementation of such policies impossible, some degree of insulation from the world economy might be desirable. In such circumstances the loss of advantage of international division of labour might be preferable to that resulting from under-utilization of resources. Some misallocation of resources might be better than their non-use.

4. THE BALANCE OF PAYMENTS ARGUMENT

In the 1930s, arguments for the protection based upon the desire for fuller employment were closely linked with those concerned with the balance of payments. If there had been no 'balance of payments constraint', Keynes' employment argument for the tariff would not have been advanced. There are other and better ways of securing a higher level of domestic demand than recourse to protection. But given balance of payments difficulties, Governments are tempted to reduce external deficits by means of domestic protection. This is especially true of less developed countries whose development programmes often entail a substantial strain on limited foreign exchange resources. In fact the GATT specifically permits a country to impose trade controls (as a temporary measure) in cases of payments disequilibrium, and in the post-war world a very high proportion of trade and payments restrictions exist precisely in order to safeguard countries' balance of payments. The UK import surcharge of 1964 was imposed for this reason and the UK exchange controls have the same objective. But similar criticisms can be levied against protective policies imposed for balance of payments reasons, as against those invoked to maintain full employment. Country A's imports are country B's exports and policies which deliberately restrict A's imports have an adverse effect upon incomes in B and hence upon B's imports. The reduction in country B's imports could well have an adverse effect upon country A. Even if B imports nothing from country A, it will almost certainly

---

[1] The evolution of Keynes' thought on the tariff question is well documented by Randall Hinshaw in his contribution *Keynesian Commercial Policy*, in the symposium *The New Economics: Keynes' Influence on Theory and Public Policy*, ed. S. E. Harris, London, Dennis Dobson Ltd, 1947. The question is also discussed by Sir Roy F. Harrod in his *Life of John Maynard Keynes*.

import from third countries which are country A's market. Of course, even if protection succeeds in correcting balance of payments disequilibrium (or unemployment) it does not follow that protection is the best policy to attain this end. It is simply one method of switching demand from imports to home produced substitutes and in this respect may be regarded as an alternative (and in many respects a second best alternative) to devaluation.

5. THE BARGAINING TARIFF

Textbooks have traditionally dealt with an argument for protection known since Adam Smith—who accepted its validity—as 'the bargaining tariff'. This refers to a country imposing customs duties in order to acquire greater leverage in persuading other countries to lower theirs. A unique version of this was the imposition of a 10 per cent surcharge by the US in August 1971 on all goods not subject to import quotas, in order to exert pressure on the other industrial countries to upvalue their currencies *vis-à-vis* the dollar, to institute negotiations for a new world monetary system and to receive trade concessions from the EEC, Japan and Canada. The surcharge was lifted in December of the same year, when agreement on a currency realignment and on the granting of some trade concessions, had been reached.

Finally, as with all arguments for protection (except perhaps those relating to infant industries and developing countries), it should be remembered that protection, by insulating in part or in whole, the industries of a country from foreign competition removes one of the strongest possible incentives for efficiency. A tariff might strengthen a country's balance of trade, but the gain is temporary if the industries fostered became inefficient, so that when protection is removed their ability to compete on world markets is diminished.

SHORT GUIDE TO THE LITERATURE

The student is strongly advised to follow up the references in the footnotes to this chapter. The terms of trade argument is dealt with in Chapter XVII of Meade's *Trade and Welfare*, and the distribution of income argument in Chapter XVIII of the same volume. Readers interested in the geometry of this subject will enjoy Meade's *A Geometry of International Trade*, London, Allen and Unwin, 1952. There are several articles reprinted in The American Economic Association's *Readings in International Economics*, London, Allen and Unwin, 1968, which bear closely on this chapter, notably L. A. Metzler, 'Tariffs, The Terms of Trade, and the Distribution of National Income', originally in *Journal of Political Economy*, vol. lvii, February 1949.

CHAPTER 9

TRADE AND FACTOR MOVEMENTS

One of the ironies of the history of economic thought is the almost complete neglect by nineteenth-century classical economists of the movement of factors between countries, in spite of the fact that they lived in an age of unprecedented international mobility, both of human beings and capital. As we have seen, however (p. 27), Ricardian doctrine was based on the hypothesis that factor movements between countries were insignificant as compared with factor mobility within countries; both he and his successors accordingly failed to work out the relationship between factor movements and commodity trade.

Pigou believed that free trade in commodities tended to equalize factor prices as between countries. He aso appreciated that duties on certain imports might raise the share of national product received by factors of production employed in the protected industries. In spite of the concern of Pigou and others, however, it was not until the Heckscher-Ohlin revolution that a systematic analysis of the relationship between trade and factor movements became possible.

1. THE HECKSCHER–OHLIN VIEW

In Chapter 3, we saw how the work of Heckscher and Ohlin suggests that trade patterns reflect factor endowments. A country will tend to specialize in producing goods made with its relatively abundant (i.e. cheap) factors of production. As the result of the opening up of trade, demand for these factors will increase. With a given supply of these factors, their prices will rise. On the other hand, as certain domestic products are displaced by imports, demand for the factors used to produce them will tend to fall. Let us assume that as compared with New Zealand, Britain is relatively well endowed with labour, but poorly endowed with land resources, whereas New Zealand is relatively well endowed with natural resources but poorly endowed with labour. Britain therefore concentrates on producing manufactured goods— which have a high labour but low land content—while New Zealand produces farm products, with a high land but low labour content.

The opening up of trade results in an increase in demand for relatively cheap New Zealand foodstuffs; hence rents in that country are likely to rise. On the other hand, demand for home-produced New Zealand manufactures will fall, since these goods are now imported on more advantageous terms from Britain. Thus while rents, i.e. landowners' incomes, in New Zealand rise, wage rates fall. In Britain, on the other hand, the reverse occurs. Increased demand for British exports of manufactures causes the price of the factor most intensively employed in manufacturing, i.e. labour, to rise, while the substitution of imported foodstuffs for those produced in Britain causes British farm rents to fall. Thus the price of labour in New Zealand falls while in Britain it rises; on the other hand the price of land in New Zealand rises, while in Britain it falls. Accordingly, there is a tendency for a narrowing of the gap between British and New Zealand rents and British and New Zealand wages. Factor prices between the two countries have moved closer together. We have approached nearer to a single wage rate and a single level of rents for the trading countries.

Is it possible that rents and wages in the two countries actually become equal? If they do, trade can be seen as leading to the equalization of factor prices. The opening up of trade might indeed lead to a situation where the price of similar types of land is the same the world over; where there is one world rate of interest and a world wage-rate for similar types of labour. The corollary is that where there is free trade in goods, factor rewards in the trading countries are equalized without the factors themselves moving. The marginal product of labour in Britain becomes equal to the marginal product of labour in New Zealand. In this situation the movement of commodities may be regarded as a substitute for the movement of factors of production. Provided free trade in products is assured, there is then no need to permit the free movement of factors. To what extent does free trade in goods in fact eliminate the need for factor movements?

Before attempting to answer this question it is worth noting that the attempt is more than academic exercise, for, if commodity movements fail to bring about complete equalization of factor prices, welfare will only be maximized if Governments and international organizations take steps to ensure that factors of production as well as commodities move freely between countries. Only if capital and labour move freely will they secure the highest possible returns. The question is also relevant to the theory of customs unions. If commodity movements alone are insufficient to secure maximum marginal returns to factors of production, then union builders ought to provide for the free movement within the union of capital and persons as well as of goods.

Heckscher himself suggested that free trade in commodities would lead to factor equalization, thus eliminating the need for movements of the factors themselves. He was, however, careful to state his assumption that similar production techniques were used in all the trading countries.[1] Heckscher believed that in practice production techniques are unlikely to be similar; he instances the United States before large-scale immigration, where foodstuffs were produced with relatively larger quantities of land and relatively less labour than in Europe. Because land was so plentiful and labour so scarce, US rents were low and wages high. But even with extensive methods of cultivation, the labour scarcity was such that there were insufficient workers to cultivate all the land which could be used advantageously for grain production. Accordingly, trade alone could not even out the discrepancy between factor returns in the USA on the one hand and in Europe on the other. Some movement of labour from the Old World to the New was necessary.

In contrast to Heckscher, Ohlin insisted that free trade could not bring about complete factor price equalization. This could be attained only by the free movement of factors. Free product mobility without free factor mobility would result in only a *tendency* towards factor price equalization. 'The mobility of goods *to some extent* compensates the lack of inter-regional mobility of the factors.'[2]

Unfortunately, Ohlin nowhere states precisely *why* the factor price equalization is only partial. We must look elsewhere for a more definitive discussion of this question. Before doing so it is perhaps worth reminding the reader that in the real world there is both factor and commodity movement, although both are seldom quite free. Moreover, an increase in trade barriers is likely to stimulate the movement of factors, while an increase in impediments to factor movements is likely to encourage commodity trade—a matter which has been argued by Robert Mundell.[3]

2. THE SAMUELSON THEOREM

The first systematic analysis of the relationship between trade and factor prices was that of Samuelson who showed that *given certain*

[1] Heckscher's words were 'under the assumption of the same technique in all countries, it follows that nothing is lost either in the individual country or in the world as a whole by the fact that factors of production remain where they are'. Eli Heckscher 'The Effect of Foreign Trade and the Distribution of Income'. *Ekonomisk Tidskrift*, vol. xxi, 1919, reprinted in *Readings in the Theory of International Trade*, London, Allen and Unwin, 1950, p. 289.

[2] B. Ohlin, *Inter-regional and International Theory*, Harvard University Press, 1933, p. 42.

[3] 'International Trade and Factor Mobility', *American Economic Review*, vol. xlvii, June 1957, pp. 321–335, reproduced in Caves & Johnson, *Readings in International Economics*, Allen and Unwin, 1968.

assumptions free trade leads to the equalization of factor prices.[1] Samuelson was careful to state his assumptions, which are highly restrictive. Indeed so much so that it is sometimes said that the conditions necessary for his proof to be valid are so restrictive, and so unlikely to be met with in the real world, that so far from proving that factor-price equalization is the inevitable result of commodity trade his work suggests precisely the opposite.

But Samuelson, while admitting the fairly restrictive nature of his assumptions, suggests that despite numerous qualifications, the gist of his discussion was to show that relatively free commodity trade was 'a better substitute for the mobility of factors than was hitherto thought to be the case'.[2]

Following Haberler[3] we can summarize the assumptions of Samuelson's theorem as follows:

(1) Free competition in all markets
(2) Absence of transport costs
(3) Incomplete specialization
(4) Production functions in both countries identical and homogeneous in the first degree
(5) One commodity is always labour intensive and the other always capital intensive
(6) Factors of production are qualitatively equal in all countries
(7) Number of factors is not greater than the number of commodities.

Let us suppose that Britain produces cars, New Zealand dairy produce. Trade between the two countries will tend to bring about equality in factor yields and returns. But will there be merely a *tendency* towards equalization or will trade continue until returns are fully equalized? By assuming perfect competition, the ratio of the price of cars to dairy produce in each country will be equal to the ratio in each country of the marginal cost of producing cars to the marginal cost of producing dairy products. Moreover, since we assume that transport costs are negligible and that trade is completely free, there will be single international prices for cars and dairy produce respectively. But since prices reflect marginal costs, if prices are equal, marginal costs must be also equal. Thus the marginal cost of producing cars and dairy

---

[1] This was set out in two *Economic Journal* articles, in 1948 and 1949. P. A. Samuelson, 'International Trade and the Equalisation of Factor Prices', *Economic Journal*, June 1948, and 'International Factor—Price Equalisation Once Again', *Economic Journal*, June 1949.

[2] *Economic Journal*, June 1948, p. 183.

[3] *A Survey of International Trade Theory*, Princeton 1951, p. 18.

produce is the same in both countries. Furthermore, since we have assumed identical production functions, it would be impossible for, say Britain, to use more labour in producing butter than New Zealand. Accordingly, the marginal productivity of labour must be the same in the two countries, and since factor rewards reflect marginal products, wages in the two countries must be equal. This reasoning applies to other factors.

In order to test Samuelson's reasoning, let us assume for a moment that the wage rate in Britain is in fact lower than in New Zealand. Such a gap is compatible with equal product costs and equal prices only if compensated by a gap in rents; for if we assume identical production functions and constant returns to scale, costs must be determined solely by factor prices. If British wages are lower than those in New Zealand, the cost of labour-intensive British cotton goods would be lower than if wages in the two countries were equal. There is accordingly a tendency for demand to switch from New Zealand to British made cottons, and away from British produced foodstuffs. This demand switch continues until the price equilibrium is restored. Thus the movement towards factor price equalization will persist until factor prices are actually identical as between trading countries.

The logic behind Samuelson's reasoning is impeccable. But the assumptions upon which the reasoning rests are so restrictive that they should be examined closely in order to see how far they correspond to reality. Samuelson himself was well aware of the fact that in the real world differences in wages and other factor prices exist and indeed would continue to exist even in a regime of complete free trade. For example, in the first of his two *Economic Journal* articles he drew attention to transport costs as an obstacle to trade, to the fact that one country might become completely specialized before factor rewards had become equalized, and to the unrealism of the assumption that production functions were everywhere the same.[1] He also stressed that even when technical production functions were alike, the 'same' labour working in one place with the 'same' kind of equipment and other resources produces substantially different output than elsewhere. Perhaps the most systematic examination of the limitations of Samuelson's analysis is that of Professor James Meade.[2]

[1] *Economic Journal*, June 1948, p. 178.
[2] J. E. Meade, *Trade and Welfare*, London, Royal Institute of International Affairs, 1955. Chapters XX and XXIV.

3. WHY FACTOR PRICE EQUALIZATION IS PARTIAL

Differences in Atmosphere

Meade suggests that there are six reasons why the assumptions made in the Samuelson theorem are unlikely to be valid in the real world. Firstly, the theorem assumes that production functions are identical as between trading countries. We have already noted that Heckscher argued that because these functions were not identical, factor movements had a useful role to play in maximizing welfare. A given set of resources does not necessarily produce the same output in one country as in another. Taussig recognized this when he saw that although a country might have an absolute superiority over another in all lines of production in such a situation labour might benefit from moving from the less to the more productive country. Workers migrating in this way would benefit from the existence of a more productive 'climate' in the country to which they moved. Taussig uses the term 'climate' to include not only physical climate but also the social and intellectual atmosphere in which production is taking place. Meade takes over the point by suggesting that 'the same textbooks and the same brains would not produce the same thoughts in Chicago and in London.' Of course it may be that the atmosphere for the employment of one factor (e.g. labour) may be better in one country than in another, while the atmosphere for the employment of another (e.g. capital) might be better in the latter country than in the former. Whether the atmosphere of one country is absolutely superior, either for the employment of all factors or for the production of all goods, or whether it is superior in only a limited number of factors and goods, output will not be maximized until some of the factors have moved from the climatically less attractive to the climatically more attractive country. Differences in atmosphere between countries 'may clearly make it a matter of real importance that certain factors should be employed in one country rather than in the other.'

Returns to Scale

One of Samuelson's significant assumptions was of constant returns to scale. Now if this condition is not fulfilled, Meade shows that it might be advantageous to encourage the international movement of factors as well as of goods. Suppose that before trade Britain and New Zealand both produce cars and dairy products. Britain is better endowed than New Zealand with the factor (labour) needed in relative abundance for car production, but relatively less well endowed with land, necessary in relative abundance for dairy farming. The movement of cars and dairy products will, however, tend to offset the effects of these differing endowments upon factor rewards. Thus in Britain wages will rise and rents fall, while the opposite will happen in New Zealand. Given constant costs (and his other assumptions), Samuelson's argument suggests that adjustment will continue until the factor rewards are the same in both countries. At this point, the marginal product of labour is equal in both countries. But suppose that Britain (a relatively large producer of cars) has exhausted all the economies of large scale production in car manufacturing while New Zealand although a small producer, is on the verge of very substantial economies. Thus although the *average* productivity of factors of production in car manufacture in Britain might be higher than in New Zealand (because the absolute scale of operations is greater in the UK), the marginal product of the factor labour might be higher in New Zealand.

On the other hand, the scale of output in Britain might be such that more substantial scale economies were made there than in New Zealand, perhaps because economies only became significant when a relatively large output was being produced. In these situations it is conceivable that in a regime of free trade there will be a single price for both cars and dairy products and internal equilibrium in both countries although factor rewards still differ. It may be that in New Zealand, the *marginal* productivity of factors is higher than in Britain; or it may be lower. But where increasing returns are important it would be coincidental if the marginal productivity of factors were the same in both countries. In the absence of this coincidence it will be worth while factors moving from where their productivity is relatively low to where it is high. Only in this way will equality of factor returns be achieved.

Transport Costs

The third reason for factor mobility identified by Professor Meade relates to transport costs. So far we have assumed that there are zero costs in sending butter from New Zealand to Britain and in sending cars from Britain to New Zealand. There is thus a single international price for butter and for cars. But this is unrealistic (particularly in our example of trade between Britain and New Zealand!) It normally costs something to send goods from one country to another. Accordingly, the price of butter will be higher in London than in Auckland, and the price of cars higher in Auckland than in London. Thus both the British dairy farming industry and the New Zealand car manufacturing industry will be bigger than in a situation of costless transport. The corollary is that wages remain somewhat lower in Britain and higher in New Zealand than under costless trade. Thus equilibrium is established where butter is selling at a higher price in Britain than in New Zealand (and cars at a higher price in New Zealand), but where the marginal product of labour—and hence the wage rate—remains lower in Britain than in New Zealand. Thus free trade has not secured equality of factor returns. There is accordingly some advantage in labour moving from Britain to New Zealand. In this case maximum welfare is obtained only if the movement of commodities is supplemented by the movement of factors. In practice, of course, the movement of factors (especially labour) is not costless, and the cost of transporting goods must be weighed against the cost of moving productive factors.

Complete Specialization

A fourth reason why the movement of goods alone will not always bring about equality of marginal products arises from the fact that a trading partner may have become completely specialized in the production of one of the traded products before equality of factor returns is reached. This is especially likely if one of the industries concerned is very small. Suppose that Britain has a tiny high-cost wine producing industry, for which she has a relatively poor factor endowment, but a very large low-cost brewing industry, for which she has an excellent factor endowment. When trade is opened up with say, France, which is well endowed for wine production but poorly endowed for beer production, all the factors might have been transferred out of Britain's minute wine industry long before their marginal products are equalized between the two countries.

Numbers of Products and Factors

We have so far assumed there are only two products traded and only two factors of production. Then given all the other assumptions discussed in this chapter, free trade will ensure that the marginal products of factors in both countries will be equal. But will this necessarily be so if there are more than two factors? Let us go back to our example of Britain and New Zealand, specializing respectively in labour-intensive car manufacture and land-intensive dairy farming. But this time we introduce a third factor of production, namely capital, which is used in both car manufacture and dairy farming. Let us assume that Britain is more richly endowed with capital in relation to other factors than is New Zealand. The rate of interest will then tend to be lower in Britain than in New Zealand. In producing both cars and butter, therefore, much capital is used in Britain, relatively little in New Zealand. Now the relative cheapness of capital in Britain might offset, for example, the relatively high cost of land in Britain, so that prices of cars and dairy products would be equalized and a free trade equilibrium established long before the marginal productivities of three factors were equal. Marginal products of factors would in fact be equal only if there were a third, capital intensive, product introduced into the countries' trade. Let us suppose that Britain possesses a highly capital-intensive electronic equipment industry, and is much better endowed with capital than with labour or land. In this case Britain can concentrate upon producing electronic equipment, while New Zealand concentrates upon dairy produce and cars. The addition of another product has permitted marginal products of factors to become equal. We can in fact generalize by stating that for equality in factor rewards, there should be as many tradeable products as there are factors.

Factor Substitution

The last case with which we shall deal arises from the fact that for some commodities the possibility of substituting one productive factor for another is greater than for others. The production of butter, for example, can be more or less capital intensive. If any given country is well endowed with capital, e.g. the United States, dairy farming is likely to be capital intensive, but if ample land resources are available it will be land intensive. On the other hand, for technical reasons motor manufacturing might not be susceptible to substantial factor substitution. In this situation, Britain might establish a competitive dairy farming industry, based on relatively abundant capital. There could, moreover, be an international price for dairy products in the two countries, based upon capital intensive methods in Britain and upon land intensive methods in New Zealand. But the marginal product of labour might well differ between the two countries. Thus, again, free trade equilibrium could become established without marginal products being equalized.

The six qualifications to factor price equalization are probably of considerable significance in the real world. They are certainly sufficiently realistic to explain why full factor price equalization does not occur. From the point of view of policy, they provide a powerful justification for allowing the free mobility of factors between nations.

SHORT GUIDE TO THE LITERATURE

All students should read Samuelson's path-breaking articles on this subject. His second paper, which restates briefly the theorem developed in the first, is reprinted in *Readings in International Economics*, ed.

R. E. Caves and H. G. Johnson, cited above. Samuelson's original articles appeared in the *Economic Journal* in 1948 and 1949. They are 'International Trade and the Equalisation of Factor Prices', *Economic Journal*, vol. lxviii, June 1948, pp. 163–184 and 'International Factor-Price Equalisation Once Again', *Economic Journal*, vol. lix, No. 234, June 1949, pp. 181–197. Another classic, already mentioned in the text, is R. A. Mundell, 'International Trade and Factor Mobility', *American Economic Review*, vol. 47, June 1957, pp. 321–337.

Meade deals with the question in some detail in *Trade and Welfare*, Chapters XX-XXIII, and at a less sophisticated level in *Problems of Economic Union* (pp. 55–85). There is a useful study of the factor-price equalization theorem in Caves, *Trade and Economic Structure*. Caves states the theorem in simple terms and then reviews the literature on the subject.

CHAPTER 10

GROWTH AND TRADE

It has been said that if a group of economists gathered together at any time in the 1950s and 1960s they would sooner or later find themselves discussing the problem of economic growth. From the point of view of both analysis and policy, growth theory today occupies the place held by employment theory in the 1930s. Growth theory has been incorporated in the modern approach to international trade questions, and no textbook on international economics is complete without some consideration of the interaction of growth and trade. As we shall see later (in Chapter 12), changes in the level of domestic income have important repercussions upon a country's balance of trade. In general, orthodox theory tells us that a spontaneous increase in domestic expenditure tends to encourage imports and in the short run at least to cause a country's trade balance to deteriorate.

In Chapter 12 we shall analyse the effect on income changes in money terms; we shall be dealing with money flows. In the present chapter, however, we are concerned essentially with structural questions, the question, for example, of the effect of an increase in a country's stock of capital upon its foreign trade. We shall consider also the implications of inventions or innovations in various sectors of a country's economy upon its exports and imports. For example, is the adoption of labour saving machinery likely to encourage or diminish a particular country's imports? Readers who have followed the first chapters of this book will realize that we are in fact discussing what is likely to. happen to a country's balance of trade when the shape of its production transformation curve, or production possibility frontier, changes either its shape or position (or both). Those who have forgotten the significance of these concepts should turn back to Chapters 3 and 5 before reading on.

1. THE HICKS APPROACH

The Dollar Surplus

Discussion of the relationship between growth and the balance of trade grew directly out of the great debate raging in the late 1940s and early 1950s on the question of the US dollar surplus. In the early post-war years, the US was running a substantial balance of payments .

surplus[1] and lending (or giving away) vast sums to other countries to aid their post-war recovery and future development. The question at issue was whether the us surplus was due simply to the deficit countries living beyond their means, or whether the explanation was a much more fundamental one; being due, for example, to a long-term tendency for productivity to rise faster in the us than elsewhere. In the former case the remedy for the world dollar problem was simple (although perhaps unpleasant), namely a general drawing-in of horns in the deficit countries so that they lived within their means. But if the cause of the imbalance were structural, the removal of the dollar gap was a more difficult task than the exponents of 'tough measures for deficit countries' imagined. The controversy was a vigorous one and continued for several years.

A variant of the 'structural' argument was that advanced by Professor J. R. Hicks in his inaugural lecture.[2] Hicks suggested that the long-run dollar problem was caused by the tendency for inventions and innovations in the us to have an import-replacing bias. Thus as time passed, the us became progressively less dependent upon imports, with serious results for the export prospects of other countries.

The debate on the causes of the dollar surplus is now a matter of history,[3] but out of the discussions, particularly from Professor Hicks' ideas on the import-saving bias of innovation in the us, there developed a wholly new understanding of the reaction of structural change in an economy upon the balance of trade.

Hicks takes two countries, A and B. Productivity increases faster in A than in B. In fact, for simplicity, he assumes that productivity does not rise at all in B. Now in country A, productivity could increase at a uniform rate in all industries, or it could rise faster in export industries, or in those industries which produce substitutes for goods imported from B. In the first case, the effect upon export industries is similar to that on import-competing industries. In the second case, exports become

[1] Considerable doubt exists as to how big the current us surplus was in those years; there are so many ways in which the 'current account balance' can be defined that he would be a brave (or foolish) man who would be dogmatic about the size of the surplus. For a discussion of the difficulties in defining a current account balance, the reader is referred to Chapter 11.

[2] J. R. Hicks, 'An Inaugural Lecture', *Oxford Economic Papers*, New Series, vol. 5, June 1953, pp. 117–135. The idea that productivity advanced more rapidly in the us than in other countries was fathered by Dr T. Balogh in 'The US and the World Economy', *Bulletin of the Oxford Institute of Statistics*, vol. 8, 1946.

[3] The significance of Hicks' contribution to the debate on the dollar problem is traced in F. Machlup, 'Dollar Shortage and Disparities in the Growth of Productivity', *Scottish Journal of Political Economy*, vol. 1, 1954, pp. 250–267, reprinted in Caves and Johnson, *Readings in International Economics*, cited above.

relatively cheaper, so that B *gains* from improved terms of trade with A. In the third case, however, country B will suffer, since there is no terms of trade gain resulting from a cheapening of A's exports, but there *is* a loss resulting from country A's increased self-sufficiency in importables. Hicks suggested that the third case was appropriate to the USA in its trade relationship with the rest of the world. Economic development in the USA caused that country to be increasingly self-sufficient. We are not here concerned with whether Hicks was right or wrong in his observations on the US economy in the post-war world, but with his lasting contribution to trade theory by the distinction he drew between import-biased and other forms of growth.

Since Professor Hicks' inaugural lecture there have been important developments in the theory of growth and trade. The fullest and most up-to-date discussions of the subject are in the works of Johnson[1] and Meier.[2] I have drawn heavily on both these authors in writing this Chapter.

2. PRODUCTION EFFECTS

Import and Export Bias

As Johnson points out, the question of economic interest is whether growth increases the demand for imports (*a*) more than proportionally to the increase in the value of the national product, or (*b*) in the same proportion as, or (*c*) less than proportionally to, the increase in the value of the national product. In the first case, growth leads to *less* self-sufficiency, in the second, the effect is neutral, in the third, growth leads to greater self-sufficiency. If growth decreases self-sufficiency, i.e. a country's demand for imports and supply of exportables is increasing, we describe growth as pro-trade biased. If, on the other hand, the country becomes more self-sufficient, that is if the increase is predominantly in import-replacing goods, then we describe growth as anti-trade biased. This is Johnson's terminology. Meier describes pro-trade biased growth and anti-trade biased growth as 'export biased' and 'import-biased' respectively.

The effect of different types of growth on imports and exports can be illustrated by means of figure 11. Let us assume that a country has a factor endowment such that XM represents its production possibility frontier for X goods (exports) and M goods (import-competing substitutes). Let us further suppose that X goods embody a relatively large amount of the factor labour, while M goods embody a relatively

[1] H. G. Johnson, *Money, Trade and Economic Growth*, London, Allen and Unwin, 1962, Chapter 3, reprinted in Caves and Johnson *Readings in International Economics*.

[2] G. M. Meier, *International Trade and Development*, New York, Harper and Row, 1963, Chapter 2.

large amount of capital. Now an all-round increase in factor endowments, namely in both labour and capital, will cheapen the cost of
producing both X goods and M goods. The effect will be a pushing
out of the production frontier from XM to say, X_1M_1, along the line
VT. This type of growth is described by both Sir John Hicks and Professor Johnson as 'neutral'; it brings about an increase in both exports
and import substitutes. But suppose that although there is an increase
in *both* factors there is a more than proportionate increase in the supply
of the factor, labour, used relatively intensively in producing exportables.
Then the output of goods X will increase more than proportionally to
M. Production will move out from V along VE. The supply of both M
goods and E goods increases, but the latter more than the former. This
sort of growth is export-biased, or 'pro-trade' biased. Our country is
less self-sufficient than before.

If, on the other hand, the increase in factor supply was in capital
rather than in labour, the output of import-saving goods (M) will rise
more than that of exportables. Growth is 'anti-trade' or import-
biased. The country is more self-sufficient than hitherto. Production
moves out along the line VM. Clearly, therefore, it matters a great deal,
not only to the country concerned but also to its trading partners, or
potential trading partners, whether an increase occurs in a factor which
is used relatively heavily or less heavily, in its export or import trade.

Inspection of figure 11 shows that in each of the cases so far discussed,
output of *both* M goods and X goods increases, but one more than the
other. This is because we assumed there to be an increase in the supply
of both factors. Let us now suppose that the supply of only *one* factor
increases, namely labour, used intensively in producing X goods. The
supply of capital remains constant. In this case, the output of X will
increase, but instead of the output of M also increasing (albeit relatively
slowly), the supply of M goods will actually decrease. This is because
some additional supplies of capital are absorbed when the output of X
goods goes up and this leaves the supply of capital available for production of M goods smaller than before. Hence the increase in X goods is
obtainable only at the sacrifice of some M goods. In other words the
supply of exportable products increases, that of import substitutes
actually declines.[1] We have here a case of ultra pro-trade biased or
ultra export biased growth—the best situation of course for other

[1] For a rigorous proof see J. M. Rybczynski, 'Factor Endowment at Relative
Commodity Prices', *Economica*, New Series, vol. 22, November 1955, pp. 336–341.
There is a mathematical proof in W. M. Corden, 'Economic Expansion and Inter-
national Trade: A Geometric Approach', *Oxford Economic Papers*, June 1956, p. 227.
Rybczynski's paper is reprinted in Caves and Johnson, *Readings in International
Economics*, cited above.

countries, which enjoy both wider export opportunities and improved terms of trade resulting from the form that growth has taken. In figure 11 the change in output mix is shown by a movement along VUE.

At the other extreme we can imagine a situation where the stock of labour remains constant, but an increase occurs in the availability of capital, used intensively in producing import-substitutes. The output

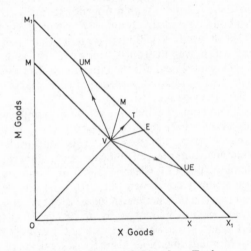

FIGURE 11. Effects of Growth on Trade.

of the import-competing goods now increases, while there is a decline in that of exportables. This is ultra-anti-trade biased or ultra-import-biased growth. It is depicted in figure 11 by a movement along the line VUM.

It should now be clear that a change in factor endowment can have one of several production effects. It can be neutral, leaving the ratio between exportables and import-replacements unchanged; it can be pro-trade or ultra-pro-trade biased, leading to a relatively greater increase in exportables than in import-replacements, or it can be anti-trade or ultra-anti-trade biased, leading to a relatively greater increase in import replacements. There are quite important policy implications of all this. If a developing country uses capital relatively intensively in its import replacement industries but labour relatively intensively in its exportable goods industries, an increased inflow of capital (perhaps in the form of aid), with a stationary working population, might result in increased import-substitution, but decreased attention to the export sector.

Innovation

So far we have considered the implications of an increase in the supply of one or more factors. Suppose growth is caused, not by a change in factor supply but by some invention or innovation which economizes in the use of one or other factor. The effects of such an innovation depend upon (*a*) whether it is labour or capital saving or neutral, and (*b*) whether it occurs in the 'M' or 'X' goods sector. Let us take first the simplest case of a 'neutral' innovation which 'saves' equally labour and capital. This might occur in either the labour-intensive industry producing X goods or the capital-intensive industry producing M goods. Suppose it occurs in the X producing industry, but not in the M producing industry. Then the effect will be an increase in the marginal productivity in the X industry. Because the marginal productivity of factors is now higher in X than in M, there will be a tendency for factors both labour and capital to move from the M to the X industries. The output of X increases, that of M declines; we have a case of ultra-pro-trade biased growth. On the other hand, if the neutral innovation occurs in the import-replacing industry, it will lead to ultra-anti-trade biased growth.

Suppose now that the innovation is not neutral but is a labour-saving one. If the innovation occurs in the labour-intensive export industry, labour will be economized and more of the goods X will be produced. This entails a shift of capital resources from making importables to making exportables. The output of import-substitutes M therefore decreases; growth is ultra-pro-trade biased. But the situation is not so clear if the labour saving innovation takes place in the capital-intensive industry, and not in the labour-intensive industry. While the output of M goods increases, it is also possible for there to be an increase in the supply of X (exportable) goods, since some labour is likely to be released by the innovation in the import-competing industry. Thus the output of both types of goods might increase and growth take any form from ultra-pro-trade biased to ultra-anti-trade biased. Similar reasoning applies to the effect of a capital saving innovation. If this is in the capital intensive industry, the production effect is ultra-anti-trade biased. If, on the other hand, it occurs in the labour intensive industry, the effect is much less easily determined, and may range anywhere from ultra-anti-trade to ultra-pro-trade biased.[1]

---

[1] As this chapter progresses I realize how much my exposition owes to Gerald Meier and become conscious of the need for the student to refer to the crystal-clear discussion of this whole subject in his book *International Trade and Development*, cited above.

3. CONSUMPTION EFFECTS

Now we have examined the effects on the balance of trade of various changes in factor supply and efficiency as they affect production. But as development occurs, changes are also likely in consumption patterns. How will the various changes we have outlined affect these patterns? An augmentation of factor supplies or an innovation will increase national income and this will possibly (or indeed probably) cause some change in the relative quantities of X and M goods consumed in the home market. If development (however caused) results in an expenditure increase which does not alter the consumption mix of M and X in our country, then the consumption effect of the development may be described as 'neutral'. This will in fact be the case only if the income elasticity of demand for X and also that for M are both equal. But if the income elasticity demand for import-substitutes (M) is greater than that for exportables (X), domestic demand for the former will rise more than for the latter. It is in fact rather unlikely that following an increase in income level there will be an absolute decrease in demand for X goods—although this would be the case if they were inferior goods.

In the more normal case there will be an unequal increase in demand for both X and M goods. If the bigger increase in demand is for import-substitutes, the effect on trade will be pro-trade biased. If X goods are inferior goods the effect will be ultra-pro-trade biased.

If the income elasticity of demand for exportable goods were greater than for import-substitutes, the consumption effect of growth is anti-trade-biased. If the income elasticity of demand for import-substitutes is negative, the consumption effect will be ultra-anti-trade biased. In the real world, development is almost certain to result in a change in incomes and tastes and such changes must be incorporated into the analysis.

Now the production and consumption changes of development react together; they can reinforce or they can offset one another. But the net result is a change in the terms upon which a country offers its goods in exchange for those of other countries—namely a shift in its offer curve.[1] Thus our discussion of one of the most recently developed aspects of modern trade theory brings us, as it were, full circle back to a thoroughly Marshallian device. It helps us to gain a fuller understanding of the real factors that lie behind the curve and of how the position of the curve can be shifted. More important than this, the developments in theory which we have outline can be of immense value in an

[1] See Chapter 4.

analysis of the development problem. As we shall see later there is growing interest in ways and means by which the exports of less developed economies can be encouraged. Modern growth-trade theory provides us with at least some of the tools to help analyse this problem.[1]

SHORT GUIDE TO THE LITERATURE

Much of the relevant literature is referred to in the footnotes. Of especial value is Professor Meier's book, *International Trade and Development*, Chapter 2. This chapter is a 'must' for all who wish to pursue the subject to an advanced level. Equally valuable is Professor Johnson's *Money, Trade and Economic Growth*. References to these works are to be found in the footnotes. There is a useful introductory summary to the whole question of trade and growth in W. M. Corden, 'Recent Developments in the Theory of International Trade', *Special Papers in International Economics* No. 7, International Finance Section, Princeton, N.J., 1965.

[1] As, for example, in H. G. Johnson, *International Trade and Economic Growth*, London, Allen and Unwin, 1958, Chapter III.

CHAPTER 11

WHAT DOES THE BALANCE OF PAYMENTS SHOW?

Most people who read the newspapers know, in a rough-and-ready way, what is meant by the term balance of payments, but if we are to use the term meaningfully some precision is necessary. Economists use the expression in more than one sense. It can be used, for example to express the relationship between the effective demand for and supply of a country's currency. In this sense we refer to a country as being in balance of payments equilibrium when (in the absence of Government intervention) the amount of its currency demanded at a given exchange rate is just equal to the supply coming on to the market. Similarly, a country is referred to as being in balance of payments deficit when demand for its currency is less than supply and in surplus when demand is greater than supply. Since this concept of the balance of payments is concerned with market demand for and supply of a currency it is sometimes known as the market balance.[1] Used in this sense the balance of payments is an analytical concept which helps us to examine such questions as exchange rate policy, the relationship between internal and external equilibrium and alternative methods of correcting disequilibrium. We shall have frequent recourse to such questions in the following chapters. But the term balance of payments is also used in a different sense, referring to the system of accounts which depicts a country's economic transactions with the outside world. It is in this somewhat more narrow sense that the term is used in the present chapter.

1. CLASSIFYING PAYMENTS TRANSACTIONS

Now it is usual to classify the various types of transaction which give rise to foreign exchange dealings and to set out under specific headings the various payments and receipts which go to make up what we call the balance of payments. The balance of payments is thus a kind of classified summary statement of all transactions determining the demand

[1] These questions are discussed fully by Professor Machlup in 'Three Concepts of the Balance of Payments and the So-Called Dollar Shortage', *The Economic Journal*, vol. lx, March 1950, pp. 46–68. Reproduced in Fritz Machlup, *International Monetary Economics*, London, Allen and Unwin, 1968.

for and supply of a given currency. If it is accurately compiled and sensibly set out it tells us not only the net position of a country in respect of all payments made to and by its residents; it also shows under which headings these payments arise during a specified period.

There is a sense in which the balance of payments always balances. If we include *all* transactions, current and capital, then the balance will be zero. If, as a householder, I spend more than I receive in a year, the excess has to be accounted for in some way; either I spend some of my savings or I incur debts to my bank or to my creditors. If account is taken of such changes in my capital position, then my outgoings are exactly equal to my receipts. In the same way, if residents in a given country spend or lend abroad more than they receive from abroad, the deficit is met by running down reserves or by adding to the country's external liabilities. If all such changes in the current, long and short term capital accounts are included, there is no residual balance, positive or negative. What then do we mean when we say that a country is in balance of payments disequilibrium and how can we tell from the figures in the balance of payments statement whether or not there is disequilibrium?

In setting out a country's balance of payments a threefold division is conventionally made between payments which arise out of (*a*) visible trade, that is those arising from the sale or purchase of goods, (*b*) invisible trade (payments arising, for example, from the rendering of financial services and from travel), and (*c*) the transfer of capital from one country to another. Item (*b*) might or might not offset (*a*) but the two items together make up the balance of current account while (*c*) is frequently referred to as the balance of payments on capital account. If there are no errors or omissions—and it is a big 'if'—the sum of (*a*), (*b*) and (*c*) will be zero. In fact errors and omissions are often considerable; in the UK accounts they are lumped together as the somewhat confusingly named 'balancing item' discussed below.

It is always tempting to think that if groups of payments relating to the current balance of payments, that is items (*a*) and (*b*), show a net surplus, all is well with the external position. Unfortunately the situation is not as simple as this, for a positive current account balance might well be more than offset by an outflow of long-term capital, in which event there may be a deterioration in the national liquidity position. This means that there is an adverse change in the relationship between the country's quickly realizable short term claims upon foreigners (i.e. holdings of foreign currency and in short term loans to non-residents) and foreigners' quickly realizable claims upon a country's residents, i.e. their holdings of the country's currency and their short term loans to the country's residents. Whether or not a deterioration in liquidity is serious depends upon the extent to which short-term claims of foreigners upon a country's residents exceeds residents' short-term claims on foreigners. If the former becomes greater relative to the latter a country may find itself in the position of being unable to meet these claims at ruling exchange rates, should they be presented. The country is in a position akin to that of a commercial bank faced with the possibility of large withdrawals but with inadequate liquid assets to meet them. Furthermore an adverse liquid position tends to be viewed unfavourably by foreign bankers and reduces a country's credit worthiness as a borrower.[1] Accordingly although a net capital outflow might represent a lucrative overseas investment, such an outflow might endanger a country's overall external liquid position if financed by a reduction in short-term reserves or by an accumulation of short-term liabilities. It is as if I have bought a piece of land—not easily resaleable at short notice—by means of running down my balance at the bank or even by increasing my overdraft. I have obtained an illiquid asset by depleting my liquid assets or by incurring an additional short-term liability. At the same time it is worth remembering that there is an essential difference in a deterioration in a country's liquid position resulting from profitable investment overseas and deterioration caused by, say, a massive exodus of British holiday makers in search of Mediterranean sunshine.

Such considerations have led in conventional presentations of balance of payments accounts to the treatment of capital transactions according to the degree of liquidity. Long-term capital has been combined with trade and services to form 'above the line' the balance of *current and long-term capital transactions*, also called the '*basic balance*' —it was at times considered *the* balance of payments, matched 'below the line' by a *short-term capital* balance, or balance of *monetary movements*. This has given the mistaken impression that the former were the active and the latter the passive element in the balance. The UK accounts followed this procedure until 1969 when a rather more useful classification was introduced.

Before going on to examine the current method, it is necessary to discuss criteria for a meaningful presentation. What ideally a balance of payments statement ought to do is to distinguish not between transactions according to their supposed degree of liquidity, but rather

[1] It has sometimes been argued that Britain's very precarious short-term liquidity position has been one of the reasons why London interest rates have tended to be relatively high in recent years. This and other questions relating to sterling are examined in Chapter 19.

between items which represent *spontaneous* or *autonomous* payments (current or capital) and those movements (current or capital) induced by these payments. These latter we refer to as *off-setting, compensatory* or *accommodating movements.*

Autonomous and Accommodating Movements

Autonomous transactions may be defined as those which take place regardless of the size of other items on the balance of payments, whereas accommodating transactions take place only because other items in the balance of payments create deficits or surpluses which have to be offset. Sometimes the offsetting process is automatic, as when gold flows out of a country in order to finance a net deficit on current account; but it can also be 'planned', as when special aid is provided by a foreign Government or bank.

There are certain items which we can readily describe as either 'autonomous' or 'accommodating'. Autonomous transactions include payment for all normal commercial exports and imports, travel receipts and expenditure, emigrants' remittances, reparations payments, purchase and sale of foreign securities when such transactions are entered into for the profit motive, and establishment abroad of a branch or subsidiary. Such autonomous items are found in both current and capital transactions.

'Accommodating' transactions clearly include the movement of monetary gold or the increase in foreign-owned liabilities to finance a deficit. They include too, grants made by Governments to developing countries to enable them to maintain balance-of-payments equilibrium. They do not include the finance by a parent company of a subsidiary in a foreign country. The purchase by British Leyland of a plant in France, in order to manufacture motor cars within the EEC, is an example of an autonomous capital outflow from the United Kingdom. The capital transfer occurs because the firm decides that this is the most profitable way of supplying the Community market. On the other hand, the increase in the United Kingdom's sterling liabilities during the Second World War is an example of accommodating finance; it occurred only because during the war years the British Government made heavy disbursements in respect of defence in certain sterling countries. These expenditures were financed by an increase in liabilities of the UK to the countries concerned. There are of course some transactions which are difficult to fit unequivocably into either category. A country's overseas defence expenditure might at first sight be regarded as an autonomous item. One would imagine that the motive behind such expenditure was political and strategic. But as every politically conscious Briton knows, balance of payments dis-equilibrium has been the reason for some cuts in overseas defence expenditure announced in 1967 and 1968.

Care should be taken in the use of the term 'payments equilibrium'. A country can have a positive balance on current account, which is purely and simply the result of the imposition of stringent import restrictions. It would, however, be misleading to describe such a country as in any fundamental sense in balance of payments equilibrium. It would be more true to say that by means of controls the authorities have suppressed the disequilibrium which would otherwise have been apparent. Similarly, it is arguable that a country which only achieves equilibrium as the result of creating substantial unused capacity is really in fundamental disequilibrium, although the balance of payments might balance.

In practice it is difficult to know the precise effect of restrictive commercial or financial policies upon a country's balance of payments, and it is not always possible to estimate the degree of disequilibrium which would exist if countries followed different policies. But there are some cases where it is clear that a balance of payments surplus would be smaller or a deficit bigger if payments restrictions were relaxed or deflationary financial policies eased. For example, there can be little doubt that the UK would have had nothing like the £950 million surplus on current account in 1971 had economic activity not been stagnating and the economy not been afflicted by a considerable degree of unused resources, shown most dramatically by the existence of close to 1 million unemployed. For 1970 the OECD estimated the 'cyclically adjusted' current surplus in the UK to be half the surplus actually shown in that year.[1]

Having noted some of the difficulties inherent in the concepts of 'balance' and 'equilibrium', we shall in the next section see how the *accounts* are classified in the UK. We shall then consider the appropriateness or otherwise of the official presentation and the changes introduced in 1970 in the light of the difficulties examined in this and other sections of the chapter.

2. THE OFFICIAL UK PRESENTATION

In the following tables we set out the accounts as recorded in the annual *United Kingdom Balance of Payments* and in quarterly issues of the monthly *Economic Trends*, both published by the UK Central Statistical Office. They are classified in the three main groups *current transactions*, *investment and other capital flows* and *official financing*. Table 4 shows

[1] OECD *Economic Outlook*, December 1971.

TABLE 4. UK BALANCE OF PAYMENTS: SUMMARY 1960–1971
(£ million)

	1960	1961	1962	1963	1964	1965	1966	1967	1968	1969	1970	1971
A. Current Account												
Imports (f.o.b.)[1]	4,138	4,043	4,095	4,362	5,005	5,054	5,255	5,674	6,916	7,202	7,882	8,585
Exports (f.o.b.)[2]	3,732	3,891	3,993	4,282	4,486	4,817	5,182	5,122	6,273	7,061	7,885	8,882
Visible balance	−406	−152	−102	−80	−519	−237	−73	−552	−643	−141	+3	+297
Government services and transfers (net)	−282	−332	−360	−382	−432	−447	−470	−464	−462	−463	−480	−521
Interests, profits and dividends (net)	+231	+252	+333	+392	+395	+442	+380	+368	+317	+462	+532	+521
Private services and transfers (net)	+192	+229	+241	+184	+161	+165	+206	+336	+469	+579	+576	+655
Invisible balance	+141	+148	+214	+194	+124	+160	+116	+240	+324	+578	+628	+655
Current balance	−265	−4	+112	+114	−395	−77	+43	−312	−319	+437	+631	+952
B. Currency flow and official financing												
Current balance	−265	−4	+112	+114	−395	−77	+43	−312	−319	+437	+631	+952
Investment and other capital flows	+286	−316	−3	−103	−289	−308	−564	−560	−1,010	−15	+499	+1,847
Balancing item	+294	−29	+73	−69	−11	+32	−26	+201	−81	+321	+157	+429
Total currency flow	+325	−339	+192	−58	−695	−353	−547	−671	−1,410	+743	+1,287	+3,228
Allocation of Special Drawing Right	—	—	—	—	—	—	—	—	—	—	+171	+125
Gold subscription to IMF	−32	—	—	—	—	—	−44	—	—	—	−38	—
Total affecting official financing.	+293	−339	+192	−58	−695	−353	−591	−671	−1,410	+743	+1,420	+3,353
Official financing (net drawings from (+)/net repayments to (−)).	−293	+339	−192	+58	+695	+353	+591	+671	+1,410	−743	−1,420	−3,353

1 Includes payments for US military aircraft.
2 Includes adjustment for recording of exports.

SOURCE: CSO *United Kingdom Balance of Payments 1971* and *Economic Trends*, March 1972.

TABLE 4a. UNITED KINGDOM OFFICIAL SHORT- AND MEDIUM-TERM BORROWING [1]

(£ million)

Drawings out-standing at end of quarter	IMF	Swiss loan	Other official borrowing			Total
			Foreign currency	Sterling	Total	
1964 4th quarter	357	28	72	116	188	573
1965 4th quarter	846	42	—	284	284	1,172
1966 4th quarter	861	42	14	564	578	1,481
1967 4th quarter	628	17	193	1,229	1,422	2,067
1968 4th quarter	1,134	11	211	2,007	2,218	3,363
1969 4th quarter	1,104	—	150	1,410	1,560	2,664
1970 4th quarter	970	—	—	399	399	1,369
1971 4th quarter	415	—	—	—	—	415
1972 2nd quarter	—	—	—	—	—	—

[1] The table shows the levels of borrowing outstanding. Figures are calculated to end-September 1967 at £1 = $2·80; from end-December 1967 to end-September 1971 at £1 = $2·40; and from end-December 1971 at £1 = $2·6057.

SOURCE: *United Kingdom Balance of Payments 1971* and *Economic Trends*, March 1972.

TABLE 4b. OFFICIAL RESERVES [1]

End of period   (£ million)

	Total	Gold	IMF special drawing rights	Convertible currencies
1964	827	763	—	64
1965	1,073	809	—	264
1966	1,107	693	—	414
1967	1,123	538	—	585
1968	1,009	614	—	395
1969	1,053	613	—	440
1970	1,178	562	111	505
1971	2,526	232	246	1,957

[1] Valued at parity of £1 = $2·80 until the third quarter of 1967; at parity of £1 = $2·40 from the fourth quarter of 1967 until the third quarter of 1971; and thereafter at the middle rate of £1 = $2·6057.

SOURCE: *Economic Trends*, March 1972.

the summary position of the UK balance of payments between 1960 and 1971 while Tables 4a to 7 provide additional data.[1]

The Current Account

The first part of the balance of payments statement concerns visible trade. Table 4 shows that since 1960 this part of the account has been in deficit with the exception of the two years 1970 and 1971. There has been a deficit on visible account for a century past and of itself this is not a matter of grave concern. In fact the net earnings from 'invisibles' discussed below enable UK residents consistently to import more goods

TABLE 5. UK BALANCE OF PAYMENTS SEASONAL ADJUSTMENTS, 1971
(£ million)

	1st quarter	2nd quarter	3rd quarter	4th quarter
Visible trade	+71	−23	+20	−68
Invisibles				
Government	+5	+1	−4	−2
Private services	+6	−13	+4	+3
Interest, profits and dividends	−35	−27	+4	+58
TOTAL	−24	−39	+4	+59
CURRENT BALANCE	+47	−62	+24	−9

SOURCE: Calculated from data in: *Economic Trends*, March 1972.

than they export. But it is apparent from the Table 4 that there have been some years since 1960 when the visible deficit has not been covered in this way. This is especially so in the later years, when very substantial overall current account deficits were incurred, notably in 1964 (£376 million), 1967 (£298 million) and 1968 (£291 million).

Too much emphasis should not be placed on monthly or quarterly changes in the visible trade balance; a month's deficit could be the result of intensive stock piling or it could be due to some quite fortuitous event such as a dock or transport dispute. In the case of the UK there is

[1] The method officially employed by the UK is described in full in the *United Kingdom Balance of Payments 1971* (HMSO, August 1971). In this publication, there is considerable detailed information on the methods used to compile the statistics.

a marked seasonal pattern in the trade balance. Holidays have a greater seasonal impact upon exports than on imports; this results in an adverse seasonal effect in the third quarter. There is also a perceptible tendency for an adverse effect in the first quarter, due to the bigger impact of bad weather upon export shipments than arrivals. Table 5 shows the magnitude of the adjustments which the official statisticians regard as necessary in order to eliminate seasonal factors. It suggests that for the two quarters of 1971 some £91 million should have been added to the balance of visible trade to make the seasonal adjustment.

The visible trade balance which appears in the annual *UK Balance of Payments* differs from that of the *Trade and Navigation Accounts* and the *Report on Overseas Trade*.[1] These latter are based upon declarations by traders (importers and exporters) to the local Customs and Excise officials who pass them on to the Statistical Office, Customs and Excise. The Statistical Office counts all documents received in a given month as relating to that month irrespective of the date when the goods actually arrive at or leave British shores. Thus a delay in despatch of documents may well result in the inclusion of export cargoes in the trade figures for the month following the actual time of shipment. Whereas trade figures relate or should relate to the actual shipment of goods, the visible trade figures appearing in the balance of payments estimates relate to the date when the goods are regarded as changing ownership. But recording change of ownership is itself somewhat arbitrary; in principle it is assumed that imports become British-owned when they leave the foreign port, while exports become foreign-owned on arrival at the country of destination. Accordingly, the balance of payments figures relate to an earlier period for imports, and to a later period for exports, than do the trade accounts.

A more serious discrepancy arises from differences in the methods of valuation of imports in the two accounts. The balance of payments estimates show trade on an f.o.b. (free on board) basis—that is valued purely on the basis of the cargo, no account being taken of freight or insurance charges. The trade accounts use this basis of valuation only for exports. Imports are valued on a c.i.f. basis; that is the value

[1] The *Trade and Navigation Accounts* are published monthly, with figures for the whole year in December. Unless they are searching for detailed breakdown, most students will find their needs satisfied in a much more convenient form in the *Report on Overseas Trade*, also published monthly. There is also a (very detailed) *Annual Statement of Trade of the United Kingdom*, which appears many months after the end of the year to which it relates. The whole question of statistical sources is dealt with by the late Ely Devons in *An Introduction to British Economic Statistics*, Cambridge University Press 1957.

includes the cost of *insurance* and *freight*. Clearly, the importance of shipping and insurance costs in relation to the value of a cargo varies with the product and distance from the supplying country; in general it is estimated that about 10 per cent should be deducted from the trade accounts to eliminate the freight and insurance elements. In the balance of payments account part of these items, those paid to foreigners, appear as invisible transactions.

Invisibles

We have already noted the importance of invisible earnings in helping to offset the deficit on the balance of visible trade. In the UK balance of payments presentation, invisible transactions appear under several headings. In general they represent the net income from services rendered by UK residents to non-residents; net income from overseas assets owned by UK residents; the balance of gifts and transfer of migrants' funds, and net grants by the British Government to overseas countries. These items are set out in some detail for the period 1963-7 in Table 6. It will be seen that under some of the headings earnings are considerable; for invisible transactions as a whole, total credits amount to more than half the total value of UK exports.

In the past, invisibles played an even more important role in the UK balance of payments than in recent years.[1] Although estimates of invisible payments and receipts for the period before 1914 are of uncertain accuracy, it seems that just before the First World War net income from invisibles exceeded one half the value of imports. The largest single item was net income from overseas assets, which in 1910-13 accounted for almost one third of the value of imports. Although in the inter-war years the net income from invisibles did not cover the trade deficit with as handsome a margin as before 1914, in the 1920s it still made an extremely valuable contribution to the balance of payments. But with the onset of the 1931 Depression there was a sharp fall in money terms in invisibles. By the outbreak of the Second World War, the surplus on invisibles was only three quarters as great as in 1927-9; although of course the fall in import prices meant that the purchasing power of the invisible surplus in terms of imports was about the same. However, as the result of a fall in exports, the deficit on visible trade was too large to be offset by the surplus on invisibles and by 1936-8 the current account as a whole was in deficit.

[1] See A. H. Imlah, *Economic Elements in the Pax Britannica*, Cambridge, Mass., Harvard University Press, 1958. The matter is also discussed by A. E. Holmans in his contribution 'Invisible Earnings' in *The British Balance of Payments*, ed. D. J. Robertson and L. C. Hunter, Edinburgh, Oliver and Boyd, 1966.

TABLE 6. UK BALANCE OF PAYMENTS, CURRENT ACCOUNT, 1967–1971
(£ million)

	1967	1968	1969	1970	1971
Visibles					
Exports (f.o.b.)[1]	5,121	6,273	7,061	7,886	8,882
Imports (f.o.b.)[2]	5,674	6,916	7,202	7,869	8,585
VISIBLE BALANCE	− 552	− 643	− 141	+ 7	+ 297
Invisibles					
Government credits	37	44	48	51	55
debits	499	510	515	537	576
BALANCE	− 463	− 466	− 467	− 486	− 521
Shipping credits	877	1,048	1,051	1,371	1,588
debits	887	1,025	1,071	1,466	1,657
BALANCE	− 10	+ 23	− 20	− 95	− 69
Civil aviation credits	109	235	287	316	354
debits	172	206	246	279	310
BALANCE	+ 27	+ 29	+ 41	+ 37	+ 44
Travel credits	236	282	359	433	469
debits	274	271	324	385	443
BALANCE	− 38	+ 11	+ 35	+ 48	+ 26
Other services credits	762	909	1,035	1,168	1,252
debits	366	435	487	513	558
BALANCE	+ 396	+ 474	+ 548	+ 655	+ 694
Interest, profits, dividends credits	984	1,115	1,342	1,365	1,441
debits	599	774	840	875	920
BALANCE	+ 385	+ 341	+ 502	+ 490	+ 521
Private transfers credits	143	161	176	182	189
debits	186	221	231	227	229

TABLE 6—continued

	1967	1968	1969	1970	1971
BALANCE	−43	−60	−55	−45	−40
Total invisibles credits	3,237	3,794	4,298	4,886	5,348
debits	2,983	3,442	3,714	4,282	4,693
INVISIBLE BALANCE	+254	+352	+584	+604	+655
All current transactions credits	8,359	10,067	11,359	12,772	14,230
debits	8,657	10,358	10,916	12,161	13,278
CURRENT BALANCE	−298	−291	+443	+611	+952

1 Including net adjustments for recording of exports.
2 Excluding deliveries, but including payments, for US military aircraft and missiles.

SOURCE: *UK Balance of Payments 1971* and *Economic Trends*, March 1972.

After the Second World War there was a marked fall in the money value of invisibles. Many overseas assets had been sold to finance war-time expenditures; others had been destroyed or neglected. In the early post-war years the British Government incurred substantial overseas military and relief expenditure. However by 1948 recovery was taking place and the invisible account was once more in surplus. But over the period 1948-52 invisible earnings financed only 12 per cent of total imports, as against 28 per cent in 1938.[1] Although in the 1950s there was a substantial improvement in the invisible balance, in the early 1960s its performance was disappointing. But net invisibles rose rapidly after devaluation in 1967 and by 1971 yielded nearly four times their value of the early 1960s.

The relative decline in net invisibles is in part due to a reduction in receipts from shipping services, in part an increase in net travel expenditure, but above all to a substantial increase in net British Government expenditure overseas.[2] Although over the last fifteen or so years the total of government overseas expenditure as a proportion of total invisible imports has not notably increased, the absolute size of the expenditure

1 A. E. Holmans, cited above, p. 50.
2 The decline in the UK net invisible earnings is examined by F. N. Burton and P. Galambos, 'The Role of Invisible Trade in the United Kingdom Balance of Payments, 1952-1966', *National Provincial Bank Review*, May 1968.

and deficit under this head is so great that a given percentage increase represents a relatively large absolute increase in the deficit—and hence a substantial reduction in the total invisible surplus. As Table 6 makes clear, Government expenditure in the late 1960s shows a net annual debit of nearly £500 million. The item includes military expenditure (in 1971 some £335 million out of a total spending of £576 million), administrative expenditure (£67 million), and cash grants to developing countries (£98 million). Clearly the most important single item under this heading is military expenditure.

Tourist expenditure was traditionally a net debit but after devaluation tourism became a net earner. In 1971 UK residents spent £443 million overseas, while visitors to the UK spent £469 million. In 1970 the respective figures were £385 million and £433 million. Two-thirds (£257 million) of overseas tourists' expenditure was in Western Europe, £23 million in North America, £56 million in the Irish Republic, only £34 million being spent in the rest of the overseas sterling area. Of the total expenditure by UK residents abroad, holidays accounted for £258 million, just over two-thirds of the total.[1] North Americans bring in the largest sum of foreign exchange (£150 million in 1970) but they are followed closely by visitors from Western Europe (£137 million). The UK is now in most years a net importer of shipping services, although the balance on this item tends to vary from year to year. There were deficits nearly all through the 1960s with near balance or slight surplus in the middle of the decade. Civil aviation, on the other hand, consistently yielded a net credit of around £40 million in recent years.

As regards those items on the invisible account which bring in substantial net foreign exchange earnings, note should be taken of the two items 'interest, profits, dividends', and 'other services'. Both of these are substantial net credits. The entry 'interest profits, and dividends' includes those payments accruing to or payable by UK residents after deduction of local taxes and after allowing for depreciation. The bulk of the earnings under this head arise from the private rather than the official sector; within the private sector, earnings from direct investment account for about four-fifths of the total. In 1971 direct investment abroad yielded no less than £709 million; payments to non-UK residents in respect of direct investment in the UK amounted to £366 million. Transactions under the head of official investment income include interest received and paid on inter-Government loans, payments to overseas holders of UK Government stock and Treasury Bills and charges on drawings from the IMF.

[1] Details are to be found in *United Kingdom Balance of Payments 1971*, C.S.O., cited above.

The category 'other services' is the most difficult to describe. It includes all transactions in services between UK private residents and overseas residents—both Government and private—which are not appropriate to other headings in the accounts. In 1971, credits under this head amounted to £1,252 million, of which £144 million was accounted for by 'financial and allied services'. This category includes brokerage, banking charges, and various insurance premia and services. About £250 million is accounted for by royalties and services rendered by UK enterprises to overseas companies. Other items are credits in respect of film and television rights, and expenditure in the UK by overseas students. On the debit side the total under this heading in 1971 was £558 million. In recent years there has been much discussion of the contribution of the various institutions in the City of London to the balance of payments.[1] It is a matter of debate whether the financial rewards in terms of the invisible account are sufficient to compensate for the additional vulnerability of the balance of payments believed to result from the status of sterling as a reserve currency and the functions of London as a financial centre. This is a matter which we shall discuss further in Chapter 19, but in passing it is worth noting that a substantial proportion of the invisible earnings under the head of financial services arise because of the experience and efficiency of various City institutions, and would undoubtedly continue if sterling ceased to be a world currency. A case in point is the Euro-currency market. City banks conduct well over half its world business. Foreign currency deposits with them had risen to over £24,000 million by October 1971.[2] For most banks in London (apart from the deposit banks) foreign currency business is now considerably more important than sterling business. It is true that about half of this is transactions by branches of American banks situated in London—there are more American banks in the City than in Wall Street! Important invisible earnings accrue none the less to the UK balance of payments as these branches are UK 'residents'.

As in the case of visibles seasonal influences are important in the UK invisible account. They are strongly adverse for travel in the third quarter and for interest, profits and dividends in the fourth quarter. Holiday expenditure abroad by UK residents is heavily concentrated in the third quarter, while receipts from overseas visitors are spread more

[1] See, for example, W. M. Clarke, *The City in the World Economy*, London, Institute of Economic Affairs, 1965, and the Treasury *Minutes of Evidence* to the Radcliffe Committee (Committee on the Working of the Monetary System), Q. 2528.
[2] *Bank of England Quarterly Bulletin*, March 1972.

evenly over the year. Net receipts under interest, profits and dividends are normally reduced in the fourth quarter, when interest is paid on the post-war North American loans.

Visibles and invisibles (overseas trade, services and transfers) together make up the current account. We now turn to the second major constituent of the balance of payments accounts.

Investment

Official long-term capital together with private investments traditionally show a net outflow. 1961 and 1971 are exceptions.

In 1964 and 1970 the net outflow was very great indeed, £354 million and £226 million respectively. International investment is carried out by Government and international bodies on the one hand, and persons and companies on the other. Capital flows in the former category are known as 'official' in the latter as 'private'. Private investment is of two main types, portfolio and direct. In the case of portfolio investments, the investor purchases securities of foreign Governments or companies, but does not exercise control. In the case of direct investment the investor (usually a company) controls the enterprise. In recent years direct investment abroad by British companies and by foreign-owned companies in the UK has been of considerable importance and has attracted a great deal of attention.[1]

From July 1965, British residents investing overseas were required to surrender 25 per cent of the proceeds of the sale of securities at the official (and less favourable) rate of exchange. A year later, the Government tightened controls on the export of capital to non-sterling countries and requested voluntary restraint on investment in the more developed countries of the sterling area. A company wishing to invest abroad more than £25,000 was required to discuss its proposals with the Bank of England which adopted the criterion of expecting the investment to provide a quick, substantial, and continuing benefit to the balance of payments. But these measures, triggered by the deficit phase of the

[1] According to Professor J. R. S. Revell's estimates, in 1961 the net worth of the overseas subsidiaries of branches of British companies was about £8·1 billion, that is rather under 20 per cent of the net worth of all British Companies, measured on a similar definition. The value of this direct overseas investment was estimated to be 9 per cent of the total wealth of the nation. See J. R. S. Revell, *The Wealth of the Nation*, Cambridge University Press, 1967. A later official estimate puts the value of UK direct investments at £4,500 million in 1962 and at £8,950 million at the end of 1970. *Bank of England Quarterly Bulletin*, June 1972.

1960s, did not in fact reduce the level of private investment overseas. In fact it rose from about £350 million in 1965 and £300 million in 1966 to over £450 million in 1967, over £700 million in 1968, over £650 million in 1969 and over £750 million in both 1970 and 1971. It is true that the *net* outflow came down to an average of little over £100 million in the late 1960s and private investment showed a net surplus of over £100 million in 1971; but that was because overseas investment in the UK private sector in its turn rose from an annual average of about £250 million in the early 1960s to about £700 million in 1969, and amounted to more than £1,000 million in 1971. Outward *direct* investment also continued to increase and had with £547 million in 1971 reached more than twice the 1964 level. If *net* direct investment rose more slowly than that, it was because inward direct investment also doubled over this period.[1]

Direct investment by British companies is not new, but whereas in pre-war years this mostly took the form of investment in mines and plantations there has been a growing tendency since the war for it to be in the manufacturing sector, and in industrialized countries, notably in Western Europe. Since 1958 the Board of Trade has made regular enquiries into the area distribution, industry composition, and profitability of direct UK investment. The results of these enquiries are published from time to time in the *Board of Trade Journal*. The motives behind direct investment are various. Sometimes it is undertaken in order to establish a plant behind a tariff wall. This is likely to be true of much direct investment in developing countries, where infant industry protection often makes it extremely difficult for exporting countries to supply the market. It is for example, almost impossible to export cars to India, where restrictions are so tight as virtually to exclude all imports. While the desire to get behind a tariff wall or to circumvent quantitative restrictions has been one of the primary motives for direct investment abroad by British firms, it has not been the only force. The desire to obtain access to raw materials; to be close to an expanding market, and to enjoy the benefits of participation in a growth area have been at least as important. Moreover, direct investment is often highly profitable. Professor John Dunning has estimated that for 1960-2 the average rate of return on UK private investment overseas was slightly higher than at home.[2]

[1] The estimate quoted above puts the increase in the value of UK direct investment between 1967 and 1970 at £2,150 million. *Bank of England Quarterly Bulletin*, June 1972.

[2] J. H. Dunning, *Does Foreign Investment Pay;* Moorgate and Wall Street, autumn 1964.

In 1966 the Confederation of British Industry requested Mr W. B. Reddaway and his colleagues at the Department of Applied Economics of Cambridge University to carry out a detailed survey of some of the effects of direct investment upon the UK balance of payments and the UK economy generally. The preliminary results of this Enquiry were published in 1967 in what has become known as the Reddaway Report.[2] It is impossible to summarize the findings of this closely reasoned Report which deals with highly complex issues. The reader interested in this field of study is strongly urged to read the Report for himself. It is however worth noting that the Reddaway team conclude that for every £100 spent on increasing the net operating assets of subsidiaries and branches, there is a once-for-all effect of an addition of £9 to British exports. There is in addition a continuing effect on British exports, resulting from the overseas operation of the parent company, but the Report puts this at an even lower figure—£1½ for every £100 invested.

Of course the choice facing a Company is often not between exporting from the UK and manufacturing locally, but between going in and establishing local manufacture or allowing an American or Continental firm to step in and secure the whole market. It should also be remembered that so far as the UK is concerned, direct investment is a two-way movement. While British companies have been establishing plant abroad, foreign companies have been doing the same thing in the UK. It is, for example, estimated that in the British pharmaceutical industry, over half the total prescription medicine sales in the UK are supplied by the US owned firms operating in the UK. Of the sixty or so members of the Association of British Pharmaceutical Industry Division B (the Division which accounts for 95 per cent of the total sales of the industry to the National Health Service), only thirty one are British owned. The presence of so many American (and Swiss) Companies is widely regarded as a spur to efficiency in the British industry and this factor should not be overlooked in weighing the merits of foreign participation in British industry.

Considerable discussion has taken place on the wisdom of curtailing the level of direct investment abroad by Britain's companies. The scale of this investment has certainly imposed a burden at times on Britain's balance of payments. It can also be argued that investment in the UK would have been greater and perhaps the domestic growth rate more rapid, if firms had invested less overseas and more at home. But against this it can be argued that there is little evidence that companies have

[1] W. B. Reddaway, *Effects of UK Direct Investment Overseas, Final Report*, Cambridge University Press, 1968.

limited real investment at home in order to export capital. Often the effect of restrictions is to make British companies raise finance abroad on terms less advantageous than in the UK. Those who advocate a more liberal approach also claim that the British company operating abroad usually acquires a great deal of technical and marketing 'know-how' from its overseas activities. But the question is not a straightforward one.[1]

Other Capital Flows

The other capital flows shown as totals for the years 1960–71 in Table 4 are detailed in Table 7 for the year 1971. They include trade credit extended by UK suppliers to overseas customers and by overseas customers to UK importers; these are items that have increased considerably over·the last few years. Export credit exceeds import credit massively and thus regularly constitutes a new outflow.

This part of the accounts also includes exchange reserves and other liabilities in sterling (the 'sterling balances'). They are discussed at some length in Chapter 19 but it is worth noting here that there tends to be a net *outflow* when the balance of payments position of overseas sterling area countries is weak, and also in times of doubt about the strength of the pound. In both cases, deposits are withdrawn from London. There tends to be a net *inflow* when overseas sterling area countries are in surplus and when the pound looks strong. In 1967 (the year of devaluation) and in 1968, sums withdrawn amounted to £284 million and £308 million respectively; in 1970, there was an inflow of £431 million and in 1971 one of £1,421 million! Some of this reflected the strong payments position of the overseas sterling area, some of it was part of the 'hot money' that arrived in the second half of 1971 with the confident expectation of a revaluation of the pound as part of the general realignment of currencies. This duly took place and a revaluation profit was made (or, in the case of US dollar holders, a devaluation loss avoided).

Two items in this part of the accounts register different types of transactions in the Euro-dollar (Euro-currency) market: the entry *foreign currency borrowing (net) by UK banks to finance UK investment overseas* (they have steadily risen from a mere £5 million in 1963 to £240 million in 1971) is self-explanatory; *other foreign currency borrowing or lending (net) by UK banks* has also become increasingly important.

---

[1] I have discussed the implications for the British Pharmaceutical Industry of the international flow of capital in *Innovation and the Balance of Payments*, ed. G. Teeling Smith, Pergamon Press, 1967.

TABLE 7. ANALYSIS OF TOTAL CURRENCY FLOW AND OFFICIAL FINANCING [1]
Not seasonally adjusted.   (£ million)

		1971
CURRENT BALANCE	1	+952
Investment and other capital flows		
Official long-term capital	2	−274
Overseas investment in UK public sector	3	+187
Overseas investment in UK private sector	4	+974
UK private investment overseas	5	−762
Foreign currency borrowing (net) by UK banks to finance UK investment overseas	6	+240
Other foreign currency borrowing or lending (net) by UK banks	7	+255
Exchange reserves in sterling:		
British government stocks	8	+47
Banking and money market liabilities	9	+639
Other external banking and money market liabilities in sterling	10	+735
Import credit	11	+85
Export credit	12	−360
Other short-term flows	13	+81
Total investment and other capital flows	14	+1,847
Balancing item	15	+429
EEA loss on forwards	16	—
TOTAL CURRENCY FLOW	17	+3,228
Allocation of Special Drawing Rights	18	+125
Gold subscription to IMF	19	—
Total (items *17* to *19*)	20	+3,353
Official financing		
Net transactions with overseas monetary authorities		
IMF	21	−554
Other monetary authorities	22	−1,263
Transfer from dollar portfolio to reserves	23	—
Drawings on (+)/additions to (−) official reserves	24	−1,536
Total official financing	25	−3,353

[1] The sum of items *1* to *5* equals the total formerly known as the 'basic balance'; the remainder (except for item *15*) makes up the total formerly known as 'monetary movements'.

SOURCE: *Economic Trends*, March 1972.

Up to 1969, flows tended to be negative, suggesting net lending of Euro-dollars overseas. In 1970, it turned into a record inflow; UK companies were borrowing foreign currencies to finance domestic investment. The 1971 inflow was lower, and mainly reflected switching into sterling by UK banks after the realignment of currencies. At the same time there was a sharp reduction in net foreign currency borrowing by UK firms for domestic investment as a result partly of restrictions imposed upon short-term Euro-dollar borrowing in January 1971 by the authorities, and partly of the easier domestic monetary conditions.

Before devaluation—partly in defence of the old parity—the Exchange Equalization Account entered into forward commitments. Settling these at the new parity involved a loss. It is this loss that is recorded by the item *EEA loss on forwards*. Entries rose (as settlements fell due) in 1967 and 1968, the year of and the year following devaluation.

For the items brought together and discussed in this sub-section (rows 2–13 of Table 7) a balance is struck giving a net *total investment and other capital flows*[1] (row 14). Combined with the current balance (row 1) and making allowance for loss on forwards (row 16) and errors and omissions (row 15), this results in the total currency flow (row 17).

Official Financing

This flow, arising out of a year's market transactions, has to be made possible, 'financed'—by the UK authorities. There are four possible ways of official financing of a surplus (a net inflow) or a deficit (a net outflow) shown in the accounts (rows 21–24 of Table 7). *Net transactions with the IMF*: in the crisis phase of the 1960s, the UK made drawings of ('borrowed') over £1,000 million and repurchased ('repaid') it in the surplus years after 1969. Similarly, *net transactions with other monetary authorities* (mostly overseas central banks): borrowing built up to more than £2,000 million by 1968 and repayments had cleared the debts by the end of 1970 (Table 4a). Up to the time of devaluation, the Exchange Equalization Account held a portfolio of dollar securities (mostly equities) vested in the UK Government and considered as nearly equivalent to assets for official reserve purposes. Over a period, the equities were sold and the proceeds invested in more liquid assets. For February 1966 and November 1967, they are entered in the accounts as transfers from *dollar portfolio to reserves*, adding over £500 million.

The final item is labelled *Drawings on and additions to official reserves*,[2]

---

[1] Inflows are preceded by a positive, outflows by a negative, sign.
[2] Drawings are shown with a positive and additions with a negative sign.

showing the changes in the level of the 'gold and convertible currency reserves', administered by the EEA of the Bank of England (Table 4b). Borrowing from the IMF and other monetary authorities, including 'swap' (delayed conversion) arrangements with overseas central banks enabled the authorities to keep drawings from official reserves modest in spite of the massive deficits of 1966, 1967 and 1968, around the level of about £1,000 million. Conversely, most of the currency inflow of the surplus years 1969 and 1970 was not added to reserves but used for the repayment of previously acquired debts. It was only the inflow of over £3,000 million in 1971 that enabled the authorities to repay short- and medium-term debts and yet add a record £1,500 million to reserves, bringing the total to £2,500 million, of which some 12 per cent was in gold and 80 per cent in convertible currencies, mostly in—in practice—inconvertible post-August 1971 dollars.

Items 21–24 of Table 7 combined show *total official financing* (row 25) which by definition equals, though with an opposite sign, *total currency flow*, so that the two add to zero.

This is, however, after allowing for two items that are shown specifically, both being transactions of a reserve nature with the IMF and arising out of the IMF system. First, in January 1970 the UK was allocated £171 million of Special Drawing Rights (SDR) and in 1971 as well as 1972 £125 million (row 18 of Table 7). Secondly, in connection with the allocation of a higher quota in the Fund, the UK had to make a gold subscription payment to the IMF, amounting to £38 million in 1970 (row 19).

The Balancing Item

In the tables, the final balance of official financing is made equal to the total currency flow only by inclusion of an entry labelled, somewhat confusingly, 'the balancing item'.

This is simply an item inserted to make recorded items balance; it is better thought of not as a balancing item but as 'errors and omissions', for it is composed of a large number of diverse items which escape the official records. Some of these errors and omissions arise because current and long term capital account figures are gathered independently of those relating to the short term capital account. Visible and invisible trade, together with long term investment estimates are calculated in the main from customs records and information returned by government departments and firms (often reporting through trade associations). These are records of 'flows'. Changes in capital account, on the other hand, are almost all deduced from information supplied by banks. These estimates are derived not from flows over a given period, but from changes in outstanding liabilities and assets between the beginning and the end of the period. In view of the diverse nature of sources and differing methods of collection it is hardly surprising that some 'balancing item' is necessary. It is as if a householder keeps a record of what he believes to be his receipts and income over the year, and this record shows that he has spent £100 more than he had earned over the period, while his bank balance at the end of the period compared with the balance at the beginning shows a deterioration of only £50.

On occasion, the size of the balancing item was found disturbing. In some years during the 1960s it was bigger than the recorded balance of current and investment capital transactions! As one commentator remarked of a slightly earlier period—1959/61—the balance of payments can be regarded 'as anything from indifferent to potentially disastrous according to the view taken of the balancing item'.[1]

Not everybody would, however, subscribe to this today. It is arguable that the shortcomings affect our knowledge of the composition but not of the size of the currency flow. Its size and so the extent of actual surplus or deficit is known, as the official financing total identically matches (with the qualifications made earlier) the currency flow, and, being based on official records, is itself precise.

A positive/negative balancing item implies that records of official financing movements show a balance of payments deficit to be smaller/ larger than appears from the recorded balance of current and capital transactions. Although the balancing item may represent errors and omissions in any branch of the recorded balance of payments on either current or capital account, attempts have been made to identify for specific periods the chief locus of the discrepancies.

In the 1950s, the balancing item was almost invariably positive, in the 1960s this was not so: but throughout the period it appeared to include a recurrent (and possibly growing) positive element believed to be attributable to differences in the measurement of current account transactions. This was partly confirmed when considerable under-recording of exports due to failure by some exporters to lodge documents with the Customs authorities was discovered in 1969 and again in 1970.[2] Adjustments were made in the accounts, increasing over the

---

[1] National Institute *Economic Review*, February 1962 quoted by C. MacMahon *Sterling in the Sixties*, Oxford University Press, 1964.

[2] The story unfolds in *Board of Trade Journal* for June 18 and September 10, 1969 and January 21, 1970, in *Trade and Industry* for November 1ϵ, 1970 and May 5, 1971. For a comment, see P. D. Balacs, 'Economic Data and Economic Policy', in *Lloyds Bank Review*, April 1972, pp. 44 ff.

period 1964–71 the value of exports and thus of the visible balance by a total of £640 million and reducing the value of the balancing item accordingly.

But while the balancing item was in earlier years ascribed to the current account, present experience suggests that the main errors in identifying fluctuations in the balances and in their levels are probably in the accounts for investment and other capital flows.

In the early 1970s, the main responsibility for fluctuation in the balancing item is ascribed to timing errors in the recording of trans-actions and the corresponding payments as well as to unrecorded capital flows. The latter include short-term 'leads and lags' in the timing of payments which, like identified flows of short-term funds, are probably influenced by the level of interest rates in the UK relative to those abroad, the relative degree of credit stringency and, on occasion, by speculation about exchange rates. In recent years, figures tend to be strongly positive when such timing discrepancies have been 'unwound', for instance in 1969 and again in 1971 when the balancing item was + £397 million and + £429 million respectively, following massive speculative movements into sterling. Over the years 1962 to 1970, how-ever, it averaged about £50 million.

It should be remembered that, however large in absolute terms the balancing item may appear in any one year, over the years it amounts to no more than half of 1 per cent of the value of the total transactions shown in the accounts.

Let us now briefly consider the appropriateness of the official balance of payments presentation currently employed in the UK, as opposed to the more conventional method used in this country between 1959 and 1969 and currently used by many other countries. The new presentation focuses on the concept of the *total currency flow* which records current as well as capital transactions and suggests that it is in some meaningful sense *the* balance of payments, representing all payments made over the year and requiring appropriate official financing; if the flow is negative, payments have exceeded receipts, there is a deficit, and official reserves or borrowing have to finance it; if the flow is positive, receipts have exceeded payments, there is a surplus, official reserves are added to and there is room for official lending or repayment. The balancing item is included in the currency flow total. So while we may not be sure to which of its sub-sections the unrecorded flows that gave rise to the balancing item belong, we do know that this will not affect the overall result, the precise value of the surplus or deficit.

In the conventional presentation, the capital account is split into long-term capital movements which join the current account transactions 'above the line', and the short-term capital movements which, together with official financing, make up the balance of monetary movements 'below the line'. The balancing item is not assigned to either.

For years it has been argued that such a presentation places too much emphasis on the balance of payments on current and long-term capital account—which it calls 'basic'—and encourages the impression that it is somehow what we mean by a 'true' balance of payments. Further, it has become progressively less meaningful as an indicator of a country's external position: the short-term movements, say international lending by banks, are certainly not purely residual, as their position below the line would suggest, and the arbitrariness of the division of capital entries above and below the line becomes worse with both the increasing importance and the increasing variety of different forms of capital which do not allow a clear-cut division according to the degree of liquidity.

Examples are the purchase of foreign shares which, as portfolio investment, are part of long-term capital as conventionally defined, but which may frequently be re-sold within days of purchase. Similarly, direct investment, also by tradition classified as a long-term capital item, sometimes represents inter-company balances of a kind that can be highly volatile in the face of such short-term considerations as the relative tightness or costliness of credit in different countries and expectations about the future movement of exchange rates. With the rapid growth and significance of multinational corporations and multinational banks, the scale of this is both large and increasing. Conversely, short-term funds borrowed on the Euro-currency market may be 'rolled over' to finance long-term investment and similarly trade credit frequently moves into a longer-term time scale.

Finally, the size of the balancing item and its position in the accounts make the 'basic balance' ambiguous in view of our lack of knowledge of the type of unrecorded transactions that give rise to it. So the 'basic balance' will either over- or understate the true payments position that needs official financing.

But in this respect the UK was not alone. Indeed there is a general feeling of dissatisfaction with the way in which most countries present their balance of payments accounts. As regards the USA, for example, Professor Machlup has shown that for any given year there appears to be not one but several 'balance of payments' figures. He instances 1951, for which year no less than twenty different phrases were used to describe the US balance—and almost as many figures were quoted. Machlup quotes figures published between 1951 and 1959 relating to the 1951 balance and finds that they ranged from a surplus of over \$5 billion to a deficit of about \$1 billion![1]

The developments which have made increasingly unrealistic and arbitrary established ways of distinguishing between long-term and short-term transactions and between 'above-the-line' transactions (which require financing) and 'below-the-line' transactions (which record this financing), have called forth a great deal of discussion on methods of presenting balance of payments statistics which take account of some of these difficulties.

The IMF has done valuable work not only in standardizing balance of payments concepts, but also in stimulating discussion of ways of defining a surplus or deficit. In the US too there has been much discussion of alternative methods of presenting the balance of payments. One of the more fruitful attempts at producing an alternative form for the balance of payments is that of Mr Walter Gardner,[2] who has tried to divide balance of payments transactions on the line suggested in the section above—that is by drawing the line between those 'autonomous' or 'market' transactions on the one hand, and compensatory official financing operation on the other. The Bank of England has attempted a reclassification of the UK balance of payments on similar lines.[3] It is on these attempts that the present method used officially in the UK is based.

The precise form of presentation of balance of payments accounts is a matter of convenience depending on the theoretical or practical issue under consideration; they alter with changing conditions. There can thus be no single, unique 'correct' classification for every conceivable purpose and every conceivable period. With this reservation, the new presentation is an important improvement. It avoids the difficulty of classifying capital movements according to their supposed degree of liquidity; it facilitates analysis because in its classification it comes very much closer to satisfying the criteria established by balance of payments theory for the distinction between autonomous and accommodating flows.[4]

[1] F. Machlup, 'The Mysterious Numbers Game, of Balance-of-Payments Statistics', Chapter VII in *International Monetary Economics*, Allen and Unwin, 1966, cited above.
[2] W. R. Gardner, 'An Exchange-Market Analysis of the US balance of Payments', *IMF Staff Papers*, vol. viii, 1961.
[3] 'The Balance of Payments: Methods of Presentation', *Bank of England Quarterly Bulletin*, December 1964. This Bulletin also contains a useful bibliography on the subject.
[4] To-underline the point that there can be no one 'correct' method which will serve for all times: economists have begun to worry about increasing difficulties in distinguishing between (autonomous) transactions that require financing and (accom-

SHORT GUIDE TO THE LITERATURE

Many conceptual problems within this chapter are discussed in Chapters I-III of J. E. Meade, *The Balance of Payments*. Professor Machlup has made some outstanding contributions in this field and the student should refer to his collected writings in *International Monetary Economics*. In particular the following should be read: 'Three Concepts of the Balance of Payments and the So-Called Dollar Shortage', first published in *Economic Journal*, vol. lx, March 1950; 'Equilibrium and Disequilibrium is Misplaced Concreteness and Disguised Politics', first published in *Economic Journal*, vol. lxviii, March 1958; 'The Mysterious Numbers Game of Balance of Payments Statistics', published for the first time in *International Monetary Economics*.

The student who wishes to understand fully the UK official presentation of the Balance of Payments accounts should read 'Notes and Definitions' at the back of the 1968 *United Kingdom Balance of Payments*. The rationale for re-arranging the accounts is discussed (for the USA) by W. Gardner, 'An Exchange Market Analysis of the US Balance of Payments', *IMF Staff Papers*, May 1961 and (for the UK) by T. M. Klein, 'The United Kingdom Balance of Payments Accounts', *Economic Journal*, no. 296, vol. lxxiv, December 1964. The student who wishes to delve more deeply into the literature of the balance of payments presentation is advised to consult Hal B. Lary, *Problems of the United States as World Trader and Banker*, New York, National Bureau of Economic Research, 1963, where alternative classifications for the US balance of payments are set out (p. 140) and W. Lederer, 'The Balance of United States Payments: A Statement of the Problem', in *The Dollar in Crisis*, ed. S. E. Harris, New York, 1961. There is a useful summary of some of the problems in Christopher MacMahon's Chatham House Essay, *Sterling in the Sixties*, Oxford University Press, 1964.

---

modating) transactions that perform the function of financing. This has led to the proposal for the introduction of a third, intermediate, category of 'compensatory corrections' to describe transactions which help to balance the accounts but which do not themselves constitute 'real' adjustment. See F. Machlup, 'Real Adjustment, Compensatory Corrections, and Foreign Financing of Imbalances in International Payments', in R. E. Baldwin *et al.*, *Trade, Growth and the Balance of Payments*, Chicago, 1965.

CHAPTER 12

INCOME CHANGES AND THE BALANCE OF PAYMENTS

1. A SPONTANEOUS CHANGE IN DOMESTIC INCOMES

One of the most significant developments in economic thinking in the twentieth century has been a growing awareness of the link between the balance of payments and the level of domestic activity in a country. Essentially the modern view is that there is a two-way relationship between internal and external economic development. An expansion of domestic incomes, resulting from some domestic development such as, say, a general reduction in interest rates, will normally have some external trade repercussions; it is likely for example, to raise imports, and at the same time reduce somewhat producers' incentive to export. The balance of trade is then likely to deteriorate. Similarly a dampening down of the level of domestic activity is likely to reduce the level of imports and at the same time force some producers more diligently to export products which can no longer be sold with relative ease on the home market.[1]

The relationship between the change in the level of aggregate domestic demand and imports has long been understood; it is normally expressed as the marginal propensity to import.[2] We can explain this by means of an example. If for every £1 million pound increase in national income (Y) imports increase by £100,000, the marginal propensity to import (m) is 0·1. The marginal propensity to import (m) can be expressed as $\Delta M / \Delta Y$. Let us now consider the effect on domestic income of a spontaneous increase in domestic investment in a country A. The increase in investment will lead *via* the investment multiplier to an increase in income of greater magnitude than the initial increase in investment.[3]

---

[1] Although the alledgedly favourable effect of domestic deflation upon the balance of trade is by no means certain. There is also evidence that a restriction of domestic demand might at times have an *adverse* effect upon the balance of trade; I have touched on this question at the end of this chapter.

[2] The subject matter of this chapter is dealt with at length by a number of writers. The fullest is Professor Fritz Machlup's book, *International Trade and the National Income Multiplier*, Blackiston, 1943. Professor Meade discusses it in his *The Balance of Payments*, cited above.

[3] The reader who wishes to refresh his memory on the working of the domestic multiplier is advised to consult F. S. Brooman's book in the Minerva Series, *Macroeconomics*, Allen and Unwin, 1962.

Since we are dealing with an open economy, the fact that some proportion of every addition to domestic income is spent on imports and therefore creates no further increase in domestic income gives rise to what is known as a 'foreign leakage'. The existence of this leakage will damp down the domestic multiplier. Given the size of the marginal propensity to save, the higher the marginal propensity to import, the lower is the domestic multiplier. For at each successive round of income spending, some will 'leak' abroad on imported goods enhancing foreign, but not domestic incomes.

In an open economy, therefore, neglecting for the moment any backwash effects which the increase in national income abroad might have upon A, we can express the multiplier in a country A as

$$k = \frac{1}{s+m} \qquad \text{equation (1)}$$

where k = the foreign trade multiplier in country A

s = the marginal propensity to save in country A

m = the marginal propensity to import of country A

If then s = 0·2, and m = 0·3, k will be equal to 2. This is to say that a spontaneous increase in investment of £1,000 leads ultimately to an increase in national income of £2,000.

Foreign Repercussions

So far we have deliberately omitted any consideration of the foreign repercussions of the increase in country A's imports. In the real world, however, it is often impossible to neglect what we might call the backwash effects of a change in national income in any particular country. Of course in the case of a tiny economy—Chad, for example—an increase in national income caused by an investment project will result in an increase in incomes in Chad. Out of higher incomes citizens in that country will purchase more goods from the outside world, in accordance with the size of their propensity to import. But Chad accounts for such a small part of overall world demand that any conceivable increase in its import demand is unlikely to have much effect upon the level of incomes in outside countries, and even less upon the outside world's demand for Chad's product. But clearly in the case of larger countries the external repercussions of a change in domestic incomes cannot be overlooked.

Let us call the home country, where the initial increase in income takes place A and designate the rest of the world as B. Some of the income increase in A will spill over in the form of additional imports from B. Since A's imports are B's exports there will thus be an additional demand for the products of B's industries, leading to an increase in the national income of that country. But it is unlikely that the marginal propensity to import of B's citizens is zero; some part of the increased incomes will be spent upon imports from A. Accordingly there will be a backwash effect, or what we call a foreign repercussion. The expansion of A's national income will increase A's imports; this increase will in turn raise incomes in B and bring about an increase in A's exports, leading to a further increase in A's national income. Thus the spontaneous increase in investment in country A brings about a consequent increase in national income, and this increase is reinforced by repercussions in the outside world. As regards country A's balance of trade the increase in exports resulting from the induced expansion of incomes in country B will offset to some extent the original increase in A's imports. There will therefore be some offset to the initial deterioration in A's balance of trade. Clearly this 'foreign repercussion' must be taken into account in considering the ultimate effects of an income increase, on both the level of income after the multiplier has worked through the system, and also upon the balance of trade.

2. AN INDUCED CHANGE IN DOMESTIC INCOMES

So far we have been concerned with the effect of an autonomous change in the level of domestic activity upon the balance of trade. The changes in imports and the consequent change in exports resulting from the foreign repercussions are 'induced'. The foreign trade changes result from, rather than themselves cause, a change in domestic incomes. But a moment's thought will show that the sequence of cause and effect need not be in this order. A change in exports induced by some external event might itself cause a change in domestic activity. In other words the expansion or contraction of exports might be the active rather than the passive factor.

A change in exports might be brought about in a number of ways; it could be caused by the modification of a foreign country's tariff, or by a change in foreign consumers' tastes or incomes. Since an autonomous change in a country's exports has somewhat similar multiplier effects as an autonomous change in investment, we refer to the operation of the *foreign trade multiplier*. Let us see how a spontaneous increase in a country's exports affects a country's national income and balance of trade. Now an increase in exports means that incomes of producers of exports goods will rise; these incomes will be spent on domestic goods, on imported goods, or saved according to the respective propensities to consume, save, and to import. The higher the proportion of the increment in incomes spent on domestic products rather than on imports at each successive round of income receipt and expenditure, the higher the value of the multiplier.

Now there will be domestic equilibrium when

$$Y = C+I+G+X-M, \qquad \text{equation (2)}$$

where Y = National Income.

C = Consumption.

I = Investment.

G = Government Expenditure.

X = Exports.

M = Imports.

When X rises, perhaps as the result of a reduction of import duties in country B, in the absence of any offset by a reduction of one of the other items in our equation, national income Y will increase in accordance with the multiplier. Since however in this case the multiplier action is triggered off by the increase in exports rather than in domestic activity, we speak of the *foreign trade* multiplier. Income will continue to rise but finally settle at a point determined by the various propensities not only in country A but also in other countries B. For the moment, however, we shall simplify our analysis by leaving these repercussions out of account.

An Example

Let us suppose that the marginal propensity to save (s) in country A is 0·1 while the marginal propensity to import (m) is 0·4. Then an autonomous expansion of exports £100 causes domestic incomes to rise by this amount. We have tried to show what happens in Table 8, which follows the lines used by Machlup in his approach. The first line in this Table shows that national income and exports both rise by £100 in the first period. Since income recipients now have more purchasing power, in period 2 they increase both domestic consumption and imports in accordance with the marginal propensities to consume and import respectively. Line 2 of Table 8 shows that out of the increase of £100 in national income, domestic consumption rises by £50, domestic savings by £10 and imports by £40. But only the £50 addition to consumption affects domestic income; the additional £40 spent on imports

TABLE 8. EFFECT OF AUTONOMOUS INCREASE IN EXPORTS ON NATIONAL INCOME AND BALANCE OF TRADE
Functional Relationships: $S = 0.1$ $M = 0.4$ $K = 2.0$
(£)

(a) Period and line	(b) Resultant change in national income	(c) Change in domestic consumption	(d) Induced change in saving	(e) Induced change in imports	(f) Autonomous change in exports	(g) Change in balance of trade	(h) Current change in national income
1	100·0	50·0	10·0	40·0	100·0	100·0	100
2	150·0	75·0	15·0	60·0	100·0	60·0	150
3	175·0	87·5	17·5	70·0	100·0	40·0	175
4	187·5	93·75	18·75	75·0	100·0	30·0	187·5
5	193·75	96·875	19·375	77·5	100·0	25·0	193·75
6	196·875	98·4375	19·687	78·75	100·0	22·5	196·875
7	198·437	99·2187	19·8437	79·375	100·0	21·25	198·437
8						20·625	199·218
'Final' period	200·0	100·0	20·0	80·0	100·0	20·0	200·0

increases foreign, not domestic incomes; and of course the £10 saved, by definition, creates no further income. Thus by the end of period 2 (the line 2 in Table 8), national income is £50 higher than at the beginning of the period.

Since £100 autonomous increase in exports is now offset by an increase of £40 in imports, the balance of trade improvement over the initial position is now only £60. The community thus enters period 3 with a cumulative increase in national income of £150. Out of this increase one half will be devoted to increased consumption, one-tenth will be saved, and four tenths spent on additional imports. At the end of period 3, then, consumption is £75 above the initial level (and £25 above the level at the preceding period); savings are £15 above the initial level; imports £60 above the initial level (and £20 above the level of the preceding period). The cumulative increase in national income by the end of period 3 is £175 while the increase in imports has gone some way to eliminating the balance of trade surplus, which now stands at £40. Now the national income will continue to increase, but at a diminishing rate, until the increase in imports and the increase in saving, catch up with the autonomous increase in exports. At this point there is no further income increase and the multiplier process is at an end.

Of course, to be precise this point will never be reached since however minute they become, increases in imports and savings are always finite. But to all intents and purposes we may regard the process as continuing until the level of national income has risen to the point where the increase in induced savings and induced imports together is just equal to the autonomous increase in exports. As can be seen from Table 8 this point is not far off at around period 8. A very large number of additional rounds create only small increments in income. In the example, income will cease to increase (perceptibly, at any rate), before the balance of trade equilibrium is restored. Although imports increase, the expansion is insufficient to offset the £100 expansion in exports. The multiplier process comes to an end *before* the balance of trade is brought to zero.

This is because at each round of income increase, part of the increment is saved; thus causing domestic expansion to come to an end before imports have grown sufficiently to offset the initial increase in exports. Increased imports will equal increased exports only if domestic savings are zero; that is if each successive increment in income is spent, either on domestic consumption or on imports. In this case, there is nothing to prevent imports increasing until the multiplier has done its work and imports equal exports. In practice, domestic savings are unlikely to be zero; thus in the real world, income changes alone are unlikely to provide an automatic corrective to the export surplus. Some price adjustment will also be necessary. Perhaps this conclusion is the most important that emerges from this chapter. Income movements alone are unlikely (indeed we can say in practice will always be) insufficient to restore equilibrium.

Foreign Repercussions Again

We have so far discussed a foreign induced expansion of exports as if there were no foreign repercussions. How can these be incorporated into the model? In discussing foreign repercussions, it is important to distinguish between two cases (1) where an expansion in A's exports is due to a foreign switch of demand in country B from their own products to those of country A and (2) where the increase in demand for A's goods is not accompanied by an equal reduction in demand for B's products Let us examine each case in turn.

In the first case, the increase in A's exports causes incomes in country A to rise, but some of the incremental income is saved, some is spent on imports from country B (assuming that country B stands for the rest of the world). There are thus two leakages; the greater their magnitude the smaller the increase in A's domestic incomes. But since at the same time foreigners substitute imports from country A for their own products, there will be a reduction in domestic incomes in B which, if the marginal propensity to import is greater than zero, in turn leads to a fall in imports from country A. This is of course the same as saying that the original expansion in A's exports will be damped down. This is the repercussion effect, which in this case is negative—and indeed can be regarded as a third leakage affecting the rate of growth of A's national income. The greater fall in foreign imports following the reduction in foreign national income, the greater the foreign repercussions leakage to A and the smaller the foreign trade multiplier. We can write the foreign trade multiplier now,

$$k = \frac{1}{s+m+f}$$ equation (3)

The factors that determine the size of f are rather more complex than at first appears. Since we can assume that the curve of the domestic consumption function rises less steeply as income increases, the reduction in B's income following the substitution of imports from A for home trade products causes a more than proportionate reduction in the level of savings, while in A, savings rise more than proportionately with income. Accordingly, the decline in savings in B offsets to some extent the decline in imports from A, while in A increased saving reduces to some extent the increase in imports from B. Account can be taken of this by building induced savings changes into the foreign repercussions factor, which we can then write as

$$f = \frac{sa}{sb} \; mb \quad \text{where} \qquad \text{equation (4)}$$

sa = marginal propensity to save in A.
sb = marginal propensity to save in B.
ma = marginal propensity to import in A.
mb = marginal propensity to import in B.

Thus the formula for the foreign trade multiplier in country A can be written

$$k = \frac{1}{sa + ma + mb \frac{(sa)}{(sb)}} \qquad \text{equation (5)}$$

Our second case is where the expansion in A's exports is not accompanied by a fall in domestic output in B. In his case there will be no dampening influence at work in B, since B's national income has not fallen. The expansion in A's exports generates higher income, part of which is spent on imports from B. This raises incomes in B; out of higher incomes, citizens in B purchase more from country A thus causing incomes in A to rise. At each round, of course, successive increases in imports and exports get progressively smaller, but the repercussions factor in this case is positive. In other words, the fact that incomes go on rising in B reinforces the expansionary tendencies in country A. The higher the marginal propensity to import and the lower the propensity to save in B, the stronger are these expansionary influences upon country A. Accordingly, we must take account of these propensities in the numerator of our equation, which we can now write:

$$k = \frac{1 + \dfrac{mb}{sb}}{sa + ma + mb \; \dfrac{(sa)}{(sb)}} \qquad \text{equation (6)}$$

Before finally leaving this chapter, there are three points which the reader should note carefully. Firstly, in the exposition I have followed Professor Machlup by assuming imports to be a function of national income. In his book, *The Balance of Payments*, Professor Meade takes imports to be a function of domestic expenditure. In analysing a practical situation the distinction could well be an important one. Second, we are dealing (for example in Table 8) with discrete time periods. We assume that an injection of income takes time to work through the economy; at the end of the period incomes, savings and imports are higher than at the beginning. But there is no instantaneous multiplier at work. In practice the interval between an income injection and its outworking in terms of the balance of trade may be several months or more. Thirdly the reader must be firmly warned against too mechanistic an interpretation of the multiplier theory. The saving and import propensities are likely constantly to be changing, and it is in practice often very difficult to distinguish between autonomous and induced changes in exports.[1]

Finally, we have implied that an increase in imports is positively correlated with an increase in domestic income and that this has an adverse effect upon the balance of trade. There is accordingly a 'balance of trade' price to pay for domestic growth. In the real world the situation is not as simple as this, for it is conceivable that the increase in domestic demand following a rise in domestic incomes might result in various economies of scale and other cost reductions, so that exports might well increase sufficiently to pay for the increased imports. In other words, in certain circumstances cost and price effects of income expansion might offset in part at least the immediate income effects. Unfortunately there is a dearth of analyses in depth on this fascinating subject of the relationship between domestic demand and exports.

The 'orthodox' view has been to assume that expanding home demand will tend to suck exportable goods out of the export into the home sector and thus re-inforce the adverse balance of trade effects on the import side, but recent research has shed some doubt on this assumption. One of the fullest and most scholarly analyses of the relationship between home demand and exports is that of Dr Ilse Mintz, who has studied the effect of cyclical fluctuations in the US upon exports of various types of products for the period 1879 to 1961. Miss Mintz concludes her study with the following words; 'repression of home demand would not, on the basis of historical experience, appear to be a promising route for achieving a rise in the total value of US exports'.[2]

---

[1] Machlup himself strongly emphasized these difficulties. See, for example, pp. 46 ff. of his book.

[2] I. Mintz, 'Cyclical Fluctuations in the Exports of the United States since 1879', *Studies in Business Cycles* No. 15, New York: National Bureau of Economic Research, distributed by Columbia University Press, 1967, p. 279.

The question as it concerns the UK is discussed by R. J. Ball, J. R. Eaton, and M. D. Steuer, 'The Relationship Between United Kingdom Export Performance in Manufactures and the Internal Pressure of Demand', *Economic Journal*, September 1966.

There is therefore considerable doubt as to whether a reduction in domestic income will always lead to an improvement in the balance of trade.

SHORT GUIDE TO THE LITERATURE

The pioneer book in this field is F. Machlup, *International Trade and The National Income Multiplier*, New York, Blakiston, 1943. There are useful discussions of many of the concepts introduced in this chapter in W. M. Scammell, *International Monetary Policy*, London, Macmillan, 1957, and in C. P. Kindelberger, *International Economics*, Homewood, Ill., R. D. Irwin, 1963. There is a diagrammation treatment of the foreign trade multiplier in R. Robinson, 'A Graphical Analysis of the Foreign Trade Multiplier', *Economic Journal*, September 1952. Meade examines the relationship between domestic *expenditure* and foreign trade in *The Balance of Payments*.

CHAPTER 13

THE RATE OF EXCHANGE

1. SOME FUNDAMENTAL CONCEPTS

We noted in Chapter 1 that one justification for a special study of international trade is the fact that countries have different currencies and monetary systems. No 'balance of payments crisis' arises if Welsh residents spend more on goods from England than English residents spend on goods from Wales; Welsh 'importers' use the same currency as English 'exporters'. Moreover, both England and Wales share a common banking system. When a Welshman buys a car made in the Midlands of England there is simply a transfer of funds from say, the Swansea branch of a London Clearing Bank to its Coventry branch. No bank is unduly worried because its customers in Wales are on balance transferring money to its customers in England. It is for these reasons that we seldom trouble to draw up a balance of payments statement for a region within a country, or between countries which, like England and Wales are parts of a single economy. But perhaps we should. If Wales is in persistent 'deficit' with England, this means automatic decline in purchasing power, contraction of economic activity, depression and unemployment. A real regional crisis will exist, even if the question of a balance of payments crisis does not arise.

On the other hand, if a Welsh resident buys a car from Western Germany the situation is quite different. The German manufacturer demands payment not in sterling but in marks; if he accepts payment in sterling, he or somebody else will convert the sterling into marks. German industrialists cannot pay for their supplies or meet their wage bills in sterling. Thus when a UK resident purchases a car from Germany, the transaction involves not only the exchange of money for a car but the exchange of sterling for marks. One question we must try to answer in this chapter is, what determines the rate of exchange between currencies.

An exchange rate is simply the price of a currency. In the absence of Government intervention, its price is determined—like any other commodity—by demand and supply. When in a given period United Kingdom residents spend more on goods and services from abroad than non-residents are spending on UK goods and services, the price of the pound in terms of other currencies will tend to fall. The demand for currency depends of course not only upon the flow of trade, but also upon the movement of capital. When, for example, a British resident buys securities of an overseas government, or when a British company purchases a factory abroad, there is a demand for foreign currency in exchange for pounds sterling. If the rate of exchange between the currencies is allowed to fluctuate the pound depreciates in terms of the mark. As depreciation continues, the rise in the value of the mark discourages the importation of goods from Germany (importers have to give up more sterling than before to obtain a given number of marks) while at the same time British goods become relatively more attractive to German importers who will have to give up fewer marks to obtain a given number of pounds to pay for imports.

If a country is in external equilibrium at any given rate of exchange and the demand for its currency falls, we can speak of a *deficit* in its balance of payments, using the term 'balance of payments' in the sense of a market balance, as opposed to the concept (used in Chapter 11) of a classification of accounts. On the other hand, if demand for the currency rises, at any given rate of exchange, we can speak of a *surplus* on the balance of payments.

In practice, governments are generally unwilling to accept the disturbances resulting from freely fluctuating exchange rates and they generally try to maintain relatively fixed rates. Minor fluctuations are allowed, but when these exceed certain predetermined limits, the authorities intervene in the exchange market by buying or selling foreign currencies in order to maintain the agreed parity. When the authorities operate in this way, the currency has a fixed rate of exchange —although in practice exchange rates are allowed to fluctuate between narrowly defined limits. Sterling, for example, fluctuated between £1 = $2·38 and £1 = $2·42. When a country with a fixed rate of exchange spends abroad more than it receives from commodities, services and capital transfers its gold or foreign currency reserves will have to be depleted if the rate of exchange is to be maintained. Disequilibrium in the balance of payments is reflected in a running down of these reserves. In a system of freely fluctuating exchange rates, on the other hand, disequilibrium shows itself in a fall in the exchange rate.

2. FREELY FLUCTUATING RATES

In Chapter 11 we outlined some of the elements which make up the balance of payments between countries. We saw that on the credit side we place the value of goods and services supplied by residents of a country, and the value of capital imports; on the debit side the value of goods and services purchased from other countries, plus the value of capital exported. Now the credit items represent demand for the currency while the debit items represent supply of a country's currency. For example, an export of goods by a UK resident entails a demand for sterling while expenditure by UK residents on overseas travel represents a demand for some other currency. In the former case there is a purchase, in the latter case a sale of sterling. In each case there is some effect upon the market price of sterling, an increase in foreign demand for UK exports tending to raise the price of sterling in terms of other currencies, whilst an increase in British residents' overseas spending tends to lower it.

A Problem in Demand and Supply

If a currency is allowed to fluctuate in value, it will find its equilibrium level in accordance with the normal forces of demand and supply. The price of the pound sterling, like the price of tomatoes, depends upon demand and supply. As we noted above the demand for sterling is determined by the desire of non-UK residents to purchase goods and services from UK residents, plus the inflow of capital funds into the UK whether short or long term. The inflow of capital funds represents a demand for sterling just as much as the export goods and services, for at some stage the currency of non-UK residents transferring funds to the UK must be converted into sterling. Likewise the supply of sterling can be thought of as the result of UK residents purchasing goods and services from outside the UK, plus the outflow of capital funds from the UK.

We can depict the demand for and supply of a currency by means of demand and supply curves. Let us consider the price of the pound in terms of the US dollar. From figure 12 we can read off from the demand curve DD, the number of pounds which will be demanded at various rates of exchange between the pound and dollar. At a rate of exchange of $9 = £1, only £100 million are demanded; this is because at this rate of exchange demand for British products and services is relatively low. US residents have to give up a large number of dollars to purchase £1 worth of British exports. At a rate of exchange of $6 = £1 however, British products appear more attractive in the US market, more of them are purchased, and the demand for pounds is greater. As the rate of exchange falls even further, more pounds are purchased; at the rate of $1 = £1, £600 million are demanded.

The supply curve represents the supply of pounds coming on to the foreign exchange market in any one period, at various rates of exchange.

At an exchange rate of $9 = £1, a very large number of pounds are offered for a given number of dollars. At the rate of $6 = £1, fewer are offered. In figure 12 the equilibrium price is $3 = £1. If the rate is 'fixed' at a level higher than this, say at £4 = £1, the pound is over-valued and supply will exceed demand.

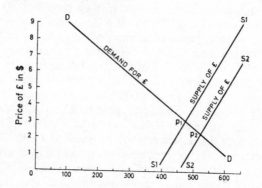

FIGURE 12. Quantity of £s Demanded and Supplied per Period.

There is of course another way of looking at the demand/supply relationship. We can think of the price of the dollar in terms of the pound; in this case we measure along the horizontal axis the dollars demanded and supplied per period. The demand for pounds is merely another way of describing the supply of dollars and *vice-versa*.

3. THE EFFECTS OF CURRENCY ADJUSTMENT

Now suppose that the UK removes all its tariffs, while other countries maintain theirs. Imports into the UK are likely to rise more than exports from the UK. In these new conditions, a new supply curve for sterling S_2S_2 (or demand curve for dollars) will be necessary, since at any given rate of exchange more sterling will be sold in exchange for a given quantity of foreign currency. In figure 12 the equilibrium value of the pound is now at P_2. Sterling has depreciated.[1]

[1] The terms depreciation or appreciation are normally used when a currency decreases or increases in value in a free market, without the authorities taking specific action to fix it at a particular new level. Devaluation or revaluation, on the other hand, normally refer to the act of the authorities in deliberately altering the rate from one fixed parity to another. When the floating Canadian dollar declined in value in the 1950s it was spoken of as depreciation. But the change in sterling parity from $2·80 to $2·40 in 1967 when the peg was, as it were, taken out at the higher level and replaced at the lower one, is described as devaluation.

Price Effects

We must now consider what happens when such a sterling depreciation takes place. Essentially what happens is a fall in the price of sterling in terms of other currencies. Foreigners have to give up less of their own currency in order to obtain a given number of pounds sterling. On the other hand, UK residents have to give up more pounds in order to obtain a given quantity of dollars. It follows that in terms of foreign currency, UK exports become cheaper, while in terms of sterling, UK imports become dearer. Suppose there is a 5 per cent depreciation of sterling in terms of the US dollar, the rate falling from £1 = $2·40 to £1 = $2·28. This means that whereas a UK-made motor car which before the depreciation was priced in sterling at £1,000 would have sold for $2,400 in the US, after depreciation it sells for $2,280. Similarly, whereas an import cargo valued at $2,400 would have sold at £1,000 before depreciation, after depreciation it will be priced at £1,050. Not only do visible imports into the UK become more expensive in terms of sterling, so also do payments in respect of invisibles and of capital flows. Thus if purchasers of goods and services—and investors—are at all sensitive to price changes the effect of the depreciation is to encourage foreigners to buy from, or remit capital to the UK, but to discourage UK residents from making payments abroad, whether in respect of visibles, invisibles, or capital transactions. Much therefore depends upon the elasticity of demand conditions in the UK and the outside world. If, for example, overseas purchasers are quite insensitive to the fall in dollar price of UK exports, they will buy no more of them in spite of the price fall.

Supply considerations are also important, in that no matter how sensitive the US demand, no increase in sales of UK goods in the US is possible unless additional supplies become available, either by an increase in total output, or by the diversion of goods from the UK home market. The elasticity of supply also helps to determine the extent to which the dollar price falls. If in the UK, supply is infinitely elastic, that is, if as many additional exportable goods can be produced as required without any price increase, then the whole impact of devaluation is on the dollar price of British exports. The dollar price falls by the whole amount of the 5 per cent depreciation. There is no increase in the sterling price to absorb part or all of the depreciation. This is in fact our assumption in the example, quoted above of a fall in the price of a UK manufactured motor car from $2,400 to $2,280. But suppose that elasticity of supply in the UK is less than infinite. Then the additional demand on UK resources resulting from increased overseas sales will raise the sterling price of British exports. Part of the dollar price effect of the depreciation is thus eroded. Instead of falling by 5 per cent the dollar price might fall by only, say, 2 per cent. The relative inelasticity of supply accordingly damps down the effect of the depreciation upon the volume of export sales. Similarly, on the import side, an infinite supply elasticity abroad implies that faced with a decline in UK demand, foreign suppliers can cut back supplies from the UK market without being forced to reduce their prices. Thus the dollar price of UK imports does not fall at all, the whole impact of the depreciation being on the sterling price, which rises by the full amount of the depreciation. If, on the other hand, the US is almost wholly dependent upon the UK market and US suppliers cannot easily switch from that market elsewhere, the elasticity of supply to the UK would be low. US producers would accordingly accept some dollar price reduction in order to keep a share of the UK market, with the result that UK import prices do not rise by the full amount of the depreciation.

It follows that if the full effect of the depreciation is to be felt on relative prices, it is not sufficient that demand conditions at home and abroad are relatively elastic. Full advantage of high demand elasticities can be taken only if supply elasticities are also high. On the other hand, a little reflection will show that this will not be the case if demand elasticities are low. If, for example, US citizens are unwilling to buy many more UK motor cars, although there is a fall in the price, it is better for the UK balance of payments if the elasticity of supply in the UK is also low. If the UK elasticity of supply is high, the dollar price of UK car exports will fall by the whole amount of the depreciation; but even so, relatively few additional cars are sold. But if the elasticity of supply in the UK is low, there will be a rise in the sterling price of British cars sold abroad. Similarly, on the import side, if UK import demand is highly inelastic, that is if the rise in sterling import price does not choke off demand to any marked extent, it is better that the sterling price rise is as small as possible. This will be the case if American supply elasticity is low, so that the dollar price falls considerably, leaving the sterling price to rise only moderately. We can generalize by saying that if demand elasticities are high, supply elasticities should also be high, but if they are low, it is better for the depreciating country if supply elasticities are also low.

We have not so far examined explicitly the precise effect of depreciation upon the foreign exchange earnings of a country, although we have seen that this will depend upon demand and supply elasticities. For the sake of simplicity let us assume that supply elasticities are infinitely great. Then the effect of depreciation upon a country's balance of payments depends upon demand elasticities at home and abroad. Taking first the export side, if the elasticity of demand in the USA is greater than one, Americans will be encouraged to buy a larger volume than before of UK exports. Since we are assuming infinite supply elasticity in the UK, the unit price of these exports, in sterling, remains unchanged. The sterling earnings from exports will accordingly rise, the amount of the increase depending upon the foreign elasticity of demand.

The effect upon import expenditure is more complicated. The sterling value of the import bill might increase or decrease, according to whether the price elasticity of demand in the UK for imports is less or greater than unity. The favourable case is where it is greater than unity. Indeed, if import elasticity of demand is infinite, imports are reduced to zero. But if the elasticity of demand is less than one, the raising of the sterling cost per unit of imports results in an increase in sterling expenditure on imports. But even if this is the case, the adverse effects upon the balance of trade can be offset by the increase in exports. Thus inelasticity on the import side can be offset by relative elasticity on the side of exports. We are in fact concerned with the sum of the elasticities of demand, at home and abroad.

Assuming that supply elasticities in the UK and abroad are infinitely great, and that the value of UK imports (M) is equal to the value of UK exports (X) before depreciation, the effect of the depreciation upon the UK balance of trade is favourable or otherwise according as ED_a plus ED_b is greater or less than zero, where ED_a is the elasticity of demand in the UK for imports from the USA, and ED_b is the elasticity of demand in the US for imports from the UK. The improvement in the UK balance is equal to $£k(ED_a + ED_b - 1)$, where k = the (small) proportional depreciation. If (X) and (M) were not in balance before depreciation—for example if the UK balance of trade were negative, that is imports exceeded exports, a 5 per cent increase in imports will be more significant for the balance of trade than a similar percentage increase in exports. Thus we are concerned, not only with elasticities, but also with the level of trade in both countries.

We have dealt so far with the bare bones of the theory of the foreign exchanges. The time has now come to examine more closely the elasticities we have been discussing, and to discuss some of the factors determining their magnitudes. Let us first examine some factors which determine price elasticities of demand.

We have worked through these calculations in terms of sterling simply because the balance of payments statistics are usually expressed in terms of sterling. However, to test his understanding, the student should satisfy himself that the same conditions for an improvement in the balance of trade (but not for imports and exports separately) is obtained if the argument is conducted in terms of dollars.

Determinants of Demand Elasticities

The most obvious is the nature of the goods imported and exported by the depreciating country. Generally speaking, in international trade the price-elasticity of demand for manufactures is likely to be rather higher than for that of foodstuffs and raw materials. If the depreciating country exports manufactures and imports foodstuffs it will probably gain from depreciation on the export side but lose on the import side. This is, however, grossly to oversimplify. Much depends upon the share of the depreciating country's exports of particular commodities in world trade. The demand for cotton in a given export market from the world as a whole might be fairly inelastic, but if the depreciating country supplies only a small part of that country's total cotton import, elasticity of demand for its cotton will be higher. The importing country will buy less from third countries and more from the depreciating country. For example, other things being equal, Brazilian cotton exports are likely to gain from depreciation, for they account for a comparatively small proportion of world cotton trade. On the other hand, demand for Indian jute products is likely to be comparatively insensitive to rupee depreciation, since India accounts for over 80 per cent of world exports of these goods. The world demand for Canadian asbestos is almost the same as the world demand for asbestos, since Canada supplies almost all world demand. A country like New Zealand which supplies only a limited amount of the world's butter imports would probably gain from depreciation at the expense of say, Denmark. Following devaluation of the New Zealand pound the total world consumption of butter might not rise very much, if at all, but New Zealand's share in providing butter might increase considerably.

The sensitivity of demand to price changes depends upon the ease with which supplies at home and supplies from competing countries are reduced when goods from the depreciating country become cheaper. If rival countries continue to press the same quantities of exports in the UK export markets following sterling depreciation, accepting smaller profit margins, the dollar price of UK exports is like to have to fall considerably for the volume of UK exports to rise very significantly. It is fairly certain that in the long run demand elasticities are greater than in the short run. Accordingly, in estimating the effects of depreciation, sufficient time should be allowed for adjustments to take place. Another important consideration is the possible range of products which although not profitable to export before depreciation become so afterwards. Perhaps the elasticity of demand for a country's present exports is fairly low, but depreciation may make profitable the exportation of a wider range of goods. It might even happen that some goods at present imported would become exports if the depreciaation were sufficiently effective.

One of the most effective limitations to an extensive increase in exports from a depreciating country in the twentieth century has been the widespread prevalence of import restrictions of various kinds. If countries allow the depreciating country a fixed quota of imports by value, depreciation will result in no increase in imports. Similarly on the import side in a regime of widespread exchange and trade restrictions it is quite possible that imports into the depreciating country would be cut to the bare minimum; this means of course, a very low elasticity of import demand. Great Britain was in some respects in this position at the time of the 1949 sterling devaluation. On the other hand the self-governing Commonwealth countries (especially Australia) had been comparatively lavish in their spending on dollar imports before devaluation; for such countries there was a fairly wide margin of imports which could be reduced as their dollar cost rose following devaluation.

The effect of depreciation is dampened down when transport and distribution costs are high. On the export side, a depreciation will not be followed by a substantial fall in export prices if exports from the depreciating country have a high import content. If, for example, half the cost of cotton goods exported from Great Britain to the dollar area consists of payments for raw cotton imported from America then (assuming infinite supply elasticity in the UK) a 5 per cent sterling depreciation will have something like a 2·5 per cent effect on the British export prices in dollar area. Finally, it should be remembered that both home users and overseas buyers might be more interested in delivery dates, spares, service and credit facilities than in prices. This again would keep the price elasticities of demand relatively low.

Some estimates

In the early post-war years it was widely assumed that demand elasticities in international trade were fairly low. At that time there was a great deal of what has come to be known as elasticity pessimism. Many economists believed that demand elasticities in international trade were relatively low, and for this reason were sceptical about the ability of exchange rate changes to correct balance of payments disequilibrium. Later, this approach gave way to greater optimism, and economists today are more willing than they were twenty years ago to believe that elasticities are relatively high. A number of estimates have been made of the price elasticity of demand for imports for various countries. These in general suggest that trade flows are sensitive to price changes; as is to be expected, demand for manufactured imports seems to be more sensitive to price changes than demand for raw materials. One of the most widely quoted estimates is that of Ball and Marwah,[1] who applied regression analysis to quarterly data of US imports covering eleven post war years. Their results show the following price import demand elasticities: Crude materials, −0·26; semi manufactures −1·38; finished manufactures −3·50. Since there is some downward bias resulting from the statistical techniques used, the authors regard these as lower limits of possible values. By adding three standard errors to their estimates they suggest that the upper limits for these values might be −0·65 for crude materials, −2·15 for semi-manufactures, −5·28 for finished manufactures.

The Ball-Marwah estimates measure the effect of import price changes over time and might well be misleading if there were significant quality and income changes. It is accordingly useful to check the estimates by means of a cross-section analysis, such as that of Professor Kreinen who compared imports into the USA of two groups of commodities, classified according to whether they had been subject to tariff reductions. The Kreinen study[2] showed an import elasticity of demand of −5·0 for all commodities excluding textiles (exports of which from Japan were subject to voluntary restraint), for the period 1954-6 and −6·0 for finished manufactures for the period 1955-9.

Another study is that of Professor L. B. Krause, who derived 'tariff' elasticities for some ninety-one categories of manufactured goods imported into the USA. This was again a cross section analysis and showed results not dissimilar to those of Kreinen.[3]

As a result of these and similar studies, it is now generally accepted that price elasticities in international trade are significantly higher than they were at one time believed to be.[4] That makes the result of a recent study all the more remarkable. At the time of the 1967 devaluation of sterling, past experience 'admittedly on somewhat shaky evidence'

[1] R. J. Ball and K. Marwah, 'The US Demand for Imports, 1948–58', *Review of Economics and Statistics*, November 1962, pp. 395–401.

[2] M. E. Kreinen, 'Effect of Tariff Changes on the Value and Volume of Imports', *American Economic Review*, June 1961.

[3] L. B. Krause, 'United States Imports and the Tariff', *American Economic Review*, May 1969.

[4] There is a vast literature on this subject. A useful summary of earlier work is in A. C. Harberger, 'Some Evidence on the International Price Mechanism', *Journal of Political Economy*, December 1957. The later studies are discussed by M. E. Kreinen, *Alternative Commercial Policies—Their Effect on the American Economy*, Michigan State University, 1967; and by Bela Balassa in *Trade Liberalization Among Industrial Countries*, New York, McGraw-Hill, 1968.

suggested to *The Economist* a price elasticity of demand for British exports of just under −2·0 and for British imports of about −0·5.[1] Other estimates used at the time for imports were between −0·5 and −1·0.[2] But when in 1972 members of the research staff of the National Institute of Economic and Social Research investigated the impact of the devaluation on the balance of payments, they found to their surprise that their numerical results implied rather lower price elasticities, of the order of −0·25 for imports and of −1·4 for manufacturing exports.[3]

Supply Elasticities

How elastic are supply conditions in international trade? While it is difficult to estimate demand elasticities in international trade, it is quite impossible to estimate supply elasticities. All we can do is to outline some of the considerations which are relevant to make a broad generalization regarding supply conditions in a particular country at any point of time. Supply of exports is likely to be greater in the long run than in the short run. It takes time for producers to switch goods from the home to the export market. Often it is necessary for overseas trading outlets and agencies to be established or expanded. In general it will be easier for goods to be switched abroad if home demand for the products concerned is relatively low than if it is buoyant.

A relevant consideration is the proportion of total output of a product exported. If practically the whole output is exported, the short-term elasticity of supply is likely to be low. Where only a small proportion is normally exported, it is likely to be higher. Accordingly the elasticity of supply of tin exports from Malaya and Bolivia, cotton exports from Brazil and Egypt, and beef from the Argentine is likely to be low, since a very high proportion of output of these commodities is exported, comparatively little being consumed in the countries of origin. In the long term, however, when it is possible for a transfer of factors of production to occur, export supplies might well increase.

Effects on Invisibles and Investment

So far we have fastened our attention on the effect of depreciation upon the balance of visible trade. There will also be an effect on

[1] *The Economist*, November 25, 1967.

[2] See G. D. N. Worswick, 'Trade and Payments', in Sir Alec Cairncross (ed.), *Britain's Economic Prospects Reconsidered*, London, Allen and Unwin, 1971, p. 90.

[3] 'The Effects of the Devaluation of 1967 on the Current Balance of Payments', *The Economic Journal*, special issue in honour of E. A. G. Robinson, March 1972.

invisibles and on the flow of capital. Following depreciation, all payments to foreigners which have to be made in foreign currency become more expensive, but foreigners find it cheaper to visit, or obtain services from the citizens of, the depreciating country. Of course, if residents of the depreciating country have undertaken fixed contractual obligations in terms of their own currency, then depreciation will not affect the payments; but if the obligations are in terms of another currency, more domestic currency will be needed to meet them. There will be a deterioration in the invisible balance. Similar reasoning applies to the effect on the capital account. Since non-residents have to surrender less of their own currency in order to finance a given level of investment in the depreciating country, they will be encouraged to remit funds to it. On the other hand, residents of the depreciating country will be discouraged from exporting capital. The NIESR study referred to earlier [1] found the demand for some of the invisible items in the British balance of payments to have been more price-elastic than that for goods, and concluded that the contribution to the total effect of devaluation of invisibles was greater than that coming from the visible items!

4. INCOME EFFECTS: THE ABSORPTION APPROACH

We have considered the effect of depreciation upon various parts of the balance of trade, but so far our discussion has been entirely in terms of price changes. It has long been realized, however, that when depreciation takes place there will be income as well as price effects. It is, for example, clear that when incomes rise in the depreciating country following the expansion of exports, this might have an important effect upon the volume of both imports and exports. Imports will almost certainly increase, and there will also be a tendency for exportable goods to be sucked into the home market. Both movements will offset the balance of trade gain resulting from the price effects of the depreciation.

In recent years it has become normal practice to discuss the effects of depreciation upon aggregate demand in terms of what is known as the absorption approach. The elements of the approach are quite simple; what is more controversial is the relative importance of price and 'absorption' effects. The absorption approach was introduced into the literature by S. S. Alexander in 1952. [2]

[1] *The Economic Journal*, March 1972.
[2] S. S. Alexander, 'Effect of a Devaluation on a Trade Balance', *IMF Staff Papers*, April 1952.

If a country has an import surplus, this means that total consumption and investment is greater than national output. Residents of that country are 'absorbing' more than they produce. If on the other hand they are consuming and investing less than they produce, there is an export surplus; they are 'underabsorbing'. In the formula

$$Y = C+I+G+X-M,$$

where Y = National output
       C = Consumption
       I = Investment
       G = Government Expenditure
       X = Exports
       M = Imports,

the sum of $C+I+G$ is equal to the total absorption which we designate A. Then if the balance of trade is B,

$$Y = A+B$$

Now let us assume that following depreciation, the trade balance B increases. If there are unemployed resources, the increase in B can lead to an increase in Y and there is no need for absorption (Government expenditure, investment and consumption) to decrease. Export-led (or import-substitution led) growth occurs and national income increases. But suppose that there are no unemployed resources—that is Y cannot increase. In this situation, the trade balance can only improve if there is an offsetting reduction in domestic absorption A. Hence, for depreciation to bring about an improvement in the balance of payments in time of full employment, some decrease in the rate of absorption must occur. Is there any automatic mechanism whereby this change in domestic absorption of resources occurs, or does the government of a country whose currency is depreciating need to take special measures to bring it about?

There are some consequences of a depreciation which might automatically reduce domestic absorption. One such is the terms of trade effect. Since depreciation makes foreign trade products more expensive than home trade goods, the real purchasing power of the population of a country with a depreciated currency falls, thus reducing effective demand for goods and services. Secondly, there is the so-called 'money illusion' effect. Although depreciation raises prices, if people are in the habit of saving a given amount of their money incomes each year they will continue to do so, reducing spending and thus absorption, rather than saving. Thirdly, since there is a tendency for consumers to maintain the real value of their cash balances, as prices rise, they will replenish them by increased saving, that is by decreasing absorption. Fourthly, it is argued that if imports account for a high proportion of the spending of citizens on relatively fixed incomes, the real income, and hence the saving, of such people will decrease. But this will be offset by higher incomes of the business community whose profits have now risen. Out of their high profits the business community will increase savings—more than those living a relatively fixed incomes decrease theirs—so that net savings increase and domestic absorption falls. This tendency is likely to be reinforced if, as is likely, the redistribution of income in favour of the business community raises the total yield of taxes.

How Great Are Absorption Effects?

It is difficult to know how much weight to give to these various 'automatic' absorption effects. Kindelberger lays stress on the income redistribution effect, arguing that some post-war Latin American currency devaluations resulted in substantial income transfers from urban to agricultural income recipients. Since the import propensities of the urban community is generally greater than that of rural interests, the real income transfer resulted in a net reduction in imports. Other writers regard all the absorption effects we have outlined as weak.

Some, notably Professor Machlup, argue that more important than the considerations normally discussed under the absorption approach is the improvement in resource allocation which might be expected to follow depreciation. If a country has a balance of payments deficit, due to an overvalued currency and it then devalues, the effect on the production side is to remove the distortion in resource allocation caused by the overvaluation. The improvement in resource allocation and hence in real income enables the trade balance to improve without any decrease in absorption being necessary. As with so many controversies in economic theory, it is not necessary for the student to take sides, it is far more important to use the insights derived from different approaches to the problem to enrich one's understanding of the issues involved. It is also important to realize that in any real world situation, attention should be paid to price, income, and reallocation aspects of depreciation. In certain countries and at certain times, one aspect will clearly be more immediately relevant than another, but it should not be considered entirely alone.

Indeed, although analytically it is useful to keep price and income effects separate, the two are closely interconnected. Depreciation alters price relationships; changing prices in turn affect savings propensities by facing income recipients with a new set of price alternatives.

Even without any income redistribution quite significant changes might occur in the savings and import functions.

Finally, and perhaps most important of all, if the degree of 'automatic' absorption is inadequate to prevent domestic inflation following devaluation, the necessary expenditure reducing measures will have to be taken. Indeed, the probability that absorption and disabsorption are not fully automatic implies that frequent recourse must be made to fiscal and monetary policies for internal balance. The choice of measures adopted to maintain domestic equilibrium is examined in Chapter 16.

We have considered at some length many of the consequences of a change in the exchange rate. We have noted that a large number of factors are relevant in determining whether a given change in the exchange rate is likely to restore equilibrium. Before continuing our discussion of the adjustment process we shall, however, briefly examine the advantages and disadvantages of an exchange rate regime in which rates are allowed to fluctuate relatively freely.

SHORT GUIDE TO THE LITERATURE

There is very full treatment of many of the questions raised in this chapter in L. B. Yeager, *International Monetary Relations, Theory, History and Policy*, New York, Harper and Row, 1966. A pioneer article which is still well worth reading is Machlup's 'The Theory of the Foreign Exchanges', *Economica*, New Series, vol. vi, November 1939, reproduced in both *Readings in the Theory of International Trade* and F. Machlup, *International Monetary Economics*. Another pioneer article which deals with the effect of depreciation is Professor Joan Robinson's 'The Foreign Exchanges', first published in *Essays in the Theory of Employment*, Oxford, and reproduced in *Readings in the Theory of International Trade*. Meade deals with the effect of depreciation on the balance of trade at several points in his *The Balance of Payments*.

There are valuable papers on this subject in Caves and Johnson, *Readings in International Economics*; by S. S. Alexander. 'Effects of a Devaluation on a Trade Balance', reproduced from *IMF Staff Papers*, vol. ii, April 1952, (on the absorption approach) and H. G. Johnson, 'Towards a General Theory of the Balance of Payments', reproduced from *International Trade and Economic Growth*, Harvard University Press, 1961, pp. 153–168. On absorption there is a useful bibliography at the end of S. C. Tsiang, 'The Role of Money in Trade Balance Stability: Synthesis of the Elasticity and Absorption Approaches', reproduced from *American Economic Review*, vol. li, no. 5, December

1961, pp. 912–936. The article itself is fairly mathematical. Students should also consult Guy H. Orcutt, 'Measurement of Price Elasticities in International Trade', reproduced from *The Review of Economics and Statistics*, vol. xxxii, no. 2, May 1950 (this article has a useful but by now very much 'dated' bibliography). They should also read F. Machlup, 'Elasticity Pessimism in International Trade', first published in *Economia Internazionale*, vol. iii (1950), and reprinted in *International Monetary Economics*. Machlup himself contributed to the absorption approach debate and his paper 'Relative Prices and Aggregate Spending in the Analysis of Devaluation', *American Economic Review*, vol. lxv, June 1955, pp. 255–278 is also reproduced in *International Monetary Economics*.

CHAPTER 14

FOR AND AGAINST FLUCTUATING EXCHANGE RATES

The first and most obvious advantage of a fluctuating exchange rate is that provided the mechanism we have outlined works reasonably smoothly, depreciation or appreciation can be expected automatically to restore equilibrium in a country's balance of payments. There is no need for unemployment to be created or restrictions to be imposed in order to reduce imports and increase exports. Of course as our discussion has shown, in a time of full employment a currency depreciation is likely to be inflationary unless accompanied by a reduction in domestic demand. But the amount of deflation required is only what is sufficient to reduce absorption to the full employment level[1]; it is not necessary for additional idle capacity to be created.

If on the other hand, a country has a balance of payments deficit and the exchange rate is not allowed to vary, in a regime of free trade the whole burden of the adjustment is on domestic incomes. Even if there is already underemployment, policies for internal deflation must be followed, in order to reduce imports and to encourage firms to export. Moreover, a flexible rate economizes foreign exchange reserves. Since there is a built-in tendency towards balance of payments adjustment *via* price effects, fluctuations in the reserves are likely to be less than with a fixed exchange rate. These considerations suggest that the authorities have rather more scope for implementing a domestic economic policy of their choice in a regime of fluctuating rates than if rates are fixed. This is not to imply that adjustment under flexible rates is painless. As we have seen, if depreciation or appreciation is to be effective, significant changes are necessary both in production and consumption. A flexible rate demands a flexible economy. But given this internal flexibility, a fluctuating rate enables a policy of internal full employment or growth to be followed at the same time as a policy of balance of payments equilibrium.

---

[1] Full employment here does not mean that every single worker and piece of capital equipment is fully employed; if reasonable mobility is to be assured a pool of unemployed resources is necessary.

1. SPECULATION

The Role of Speculators

Against the system of fluctuating rates, however, it can be argued that speculation is likely to add to the magnitude of fluctuations. If the rate is falling and there is no guarantee that the authorities will enter the market to prevent the exchange rate falling below a given point the activities of speculators might well force the rate to a level lower than required to restore payments equilibrium.[1] Similarly, if there is no 'ceiling' above which a currency cannot rise, speculators who anticipate a continued rise in the exchange rate will purchase the currency for purely speculative purposes and this way cause the price to rise more than really necessary.

On the other hand, it is arguable that the role of speculators need not be disequilibrating. If speculators correctly assess the measure of depreciation or appreciation necessary to restore equilibrium, they will be inclined to reverse their selling or buying activities as that rate is reached. Since speculators are professionals whose job it is to be well-informed, they are more likely to assess correctly the equilibrium rate than many others who operate in the foreign exchange market. The more numerous and the more well-informed the speculators, the more likely it is that some at least will call a halt as a currency approaches what they regard as its equilibrium value. As this value is approached, some speculators are likely to reverse their positions and thus reverse also the current trend. Indeed, it is possible for intelligent large scale speculation actually to reduce the size of exchange rate fluctuations.

Suppose the present (flexible) rate is \$4 = £1, but that speculators believe that over the next few months normal commercial factors will cause the rate to fall to \$3 = £1. They will immediately purchase dollars, thus causing the exchange value of the pound to drop—let us say to \$3·75 = £1. Owing to their activities, the pound has depreciated earlier than it would otherwise have done. If the relevant demand and supply elasticities are sufficiently great there will be an improvement in the balance of payments which will perhaps decrease the extent of the currency depreciation needed. Moreover, the very fact that speculators now hold larger than normal dollar balance will make others wary of purchasing too large a supply of dollars at the new rate. The realization that these dollars will be converted back into pounds at a future date will of course alter expectations about the future value of the pound. Although it is known that balance of payments considerations dictate a

---

[1] The whole question of speculation in a regime of fluctuating exchange rates is discussed by Professor Meade in *The Balance of Payments*, cited above, pp. 218 ff.

further fall to $3 = £1$, it is also widely appreciated that the selling of the speculative balances will eventually raise the value of the pound above what it would be on purely commercial grounds. Thus the rate might not fall as far as $3 = £1$. Speculation damps down, rather than increases exchange fluctuations. The incentive to speculate in dollars is also weakened by the fact that the profit margin on purchase and sale is narrowed as the pound depreciates. If in fact the pound had fallen from $4 = £1$, to $3 = £1$, the gain to speculators would have been one dollar in every pound; now that the pound has fallen to $3.75 = £1$, the profit on speculation is reduced. If the activities of speculators are on a sufficiently large scale, competition among them to purchase dollars automatically narrows the profit margin.

Of course, speculation only reduces exchange rate fluctuation if speculators correctly assess their direction and amplitude. If they incorrectly assess the direction of an exchange rate change, then their activities create greater disequilibrium than would otherwise exist— speculation becomes 'perverse'. Similarly if speculators overestimate the extent of the change, they make the change greater than would be necessary on pure balance of payments grounds.

There is reason to believe that speculation is less likely to create problems for the foreign exchange market in a regime of flexible rates than under the present IMF system. Under the IMF arrangements currency adjustments take place only at rare intervals. Because they are so infrequent, adjustments in parity are usually quite substantial and unlikely to be reversed in the foreseeable future. Thus when a currency is under pressure, speculators have a one-way option, standing to reap very substantial gains if and when devaluation takes place. Under a system of flexible rates speculators know that the movement against a currency might be reversed in the not too distant future.

Business Uncertainty

Another objection to freely fluctuating rates concerns the effect of frequent fluctuations upon the day to day business of importing and exporting. A fluctuating exchange rate adds yet another uncertainty to the business of foreign trade. It is difficult enough for an exporter to assess future market conditions for his product without being faced with the additional hazard of exchange rate uncertainty. Accordingly it is sometimes argued that a fluctuating exchange rate system might reduce the total volume of international trade. This argument should not be overstressed, for in practice, traders can insure themselves against too violent fluctuations in exchange rates by what are known as forward exchange operations.

A trader wishing to obtain a given amount of foreign exchange in say, three months' time, can arrange to purchase that currency from a foreign exchange dealer at an agreed rate three months hence. The forward exchange dealer quotes a rate which may be more or less favourable than the current 'spot' rate. If, for example, the present 'spot' rate of sterling were £1 = $2·40, and the forward price quote is the £1 = $2·41, the forward pound is said to be at a premium. More dollars will have to be given up to buy one pound sterling. If the forward quotation were £1 = $2·39, forward pounds would be at a discount. The forward rate will of course depend upon demand for and supply of forward foreign exchange. But it will also be affected by interest rate differentials between the two countries whose currencies are being traded. A forward exchange dealer who has undertaken to provide dollars in, say, three months time will cover himself by switching some of his sterling holdings into dollars. In doing so he may find that he incurs loss of interest. If short term rates are lower in New York than in London, he will require a higher premium on the sale of dollars to his customer than would otherwise have been the case. The premium will be less if the London interest rates are relatively high.

Arguing in favour of freely fluctuating exchange rates an inflationary bias for the whole international economy is ascribed to the adjustment process under a fixed exchange rate regime. The downward rigidity of wages and prices means that unless a usually unacceptably high level of *deflation* and unemployment is risked in the deficit country, most of the adjustment takes the form of *inflation* in the surplus country.[1]

A third argument against a system of fluctuating rates is what we might call the disciplinary one. Modern Governments are under constant pressure to overspend. In the inflationary world which results, those countries which have least control over inflationary spending tend to run frequently into balance of payments difficulties. If the rate of exchange is fixed, such countries are very conscious of their underlying imbalance by the decline in their reserves. If, on the other hand, the rate of exchange slides easily up and down, there is a constant temptation to avoid or postpone the domestic measures necessary to achieve internal and external equilibrium.

From these arguments the reader will appreciate that there is much to be said both for and against a system of fluctuating exchange rates.

[1] This is explained by G. Haberler in his *Money in the International Economy*, Institute of Economic Affairs, 1969, pp. 40–41.

As a matter of practical politics, however, a completely freely fluctuating system is almost certainly out of the question at the present time. There is, however, an influential body of opinion among academic economists which sees great virtue in a *modified* flexible exchange rate system.[1] It welcomed the modified floating of exchange rates that took place between the middle of August and the middle of December 1971 on a world-wide scale.[2]

Stabilization Funds

Even with a system of floating currencies, rates are seldom allowed to fluctuate without some intervention of the authorities. This intervention is usually aimed at eliminating day-to-day exchange rate variations, which are of course only a nuisance, without interfering with long term trends in the movements of rates. At times it is difficult to disentangle short term from long term trends and occasionally stabilization funds have been used deliberately to under- or over-value a currency. Intervention is usually by means of an exchange stabilization account, operated by the Central Bank or perhaps a separate body of experts responsible to the Government.

A stabilization fund consists of a mixed bag of currencies. Its power to intervene in the market is of course limited by the size of its gold and foreign exchange assets, since its business is to buy and sell foreign currencies in accordance with changing market conditions. A country's fund really operates by adding to or reducing the total demand for its own currency. For example, if on a particular day the price of a currency on the free market were falling—as the result, say, of a labour dispute or a foolish speech by a member of the Government, the fund might well decide to support the currency by purchasing it in exchange for some of the foreign currency it holds. On the other hand, if the value of the domestic currency is rising, due to a temporary inflow of capital following a short-term weakness of some foreign currency, the fund may offset the rise by selling its domestic currency. In this way, a stabilization fund irons-out temporary exchange rate fluctuations. The British Exchange Equalization Account was set up in 1932; the American Stabilization Fund in 1934. Similar arrangements were made in France, the Netherlands, and Switzerland.[3]

[1] Some such proposals are discussed briefly in Chapter 18.

[2] In the jargon of the 1971 float, this procedure was called 'dirty' floating.

[3] There are several authoritative studies of currency experience in the inter-war years. The best known is Ragner Nurkse's study, *International Currency Experience*, published under the auspices of the League of Nations, 1944. There is some extremely detailed and well-documented material in Leland B. Yeager, *International Monetary Relations, Theory, History, and Policy*, New York, Harper and Row, 1966.

2. THE CANADIAN EXPERIMENT

The most prolonged example of a freely fluctuating rate of exchange is afforded by the Canadian dollar, which was allowed to fluctuate in accordance with demand and supply between 1950 and 1962. Since the war, the Canadian dollar is the only currency of a major industrial country allowed to float for any considerable length of time. Although the Exchange Fund Account smoothed out day-to-day fluctuations, it intervened as little as possible and in general its activities seem to have been peripheral. Especially after 1952, the Canadian dollar rate was virtually a free one, determined in the market place by purely commercial considerations.

After a re-valuation to parity with the US dollar in 1946 the Canadian dollar was devalued in 1949, although to a lesser extent than sterling and most West European currencies. Following devaluation, Canada's trade balance with the USA improved considerably—especially after the Korean war boom of 1950 which caused an enormously increased demand for Canada's raw material. At the same time there was a massive inflow of capital. Although a significant proportion of this inflow represented direct investment in Canada's rapidly expanding mines and industries, by far the greater part of its was speculative. Capital was attracted in anticipation of a revaluation of the Canadian dollar. In spite of the apparent strength of the currency, the Canadian authorities were in the summer of 1950 reluctant to alter the exchange rate once more. For one thing, they found it extremely difficult to estimate the equilibrium rate of exchange in the circumstances in which they found themselves. The obvious importance of the capital account meant that an exchange rate based purely on the prices of Canadian goods compared with those of US products would be of only limited significance. Secondly, there was some doubt about the future of the trade balance. Most observers thought that exports would fall very markedly when the commodity boom broke. In these circumstances the Government decided that the wisest course would be to set the currency free to find its own level. Accordingly, from September 1950, the Canadian dollar was allowed to float although it was announced that the new policy was 'experimental'. In fact the experiment lasted eleven years.

From 1949 to the autumn of 1950, the par value had been fixed at Can $1 = 90·9 US cents. When it was left to float, the Canadian dollar immediately rose to 93·5 US cents, and from 1952 on was at a premium. The highest point reached was over 106 US cents. Throughout the period exchange rate fluctuations were moderate; from 1952 to 1960, the change from one quarter to another never exceeded 2 per cent. In fact the moderate fluctuations in the exchange rate were in marked contrast to fairly substantial swings in the balance of trade and long-term capital. This balance varied between + $ Can 200 million and − $ Can 200 million a quarter. In more than half the quarterly periods, the variations was greater than 10 per cent of the export receipts. This relative exchange rate stability was said to be the result of speculative activity, which so far from being disequilibrating, actually helped reduce fluctuations in the exchange rate. As one authority on the Canadian experience in these years remarked

'stabilising exchange speculation appears to have been much more instrumental in keeping the fluctuations of the Canadian dollar within relatively narrow limits than either official intervention in the exchange market or the price effect of exchange variations on imports and exports . . . short-term capital has been the true stabiliser of the Canadian exchange rate.'[1]

Commenting on the early years of the Canadian experiment—when exchange fluctuations were greater than they later became, the IMF concluded that speculation had been 'equilibrating rather than disequilibrating'.[2]

One of the objections to fluctuating exchange rates arises from the allegedly unfavourable effects upon long-term capital flows. It is said that private investors and firms will be reluctant to invest in enterprises in a country whose exchange rate is free to fluctuate. The experience of Canada in the 1950s gives little support to this view. There was a rapid increase in long-term (including direct) investment in Canada, throughout the period; at no stage did potential investors appear to be discouraged from their activities by the prospect of exchange rate instability. Of course, Canada in the 1950s was a strong magnet for capital. Discoveries of new sources of mineral wealth were being made continually and manufacturing industry was growing apace. It would accordingly be unwise to argue a general case for fluctuating exchanges from the special case of Canada in the 1950s. But such evidence as there is suggests that two of the dangers which are alleged to beset fluctuating rates—namely perverse speculation and the discouragement of long term capital flows—were not apparent in the Canadian case.

The Canadian experiment came to an end in 1962, but the circumstances surrounding the return to a fixed rate were such that it is difficult

[1] R. R. Rhomberg, 'Canada's Foreign Exchange Market: A Quarterly Model', *IMF Staff Papers*, vol. vii, April 1960, p. 447.
[2] *IMF Annual Report*, 1953, p. 70.

to argue that the fluctuating rate had been proved a failure. Towards the end of the 1950s, there were serious difficulties in the current account; there was a massive trade deficit and a substantial increase in net out-goings on the invisible account. But the continuing inflow of capital kept the rate of exchange from falling. This inflow was, as always in the Canadian case, partly accounted for by direct investment; but it was also encouraged by the relatively high long term interest rate in Canada. At the end of 1960, the long-term bond rate was 5·41 per cent, as against 3·80 per cent in the USA. Thus the Canadian dollar was at a level which although an equilibrium level for current and long-term capital trans-actions, seriously overvalued the currency on the trade account. This overvaluation was recognized as an important cause of the mounting unemployment in the last years of the decade. Accordingly, in 1961 the authorities deliberately tried to force down the parity of the Canadian dollar, finally notifying the IMF in 1962 that the currency would once more be fixed.

This is not the place to discuss the merits of the decision to restore the fixity of the exchange rate.[1] But it is worth pointing out that if unemployment were the worry, the correct policy in a regime of flexible exchange rates would be one of monetary and budgetary expansion. If the expansion resulted in balance of payments difficultes, this would be looked after by a depreciation of the currency. In fact, the Canadian authorities followed the opposite policy of tight money, resulting in high interest rates, which attracted foreign funds and thus kept the exchange rate from falling as far as was desirable for balance trade equilibrium. An expansionist domestic financial policy would have lowered the Canadian rate of interest, discouraged the inflow of capital, and caused the Canadian dollar to depreciate. The experience of Canada points to a very important lesson—that a fluctuating ex-change rate cannot of itself maintain domestic equilibrium. It can only provide the mechanism allowing a Government to carry out the most appropriate domestic policy without undue fears as to its repercussions on the balance of payments. It was not the fluctuating dollar which was found wanting in the late 1950s, but rather the policies and attitudes of the Canadian monetary authorities.

The Experience of the Float in 1970

There is evidence to suggest that this lesson had been learned when in June 1970 Ottawa returned to a freely floating exchange rate. This was

[1] The circumstances surrounding the ending of the experiment are discussed by R. E. Artus, 'Canada Pegs its Dollar', *The Banker*, June 1962, and by Leland B. Yeager, cited above, pp. 423 ff.

in response to foreign exchange (mainly US dollar) inflows that were beyond the ability of the Bank of Canada to control or to 'sterilize'. At the same time, the authorities felt that it would be impossible to choose a higher *fixed* exchange rate with any confidence that it could be defended in the short run and that over the long run it would remain appropriate to economic developments in the US and in Canada itself.

The inflows resulted from inflationary effects on the US economy associated with the American involvement in Vietnam and took the form of financing an extremely strong Canadian trade surplus and, additionally, of speculative moves into Canadian dollars.

The pressures served to underline the existence of a conflict for Canadian monetary policy between the requirements of the exchange rate and the domestic economy equilibrium, given the close integration of the North American market through extensive trade and the high mobility of interest-sensitive funds. These respond to even slight yield differentials and tend to eliminate them, with the result that, given a fixed exchange rate, the Canadian interest rate structure is assimilated to the US structure, irrespective of domestic needs, and Canadian monetary policy tends to be frustrated. By contrast, Canadian monetary policy shifts in the 1950s have been shown to have been much more powerful with the existence of fluctuating exchange rates.

Similarly, a flexible exchange rate breaks the rigid linkage between the business cycle of the US and Canada (which with fixed exchange rates operates via the extensive trade and finance ties) and protects Canada from importing whatever cyclical instability develops in the US.

The Canadian authorities have been so conscious of the additional effectiveness of monetary policy instruments available to them through floating exchange rates that they were not only prepared to ignore the disapproving noises made by other industrial countries and by the IMF in 1970 but to maintain their float even after the Smithsonian Agreement of 1971, when the other industrial countries returned to fixed parities.

The constraints on domestic monetary policy arising out of fixed exchange rates in conditions of capital mobility is of course very relevant to the situation of Western Europe and Japan during the dollar crises of the late 1960s and early 1970s, discussed in a different chapter. The Canadian experience shows the issues that much clearer because the integration in trade and financial terms between Canada and the US are so much closer even than between any other industrial country and the US.

SHORT GUIDE TO THE LITERATURE

L. B. Yeager's *International Monetary Relations, Theory, History and Policy* is useful, especially the chapter on Canada's fluctuating exchange rate. There is a defence of relative stability of exchange rates in R. Nurkse, *Conditions of International Monetary Equilibrium*, Essays in International Finance No. 4, Spring 1945. International Finance Section, Princeton University, reprinted in *Readings in the Theory of International Trade*. The argument for exchange rate flexibility is put lucidly by Meade, *The Balance of Payments*, especially Chapter VII, on Speculation, and by Milton Friedman, 'The Case of Flexible Exchange Rates', *Essays in Positive Economics*, Chicago, Chicago University Press, 1953, pp. 157–203, reprinted in an abridged form in Caves and Johnson, *Readings in International Economics*. E. V. Morgan, 'The Theory of Flexible Exchange Rates', *American Economic Review*, vol. xlv, no. 3, June 1955, is also very useful.

The case against flexible exchange rates is argued by Sir D. MacDougall, *Westminster Bank Review*, 1954. H. G. Johnson and J. E. Nash discuss the theoretical and practical implications of fixed versus fluctuating exchange rates with regard to the UK in *UK and Floating Exchanges*, Institute of Economic Affairs, 1969. New studies by R. M. Dunn, Jr, *Canada's Experience with Fixed and Flexible Exchange Rates in a North American Capital Market*, Canadian–American Committee, 1971, and A. F. Wymme Plumptree's, 'Exchange Rate Policy. Experience with Canada's Floating Rate', in *Essays in Honour of Thorkil Kristensen*, OECD, Paris, 1970, show the wider significance of the Canadian experience.

CHAPTER 15

FIXED EXCHANGE RATES

We have seen that under a system of flexible exchange rates, provided
the demand and supply elasticities are appropriate and speculation is
not disequilibrating, there is a built-in mechanism of balance of payments adjustment. This mechanism operates through the price system
and to this extent is 'automatic'. We come now to consider the balance
of payments adjustment process when exchange rates are no longer
free to vary. To what extent is the mechanism automatic?

If a country's exchange rate is not allowed to alter, or allowed to
change only at rare intervals the country is said to be on a fixed external
standard. As we shall see in Chapter 17, most countries are at present
on a modified fixed standard—the IMF system. In the present chapter,
however, we are concerned with the implications of a rather more
rigid standard, in which, unlike in the IMF system, there is no provision
for occasional exchange rate adjustments and where no special provision
is made for assisting countries in temporary balance of payments difficulties. In fact we shall be examining the process of adjustment under a
fixed exchange rate system as typified by the traditional gold standard.
Although the standard in this form is no longer in operation it is
essential for the student to grasp its *modus-operandi* before moving on
to consider the present system. In this Chapter we shall first give a
grossly simplified account of how the nineteenth-century gold standard
was supposed to work—even these simple elements were not fully
understood by contemporary observers—and then modify the analysis
to make it approximate more closely to real world conditions. First,
however, we must explain what is meant by a fixed external standard
and consider some of its variants.

1. THE GOLD STANDARD SIMPLIFIED

The Exchange Parity

Under a fixed exchange rate system, each country keeps the value of its
currency fixed in terms of some external standard. This external standard
can be gold, silver, other precious metal, another country's currency,
or even some internationally agreed unit of account. The essential
element is that a country ties the value of its currency to that of some
external unit. Let us suppose that this external unit is gold.

Now if a group of countries maintain a fixed rate of exchange (or 'parity' as it is called) between their currencies and gold, the rate at which their currencies exchange against one another is also fixed. Thus the group is bound together by a system of fixed exchange rates.. For example, before 1914 the Bank of England undertook to buy and sell gold at a rate of 113 grains of fine gold to £1, whereas the US authorities were prepared to buy and sell at a rate of 113 grains to $4·86. Thus £1 would exchange against $4·86. A British resident could always obtain $4·86 for £1; if the rate diverged far from this, he could obtain his dollar at approximately the $4·86 rate simply by purchasing gold, shipping it to the US, and presenting it to the authorities there who would surrender $4·86 for every 113 grains of gold. So long as the authorities in the participating countries accept the obligation to maintain the gold parity of their domestic currencies, and so long as movement in gold is free, the rate at which one currency exchanges against another cannot move far from the rate determined by the gold parities of the respective currencies.

Although exchange rates cannot diverge far from these cross rates determined by gold parities, there is likely to be some divergence. This is because it costs money to ship gold from one country to another; there is, too, a loss of interest earnings when a currency is converted into gold. Unless the rate of exchange diverges more than a certain amount of parity, it is worthwhile accepting the less favourable rate of exchange rather than going to the expense of temporarily converting into gold and shipping the gold abroad.

Let us suppose the UK demand for imports from the US rises; demand for dollars in terms of pounds will increase, there is accordingly a tendency for the price of the dollar in terms of pounds to rise. Under the gold standard, however, there is a ceiling above which the value of the dollar cannot rise; for if it did, UK traders would find it cheaper to finance imports by the purchase of gold rather than dollars. The height of this ceiling is determined by the cost of shipping gold (including freight, insurance and loss of interest). The point at which it becomes cheaper to buy and export gold rather than foreign currency is known as the gold export point. On the other hand the rate at which it becomes profitable for foreigners to send gold to a country rather than to purchase its currency is known as its gold import point. Thus the rate of exchange cannot fluctuate outside these two points known as the gold specie points.

During the Middle Ages—indeed down to the middle nineteenth century—silver was in many countries more widely acceptable than gold as the external standard. In a number of European countries, notably

France, gold and silver were equally regarded as the standard. It was only after the great gold discoveries in Australia and California around 1850 that Paris became a gold centre and the franc was generally regarded as convertible into gold rather than into silver. Legally, however, bimetalism persisted for many decades. In Western Europe the pre-eminence of gold was established fully only as the result of the adoption by Germany in 1871 of a new currency, the mark, based on gold. Within a few years the Germany currency reform was followed by the suspension of free coinage of silver in Holland and the Scandinavian countries. France and her bimetallic associates in the 'Latin' union, Belgium, Switzerland and Italy, followed a few years later. It was only after the defeat of the silver interests at the United States Presidential election of 1896 that the United States was placed unequivocally on the gold standard.

In the United Kingdom gold was established as the primary standard in the eighteenth century, and when the wartime paper currency was abandoned in 1819 the gold standard was officially accepted. The guinea was abandoned in favour of the 20s sovereign, containing just over 113 grains of fine gold; thus a standard ounce of gold was equivalent to £3 17s 10½d. There was no free coinage of silver, the government deciding the amount of silver to be minted at its discretion. In practice this meant that any resident of the United Kingdom could present gold at the Bank of England, and have it coined into sovereigns; similarly he could require any sovereigns he presented to be melted into gold bars. Accordingly, from 1819 onwards (indeed until 1914) notes were convertible into gold sovereigns.[1]

Types of Gold Standard

It is clear that for a gold standard to function properly certain requirements have to be met. Firstly, a country's currency unit, be it the pound, dollar, or any other currency, must be convertible into gold at a fixed price, and secondly, there must be free trade in gold. It is by no means essential for all domestic currency units to be freely convertible into gold in any quantities. There are in fact different degrees of

[1] This does not mean that in England the note was backed by gold to the extent of 100 per cent. In the case of many Banks of Issue, it was normal practice for the note issue to exceed the gold reserve; after 1844 the issue of notes by the Bank of England in excess of its gold holdings was legalized. Notes not covered by gold were known as the fiduciary issue.

Before 1925 the Bank of England made no charge for coinage, but the seller lost his entitlement to interest while gold was being coined, a process taking about three weeks.

convertibility depending upon the type of gold standard in operation. In the case of a 'full bodied' gold standard, the monetary authority is compelled to convert the most important kind of domestic currency into gold, and to exchange even the smallest quantity of notes or coin into gold. This type of full gold standard which the late Sir Dennis Robertson called a 'gold circulation system' is the most rigorous form of the gold standard. It was the form in which the United Kingdom operated the gold standard before 1914.[1]

When the gold standard was restored in the 1920s it was no longer possible for the monetary authorities of most countries to undertake to convert domestic paper money into gold; internally they were off the gold standard. But many such countries including Britain, wished to retain the external link between their currencies and gold. Accordingly their monetary authorities undertook to convert domestic money into gold bars of a minimum size. For the UK this minimum size was 440 ounces, and such bars could be freely shipped overseas. This system, operating in the UK between 1925 and September 1931, was known as the gold bullion standard.

Another major variant of the gold standard is the gold exchange system, under which a country does not maintain convertibility between its own currency and gold but between its currency and another currency itself convertible into gold at a fixed parity. Such a country keeps its reserves, not in gold, but in a foreign currency which is always freely convertible into gold at a known price. The country is, as it were, on the gold standard at one remove. The system commends itself to Governments wishing to enjoy the stability conferred by the gold standard without the loss of interest earnings incurred by holding external assets in gold rather than in interest yielding foreign balances or securities. The system was in operation in India before the First World War, but was more widely adopted in the inter-war years. It is particularly appropriate for poorer countries having close economic and political ties with a country whose currency is tied to gold. But the system has by no means been confined to such countries.

The Nineteenth-Century View

In its external aspects, the *modus-operandi* of the gold standard is similar, whether a full circulating standard, a gold bullion standard, or a gold exchange system is in operation. Let us suppose that two countries, the UK and the USA are in payments equilibrium. A change takes

[1] The late Sir Dennis Robertson's little book on *Money*, published in 1923 and revised in 1948, is still a first-rate text on the operation of the gold standard. D. H. Robertson, *Money*, Cambridge University Press.

place in the UK economy causing an increase in imports from the US; the dollar rises above par and will continue to do so until it becomes cheaper for the United Kingdom importers to finance imports by the export of gold instead of by purchase of dollars. Gold will flow from the UK to the US; the UK reserves will be depleted while those of the United States are augmented. Under a gold circulation system which pre-dominated in the nineteenth century, the reduction in the gold reserves of the United Kingdom would automatically result in a reduction of the domestic money supply. Under a gold exchange standard, this effect is not automatic but depends on appropriate action by the monetary authorities. This is the main difference in the operation of the gold circulation system and the gold exchange system. Now before 1914 economists were much more willing to accept the Quantity Theory of Money than they are today, and they accordingly believed that a reduction in money supply in the UK would cause UK prices there to fall, while the increased money supply in the US would cause US prices to rise. UK exports would become relatively cheaper while US exports became relatively dearer. The change in relative price levels would improve the UK balance of trade, and worsen that of the US. As we noted in Chapter 2, it was because David Hume believed that the sequence of events would occur on these lines that he argued that any attempt to foster a balance of trade surplus on mercantilist lines was doomed to failure.

Now as the movement of gold takes place, the central monetary authorities in the deficit country have a clear inducement to protect the reserves by raising interest rates whilst in the surplus country, the authorities are constrained to lower rates. The resultant changes in the interest rate pattern would encourage a flow of capital from the surplus to the deficit country. Clearly this would take place only if not offset by inappropriate interest rate policies. Hence it was necessary for countries on the gold standard not only to allow the free movement of gold—the first 'rule' of the standard—but to follow also another 'rule', namely to allow interest rates to fall when a surplus was developing, and to rise in a period of deficit. The authorities in the deficit country would do this anyway, since the depletion of reserves would indicate the need to stimulate an inflow of funds. But there is less constraint upon the authorities in the surplus country to lower their interest rates.

In following the rule of the gold standard, it is vital for governments to give priority to the maintenance of external equilibrium, even if domestic considerations indicate the need for a quite contrary policy. Thus, although a higher level of domestic unemployment might suggest a lowering of interest rates in a deficit country the rules of the gold standard require a raising of interest rates. Indeed, the need to gear internal financial policies to the requirement of the balance of payments rather than that of domestic stability is the price that a country must be prepared to pay to remain on the standard.

Now it was widely believed in the nineteenth and early twentieth centuries that under the gold standard the balance of payments adjustment process was firstly through interest rate changes causing equilibrating capital movements and in the longer run (but more fundamentally) through price adjustments brought about by the changes in money supply in the deficit and surplus countries. Little attention was paid to the role of income changes. It was only after the First World War, that a fuller and more accurate understanding was reached of the gold standard adjustment mechanism. A number of studies carried out after 1920 confirmed the traditional view that following a deficit in a country's balance of payments, there tended to be an outflow of gold and a reduction of prices. But the price reductions were small and appeared to take place some time after the initial outflow; even more surprising was the fact that equilibrium seemed often to be restored long before the relative price changes could possibly have affected the balance. In other words, the adjustment seems not to have been solely caused by changes in relative price levels. Taussig, who with his colleagues[1] had carried out some studies of the adjustment mechanism shows his surprise at the results by remarking that 'here we have a phenomena not fully understood'. Somewhere was a missing link.

We now know what that missing link was; it was the adjustment resulting from changes in relative incomes and employment. In the surplus country, increased exports would cause incomes to rise relative to those in the deficit country. Out of their higher national income, residents in the surplus country would buy more of the product of the deficit country. In this way an adjustment in the balance of trade between the two countries would be achieved—an adjustment often quite independent of relative price changes.

2. A MODEL OF THE GOLD STANDARD

In the light of developments in economic thinking it is now possible to see more clearly how the gold standard adjustment process really operated. We shall accordingly outline the modern approach to the theory of the gold standard adjustment. It is widely agreed that the

[1] See F. W. Taussig, *International Trade*, cited above, Chapters 20–25. The best known of these studies are by Jacob Viner, *Canada's Balance of International Indebtedness 1900–1913* (1924), J. H. Williams, *Argentine's International Trade under Inconvertible Paper Money 1880–1900* (1920), and H. D. White, *The French International Accounts 1880–1913* (1933).

gold standard adjustment process is considerably more complicated than our analysis so far has suggested. Let us suppose that under the gold standard the United Kingdom has a payments deficit with the USA. There will be an outflow of gold; if the domestic money supply is linked to gold either by a 100 per cent currency gold cover requirement or some fixed proportionate reserve arrangement, the domestic money supply will be automatically reduced. In the absence of off-setting policies, a rise in interest rates will follow. The raising of these rates attracts funds from abroad, at the same time discouraging the outflow of capital. There will thus be an improvement in the UK capital account. This is the first element in the adjustment process.

If, however, the deficit has been caused by a change in the balance of trade (perhaps due to a change in incomes or tastes) the improvement in the capital account will not remove the fundamental *cause* of the disequilibrium. The capital flow has a gap-filling rather than a curative function. But provided the level of investment is not entirely insensitive to rate of interest changes, the raising of interest rates will also cause some degree of domestic deflation, bringing about a more fundamental adjustment.[1]

As domestic expenditure declines, UK residents purchase less from abroad—provided of course their marginal propensity to import is greater than zero. Accordingly there is an expenditure-reducing movement at work which brings about a fundamental improvement in the balance of trade. Meanwhile an opposite movement will occur abroad, where, given appropriate elasticities, interest rates will fall, domestic expenditure increase, and imports be stimulated. This is the 'income' adjustment element, which we discussed in Chapter 12. There is, however, a third, and rather more complicated adjustment, operating through relative price changes. This was the adjustment element most stressed by the classical writers. But it operated in a much more complex manner than they imagined.

If expenditure in the United States rises very substantially and a considerable part of this increase is on imports from the UK (that is if the United States marginal propensity to import from the United Kingdom is high), the increase in demand for UK products might be substantial. Indeed it might even go some way towards off-setting the deflationary effect in the UK of the raising of interest rates. If the reduction in domestic expenditure in the UK results in a marked fall in imports, that is if the UK marginal propensity to import is high, the net deflationary effect will be less than if the marginal propensity to

[1] The analysis is based upon Professor Meade's *The Balance of Payments*, cited above.

import is low. The greater the reduction in imports, the more purchasing power will UK residents have left to spend on home-produced goods; hence the less the domestic deflation. Likewise, if the US marginal propensity to import is high, the resulting expansion of incomes would result in a relatively substantial increase in demand for UK products. Accordingly, high import propensities in both the US and UK damp down the deflationary effects of the raising UK interest rates. We can summarize by saying that the deflationary effects of income reductions in the deficit country induced by the raising of interest rates will be less, the higher the marginal propensities to import of both deficit and surplus countries. It is probable that the sum of the marginal propensities to import is less than unity, but even if the sum were greater than unity, income adjustments alone would be insufficient to restore balance of payments equilibrium, for reasons explained in Chapter 12.

Given some flexibility in prices and wages, the net fall in demand for UK goods and the net increase in demand for US goods will cause a fall in the UK price level relative to that of the US. Accordingly UK products become cheaper in relation to those of the US. Now if the price elasticities of demand for UK and US products in each other's import markets are sufficiently high (to be precise if the sum of these elasticities is greater than unity) there will be a further improvement in the UK balance of trade. This is our third adjustment and results from relative price changes. Accordingly, following the movement of gold we can distinguish three separate adjustment processes at work. There is first the capital account adjustment resulting from the transfer of capital from the surplus to deficit country, secondly there is the balance of trade adjustment brought about by income changes; finally there is the adjustment resulting from the change in relative prices. But these changes do not always operate as smoothly and certainly as the textbooks sometimes suggest.

3. HOW THE GOLD STANDARD WORKED IN PRACTICE

Before examining more basic criticisms it is worth noting that the nineteenth-century gold standard that we are now discussing is perhaps in some respects more accurately described as the sterling standard. In practice a large number of countries held their reserves in the form of sterling rather than gold, and sterling certainly moved much more actively than gold in settlement of international indebtedness. As events following the 1931 British departure from gold showed, many sterling using countries were more anxious to tie their exchange rates to sterling rather than to gold.

Asymmetrical Adjustments

Perhaps a major criticisms of the text book formulation of the gold standard operation is the impression given of a relatively smooth adjustment process. Capital flows, income and price changes, all seem to work together to bring about the necessary adjustment. It seems that all Governments need to do is to keep the few simple rules. One qualification to the simple textbook story arises from the fact that even in the nineteenth century such changes as took place in relative costs and prices were by no means as frequent or of such amplitude as might have been expected. Neither was there in practice the expected degree of symmetry in price changes as between surplus and deficit countries. According to the simple theory of the gold standard prices in deficit countries should fall while those in surplus countries rose. In fact research suggests that even in the heyday of the gold standard export prices of the leading trading countries normally moved in the same direction, irrespective of their balance of payments positions. Thus the prices of both surplus and deficit countries rose and fell more or less in unison.[1] Linked to this is the fact that contrary to what is often alleged, even at the end of the nineteenth century, downward wage-adjustments were the exception rather than the rule. As Triffin remarks, it may be doubted whether money wage reductions were much more acceptable in the nineteenth century 'economically, politically and socially' than they are today.[2]

The Peripheral Countries

Secondly, there is evidence that the gold standard functioned less smoothly and with more jolts and strains in the then less developed countries than in the financial centres such as Britain. It is obviously easier for a country, which normally has a substantial outflow of capital but is in temporary deficit, to make adjustment by raising its interest rates and stemming the outflow of investment funds, than for a deficit country which normally depends upon an inflow to attract additional finance. The effect of a deficit in the UK could be serious for many countries dependent upon the UK for capital. If the UK was temporarily in deficit on current and capital account, the raising of London Bank Rate would of itself often be sufficient to arrest the outflow of capital,

---

[1] C. A. Maddison, 'Growth and Fluctuations in the World Economy', *Banca Nazionale Del Lavoro. Quarterly Review*, June 1962, quoted by R. Triffin, 'The Evolution of the International Monetary System: Historical Reappraisal and Future Perspective', *Princeton Studies in International Finance* No. 12.

[2] R. Triffin cited above.

buttressing the reserves until the crisis had passed. No significant deflation would be necessary. But the effect on those poorer countries dependent upon a steady flow of these funds from London could be serious. Faced with difficulty in obtaining short term finance, they might be compelled to deflate incomes, perhaps undergoing drastic cuts in living standards.[1]

Thus even in the nineteenth century the operation of the gold standard in the real world was far from automatic and not as painless as beginners in international monetary economics are sometimes led to believe. In the twentieth century, the strains were even greater. Not only were prices and wages even more rigid than in the nineteenth century; political and economic uncertainties caused capital flows to be much less sensitive to interest rate changes than had been the case before 1914. Indeed the flight of hot money and 'funk' money often caused perverse capital movements and prevented changes in interest rates from influencing the flow of short-term capital. The experience of the 1930s showed that some alternative to the historic gold standard needed to be devised. In the following chapters we consider the machinery devised in the war years which operates today.

SHORT GUIDE TO THE LITERATURE

A 'classic' work on the gold standard is W. R. Brown Jr, *The International Gold Standard Re-interpreted, 1914–1934*, New York, 1940. A more recent and specialized study is by A. G. Ford, *The Gold Standard, 1880–1914: Britain and Argentina*, Oxford University Press, 1962. Two works by A. Bloomfield are also work consulting: *Monetary Policy under the International Gold Standard, 1880–1914*, New York, 1959, and 'Short-term Capital Movements Under the Pre-1914 Gold Standard', *Princeton Studies in International Finance*, no. 11, Princeton University, New Jersey, 1963.

[1] For a full length study of the operation of the Gold Standard as it affected a developing country in the nineteenth century see A. G. Ford, *The Gold Standard 1880–1914, Britain and Argentina*. Dr Ford has also written a very informative short article on this question in *Lloyds Bank Review*, July 1965, entitled 'The Truth about Gold'.

CHAPTER 16

INTERNAL AND EXTERNAL EQUILIBRIUM

1. A NEW BRANCH OF THEORY

The last few chapters have been devoted to an examination of the adjustment process in the balance of payments, and we have seen how external equilibrium is maintained in various exchange rate regimes. So far, however, we have concerned ourselves almost entirely with the mechanism for maintaining or achieving external equilibrium, giving little consideration to the question of conflict arising from the attempt to maintain simultaneously both external and internal equilibrium. But Governments are concerned not only with the balance of payments, i.e. external equilibrium, but also with internal equilibrium. Now the attempt to satisfy the requirements of both internal and external equilibrium often gives rise to serious policy problems. Moreover, while in this book we have from time to time implicitly assumed that Governments follow appropriate policies for internal balance, we have nowhere analysed them in detail. For example, as regards the effect upon the balance of payments, does it matter, and if so why, whether a Government uses fiscal or monetary policies for internal balance? In this chapter we shall try to remedy these deficiencies.

The present day student may find it difficult to realize that only in and after the 1950s was a systematic attempt made by economists to examine problems arising when Governments have to reconcile policies for internal and external equilibrium. The pre-war and wartime literature was primarily concerned not so much with policy as with the automatic adjustment mechanisms. In his path-breaking book on the National Income and the Balance of Trade published in 1943[1] Machlup was concerned almost entirely with the automatic adjustment mechanism, and paid virtually no attention as to how policy measures might be taken to speed up the adjustment process. Neither did he consider the conflict which might arise between the claims of internal and external equilibrium.

A Problem in Reconciliation

Since 1950 there have been very important developments in this field of International Trade theory. Firstly there has been growing

[1] Discussed in Chapter 12.

awareness both of the repercussions of domestic policy upon the external balance, and the difficulty of reconciling the objectives of domestic and external equilibrium. Secondly the attempt has been made to create a synthesis of the theories of price and income adjustment. No longer are income and price changes regarded as quite distinct mechanisms in the balance of payments adjustment process. The modern view is to regard economic policy as having the objective of internal and external balance and to examine fiscal, monetary and exchange rate policies in the light of the objective.

The earliest systematic account of the difficulties in reconciling policy objectives is to be found in J. E. Meade's *The Balance of Payments*. Basically, the argument is that if two policy targets are to be hit simultaneously, two policy weapons, or to use more elegant language, two policy variables, may need to be employed. Thus if both full employment and payments equilibrium are to be secured, two policy weapons are required, one to hit the full employment target, the other to achieve balance of payments equilibrium.

Professor Meade assumes that there are two types of policy variables (*a*) income adjustments, working through changes in domestic expenditure, and (*b*) price adjustments, which can be brought about in various ways but particularly by means of operating on the rate of exchange. In some circumstances, of course, the employment of only one of these policy variables may be adequate. For example, in the case of a country in balance of payments surplus and domestic unemployment, policy measures are relatively simple. An expansion of domestic demand, by means of fiscal and/or monetary measures will mop up domestic unemployment and at the same time increase imports. There is no clash of objectives—although even in such a case it is unlikely that both full employment and payments equilibrium will be reached at exactly the same time. If, say, full employment is attained before the surplus has disappeared, the continuation of the expansionary policy will lead to domestic inflation; on the other hand, if the brake is applied to domestic expansion, the balance of payments surplus will continue. In the case of a country in balance of payments deficit with domestic inflation the remedy is also relatively simple. Domestic deflation will reduce the deficit as well as ease the strain on domestic resources—although here again a difficulty will arise if the external equilibrium is secured before internal equilibrium has been achieved.

The situation is, however, quite different if a country is in balance of payments deficit but has domestic unemployment. An expansion of demand will cure the unemployment, but make the deficit worse, while a policy aimed at removing the deficit will create even more unemployment.

Equally difficult is a situation where a country has a balance of payments surplus and overfull employment. An expansionary policy will remove the surplus but make the domestic imbalance more intractable. It is in cases like these that two policy variables must be employed. Meade suggests that the appropriate technique is to use one set of policies, namely financial policies, to look after internal equilibrium while employing price policies, as exemplified by exchange rate adjustment, to achieve external balance.

Let us take the case of a country in balance of payments deficit but with a relatively high level of domestic unemployment. The employment of financial policies for internal balance can be relied upon to fill the employment gap, but as we have seen, such policies will widen the deficit. Meade accordingly suggests that this is a case where the price or exchange rate policy weapon should be invoked. By *lowering* export prices at the same time that domestic demand is increased, the deficit can be corrected simultaneously with the absorption of the slack in the domestic economy. The obvious (but not necessarily the only) way to bring about a reduction in export prices is by currency depreciation. Similarly in the situation where a country has a payments surplus with overfull domestic employment, the correct policy would be a disinflationary financial policy, to dampen down home demand, accompanied by an appreciation of the exchange rate. The employment of two policies makes it possible to hit two targets simultaneously.

In Meade's approach there is a distinction between what we might call 'relative cost' or price changes on the one hand and 'domestic expenditure' changes on the other. The former are used to maintain external, the latter, internal balance. Accordingly there is a distinction between price and income effects. While this distinction is useful in analysing policy problems, it should be remembered that the two effects cannot be placed in watertight compartments. As we saw in Chapter 13, a change in exchange rates can have quite important income effects ('the absorption approach'). Similarly, domestic expansion might bring about price increases in certain export products long before full employment is reached. Moreover, it would be misleading to assume that the effect of one set of policy variables can be confined to either the domestic or external sector. A Government may decide to cope with domestic disequilibrium by means of appropriate financial policy, leaving the exchange rate to look after the external situation. But if it decides to rely upon monetary (i.e. interest rate) policy rather than fiscal policy, there may be important effects upon the capital account. A raising of interest rates in order to reduce domestic demand could well have a very marked effect upon the balance of payments by attracting short-term capital. Perhaps the most substantial advance since Meade's *The Balance of Payments* in the theory of policy for balance of payments is the awareness that whatever their motive, price and income policies do in fact influence both internal and external equilibrium.

The Diagrammatic Approach

Professor Meade illustrates his discussion of the relationship between policies for internal and external balance by means of numerous tables which show in schematic form the appropriate set of policy measures which a pair of countries should adopt if they are to be in payments equilibrium with one another and at the same time each enjoy internal balance.[1] A slightly different approach is that of Corden[2] and Swan[3] who employ simple diagrams to make somewhat similar points. In what follows we examine the approach of Professor T. W. Swan, who uses a piece of diagrammatic apparatus which is now well established in international trade theory, and with which the student should be familiar.

Figure 13 is built up in the following manner. The level of domestic employment and the state of the balance of payments both depend upon the level of domestic spending and the cost position of a country's exports *vis-à-vis* those of its competitors. Let us take first the level of domestic employment. If a country's competitive position is favourable, i.e. if the cost ratio of foreign prices to domestic prices is high, then a given level of employment can be supported with a relatively low level of domestic demand, for exports will be high in relation to imports. On the other hand, if the cost ratio is unfavourable (if C is near to O in Figure 13), employment generated by export activities will be small, and a high level of domestic expenditure necessary to maintain a given level of employment. The relationship between export competitiveness and domestic expenditure at various levels of employment is shown by the I family of curves (I standing for internal balance). These curves slope from north-west to south-east We can let the curve IF represent full employment, IO represent overfull employment and IU underfull

[1] The student is strongly urged to ponder over Tables X, XI and XII of *The Balance of Payments* (pp. 117, 154, 156).

[2] W. M. Corden, 'The Geometric Representation of Policies to Attain Internal and External Balance', *Review of Economic Studies*, vol. 28, October 1960, pp. 1–22.

[3] T. W. Swan, 'Longer-Run Problems of the Balance of Payments', in H. W. Arndt and W. M. Corden (eds), *The Australian Economy: A Volume of Readings*, Melbourne, Cheshire Press, 1963, reprinted in Caves and Johnson, *Readings in International Economics*.

employment. As regards internal equilibrium, therefore, the object of policy makers should be to keep on the curve IF. If, by currency adjustment or incomes policy, a relatively favourable cost structure is established, there is less need for expansionary financial policies

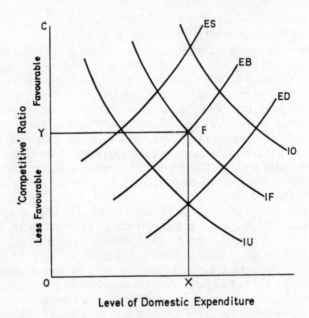

FIGURE 13. Determinants of Internal and External Equilibrium.

to secure buoyancy of domestic expenditure. So much for internal balance.

What about external equilibrium? Here we represent various degrees of balance of payments equilibrium by the E family of curves (EB symbolizing external balance). A given degree of external equilibrium requires various combinations of 'competitiveness' and domestic expenditure. If a country's economy is very uncompetitive, that is if the value of C is low, then a given degree of external equilibrium is compatible with a lower level of domestic expenditure than if the country's cost structure is more favourable. Accordingly the E curves slope from south-west to north-east. Only one of them (EB in our figure) represents external balance. The curve ES represents balance of payments surplus; ED represents a deficit. The object of policy makers is to keep along the EB curve. Clearly there is only one point at which the requirements of both internal and external equilibrium can be met, that is at F. Thus the combination of policies which may be expected to achieve both full employment and balance of payments equilibrium targets is that which achieves a competitive cost ratio represented by OY (perhaps achieved by an appropriate exchange rate/wages policy) and a level of domestic expenditure of OX (achieved by fiscal or monetary measures).

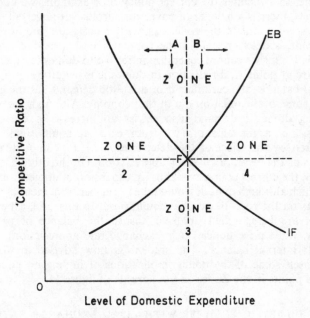

FIGURE 14. Policy Criteria for Internal and External Equilibrium.

Professor Swan uses this apparatus to examine some of the policy dilemmas resulting from difficulties in reconciling the requirements of internal and external equilibrium. Figure 14 consists essentially of the two curves for internal and external balance, IF and EB, respectively. To use Swan's expression, these curves 'divide existence into four zones of economic unhappiness'. In Zones 1 and 2 there is an external surplus, but whereas in Zone 1 the surplus is accompanied by overfull employment, in Zone 2 it is accompanied by underemployment. In Zones 3 and 4 there is a balance of payments deficit, but whilst in Zone 4 there is overfull employment, in Zone 3 there is unemployment.

The student should make sure he realizes why this is so; reference back to figure 13 should clear up any confusion. Now although we know that there is disequilibrium within 'each zone of economic unhappiness', how is the policy maker to know whether the disequilibrium is caused by 'cost' of 'expenditure' influences?

Professor Swan's answer is to divide the figure into four quadrants, the lines forming the quadrants then subdivide each zone. It is the position of a country in relation the lines forming the quadrant within the zone, that dictates the correct policy. For example, we know that in Zone I, there is a balance of payments surplus with overfull employment. At all points in the zone, competitive costs are 'too low'. From any point, a deterioration in the country's cost structure brings us towards F. But we cannot generalize in regard to domestic expenditure. If we are at point A, a reduction in domestic expenditure brings us to internal balance; the curtailment of domestic demand has the effect of taking some of the inflation out of the economy. Although the effect of reducing domestic demand also causes an increase in the external surplus, i.e. a movement *away* from external equilibrium, this is countered by the effect of the deterioration in the competitive ratio, perhaps as the result of currency appreciation. On the other hand, at a point B, the correct course would be an expansion of domestic expenditure which although of itself would take us further from internal balance helps us on the road to external equilibrium. In this case, expenditure policies are being relied upon to absorb the balance of payments surplus, while price policies (e.g. exchange rate appreciation) take us towards internal balance. The student is now advised to work out for himself some of the policy implications of finding his country at various points in the Zones and quadrants of figure 14.

2. DOMESTIC POLICIES WITH FIXED EXCHANGE RATES

So far in this chapter we have assumed that our two policy variables are price and income adjustments. But elsewhere in this book we have seen that in the post-war world, international price adjustments have been very difficult to engineer, due to the relative fixity of exchange rates. How then have policy makers set to work to secure both internal and external equilibrium when one of their policy tools has been virtually denied them? There are several possible answers to this conundrum. The answer given by Professor Johnson in his *The World Economy at the Crossroads*[1] is that some adjustment occurs by natural

[1] *The World Economy at the Crossroads—A Survey of Current Problems of Money, Trade and Economic Development*, Oxford, Clarendon Press, 1965, Chapter 3.

competitive realignment of prices and costs, there being differences in the relative rates of inflation of deficit countries on the one hand, and surplus countries on the other. But this adjustment process is slow and halting; at times, indeed, it becomes overwhelmed by, for example, surges of inflationary pressure in the deficit countries. When these occur, either some kind of *ad hoc* intervention is necessary, e.g. a currency rescue operation mounted by central bankers, or in the last resort that rare event, regarded in the post-war world as almost a catastrophe—currency devaluation—becomes unavoidable.

There is, however, another sense in which some kind of 'adjustment' can be brought about, even when price policies cannot be operated. This possibility arises from the fact that what we loosely describe as financial policy has two main elements—fiscal policy and monetary policy. In a world of relatively free capital movement, monetary policy can be used quite effectively to influence the external position *via* the balance of payments on capital account, while fiscal policy can be used to maintain domestic balance. Thus both internal and external equilibrium might be secured even with a fixed exchange rate by a judicious combination of fiscal and monetary policies.[1] Unfortunately, however, such a system has within it nothing which restores true equilibrium. A given level of domestic employment, for example, can be secured only so long as interest rate policy is such that a given rate of capital inflow is assured. Johnson suggests that so far from aiding adjustment, manipulation of the rate of interest to secure a capital inflow might actually increase the degree of fundamental external imbalance. For it is likely that such a country is one which at full employment finds its costs and prices rising faster than those of its competitors (otherwise it would not be the kind of country to get into deficit at full employment), and the cushion provided by the steady inflow of capital delays any fundamental readjustment. Secondly, the high level of interest rates necessary to maintain the capital inflow is likely to have an adverse effect upon domestic investment, growth and international competitiveness.

There is another very important welfare consideration relevant to this discussion. If interest rates are used primarily to influence capital flows, in the context of a country's overall balance of payments position,

---

[1] The question is discussed by Professor H. G. Johnson in 'Theoretical Problems of the International Monetary System', *Journal of Economic Studies*, vol. 2, no. 2, January 1968.

The development of this aspect of theory owes much to R. A. Mundell. The first systematic treatment was in his 'The Appropriate Use of Monetary and Fiscall Policy for Internal and External Stability', *IMF Staff Papers*, vol. 9, March 1962, pp. 70–79.

there will be a tendency for capital to flow towards countries in deficit on current account and away from those with current account surpluses. The resulting pattern of capital resource allocation is not necessarily the optimum. Capital should in fact move to countries where its real return is relatively high; these are not necessarily those where current accounts and domestic employment situations are such that interest rates happen to be relatively high.[1]

The Assignment Problem

Another set of problems in regard to the choice between fiscal and monetary policy arises from the fact that usually the policies are implemented by different sets of people—the Central Bank controls interest rate policy, the Treasury budgetary policy. Since policy implementation, indeed often policy decision making, is in the hands of separate agencies there is a danger of policy clashes occurring; for example the actions of the Central Bank might well defeat the purposes of a particular budget measure. There is more than a purely administrative problem here, for unless it is clearly established which set of policy measures is to attain a particular object, e.g. internal full employment, the most efficient use of the policy weapons will not be attained. R. A. Mundell has described this as 'the assignment problem'.[2] He suggests that policy objectives should be 'assigned' to various policy measures in accordance with the principle of 'effective market classification', that is, each policy measure should be given the task of attaining the objective upon which it is likely to have relatively the greatest impact. Accordingly, if the exchange rate cannot be altered, and if other price adjustments are impossible or likely to be inadequate, monetary policy should be given the task of ensuring external equilibrium while to fiscal policy is assigned the work of maintaining internal equilibrium. If the tasks are assigned otherwise, the actions of the two authorities may move the economy further and further away from equilibrium.

So far in this chapter we have omitted all reference to the use of direct controls as a means of restoring external equilibrium. Such measures are of course frequently resorted to for this purpose—not

[1] This question is analysed by Professor Harry Johnson in 'The Welfare Costs of Exchange Rate Stabilisation', *Journal of Political Economy*, vol. lxxiv, no. 5, October 1966, pp. 512–518.

[2] R. A. Mundell, in 'The Appropriate Use of Monetary and Fiscal Policy for Internal and External Stability', *IMF Staff Papers*, vol. 9, no. 1, March 1962, pp. 70–77, and in 'The Monetary Dynamics of International Adjustment under Fixed and Flexible Exchange Rates', *Quarterly Journal of Economics*, vol. lxxiv, no. 2, May 1960, pp. 227–257.

only to remove or reduce a deficit, but sometimes to reduce a balance of payments surplus. It is of course arguable as we noted in Chapter 11, that balance of payments equilibrium achieved by means of direct controls is not really equilibrium at all. A discussion of the fascinating question of when equilibrium is not really equilibrium would however require a chapter to itself! Fortunately there is little need for the student to feel cheated that such a chapter does not exist in this book, for there is a tendency today for economists to make the distinction, not so much between direct controls on the one hand and income and price measures on the other, 'but between what are known as expenditure-reducing devices and expenditure-switching devices.[1] The former clearly *reduce* overall expenditure; deflation is an obvious example. Expenditure switching devices on the other hand, *divert* expenditure from one field to another. Such devices include depreciation; direct controls on imports and exports, subsidies and tariffs. Normally the imposition of these measures results in a switch of expenditure from say imports to home-trade products, and from the latter to exports.

SHORT GUIDE TO THE LITERATURE

The reader is referred to the footnotes, especially to the works of Meade, Johnson and Swan. See also Dr Corden's *Recent Developments in the Theory of International Trade*. Dr Corden's own contribution to the discussion is in his *The Geometric Representation of Policies to Attain International and External Balance*. Review of Economic Studies, vol. 28.

[1] The distinction between expenditure-reducing and expenditure-switching devices was first developed by Professor Harry Johnson in his *International Trade and Economic Growth*, London, Allen and Unwin, 1958, Chapter 6.

CHAPTER 17

THE INTERNATIONAL MONETARY FUND SYSTEM

The post-war international monetary system, known variously as 'the IMF system', 'the adjustable-peg exchange rate system', or 'the gold exchange standard', was devised during the Second World War in an attempt to avoid on the one hand the rigidities of the gold standard of the 1920s (and the need completely to subordinate domestic economic policy objectives to the requirements of external balance at unchangeable exchange rates), and on the other, the chaos of the competitive devaluations and other beggar-my-neighbour policies of the trade and exchange control ridden world of the 1920s.

The IMF aims at relative stability of exchange rates. Members are required to notify the Fund of their exchange rate parities and to keep fluctuations to within a stated percentage around parity, although in practice the permitted fluctuations are often somewhat wider. Members undertake to alter rates only in case of fundamental balance of payments disequilibrium; the Fund articles, however, nowhere define what is meant by this.

On the other hand, it would be misleading to regard the IMF system as simply a gold standard in which exchange rates are sometimes changed. The Fund plays a much more active role. It is perhaps better to think of the Fund basically as a mechanism of multilateral co-operation in the international monetary field. It aims at promoting good neighbourly policies by encouraging exchange rate stability, by providing temporary assistance to member countries in balance of payment difficulties and by discouraging discrimination in international payments. Although the Fund in general frowns upon exchange controls on current transactions, it specifically allows control of capital movements. In these respects the constitution of the Fund reflects the reaction against the practice of the 1930s.

1. THE GENESIS OF THE FUND

The IMF arrangements were devised in the darkest years of the War by economists and statesmen on both sides of the Atlantic; the plans were part of what many hoped would be a kind of New Deal in international trade and monetary arrangements. During the Second World War, some of the ablest economists and civil servants devoted themselves not only to helping to win the war, but to planning the shape of the international economy which they hoped to see established when the fighting was over. On the American side, President Roosevelt gave a high priority to planning for the peace, affording every encouragement to those advisers and civil servants anxious to devote themselves to this cause. Although Winston Churchill was never as interested as Roosevelt in post-war planning he gave support to the civil servants and economists of the War Cabinet Secretariat[1] especially concerned with the shape of the post-war world economy. These experts were concerned not only with future international financial arrangements, but with the future of trade and international investment. Indeed, they hoped to see established three pillars of post-war co-operation: an International Monetary Fund and an International Bank for Reconstruction and Development to provide for the financial needs of the expanding world economy, and an International Trading Organization to be the focal point of co-operation in trade matters. In a number of respects the international economic institutions established at the end of the War disappointed those early hopes.

As we shall see in Chaper 18 there is widespread doubt as to the ability of the Fund in its present form to meet the pressing needs of the world economy. As for the International Bank for Reconstruction and Development, it has fulfilled a useful role in helping solve the problem of development, but this has been possible as the result of considerable modification of its original structure and policy. For example, it became necessary to supplement the IBRD by the establishment of the International Finance Corporation in 1956 and the International Development Association in 1958.

Bretton Woods

The proposed International Trade Organization never came into being: the GATT originally intended as a stop-gap until the ITO could be set up has fulfilled a useful function—but by its very nature the GATT has been but a pale shadow of what the designers of the ITO hoped that organization would become. Both the IMF and IBRD were established following a Conference of the allied nations held at Bretton Woods, United States, in July 1944—a full nine months before the ending of the war in Europe. This Conference was itself the result of a series of trans-Atlantic talks and negotiations between the experts.

[1] Among them Lord Robbins, Professor James Meade, Professor E. A. G. Robinson, the late Lord Keynes and the late Sir Dennis Robertson.

The British Proposals

The British proposals for the setting up of an International Monetary Institution were published in 1943, in the form of an official Government White Paper, widely known to embody the ideas of Keynes. Essentially, it advocated the establishment of an International Central Bank to operate much like a National Central Bank. In some respects the International Monetary Fund as it finally emerged from the Bretton Woods negotiations fell short of British hopes.[1] In *Proposals for an International Clearing Union*[2] the British advocated a Clearing Union, able to create international purchasing power by allowing member countries overdraft facilities. These would take the form of currency balances, known as bancor, the value of which would be fixed, but not unalterably, in terms of gold. The scheme required members to accept bancor as equivalent to gold as a means of international payments. National Central Banks would keep accounts with the Clearing Union. Countries with a favourable balance of payments with other members would build up a credit with the Clearing Union, while those with unfavourable balances of payments would accumulate debits. Member countries would have the right to run up their debit balances in accordance with an agreed formula. The scheme proposed that the initial quotas should be fixed with reference to the sum of a member country's exports and imports on the average of (say) the three pre-war years and might be (say) 75 per cent of this amount.

A number of checks were designed to come into play long before the limit of a country's quota was reached, so that there were built-in devices to help restore equilibrium. A charge of 1 per cent per annum was proposed on the amount by which a country's balance in the Union exceeded one quarter of its quota, and one of 2 per cent on the amount by which the balance exceeded one half of a country's quota. The draft Plan also required a member country to obtain the permission of the Governing Board—established to administer the Union—before

[1] There are some interesting accounts of the negotiations leading to the establishment of the IMF. Among them W. M. Scammell, *International Monetary Policy*, London, Macmillan, 1961, and R. F. Harrod, *The Life of John Maynard Keynes*, London, Macmillan, 1952.

[2] The *Proposals* originally appeared as a British Government White Paper, Cmd. 6437, HMSO, April 1943. A somewhat abridged statement of the *Proposals*, quoted from the original White Paper, constitutes Chapter XXIV of S. E. Harris, *The New Economics: Keynes' Influence on Theory and Public Policy*, London, Dennis Dobson, 1947. There is also in Professor Harris' book a penetrating analysis of the British and American proposals by Professor Joan Robinson, under the title *The International Currency Proposals*. Both the official White Paper and Professor Robinson's article are well worth reading by the student who wishes to grasp some of the issues surrounding the origins of the present international monetary system.

increasing its debit balance by more than one quarter of its quota within a given year. As a condition of allowing a debit to exceed half a member's quota, it was envisaged that the Governing Board might require the devaluation of the member's currency, controls on the outflow of capital, or even the outright surrender of a suitable proportion of the member country's external reserves. The Governing Board would have authority to recommend the adoption of appropriate internal policies to correct the disequilibrium.

If a member's debit balance exceeded three quarters of its quota for at least a year, or if the debit was increasing unduly rapidly, the Governing Board might, after a two-year interval, declare the member in default. A member country would then no longer be entitled to draw against its account except with the specific permission of the Board. Thus there were a series of checks to prevent abuse of a country's drawing rights, and to prevent the Union degenerating into a spendthrift's paradise. An interesting feature of the Clearing Union Proposal was the built-in deterrent against the piling up of surpluses, achieved by requiring a country to pay an interest charge on its credit balance. The Plan provided that where a country's credit balance exceeded half of its quota on the average of at least a year, the Governing Board and the country together should determine appropriate measures to restore equilibrium; such measures might include currency appreciation, internal reflation; or the removal of import controls and tariffs.

The Keynes Plan did not do away with gold as an international store of value; indeed it recognized that gold would still have a useful role to play in providing a means for settling international indebtedness. Central banks would be entitled to retain their separate gold reserves and ship gold to one another, provided they did not do so at a price above parity; they could even mint and put into circulation gold coins. Essentially, however, the Clearing Union aimed at providing a means for ensuring that the volume of international purchasing power available was sufficient to finance as large as possible a quantum of international trade. Gold was to be supplemented rather than entirely displaced as an international medium of exchange. Just as an efficient banking system ensures the maximum utilization of domestic resources, so it was hoped that the Clearing Union arrangements would ensure the highest possible level of international trade and employment.

The American Plan

Perhaps many of the strains and tensions which have plagued the post-war international economy would have been less had Keynes'

Clearing Union been established. But this was not to be; for the arrangements adopted at Bretton Woods were based less upon the expansionist ideas of Keynes than upon the more conservative ideas of the United States Treasury. The American proposals were founded upon a draft plan for an International Stabilization Fund, drawn up largely by Harry Dexter White.[1]

The American Plan envisaged an international exchange stabilization fund, which like the national Exchange Equalization Funds of the 1930s would consist of assets composed of various currencies. These would come into the possession of the fund as the result of contributions of members, fixed in accordance with predetermined quotas. Member countries in deficit would be allowed to draw on the Fund's resources within limits based upon their quotas. In the American Plan these quotas were based not only upon the volume of a member's foreign trade, but also on the size of its gold holdings and national income. This meant a much larger American quota than would have been the case under the British Plan.

Although at Bretton Woods it was often stated that whatever the merits of the British Clearing Union Plan its objectives could also be achieved by the American Proposal, there were certain fundamental differences between the two schemes. Firstly, the resources of the British Clearing Union were greater than those proposed for the American Fund. The US proposed that the total of the Fund's resources should be $5 billion, while the British Clearing Union Plan envisaged a total credit creating capacity five times as great as this—of about $25 billion. The difference in the size of the resources envisaged in the two Plans was such as to be a difference of kind rather than of degree. Keynes wanted a Fund so large that its very existence would give Governments sufficient confidence to relax trade and other controls and to implement full employment policies. He hoped that his Clearing Union would be one of the foundation stones of a better, saner world. The US Plan, on the other hand, based on more modest resources, could

---

[1] Although the so-called White Plan was less ambitious than Keynes' proposal, it should be remembered that White envisaged that the International Bank for Reconstruction and Development would be conceived on much bolder lines than turned out to be the case at Bretton Woods. The Bank was to have been a real international Central Bank with power to grant loans, finance international commodity stabilization schemes, issue notes—and in fact undertake many of the functions which Keynes' plan had assigned to the Fund. Had White's proposals for both institutions been adopted an ambitious system of international financial arrangements would have resulted. The contribution of Harry Dexter White to post-war international economic planning is outlined by Sir Roy Harrod in his *Life of John Maynard Keynes*, cited above.

do little more than provide deficit countries with an 'iron ration' to tide them over periods of immediate but temporary difficulty. In the event, when the International Monetary Fund was established, its total assets were rather greater than the Americans had envisaged, but at US $ 8·8 billion they were still below what Keynes considered adequate.

A second difference between the schemes was that the British scheme, unlike the American, did not require the immediate surrender of assets by member Governments. An absorption of part of countries' gold reserves was necessary under the US scheme but under the British proposal, assets would be 'created' as and when required. The credit creating powers of the British Clearing Union could become a powerful engine of world economic expansion. Looking even further ahead, Keynes believed that the Union could fulfil a vital role in helping combat the international trade cycle, and in financing international commodity buffer stocks. A third difference is in the relative position of the United States in the two schemes. The fact that under the US Plan, the size of member countries' quotas and voting rights took into account their national incomes and reserves as well as their importance as trading nations gave the United States more influence than the British scheme, where Britain and the United States would have had roughly similar status.

We have outlined the two major schemes discussed at Bretton Woods, not only because of their intrinsic interest, but also because the controversies of the 'forties throw some light on the disputes of the 'sixties. The International Monetary Fund, based largely upon the US proposed Stabilization Fund, has now been in operation some twenty years, yet still the clash between conservatives and expansionists continues. Today, however, the *personae* of the drama have changed. In the 'sixties the Americans are the expansionists, the Europeans the conservatives. In 1943, however, it was American power which was in the ascendant; accordingly it was hardly surprising that the arrangements finally hammered out at Bretton Woods reflected the viewpoint of creditor America rather than of debtor Britain. Keynes and his colleagues secured a number of amendments to the original American Plan, and in a speech commending the final Agreement to the House of Lords, Keynes described it as 'a dog of mixed origin which in some important respects was a considerable improvement on either of its parents'.[1] But it cannot be denied that the International Monetary Fund as it

[1] Speech to the House of Lords, May 23, 1944, reproduced as Chapter XXVII in S. E. Harris, *The New Economics, Keynes' Influence on Theory and Public Policy*, cited above.

subsequently developed, far from satisfied the forward-looking aspirations of Keynes and his colleagues. In the light of these considerations we shall now examine the IMF arrangements and the way they have operated over the last two decades.[1]

2. THE IMF

Constitution and Objectives

The Fund commenced operations in 1947. Originally, there were forty-four members; by late 1972 there were no less than one hundred and twenty-four, the most notable non-members being the CMEA countries and Switzerland. The Fund is controlled by a Board of Governors, who meet once a year to take major policy decisions. Among their tasks is to appoint the Executive Board, members of which (the Directors), are responsible for detailed policy decisions. The Directors are served by a full-time Managing Director, at present Dr Pierre-Paul Schweitzer, who succeeded the late Per Jacobsson in 1963.[2]

According to its Articles, the object of the Fund is to lessen the duration and reduce the degree of disequilibrium in members' balances of payments. This is achieved by making available international resources in case of need. Such assistance is designed to help members avoid recourse to mutually harmful policies such as frequent and competitive devaluation, exchange controls on current payments and devices such as multiple exchange rates. Before the war a great deal of damage was caused by frequent recourse to exchange controls (often of a highly discriminatory nature) on current payments, a device frequently used by the Nazis in their attempts to dominate their Eastern neighbours. On the other hand serious economic difficulties were created in the 1930s by massive movements of short-term capital (often politically motivated) which not only depleted countries' reserves but hampered the function of the rate of interest as the regulator of the international flow of capital. Accordingly, while the architects of the IMF forbade restrictions or exchange controls on current payments (except in carefully defined circumstances), controls on capital movements are specifically permitted.

[1] One of the clearest expositions of the precise significance of the actual Fund Articles is in S. Horie, *The International Monetary Fund. Retrospect and Prospect*, London, 1964 and H. Aufricht, *The International Monetary Fund, Legal Bases, Structure, Functions*, London, 1964.

[2] Each member country appoints one Governor who normally serves for a period of five years.

The Fund's Resources

The IMF follows the American Stabilization Fund proposal in that it consists of gold and currencies contributed by members. On joining, each member country is allotted a quota, which determines both its initial contribution to the Fund and its drawing and voting rights. A member is required to contribute in gold or convertible currency the equivalent of 25 per cent of its quota or 10 per cent of its official gold and convertible exchange reserves.

The Fund Articles provide for an adjustment of quotas every five years, but it was only in and after 1959 that substantial increases have been made. In that year, most quotas were raised by 50 per cent, while for some countries, notably Western Germany, larger increases were agreed. In 1965 and 1970 there was a further general increase. After these increases, the total quotas—and hence resources—of the Fund amounted to just under $29 billion. This is a substantial increase on the original $8 billion, but little more than the $25 billion proposed by Keynes in his Clearing Union Plan of 1943—when prices of internationally traded goods were perhaps a third of what they are today. On the other hand, as we shall see below, the 'quota' resources of the Fund have been supplemented by various other devices and a crude comparison of this kind does not really throw a great deal of light on the potential of the Fund as a provider of foreign exchange. The United States still has easily the largest quota—$6·7 billion (about one-quarter of the total), followed by the United Kingdom with $2·8 billion, Germany with $1·6 billion, and France with $1·5 billion. Fifth in order of size is Japan's quota ($1·2 billion), followed closely by Canada ($1·1 billion) and India ($940 million).

In general a member may call upon the Fund to finance temporary balance of payments disequilibrium, within the limits determined by its quota, but the Fund is not designed to finance long-term deficits, caused for example, by a large scale domestic development programme. The Fund is a 'mixed bag' of gold and national currencies and its rules have been devised to prevent a depletion of any one currency. A member normally draws on the Fund's resources by purchasing a particular currency in exchange for its own currency. In determining a member's right to purchase from the Fund, account is taken by the Fund of its holding of that member's currency. Accordingly, a member may purchase another's currency from the Fund, provided that transaction does not lead to an increase in the Fund stock of the drawing member's currency by more than one quarter over a twelve month period, or to a level twice as high as its quota. Thus the ability of a member to draw on the Fund's resources depends not only on the member's previous drawings, but also upon the borrowing activities of other members. If a member country's currency has been in heavy demand and the Fund's supply of that currency is accordingly low, that member can draw more freely than if the Fund is well supplied with the currency.

In the early days the Fund was very stringent in its interpretation of the rules in regard to drawing. Assistance was granted only in the

TABLE 9. SUMMARY OF FUND TRANSACTIONS, 1948–1972[1]
(In millions of SDRs)

	Total purchases by members	Total repurchases by members
1948–1952	852	79
1953–1957	1,499	953
1958	665	86
1959	263	537
1960	165	522
1961	577	658
1962	2,243	1,260
1963	579	807
1964	625	380
1965	1,897	516
1966	2,817	406
1967	1,061	340
1968	1,348	1,116
1969	2,839	1,542
1970	2,996	1,671
1971	1,167	1,657
1972	2,028	3,122
Total	21,626	15,656

[1] Fiscal years ending April 30th.
Totals may not equal sums of items because of rounding.
SOURCE: *IMF Annual Report*, 1972, p. 78.

case of proven need, and where it was clear that the recipient country was prepared to take steps to restore equilibrium. Following the institution of the European Recovery Programme in 1948/9, the IMF temporarily ceased to assist countries receiving Marshall Aid. In fact the Fund was virtually dormant in the early years of its life. After 1952, however, the Fund followed a somewhat more liberal line, and since that date a member has been allowed as of right to purchase foreign exchange up to 25 per cent of its quota.[1] The Fund also looks relatively favourably on a drawing in the next 25 per cent *tranche* of a member's quota, but beyond this point it requires clear evidence that the country is taking steps to correct the disequilibrium. A further element of flexibility was introduced in 1961 when the Fund announced that it would allow member countries to draw more freely on its resources where balance of payments disequilibrium was due to an outflow of short term capital.

Table 9 gives an indication of the extent of members' purchases from the Fund since its inception in 1948. Before 1958 most of the drawings were in United States dollars, but in recent years US dollars accounted for only about one-sixth of total drawings, while about one third was in German DMs. The Fund will normally advise members which currencies they should purchase from them and in this way it can not only secure an equitable use of its resources, but also prevent a currency from becoming 'scarce'. Some indication of the widespread use of the Fund's resources is given in Table 10 which shows the drawings of member countries for the year 1970—which of course included massive UK drawings.

Stand-by Facilities

An important development in Fund policy was the introduction in 1952 of a system of stand-by arrangements, whereby member countries are given assurance of assistance, should they need it, for a given period, usually six months or a year. The knowledge that the Fund has declared its willingness to support a member in this way acts as a stabilizing influence. It often helps to deter adverse speculation. The existence of a standby pledge by the Fund may also facilitate the raising of further external credit. A stand-by credit is sometimes needed purely as a precautionary measure, with little expectation that it will be drawn upon. Between the introduction of the device in 1952 and the end of 1972, some 319 arrangements were successfully negotiated, on behalf of fifty-eight member countries. Approximately one-third of the total Fund drawings have been made in accordance with these arrangements. Some member countries have maintained successive arrangements over

[1] Provided the country had initially contributed 25 per cent of its quota in gold and had not exercised the option of contributing gold only to the extent of 10 per cent of its reserves. It should also be noted that if other members have purchased the currency, what is called the 'gold tranche' is increased by an equivalent amount.

TABLE 10. PURCHASES OF CURRENCIES FROM THE FUND, YEAR ENDED APRIL 30, 1970

(In millions of us dollars)

Member purchasing	Under stand-by arrangements	Total
Afghanistan	9·75	9·75
Belgium		46·50
Burma	11·99	12·00
Burundi	1·50	1·50
Ceylon	15·00	15·00
Chad		3·78
Chile	20·00	20·00
Columbia	33·25	33·25
Denmark		45·00
Dominican Republic		8·00
Ecuador	8·25	11·00
El Salvador	6·00	12·25
France	985·00	985·84
West Germany		540·00
Ghana	3·00	3·00
Guatemala	6·00	6·00
Guinea		3·80
Haiti		1·50
Indonesia	59·00	59·00
Ireland		20·00
Israel		45·00
Liberia	1·40	1·40
Mali	2·25	2·25
Nicaragua	14·00	14·00
Pakistan	35·00	35·00
Peru	15·00	15·00
Philippines	18·00	18·00
Rwanda	2·00	2·00
Syrian Arab Republic		9·50
Tunisia		4·50
Turkey	10·00	10·00
United Kingdom	1,000·00	1,000·00
Uruguay		1·84
	2,260·89 [1]	2,995·65 [1]

[1] Total does not equal sum of items because of rounding.

SOURCE: *IMF Annual Report*, 1970, p. 137.

periods of as long as eight or nine years.[1] The significance of stand-by arrangements is seen from Table 10.

For stand-by arrangements repayment terms (three to five years) and interest charges are generally the same as for normal drawings from the Fund, which always requires from the member requesting the facility a statement of policy intentions. The largest stand-by arrangements in the early years was at the time of Suez crises when stand-by facilities for $738·5 millions were put at the disposal of the UK. Together with an immediate drawing of $561·5 million, the UK thus had available no less than $1,300 million—an amount equivalent to its quota. Massive support was also given to sterling through stand-by facilities in the British external crises of the 1960s.

Less Developed Countries

The Fund has provided valuable stand-by facilities to less developed countries. In 1967, for example, South Korea made an arrangement with the Fund to support its unitary but fluctuating exchange rate system. In the same year an arrangement with Burundi helped that country to meet temporary balance of payments difficulties caused by a decline in the world price for coffee; Guyana's stand-by arrangement for $7·5 million made possible domestic stabilization policy. When the Fund was established, no special arrangements were considered necessary for the provision of finance to less developed countries. As the years passed, however, there was an increasing awareness by Fund members of the special problems of these nations, whose drawings in the 1960s were four times the 1950s total.

Some of the balance of payments problems facing developing countries arise from the very considerable fluctuations in their export earnings resulting from the instability of commodity prices. Since 1960 the Fund has given a great deal of attention to this problem, and in 1963 launched a scheme for the provision of compensating finance to developing countries whose export earnings fall abnormally low.[2] Accordingly, a country suffering from a temporary decline in its export earnings may apply for a special drawing (additional to its normal drawing right), to compensate for this decline. Such a special drawing must not normally exceed one fourth of its quota. In such cases, the

[1] *Finance and Development*, Review of the Fund and Bank, vol. iv, no. 2, June 1967.
[2] The background to the discussions leading to these new arrangements is to be found in the IMF Report, *Compensatory Financing of Export Fluctuations*, Washington D.C., February 1963, and also 'Fund Politics and Procedures in Relation to the Compensatory Financing of Commodity Fluctuations', *IMF Staff Papers*, vol. viii, 1960–1, pp. 1–76.

Fund waives the rule requiring that the total of a member's currency held by it should not exceed twice the quota. In order to identify export short-falls of a short-term character, the Fund, in conjunction with the member concerned, makes estimates of the medium-term trends in a member's exports.

In general, less developed countries are still unsatisfied with the Fund arrangements for the compensation of export short-falls; many would prefer their drawing rights to be related rather to the actual gap in any year between export proceeds and the medium-term trend than, as at present, to the size of their extremely modest quotas.

The General Arrangements to Borrow

Since 1962, the Fund has acted as intermediary in the provision of mutual credit facilities among its industrialized members, the so-called 'Group of Ten'. Under these General Arrangements to Borrow, as they are known, any member of the group can call upon its fellow 'group' members to provide finance additional to that available under the normal Fund rules. Members of the group undertake to give one another assistance to certain predetermined limits. Loans made under such arrangements must be repaid through the Fund within three to five years. They bear interest at relatively low rates. The United Kingdom had recourse to the General Arrangements to Borrow in December 1964, in 1965 and 1969. Assistance under these arrangements is provided from members' own resources, not from the Fund. Indeed, Switzerland, although not a member of the Fund has provided up to $200 million under the scheme. When in August 1971, the Fund repaid the equivalent of $152 million under the GAB, this settled outstanding claims related to a further borrowing by the UK in June 1969. This was the first time since their initial activation in December 1964 that the Fund had no outstanding debts under the Agreements.

The Fund does not have any direct control over the decision on whether a request for assistance should be acceded to. On the other hand, the loans are guaranteed by the Fund, and a member country which has made a loan under the General Arrangements may request repayment from the Fund itself. The General Arrangements to Borrow should not be confused with the Basle Agreements of 1961, under which member countries of the Bank for International Settlements may request short term credits from other members.[1] These Agreements are, however, quite outside the jurisdiction of the Fund.

[1] The Bank for International Settlements was set up in 1930 to facilitate the collection of Germany's reparation payments: it consisted of Central Bank representatives of Belgium, Germany, France, Italy, Japan, the United Kingdom and the

Exchange Control

An objective of the IMF is the progressive elimination of exchange controls on current payments. Such controls were permitted in the early days of the Fund as a transitional measure, but the Fund has worked for their removal, particularly where they were discriminatory. Since 1952 the Fund has carried out a regular review of exchange restrictions with member countries imposing them. Member countries may impose discriminatory exchange controls against a country whose currency has been declared scarce in the Fund. Article 7 lays down the procedure for such a declaration. At the time of the Fund articles, this was hailed as a great victory for the non-American negotiators, who in this way might obtain permission to discriminate against the dollar if the United States continued to accumulate surpluses.[1]

In the event, the scarce currency clause has not been invoked, for even in the days of acute world dollar shortage, the Fund itself was never short of dollars. Simply because in the early years the Fund operations were on such a small scale; its dollars resources remained virtually intact. Twenty odd years after the ending of the war, many countries continued to apply exchange controls on current transactions. As we noted in Chapter 6, many countries not only use such controls but operate them on a discriminatory basis. Each year the Fund in its *Annual Report on Exchange Controls* lists the exchange controls in force in various countries. In some years the Report has been able to announce a reduction in their extent and severity; in others it has been forced to deplore their extension. But the Fund has at least provided a forum where such restrictions can be discussed and by naming the countries where restrictions are rampant it does at least provide the elements of a confrontation on the subject.

SHORT GUIDE TO THE LITERATURE

See Short Guide to Chapter 18.

United States. The B.I.S. has been an influential international maid-of-all-work; for example, it acted as a clearing office for European Payments Union settlements. Every year the B.I.S. publishes a most informative Annual Report on developments in the international monetary field.

[1] In his *Life of John Maynard Keynes* (cited above) p. 545, Sir Roy Harrod tells how he first came across the draft Article 7 in a crowded war-time train to Oxford. His exhilaration on reading the draft was such that he wanted to wake the soldiers sleepily sprawling over their seats to tell them that here was 'the real thing', which might save Britain from a post-war slump and make possible the social reforms upon which so much store was being set at that time. It seemed that at last the United States was fully alive to its responsibility as a creditor country.

CHAPTER 18

THE INTERNATIONAL MONETARY SYSTEM IN TRANSITION

The International Monetary Fund has for many years performed a useful role by supplying additional reserves for *deficit* countries. This allowed them to spread the adjustment of their balance of payments over a longer period. The 'breathing space' function has undoubtedly decreased the need for trade and exchange controls; but the responsibility for and the burden of adjustment remained with deficit countries; the Fund has been less successful in getting *surplus* countries to make a contribution to the return to equilibrium. No doubt in the context of a world of fixed exchange rates, the degree of domestic deflation in member countries would have been greater but for the Fund. It has also shown a degree of flexibility in meeting changing circumstances of world trade over the last turbulent decades.

But there has been growing dissatisfaction in many quarters with the Fund's inability to provide appropriate amounts and appropriate kinds of means of international settlement in line with the changing needs of international trade and economic growth as an alternative to having to rely for reserve creation on the accidents of gold mining and on US balance of payments deficits. At other times, it was the trend to international inflation, ascribed in part to the dollar flood and the inflexibility of exchange rates, on which major criticism focused. And finally there was growing unease about the consequences for international equilibrium of the 'asymmetry', the differential role assigned by the system to the US dollar and to other currencies in the adjustment process.

In the late 1960s, the international monetary order moved into a period of crisis and in 1971 one could speak of a breakdown. For some months, the major currencies had given up their official par value and the system turned into one of floating exchange rates; even after a return to formally fixed parities, the gold exchange standard had been finally transformed into a dollar standard as dollar inconvertibility was maintained 'for the time being'.

1. THE LIQUIDITY PROBLEM

In spite of the rapid growth of international trade in the late 1940s and 1950s, by about 1960 there was a growing feeling of disquiet at many aspects of the international economy. One matter of grave concern was the apparently slow growth of international reserves. Although the total volume of liquid resources has generally increased since the Second World War, the rate of growth has been slower than the expansion of world trade. Moreover, the growth of liquidity in the non-Communist world has been of a somewhat haphazard nature. It has tended to depend upon such accidents as gold mining developments, the sales of gold from the USSR, and the willingness of people in various countries to hold their international reserves in dollars. There has been no conscious policy of relating reserve growth to the expansion of international trade.

Now the development we have mentioned need not necessarily be disastrous. Provided reserves are well-distributed and that swings in countries' balances of payments are moderate, the world could manage with relatively small reserves. There is no fundamental sense in which reserves are 'adequate' or 'inadequate' and no generally accepted criterion by which this adequacy can be measured. Certainly, a slavish adherence to a fixed ratio of world imports to world liquidity could be misleading. But when large numbers of countries are compelled to slow down domestic growth or impose restrictions on imports and on capital movements in order to safeguard their reserves, there is *prima facie* evidence that international liquidity is insufficient to maintain the maximum possible growth rate or the largest possible volume of trade. This was the situation that seemed to threaten the world economy in the early 1960s. Table 11 shows how after 1951 reserves declined as a percentage of imports for all groups of countries. Evidently in the case of some countries, especially the less developed ones, the implications

TABLE 11. CHANGING PERCENTAGE OF RESERVES TO ANNUAL IMPORTS EXCLUDING CMEA COUNTRIES AND PEOPLE'S REPUBLIC OF CHINA

	1951	1960	1970
'The Ten'	73	60	31
USA	204	117	34
UK	22	29	13
All developed countries	68	57	32
Less developed countries	64	44	33
Total	67	55	32

Reserves = Gold, foreign exchange holdings and reserve position with the IMF.

SOURCE: *IMF Annual Report*, 1970.

of this trend are quite serious. Even more dramatic, although in terms of immediate domestic hardship less serious since reserves were initially at a much higher level, was the decline in the reserve position of the USA. In 1951 reserves were sufficient to cover two years' visible imports. By 1960 they covered fourteen months' imports, and by 1970 imports for only four months.

After 1971 the relevant indicators pointed in the opposite direction; countries were suffering partially 'imported' inflation and many felt compelled to impose restrictions on speculative capital inflows in an attempt to avoid further deterioration: there was *prima facie* evidence of an abundance of international liquidity. We have seen how for many years the growth of reserves had lagged seriously behind the growth of trade; but in 1970 and 1971, the value of world exports increased by about 28 per cent, the value of reserves by over 70 per cent. Between 1961 and 1969, total liquidity had increased by $13,000 million; between 1969 and 1971, the increase amounted to $52,000 million!

As important as the change in the amount of international liquidity was the change in its composition. Whereas in 1951 some 69 per cent of the world's monetary reserves consisted of gold and about 9 per cent of US dollars, by 1971 30 per cent consisted of gold and 39 per cent of US dollars. Table 12 emphasises this point, namely the growing significance of claims on the US as a proportion of international reserves—and of course these additional dollar holdings came into being only as the result of a massive and continuing US payments deficit. It is not too much to say that the rate of growth of world trade—and of world output—in the earlier part of that period would have been impossible but for the purchasing power and the liquidity provided by the US; Western Europe and Japan experienced export-led growth and all countries were glad to add dollars—which were convertible into gold— to their reserves. In the latter part of the period, the demand exercised by the US tended towards world inflation and the dollars became an embarrassment. Swelling dollar balances outside the US contrasted with dwindling gold reserves in the US and made their convertibility into gold less and less credible and thus shook confidence in the central tenet of the world monetary system.

Thus the international liquidity problem is not a simple one. It would clearly be impossible in a volume of this length to give a full discussion of the international liquidity problem; indeed any such discussion would rapidly become out of date. But every student of international economics should at least realize that the problem exists and that in looking for solutions one must keep in mind the twin dangers of world deflation and world inflation that can result from inappropriate amounts and in-

TABLE 12. GROWTH OF WORLD LIQUID RESERVES, 1951–1971
(billion $ US and percentages)

	Reserves at end of year 1951		Reserves at end of year 1960		Reserves at end of year 1971		Percentage increase 1951–1971
	$^b	Percentage of total	$^b	Percentage of total	$^{b1}	Percentage of total	
Gold	33·9	68·8	38·0	63·8	39·3	30·2	+ 16
Reserve position with MF	1·7	3·4	3·6	6·0	6·9	5·3	+ 306
SDR	0·7			6·4	4·9		
Foreign currency	13·7	27·8	18·9	31·2	77·6	59·6	+ 466
of which: US	4·2	8·8	11·1	18·3	51·0	39·2	+ 1,114
UK	8·2	16·7	7·1	12·1	7·1	5·5	− 13
Total	49·3	100·0	60·5	100·0	130·2	100·0	+ 164

1 In terms of SDR which at the beginning of the year were equal in value to the $, at the end of the year all figures would be about 8% lower.

SOURCE: *IMF Annual Reports and International Financial Statistics and NIESR estimates.*

appropriate kinds of liquidity and, as we shall see, from a reluctance to alter exchange rates in either an upward or downward direction.

2. SOME REMEDIES

Since the 1950s, a number of ways of tackling the liquidity problem have been suggested—apart from saying it does not exist! Originally, remedies fell broadly speaking into two groups, those which aimed directly at augmenting international liquidity and those involving what we might call a more economical use of existing liquidity, for example by increasing exchange rate flexibility. Later, there was greater emphasis not simply on increasing but on controlling the amount of liquidity and on its composition.

The Price of Gold

Perhaps the most direct way of creating more liquidity, and one advocated in various quarters since the early 1950s is a raising of the official gold price, which is the dollar price at which the US had undertaken as part of the IMF system to purchase gold from or sell it to central monetary institutions before suspending such transactions in August 1971 and thus making the dollar 'inconvertible'. This price was fixed at $35 an ounce as long ago as 1934 (and marginally raised to $38 early in 1972). So the official price of gold has remained virtually fixed for decades, while the prices of practically all other commodities in world trade have trebled or quadrupled. The effect of the fixed price of gold, it was argued, is to prevent a rise in the 'real' value of the world's gold reserves, to discourage production and to encourage consumption of the metal. A low gold price furthers its ever-growing use for jewellery and industrial purposes. Moreover, since from time to time it becomes widely believed that some increase in the official price is inevitable, there is a very large speculative demand for gold; a further significant proportion of annual output disappears into 'traditional' hoards. If the US gold price, and with it the price of monetary gold, were raised substantially, not only would real purchasing power of official gold holdings increase overnight; there would be an incentive to expand gold output, a disincentive to acquire gold for industrial use and speculators as well as 'ordinary' hoarders would be encouraged to disgorge their holdings.

Up to December 1971, US administrations had been adamant in their refusal to countenance any increase in the price of gold. Apart from economic considerations, they were reluctant to 'devalue' the dollar in relation to gold and had a political objection that an increase in the price of gold would help countries which least 'deserve' assistance, namely the major gold producers, the USSR and the Republic of South Africa, and the main gold 'hoarding' countries, for instance France.

Although a raising of the price of gold can provide an immediate increase in liquidity, it could have the serious side-effect of discouraging the development of new reserve media not direclty linked to either gold or individual currencies. In terms of overall reserves, what was gained in the short term on the gold front might be lost on the long-term front of monetary reform, as it would go no way at all towards establishing a more rational system of international reserve control. The volume of world reserves would still be a hit-and-miss affair, subject to the vagaries of gold output. Unless the gold price were constantly to be changed, there would be no mechanism for controlling the supply of international media of exchange. Partly for this reason, economists (but not central bankers!) outside France generally tended to reject the idea of a raising of the dollar price of gold.[1] Instead they tend to advocate one or other of the more sophisticated schemes for the solution of the international liquidity problem.

But while the advantages of a large increase in the official price of gold are arguable, a small increase of the kind effected in 1972 appears to have no (economic) merit whatever. If anything, it encouraged speculators in their belief that in spite of all the brave talk about 'demonetization', gold would continue as the base of the international money order and that eventually its official monetary price, as well as its private market price, would rise substantially.

In the past decade, continuing pressure by private demand on the supply and price of monetary gold has led to varying policy responses by monetary authorities. When the price came under heavy attack, in 1962 for instance, the US took the initiative in establishing the 'gold pool' formed by a group of central banks which were prepared to sell gold to private users outside the official monetary system at the same official price of $35 an ounce that served for transactions between central monetary institutions.

Sales were particularly high at times of lack of confidence in the monetary system generally and its key currency, the dollar, in particular. After a number of lesser 'runs into' gold, demand spiralled in 1968, following the devaluation of sterling before the operation could be seen

[1] There are of course some notably exceptions to this generalization. No less eminent an economist than Sir Roy Harrod has consistently advocated the raising of the dollar price of gold, e.g. in *Reforming the World's Money*, Macmillan, 1965.

In France the most distinguished advocate of raising the dollar price of gold is M. Jacques Rueff. He has set out his ideas on the whole gold question in *The Balance of Payments*, London, Macmillan, 1967.

to be successful, and when the dollar appeared the reserve currency next in line for devaluation.

At that time, the drain on the gold pool became so great that the total amounts inside the world monetary system declined, and the gold pool discontinued its policy of selling at the official price. Some 3,000 tons of gold, nearly two years' production, is believed to have gone to speculators. In March 1968, a two-tier gold market came into being with a price of $35 an ounce used for official transactions and for IMF accounting purposes, and a second market at which private demand and private supply match at a free price.

From then on, it was the *price* on the free gold market which indicated the state of confidence in and expectations of the dollar and the international monetary system as a whole, just as under the gold pool it had been the *quantities* demanded and sold that acted as signals.

In fact, the gold price rose sharply in 1968 to $42 an ounce, fluctuated between $32 and $39 for some time in 1969 and rose to what was then a record high of nearly $44. In 1970, a year of comparative calm in the international monetary field, the price plummeted and seemed to settle at $35 before, in 1971, it took off again, accompanying the various dollar crises of the year in a barely interrupted rise to reach the new record level of over $65 early in 1972 with 'informed' observers arguing about the future. Estimates have to take into account not only the state of confidence in the international monetary arrangements, but also the continually rising demand for industrial gold which by 1971-2 was assumed to have outpaced slowly rising—if not falling—production, and the narrowness of the gold market. Such developments are bound to call into question the monetary authorities' gold price policy and current forecasts in a field in which expectations tend to be self-realizing.

Stamp and Triffin

In the ferment of ideas on reforming the IMF that were current in the early 1960s, one of the most radical was that of the Hon. Maxwell Stamp, who advocated a scheme which at one blow would create additional international liquidity and put it into the hands of the countries who needed it most, namely the less developed countries. Stamp first put forward his proposals in the British press in 1960. He originally envisaged that some $3 billion of additional purchasing power would be created by the issue of fund certificates over say a twelve-month period. All of these certificates would be passed on to the developing countries, perhaps through an additional leading agency such as the IDA.[1] Each member of the Fund would accept these certificates when

[1] The functions of IDA are discussed in Chapter 24.

tendered by the Fund or by a Central Bank of a member country. They could be exchanged into any convertible currency.

In this somewhat radical form the Stamp proposals were hardly likely to be acceptable. Accordingly, to make them more attractive to orthodox financial interests, Stamp suggested[2] that certain countries suffering from inflation might be allowed to opt out of accepting the certificates. He further proposed that Fund certificates could be lent, not given, to developing countries. Such certificates might be loaned for a five-year period, during which time the IDA would pay interest on them. In his modified proposals, Stamp also accepted that some limit might reasonably be placed on the extent to which fund members were automatically obliged to accept certificates, which might carry a modest rate of interest. One of the attractions of the Stamp Plan is that it would ease the problem of world liquidity, and at the same time provide much needed assistance to developing countries. However the Plan has received relatively little support and has been much less discussed than another 'radical' proposal, that of Professor Triffin.

Triffin's proposals aim at an overall—and controllable—increase in international liquidity, together with the transfer of reserves in the form of dollars and sterling to the IMF. Triffin believes that the use of national currencies as international reserves is inherently destabilizing. As soon as confidence in a reserve currency wanes, holders will try to switch their reserves from the currency into gold, thus precipitating a scramble for gold or some other currency. Triffin accordingly advocates the gradual transfer of dollar and sterling holdings to the IMF. As time passes, he envisages that member countries of the IMF will hold an increasing proportion of their international reserves in the form of IMF deposits; indeed he suggests that every member of the IMF should keep at least 20 per cent of its reserves in the form of such deposits. Unlike the present holdings, these deposits would be guaranteed against devaluation and—unlike gold—would bear interest. On the basis of these deposits the IMF could then act as a true international central bank. It could add to these deposits by making loans in the form of 'created' deposits—just as a commercial banker in this way increases his deposits. There would, however, be a ceiling on the size of this credit-creation. Triffin suggested that the Fund should limit its net lending to a total which, over a year, would increase total world reserves by no more than, say 3 per cent. Secondly, Triffin wishes the Fund to be able to purchase or sell securities in the financial markets of the member countries. In this way, The Fund, again like a Central bank, would engage in open market operations.

[1] In *Moorgate and Wall Street*, autumn 1962.

If the Fund operated in the way Triffin suggested, it would be acting very much like a Central Bank. As a Central Bank controls domestic purchasing power, so would the IMF control international purchasing power. The reformed IMF would also gradually take over the dollar and sterling balances, thus relieving the US and Britain of what many people (but not all) regard as a destabilizing burden in modern conditions.[1] Triffin's Plan, although widely regarded as a brilliant piece of economic thinking has not met with a favourable response in Western Government circles. Many critics, particularly in Continental Europe, regard the Plan as a blue-print for international inflation—in spite of Triffin's insistence on the limitation of deposit expansion. In the event, reform of the IMF is now taking place along somewhat different lines than advocated by either Stamp or Triffin.

Special Drawing Rights

Lengthy discussions, which largely took place among the industrial country members of the IMF, finally resulted in the acceptance by the Fund of a scheme for the creation of what are now known as Special Drawing Rights (SDR). The scheme was formally outlined at the 1967 Annual Meeting of the IMF at Rio de Janeiro, and detailed proposals were approved by the Board of Governors in April 1968.

Such an SDR is not a line of credit, or part of a 'pool' of resources. It is simply an obligation to accept a drawing right from another member in exchange for an equal amount of convertible currency.

The basic difference between the SDR scheme and the other arrangements of the Fund is that the issue of a Special Drawing Right means an increase in the world's monetary reserves without any deposit of gold or currency by the participating countries. In other words, while the IMF in general enables better and fuller use to be made of existing monetary reserves, SDRs actually bring about an increase in reserves. Whereas drawing on the IMF have to be repaid, SDRs, once allocated continue permanently in existence.

Every member of the IMF has the right to participate in the newly

[1] Triffin's ideas are available in a number of publications. His original Plan is set out in his *Gold and the Dollar Crises*, Yale University Press (Paperback) 1961. The Triffin Plan is summarized and commented upon in H. G. Grubel's *World Monetary Reform. Plans and Issues*, London, Oxford University Press, 1963. Professor Grubel's book is an extremely valuable survey of various proposals for the reform of the international monetary system. It contains extracts from or summaries of the writings of Stamp, Harrod, Bernstein, Machlup, Roosa, Meade and Rueff, among many others. The book is a 'must' as a reference volume for all students who wish to fully understand this question.

created Special Drawing Account and is then entitled to share, in proportion to its Fund quota, in any allocation of SDRs which the Fund decides to make. These SDRs can be freely exchanged into foreign currency either by arrangement with another participant or by transfer to other IMF members *designated* by the Fund for this purpose. These are generally chosen from among those countries whose combined balance of payments and reserve positions are considered sufficiently strong. Also taken into account is the amount of SDRs countries already hold; where holdings are relatively low (because wide use has been made of SDRs) they can be 'reconstituted' to a level not below 30 per cent of original allocations; where holdings are high (because additional SDRs have been accepted and foreign currency given up in exchange) exemption from designation may be granted to allow the equalization of excess holdings.

Designated participants are obliged to supply any one of eight currencies which the Articles of Agreement call 'currencies convertible in fact'. The issuers of five of these have undertaken to convert balances of their currencies so supplied further into US dollars. The other three (the French, the UK and the US authorities) have undertaken to convert balances of their currencies into any one of the other two.

This somewhat complicated mechanism is intended to ensure that all participants have access to whichever of the three reserve currencies (which the Articles of Agreement in this context call the 'interconvertible currencies') it needs for the purpose of financing balance of payments outflows.

The so-called 'equal value' principle is fundamental to the scheme; it provides that it should make no difference to the users of SDRs whichever currency is provided and by whom. To give effect to it, conversions take place at foreign exchange rates obtaining on a specified date. The value of SDRs is defined as: SDR1 = 0·88671 grams of fine gold, which equals the gold content of 1 (1934) dollar. With the raising of the official dollar price of gold in 1972, 1 SDR is of course no longer equal to 1 US dollar but to about US $ 1·08.

The first allocation of SDR 3,414 million was made on January 1, 1970 to the 104 member countries who had elected to participate in the scheme and was entered in the Special Drawing Account. It was then divided among the participants in equal proportion to their Fund quotas so that each had its SDR holdings account credited with SDRs equal to 16·8 per cent of its quota. When the second allocation of SDR 2,949 million was made on January 1, 1971, 109 participants received SDRs equal to 10·7 per cent of that quota. SDR 2,952 million, equal to 10·6 per cent of their quota, was allocated on Janaury 1, 1972. By that time, the participants numbered 112 and accounted for 99 per cent of total Fund quotas.[1]

In these first two years, total transactions in SDRs amounted to near enough SDR 2,500 million, about 60 per cent of which consisted of transfers between participants (by designation or on a bilateral basis), 30 per cent of transfers from participants to the General Account of the Fund in respect of repurchases (repayments) of currencies borrowed and of borrowing charges; the rest were transfers from the General Account to participants.

Almost all countries made some use of SDR facilities in the first two years of operation, but to widely differing extents. The primary producers as a group, for instance, used a net third of their Special Rights in exchange for foreign currency. Among the industrial countries, the US used nearly one-third, the UK nearly one-fifth of their respective allocations. The other industrial countries as a group were the main net acceptors of SDRs and providers of foreign currency and ended the two-year period with SDRs amounting to one-and-a-half times their original allocation.

SDRs have thus made a definite if modest contribution to the solution of the international liquidity problem. At the end of 1971, they accounted for nearly 5 per cent of the world total of reserves, nearly double the liquidity provided directly through the Fund.

The amount of new SDRs to be created in each 'basic' period of five years (after the initial three year period 1970–2) can be varied, taking into account the world liquidity position and the level of aggregate world demand. It is thus conceivable that in view of the inflationary glut of inconvertible dollar reserves existing in the monetary system, allocations for the period commencing 1973–4 may be of token amounts only.

In any case, SDRs provide the first example of consciously created international liquidity, the amount of which can be decided in accordance with international policy and hopefully in accordance with the need or otherwise for additional world purchasing power.

Future allocations of SDRs could be made on a selective basis, rather than according to members' Fund quotas which by their very nature heavily favour the wealthy over the poor countries (the 1972 allocation to the US of SDR710 billion, for instance, equals that of all less developed countries taken together). At the third UNCTAD in 1972, it was proposed

[1] D. S. Cutler, 'The Operations and Transactions of the Special Drawing Account' Finance and Development, no. 4, 1971, gives an analysis covering the first 21 months. Later data will be found in further issues of Finance and Development and in IMF International Financial Statistics.

to distribute SDRs either directly to less developed countries or through multilateral agencies and aid schemes. Third World purchasing power and total world reserves would increase. This has become known as 'the link' between aid and liquidity. No agreement was reached on this proposal in the 'Stamp' tradition,[1] and it was referred to the IMF for further consideration.

SDRs have been cast in further and significant roles at the centre of a reformed international monetary order, following the breakdown of the traditional IMF system in 1971. It is proposed that SDRs should act as the standard of international value in which countries could express their parities, and provide the 'pivot' of the structure of international currencies and cross rates, a function which has hitherto been carried out by the US dollar.[2] Perhaps as a 'dry run' for its future function, the IMF has since early 1972 expressed the value of its transactions and account entries in terms of SDRs rather than of US dollar equivalents.

It is further suggested that SDRs might evolve from a marginal to the principal international reserve asset. Ultimately, the existing reserve currency balances could be funded into special allocations of SDRs. To show the order of magnitudes involved: at the beginning of 1972, the number of SDR units outstanding amounted to 9,400 million; US dollar reserve liabilities to \$50,000 million (= SDR46,000 million); the sterling balances to about SDR6,000 million. Clearly SDRs still have a long way to go.

3. THE PROBLEM OF EXCHANGE FLEXIBILITY

The founders of the IMF had been extremely conscious of the instabilities experienced in the pre-war period and opted strongly for fixed exchange rates, with parity changes as a last resort. But they were less conscious of the consequences of insufficient flexibility. In the event, stability turned out to be rigidity. This favoured the emergence of balance of payments disequilibria, made them more intractable and increased the need for international liquidity. While the decision to alter a rate of exchange is taken by a member government, Article 4 lays down that the Fund must be notified in advance.

If the proposed change, together with cumulative previous changes alters the parity by less than 10 per cent, the Fund can raise no objection. If it exceeds 10 per cent, the Fund's consent is required; the time allowed for the Fund to make up its mind varies with the magnitude of

[1] See pp. 242 ff.
[2] This question is discussed by J. Williamson in 'The Choice of a Pivot for Parities', *Princeton Essays in International Finance*, no. 90, November 1971.

the proposed change. For example if the change is greater than 20 per cent the Fund may ask for a period of at least three days in which to communicate its position. In practice it is impossible for the Fund to carry out a lengthy inquisition into the merits of a proposed change in parity and in any case the final decision rests with the Government of the member country.

Nevertheless, it is a fact that in the first twenty years of the existence of the Fund, exchange rate alterations of the major currencies had been very rare indeed. The situation changed after 1967 and by the end of 1971 the whole world currency structure had been modified in such a way as to devalue the dollar by about 9 per cent and to assist the US to shed its payments deficit and stop the 'dollar flood'. The last comparable realignment had taken place in 1949; at that time most countries devalued against the dollar and ultimately closed the 'dollar gap'. In the intervening period, the only notable changes had been the devaluation of the French franc in 1957–8, the revaluation of the German mark and with it the Dutch guilder in 1961, and the 10-year-long float of the Canadian dollar (discussed in Chapter 14) which came to an end in 1962.

As currency adjustments made under the IMF regime were infrequent, drawings on the Fund had to be greater than if exchange rates had been more flexible and additional resources had to be found. The large number of *ad hoc* methods used to make further reserves available through and under the auspices of the Fund enabled countries to ride out speculative pressures but also to avoid exchange variations even in the case of 'fundamental imbalances'. Indeed, advocates of greater flexibility claim that the system has been altogether too successful in preventing recourse to currency adjustment as a corrective for balance of payments disequilibrium, whether a deficit or a surplus, and for 'unrealistic' exchange rates, whether overvalued or undervalued.

Accordingly, countries had to rely almost entirely on domestic financial policy as regulator of the balance of payments. It is arguable that deficit countries have been compelled to resort to domestic deflation and that surplus countries have suffered inflation more frequently and more damagingly than would have been necessary in a regime of more flexible rates or a more flexible attitude.

At different times, both deflationary and inflationary dangers were said to be inherent in the fixed exchange rates system. In this context, Joan Robinson has identified a deflationary kink in the 'new mercantilist' system of the 1960s in which every country likes to have a surplus,[1] and G. Haberler a world inflationary bias in a system in which wages,

[1] Joan Robinson, *The New Mercantilism*, Cambridge, 1966, pp. 12 ff.

costs *and* exchange rates are inflexible in a downward direction in deficit countries and adjustment is left to rising wages and costs in surplus countries.[1]

Certainly, both deficit and surplus countries have been unhappy applying with full force the contraction or expansion policies traditionally associated with their relative positions, fearing they would result in deflation or inflation instead of the desired disinflation or reflation. As they have also been reluctant to use alterations in the exchange rate as alternatives in such circumstances, the adjustment process under a rigid exchange rate system was bound to work badly or break down completely, leaving a tendency to polarization between persistent deficit and surplus countries and contributing to the world inflationary pressures experienced by the international economy during the late 1960s and the early 1970s.

In the late 1960s exchange rate alterations became much more frequent. But that did not at first reflect a major change in attitudes towards flexibility. When devaluations or revaluations came, they had not been chosen but suffered, with national authorities conceding defeat after a costly defence of (unrealistic) parities. They submitted to the pressures of speculative capital flows across the exchanges which anticipated or imposed the alterations.

After years of applying income-reducing and income-switching policies, massive borrowing and a number of expensive defensive actions against runs on the pound, sterling was devalued in 1967 and a number of other currencies followed suit. In 1968 it took a massive leakage of gold from the international monetary system to private purchasers before the official gold price was abolished as far as private demand was concerned and the two-tier gold market introduced. France lost four-tenths of her substantial official reserves in 1968 before devaluing the franc a year later; Germany suffered inflationary inflows amounting to more than $12,000 million in the six months before the mark was floated in September 1969 in anticipation of the formal revaluation in the following October. In 1971, Germany took in $10,000 million in defence of the parity during the first four months. Over the two days May 3 and May 4 the German Bundesbank had to absorb an additional $1,000 million and on the morning of the 5th a further $1,000 million was taken in within the first forty minutes of trading—all this pressure was needed to make the German authorities give up maintaining the parity and allowing the mark to float. Similarly, in August 1971, it needed more massive flows of inconvertible dollars before the major

[1] G. Haberler, *Money in the International Economy*, Institute of Economic Affairs, 1969, pp. 40–41.

industrial countries began their four months' float. In June 1972 the pound sterling was allowed to float after only a week of persistent selling by external holders, but even by then the reserves had lost £1,000 million.

Official attitudes towards exchange rate flexibility are clearly changing, however. The promptness with which Britain initiated a currency float in June 1972 followed the statement by the Chancellor of the Exchequer in the Budget Debate that he would not let an inappropriate exchange rate stand in the way of the needs of an expanding economy. Similar attitudes have been expressed by the authorities of other countries. At their Washington meeting in December 1971 the ministers of the Group of Ten countries expressly linked their support for the principle of stable exchange rates with a wish to see a 'suitable degree of flexibility' established as part of the reform of the international monetary system. 'Pending agreement on longer-term monetary reform' an automatic element of flexibility was also built into the IMF system by the provision for $2\frac{1}{4}$ per cent margins of exchange rate fluctuations either side of parity instead of the 1 per cent limit applicable up to then. This modification of IMF procedure had long been suggested as a means of increasing flexibility and thereby counteracting a possible liquidity shortage.[1]

Another idea was the scheme for getting some degree of exchange rate flexibility while avoiding the alarums and speculative strains which accompany present adjustments in exchange rates. As we saw in Chapter 17 part of the difficulty of the present system arises from the almost inevitable delaying of exchange rate adjustments until they are overdue, with the consequence that very large adjustments become necessary.

To avoid some of the difficulties inherent in the present system Professor Meade has suggested that in any year parities of Fund members might be changed by, say 2 per cent above or below the previous years' parity. This arrangement would certainly provide for ease and smoothness of adjustment, although it would still be exposed to the criticism that it leaves the door open to speculation, just as does the present scheme.

Meade's proposal has been developed in some detail by Dr J. H. Williamson[2] of York University who suggests that a country desirous of changing its parity should announce its intention in advance, but

[1] G. N. Halm, 'The Bank Proposal: The Limits of Permissible Exchange Variations', *Special Paper* no. 6, International Finance Section, Princeton University 1965.

[2] J. H. Williamson, 'The Crawling Peg', *Essays in International Finance*, no. 50, December 1965, Princeton University.

change the parity in small amounts say 1/26th of 1 per cent per week. The small size of the adjustments would make speculation very much less attractive than at present, although of course countries operating the arrangement would have to follow appropriate interest rate policies. At the same time, the exchange rate alteration would influence payments flows by slowly bringing about price adjustments. This proposal has been christened the 'crawling peg' method of adjustment. So far the scheme has not become practical politics, although among many economists it is regarded as an ingenious method of tackling a very intractable adjustment problem. The only country applying such a 'crawling peg' or sliding exchange rate method is Brazil.

4. SHORT-TERM CAPITAL MOVEMENTS

The more pronounced disequilibria of the late 1960s and the emergence of funds highly mobile internationally and on a scale not previously experienced resulted from a combination of changes of substance with developments of a technical nature: the polarization in balance of payments persisted with the US deficit continuing and deteriorating and the corresponding surplus of other industrial countries growing. This created a situation in which specific currencies were consistently identified with potential revaluation while others were near-permanent candidates for devaluation. Cycles of economic activity and associated policies tended to be out of phase between countries and by 1970 resulted in interest rate differentials which set off or contributed to destabilizing capital flows. The increasing economic interdependence and integration through trade and investment favoured the international transmission of domestic disequilibria; after the restoration of convertibility of the major currencies in 1958, parities were no longer protected by the extensive system of trade and payment controls in force until then; convertibility and the formation of the EEC and EFTA after 1958 considerably raised the level of activity of capital movements by reducing the risks and increasing the potential returns of international investment; the intermediation process became more efficient with the emergence and growth of institutions that facilitate international investment.

The Euro-Currency Market

In this connection, we have to mention, though we cannot discuss in any detail, two closely linked channels through which funds move with particular ease: the Euro-dol'ar and Euro-currency markets, the size of which was estimated to have risen from \$57,000 million at the end of 1970 to \$71,000 million in 1971,[1] and the inter-company accounts of the multinational corporations.

Euro-dollars are dollar balances deposited with commercial banks outside the USA, not being exchanged into local currency but remaining denominated in dollars. These banks—which also include overseas branches of American banks—constitute the Euro-dollar market. The Euro-currency market includes in addition other currencies deposited outside their national areas and maintaining their original denomination.

After the Second World War, the Soviet Union and other East European countries placed dollar balances with London and Paris banks rather than with banks in the US for fear of their 'attachment' by American courts; when such balances were lent to borrowers outside the US in the form of dollars, the first step towards the Euro-dollar market had been taken. Two monetary policy measures furthered its development on a large scale. 1957 saw a sharp rise in UK interest rates and the imposition of restrictions on the use of sterling credits to finance trade between non-sterling countries. This brought a demand for dollars, the supplies being based on the US balance of payments deficit. The resulting business has tended to be transacted in Europe rather than in the US because of the existence of a regulation made by the Federal Reserve System (regulation Q) which limited the amount of interest banks may pay on deposits inside the US. Euro-dollar transactions remain competitive partly because of the smaller margins on which the banks are able to operate as dealings in the market are confined to large lots, usually \$1 million or more.

The chief use made of short-term Euro-dollar or Euro-currency loans is the financing of international trade. Medium-term finance for up to five years is now also provided partly by the method of 'rolling over' shorter-term credit. This is used to finance investment in any country where domestic credit policies make for tight or expensive credit conditions. Still longer-term facilities are provided by the Euro-bond end of the market with users ranging from big firms to local authorities and national Governments. In the five years ending 1972 the total value of such loans amounted to about \$16,000 million, over a period of approximately twenty years. The market has grown rapidly and almost continuously since 1957 from a few hundred million dollars to its present size. There is some uncertainty about the precise figures for total assets and liabilities, partly because it is necessary to dis-

[1] Bank for International Settlements, 41st Annual Report, Basle, June 1971, and 42nd Annual Report, Basle, June 1972.

tinguish between credit available to final borrowers and gross credit which includes inter-bank lending.

The main *theoretical* issue on which interest has centred is the extent of growth of credit not due to additional primary deposits but to a credit 'multiplier' analogous to that which operates in ordinary domestic monetary systems. A related question is how and to what extent the market reflects or affects the US balance of payments deficit.

The chief *policy* issue raised by the existence of the Euro-currency market concerns the way in which it has added a new dimension to the mobility of short-term funds which have tended to overwhelm or at least strongly to limit the effectiveness of national monetary and exchange rate policies.

The big international companies have a voracious appetite for capital; but they also have substantial temporary surpluses. The Euro-currency market grew around this dual need for opportunities for profitable short-term lending and for cheap short- to medium-term borrowing. At times these companies use the market to switch funds out of one currency and into another in response to interest rate differentials or parity change expectations. These speculative and precautionary transfers—aiming at making a profit or avoiding a loss—also take the form of leads and lags in inter-company payments. What makes the impact in times of crisis so devastating to the currencies on which their attention focuses is that both interest rate differentials and currency change expectations suggest the move of such funds in the same, easily foreseeable and therefore 'speculatively safe' and profitable, direction.

We can illustrate the situation with the build-up of the crisis in 1970–1. Domestic economic developments had led to a progressive easing of money rates and credit conditions in the US. In most European countries, the economic cycle was in a different phase, interest rates were high and short-term money flowed in heavy volume from the US to the Euro-dollar market, bringing down its rates. This in turn widened the rate differential between the Euro-dollar market and the domestic markets of the Continent and so the US money moved onto the national money markets and central bank reserves of Europe and, most of all, of Germany. As through most of the period the German authorities maintained stringent credit conditions and high interest rates as an anti-inflationary measure in the final phase of a boom period, German banks and industrial firms found the Euro-dollar market attractive and borrowed over $6,000 million direct.

A number of important consequences can be identified. Firstly, the low interest rate policy in the US, intended to encourage domestic investment for expansion, was in part frustrated by the outflow of funds in search of high interest rates; the high interest rate policy in Germany, intended to discourage investment, was in part frustrated as firms borrowed more freely and more cheaply abroad: reflation in the US was delayed, inflation in Germany aggravated. Secondly, the US balance of payments position deteriorated, the German reserves increased by about $6,000 million. Thirdly, the changes in the reserve position in the two countries led to pressures in the direction of depreciation of the dollar and appreciation of the mark. Fourthly, as these pressures continued, parity change expectations reinforced the flows and led to the decision of the German authorities in May 1971 to let the mark float up and prepared the decision taken in August 1971 by the US authorities to let the dollar float down.

A Theory of International Capital Flows

The way in which even before 1970 the wide disparities in the relative position of monetary policies in different countries have led to substantial capital flows which in their turn have tended to frustrate national monetary and exchange rate policies, has led in Canada to the suspension of fixed exchange rates and in many countries to widespread demand for the introduction of more or less stringent controls of short-term capital movements.

The problem has furthered theoretical and empirical study of the relationship between international capital flows and domestic monetary variables, not least in the hope that ultimately it may be possible for the authorities to predict the effects of domestic and foreign monetary policy changes so as to deal with or avoid undesirable effects of such capital movements, possibly without the application of exchange controls. A study commissioned by the OECD [1] brings out clearly the high degree of sensitivity of capital movements to changes in interest rates in various individual countries and to other aspects of monetary policy. More specifically, it gives a picture of the consequences of a change in US monetary conditions—via the Euro-dollar market—on the capital account of the balance of payments of other countries.

It also comes to the not altogether surprising conclusion that the US interest rate changes provide a most powerful influence on Euro-dollar rate changes, while domestic rates of the UK and Germany modify the Euro-dollar rate only marginally. For other countries, like Italy, the relationship is all one way from the Euro-dollar market to the Italian domestic money market. The study accepts earlier estimates that a

[1] W. H. Branson and R. D. Hill, Jr, *Capital Movements in the OECD Area*, December 1971.

one-percentage-point change in the US short-term rate generates a one-point change in the Euro-dollar rate with a slight lag.[1]

The traditional theory of international financial capital movements relates capital *flows* to *levels* of interest rate differentials and suggests flows continuing as long as the differences in rate levels continue. On this view a country could derive a continuing improvement in the capital account position of its balance of payments as long as its interest rates are raised and maintained above relevant rates abroad.[2]

In contrast to such 'flow theories', the OECD study is based on a theory of international capital flows which relates *stocks* of assets to *levels* of interest rates or capital *flows* to *changes* in interest rate differentials. It is assumed that there is an optimum composition of portfolios made up of domestic and foreign assets and that the fraction of total assets held abroad is in part a function of the level of respective interest rates.[3]

On this view an increase in domestic interest rates will cause a shift in the *stock* of portfolios towards domestic assets and to the extent that total assets grow an equivalent reallocation of marginal additions to portfolios towards domestic assets.[4] This 'continuing flow effect' is presumed to be modest relative to the once-and-for-all 'stock-shift effect'. This view has obvious implications both from the viewpoint of the kind of financing that countries may require and for the role to be assigned to monetary policy as an instrument of domestic stabilization, as the foreword to the study points out.

5. THE DOLLAR AND THE IMF SYSTEM

We have already mentioned the 'asymmetry' in the roles assigned to the US dollar and to other currencies in the adjustment process by the IMF system. Its position at the centre of the system gave a number of international roles to the dollar. It was to serve as an international *unit of*

---

[1] P. H. Hendershott, 'The Structure of International Interest Rates: The US Treasury Bill Rate and the Euro-dollar Deposit Rate', *Journal of Finance*, September 1967; and S. W. Black, 'An Econometric Study of Euro-dollar Borrowing by New York Banks and the Rate of Interest on Euro-Dollars', *Journal of Finance*, March 1971.

[2] For this view see, e.g., R. A. Mundell, 'The Monetary Dynamics of International Adjustment under Fixed and Flexible Exchange Rates', *Quarterly Journal of Economics*, May 1960.

[3] Other considerations, abstracted from in this context, include risk evaluations.

[4] This 'portfolio-equilibrium stock-adjustment' model of capital movements was developed by T. D. Willett in his 'A Portfolio Theory of International Short-Term Capital Movements', Ph.D. Thesis, University of Virginia, 1967, and by W. H. Branson in his *Financial Capital Flows in the US Balance of Payments*, Amsterdam, 1968.

account in the sense that most other currencies expressed their parities in terms of the dollar as well as in terms of gold. The declared parities of currencies was made effective by the intervention of the respective monetary authorities who buy and sell their own currencies at all times at par (allowing for a margin of fluctuation), using the dollar as *intervention currency* for this purpose in most cases and losing and gaining external reserves in the process. As other currencies actively adjust to the dollar, its own value is maintained without any intervention by the US authorities who gain or lose reserves in passive response. In a sense, the US is the only country without an exchange rate policy.

This role as the pivot around which the system moves presupposes a fixed relationship between the dollar and gold. This is made effective by the US authorities' at all times buying gold from and selling it to central monetary institutions at the official price. This guaranteed convertibility —which was suspended in August 1971—had made the dollar 'as good as gold', an acceptable part of a country's official reserves, and added the role of *reserve currency* to its other functions. Of course each dollar so added to reserves originated in and is an expression of a US balance of payments deficit. Insofar as other countries are prepared to accept dollars in this way (and so increase international liquidity) the US can run a greater cumulative deficit than would otherwise be the case and obtain in effect 'free' command over real resources.

It has become customary to describe such a benefit as the gain from 'seignorage'.[1] According to a dictionary definition, this is the difference between the circulation value of a coin and the cost of bullion and of the minting. The meaning of the term has been generalized as the net value of resources accruing to the issuer of—in this case international— money. One can distinguish[2] between its 'current' portion—the increase of real absorption made possible by the cumulative deficit in the balance of payments, and the 'capital' portion—the yield on the additional investment of resources abroad made possible by this deficit.[3] Through years of US deficit, the acceptance of large dollar flows by Western Europe and Japan enabled the US administration to finance military expenditure and development assistance abroad and the big US firms to build up a wide network of overseas affiliates without running

[1] H. G. Grubel, 'The Distribution of Seignorage from International Liquidity Creation', *Monetary Problems of the International Economy*, Chicago, 1969, pp. 269 ff.

[2] H. G. Johnson, 'Appendix: A Note on Seignorage and the Social Saving from Substituting Credit for Commodity Money', op. cit., pp. 323 ff.

[3] See also B. J. Cohen, *The Future of Sterling as an International Currency*, Macmillan, 1971, pp. 35 ff. Cohen discusses seignorage and the costs and benefits of a reserve currency from the point of view of the pound sterling.

into serious shortages of foreign exchange. The value of assets so acquired by US firms increased from $16,000 million in 1955 to $71,000 million at the end of 1969 and $76,000 million at the end of 1970.[1] The calculation of the continuing benefit to the US must take into account the annual income receipts from US international investments which between 1960 and 1971 increased from over $3,000 million to just under $13,000 million.[2]

The Dollar Standard

The cumulative net outflow of dollars into foreign reserves had, by the end of 1971, reached $51,000 million. Set against the total of $12,500 million in official US reserves, the dollar had for all practical purposes become inconvertible into gold even before President Nixon suspended convertibility officially in August 1971. This meant that the world payments system was in effect on a dollar standard. But this did not end the asymmetrical position of the dollar in the world monetary system. It was suggested[3] that the US was now relieved of having to manage its domestic policies with the goal of balancing its international accounts and that it is, on the contrary, up to the other countries to adjust to the US payments situation. In the case of a US deficit, surplus countries must either accumulate dollars or inflate, appreciate their currency, or impose exchange controls.

That this is the choice facing surplus countries is confirmed by the events of the crisis year 1971. In that year the US balance of payments deficit amounted to nearly $30,000 million on the 'official transactions balance'. This included $3,000 million deficit on trade and an outflow of more than $21,000 million of short-term capital as well as over $4,000 million on private long-term investment. In the run-up to the crisis the surplus countries of Western Europe and Japan chose to take in dollars corresponding to this deficit and to transfers from the Euro-dollar market into national currencies—and they 'imported' inflation. After August of that year, they allowed their currencies to appreciate against the dollar and in December they accepted differential revaluations against the dollar to enable the US to shed its deficit. The arrangements of the 'Smithsonian agreement' included the increase in the dollar price of 'official' gold from $35 to $38 an ounce, that is, by 8·57 per cent, a realignment of the parities of the major world currencies

[1] US Department of Commerce, *Survey of Current Business*, October 1970, and *Economic Commentary*, Federal Reserve Bank of Cleveland, 1972.

[2] US Department of Commerce, *Survey of Current Business*, September 1972.

[3] G. Haberler and T. Willett, *A Strategy for US Balance of Payments Policy*, Washington, 1971.

which was almost immediately followed by exchange rate changes of other countries and provision for a widening of the permissible margin of fluctuation to 2·25 per cent either side of parity from the 1 per cent in force before August 1971. Individual parities were to be expressed either (finally) in a specified amount of gold or as a temporary 'central' or 'middle' rate, a legal distinction without analytical difference.

The realignment represented the most comprehensive parity change since the 1949 devaluation of most major currencies against the dollar which in practice brought the 'Dollar Gap' to an end and ushered in a twenty-year balance of payments deficit for the United States. Twenty-four countries including France, the UK and a number of sterling area countries maintained unchanged par values in terms of gold which in effect revalued their currencies against the dollar by 8·57 per cent. Twelve countries including sterling area countries but also Yugoslavia set new par values, most of which devalued against both gold and the dollar by varying amounts; twenty-eight countries, including most industrial countries of Western Europe, fixed new central rates, many of which were higher than their gold parity and corresponded to a re-valuation against the dollar of between 2·44 per cent in the case of Finland, 11·57 per cent for the Benelux Countries and Austria (all countries with a very high degree of trade dependence on West Germany), 13·58 per cent for West Germany and 16·88 per cent for Japan. Most Latin American and other countries with a high degree of trade dependence on the United States, like South Korea, Thailand, etc., maintained unchanged dollar parities, and a few countries like Canada continued a floating rate. The Soviet rouble maintained its relationship to gold and thus in effect revalued against the dollar.

To translate these 'nominal' parity changes into 'effective' changes that express the alterations in the competitive position and thus allow us to evaluate the likely impact on the balance of payments situation we have to weight the new parities in accordance with the trade pattern of the individual countries. This suggests an effective rate of devaluation of the dollar of 7 per cent against all currencies and of 12 per cent against the currencies of the Group of Ten countries, and a hoped for turn-around of the payments position of the order of $8,000 million over the years 1972 and 1973.[1]

While the Smithsonian agreement brought about a currency realign-ment to enable the US to shed its deficit and introduced a wider fluctua-tion margin around fixed parities, there remained the need for a long-term reconstruction of the international monetary system that had been

[1] G. Haberler, 'Prospects for the Dollar Standard', *Lloyds Bank Review*, July 1972, p. 2.

brought close to collapse. Even the most optimistic did not envisage a solution for some years, especially as it was widely recognized that new monetary rules would have to be complemented by new and improved trading rules at a rather unpropitious moment when the commitment to liberalization was less than universal.

For a time, however, consensus appeared at least to exist on a number of key points. A new monetary order will have to incorporate a fixed exchange rate system operating with greater flexibility and provisions for more frequent and therefore smaller and less dramatic changes of parity; a system that would allow the dollar to exercise an active national balance of payments and exchange rate policy rather than the traditional approach of 'benign neglect' which leaves to other countries the burdens of adjustment; the reintroduction of dollar convertibility, a reserve medium, the quantity of which would be subject to conscious control rather than reflect passively the balance of payments position of a single country or the accidents of gold mining, and which would ultimately move forward from being a marginal and supplementary means of liquidity to exercising the functions of the existing reserve currencies and of gold. Increasingly informed discussion is casting the SDR in the role of the 'pivot' around which the international currency structure can move.

SHORT GUIDE TO THE LITERATURE

I have given fairly extensive footnote references, which the keen student will wish to follow up. In particular I would commend S. Horie, *The International Monetary Fund, Retrospect and Prospect*, London, 1964. It is possible to keep abreast of developments in the Fund organization by consulting the Fund's *Annual Reports*. There are numerous books and articles on proposals for reforming the IMF system. The reader will wish to consult Triffin's proposals in one of the original sources (see footnote, p. 244); I also commend the booklet published by the International Finance Section, Princeton University, *International Monetary Arrangements: The Problem of Choice, Report on the Deliberations of an International Study Group of 32 Economists*, 1964.

A most authoritative work of reference is *The International Monetary Fund, 1945–1965, Twenty Years of International Monetary Co-operation*, vol. I, *Chronicle*, vol. II, *Analysis*, vol. III, *Documents*, IMF, Washington, 1970. F. Hirsch, *Money International*, Pelican Books, 1969, surveys later problems, policies, and prospects in a very readable form. A theoretical and analytical approach rather than a policy-related approach to a later generation of issues concerning the international monetary system is taken in the symposium *Monetary Problems of the International Economy*, edited by R. A. Mundell and A. K. Swoboda, University of Chicago Press, 1969, and in the monograph *International Monetary Reform* by G. Walshe, Macmillan, 1971. For a study of the current developments, on the other hand, the following are recommended: the annual reports of the Federal Reserve Bank of New York for 1970 and 1971, and of the Bank for International Settlements for the same years; this latter gives the most comprehensive accounts of the movements of the Euro-dollar and Euro-currency markets. The theoretical issues of the Euro-dollar system are discussed in A. K. Swoboda, 'The Euro-dollar Market: An Interpretation', February 1968, and F. H. Klopstock, 'The Euro-dollar Market: Some Unresolved Issues', March 1968, both essays in *International Finance*, Princeton University, and R. N. Cooper, 'Notes on Euro-dollars, Reserve Dollars and Asymmetries in' the International Monetary System', in *Journal of International Economics, 1972*, which latter also deals with the wider issue of the 'dollar standard'.

CHAPTER 19

THE PROBLEM OF STERLING

1. THE BACKGROUND

In Chapter 15 we noted that the gold standard of the latter nineteenth century could with accuracy be described as a sterling standard. Sterling was used widely both as a store of value—or to use more modern terminology as an international liquid asset, and as a medium of international exchange. It was able to fulfil the former role because the whole world had confidence in the stability of sterling in terms of gold; there was little fear of a change in the sterling-gold parity. Neither did it seem likely that goods and services purchased in the United Kingdom for sterling would undergo rapid and violent price changes.

Sterling was more profitable and convenient than gold as an international asset and as a medium of exchange. Unlike gold, sterling investments earned interest. Sterling was also a more acceptable medium of exchange, since it was obviously easier and cheaper to transfer money balances from one country to another than to transport gold. Furthermore, since London was the financial centre of the world, and British banks had offices in the capitals and major cities of most countries, the transfer of funds could be effected relatively easily. A bill accepted by a London Banker or recognized Accepting House could be used to finance transactions not in any way involving the trading of goods with the United Kingdom. In the nineteenth century a number of developing countries borrowed heavily from London, undertaking to service their debt in sterling. This provided them with a further motive for holding sterling reserves. The very fact that sterling was used so widely had a cumulative effect; once London was established as the leading financial centre and the pound widely regarded as 'good as gold', it became difficult for any other centre to develop. Even countries wishing to hold a substantial proportion of their reserves in gold found it convenient also to supplement them with holdings of sterling, since London was the main distribution centre of newly mined gold. There were also political reasons for the pre-eminence of sterling; the colonies were compelled to back their currencies by sterling. Even when they became Dominions with their own banking systems, such countries usually retained strong sterling links.

Before 1914, and indeed for many years after, there was no formal

sterling area. At that time sterling-using countries were more appro‹
priately regarded as belonging to a circle of nations with a commo›
interest in holding and using sterling. At the centre of the circle wa.
Britain, closely surrounded by the colonies and later the Dominions›
which with the exception of Canada were always prepared to hol‹
sterling without limit. Outside the group, but still part of the circl‹
were the Latin American countries and Japan; countries which nor
mally held reserves in sterling, and accepted sterling without limit. Th‹
membership of this group fluctuated; there was a tendency for member
to adhere to or to drop out of the circle for various periods. Finally, o›
the edge of the circle were countries (mostly in Europe) which althougł
not normally accepting sterling without limit, used it widely and nor
mally held part of their reserves in sterling.[1]

Between the Wars

During the 1914–18 War the growing political and economic strengtł
of the United States changed the centre of gravity of the world economy
this change was reflected by the fact that the pound had to share it‹
role as an international currency with the dollar. What Professor Alar
Day has described as 'an uneasy and half-realized dyarchy' was created.²
The bi-polarization of financial centres created serious difficulties fo›
the pound. A deterioration in the external position of the USA migh‹
be the signal for a flow of capital to London, but one all too likely tc
be reversed as the US position improved. In the late 1920s the problen
became even more acute as the result of the growth of Paris as an inde
pendent financial centre. At that time there were three currencies anc
three currency centres subject to the ebb and flow of capital movement‹
resulting from the all too frequent speculative tensions.

Somewhat ironically, it was the retreat of Britain from the gold
standard in 1931 which saw the establishment of a reasonably recog‹
nizable sterling area, although lacking a legal constitution and any
institutional organization. When Britain left the gold standard, a
number of countries with close economic relations with the UK decided
to cut their formal link with gold but to retain the link between their
currencies and sterling. Such countries no longer declared an official
exchange rate with gold, but with sterling. Normally this rate was kep‹

[1] The role of sterling in the pre-1914 era is discussed by Professor Brian Tew in
International Monetary Co-operation 1945–65, Hutchinson University Library, and
Professor A. C. L. Day, *The Future of Sterling*, Oxford, Clarendon Press, 1953. In
particular the preceding and following paragraphs follow closely Professor Day's
analysis.
[2] Ibid. p. 31.

stable in terms of sterling, although in the 1930s there were a number of cases of parity changes. For example, in 1933 New Zealand devalued the New Zealand pound in terms of sterling in order to compete more successfully with Denmark in the dairy produce market. The sterling group also tended (as before the 1931 devaluation) to hold reserves in the form of sterling balances in London. These members of the pre-war sterling area consisted of most Commonwealth countries, with the exception of Canada and South Africa,[1] and the addition of Egypt, Iraq, Eire and Scandinavian countries. Although these countries were generally regarded as constituting the sterling system other countries continued to use sterling. Some, notably Japan and the Argentine, tried to maintain their currencies at par with sterling and also held considerable sterling reserves. Such countries, however, also held substantial holdings of gold and dollars, and would adjust these holdings in accordance with changes in their balances of payments. The less peripheral members on the other hand, absorbed fluctuations in their balance of payments by varying their sterling holdings.

A country holding a sterling balance in London could convert that balance into gold or dollars without hindrance. Thus if one member country of the system, say Australia, had a deficit in any year it would normally finance this by running down its sterling holdings. It could if it wished convert some of its sterling into gold in order to make this payment, with a consequent depletion of the UK gold reserves. If a large number of sterling countries are undergoing balance of payments deficits, the drain on the reserves might be serious. It would however be mitigated if another sterling country or group of countries was at the same time running a surplus in its balance of payments, thus augmenting the dollar holdings in London. In this way there was a pooling of reserves among the sterling countries. To many member countries of the sterling system, one advantage conferred by the arrangements was the added stability they enjoyed as the result of this system, especially in the disturbed years of the 1930s. At that time it was unlikely that all countries would simultaneously want to draw on their reserves.

In the 1930s, most overseas sterling countries were primary producers while the United Kingdom was an exporter of manufactured goods; thus improvements in the terms of trade of overseas sterling countries tended to be offset by a deterioration in the terms of trade with the United Kingdom. Today, however, it is doubtful how far this

[1] Canada always had strong economic links with the United States. South Africa, although in many respects a member of the sterling area, kept official reserves in the form of gold, holding sterling only for working balances.

pooling of reserves arrangement may be regarded as a justification for the sterling area. Perhaps it was more so in the 1930s than in the post-war era, during which period there has been a tendency for member countries' balances of payments to lurch together rather than to offset one another.

The War and After

With the outbreak of the Second World War the sterling area lost its European members. During the war, however, links between remaining members were strengthened by their designation as scheduled territories; for the first time the sterling area received legal recognition. The UK authorities were responsible for payments involving residents of the United Kingdom and of the colonies, while the Governments of the self-governing Dominions exercised control over their own residents. There was no central decision-taking body to allocate scarce foreign exchange reserves to members of the area. The Dominion Governments were free to authorize the making of·payments by their residents to anywhere within the sterling area or outside it and they enjoyed unrestricted access to the gold and dollar reserves of the Exchange Equalization Account. This was the account to which the official UK external reserves were transferred from the Bank of England at the outbreak of the war. There was, however, an understanding that these rights should be exercised with restraint.[1] An important benefit of the system to the overseas member countries was access to the London capital market. This privilege was especially important in the post-war years of large scale investment in many overseas sterling countries.

The most significant war-time development in sterling was the steady piling up of the balances held by overseas residents. At the end of 1938, these sterling balances were just less than £600 million. By the end of 1943 they had grown to £2,350 million, and in December 1945 they were £3,567 million. Nearly two-thirds of this sum represented liabilities to the 'scheduled territories', notably India and the Middle East. During the war the United Kingdom not only purchased vast quantities of war supplies in these territories for sterling; large sums were also disbursed in local currency as pay to British servicemen. Britain financed these transactions by crediting the London accounts of the countries concerned, that is by accumulating sterling liabilities.

The significance of this increase in the sterling balances is to be seen in the change in the ratio between British short-term assets and liabilities

[1] There is a very interesting decription of the machinery of exchange control during the war years in Professor Tew's *International Monetary Corporation*, cited above, pp. 124 ff.

before and after the Second World War. In 1935, when short-term sterling liabilities were £598 million, the gold and convertible currency reserves were £615 million. At the end of 1945, gold and convertible currency reserves at £610 million were actually a little less than in 1938; short-term liabilities had, however, reached £3,567 million—nearly six times as great as before the war and also six times as great as short-term assets in 1945. It is true that as the years passed, reserves climbed from the appallingly low level of the early post-war years but while in the 1960s reserves fluctuated around £1,000 million the sterling liabilities were never less than £3,000 million. Thus Britain was often described as a banker whose immediately available assets are equal to only one third of his immediate liabilities. Moreover, the general raising of interest rates in the 1950s resulted in a substantial increase in the foreign exchange burden of the liabilities. In 1950 interest payments on the sterling balances amounted to £33 million; in the 1960s such payments were around £100 million.

2. THE PICTURE BEFORE THE 1967 DEVALUATION

The deterioration in the short term assets/liabilities ratio since the pre-war years has had serious consequences for confidence on the many occasions in the post-war period when the pound has been under strain. In framing policy the British authorities simply cannot ignore the fact that a weakening of confidence in the pound might lead to the massive conversion of sterling held by foreigners into gold or some other currency, with disastrous consequences for the pound. On the other hand there are a number of considerations which are too seldom taken into account in regard to the position of the pound.

The Balances up to the Mid-Sixties

Firstly, although since 1945 there has been virtually no progress in reducing the sterling liabilities, the real burden of these has become less to the extent that world prices have risen by about 80 per cent since the end of the war. Secondly, there has been a marked change in the ownership pattern of the sterling balances. In 1945 liabilities to non-sterling countries accounted for 34·8 per cent of sterling liabilities to all countries; by the end of 1966 such liabilities had fallen to 26·2 per cent of the whole. The significance of this change is that balances held by sterling area countries are generally less volatile than those in the hands of non-sterling countries. Thus since 1945 balances in the hands of sterling member countries have fluctuated at around £2,500 million; the lowest figure at any year end being £2,108 million, while the highest was £2,833 million. Balances owned by non-sterling countries have fluctuated more than this; the end-year balances ranging between £665 million and £1,405 million. Since 1962 fluctuations in US-owned sterling balances have been particularly great. One explanation for the relative stability of holdings of sterling area member countries is that whereas for sterling countries, over 60 per cent of the balances are held by central monetary institutions, and less than 40 per cent in the hands of other holders, in the non-sterling countries these proportions are reversed.[1] The decreasing proportion of total liabilities in the hands of non-sterling countries could well indicate that the large scale running down of sterling balances is less likely than in the early post-war years.

Thirdly, a high proportion of the sterling balances are working balances, the owners of which are unlikely to run them down below a certain minimal level, especially since most countries of the overseas sterling area are primary producers and therefore need to hold substantial reserves to offset fluctuations in export earnings. It is, however, by no means certain just where this level lies. In a paper submitted to the Radcliffe Committee the Bank of England judged that in 1956, when holdings of non-sterling countries were between £600 million and £700 million 'they had been reduced to a natural (perhaps low) working level'. As for sterling area countries the Bank considered that, in the case of the independent Commonwealth countries, none except India appeared to hold sterling much above a reasonable minimum. At that time the sterling reserves of India, Pakistan and Ceylon together amounted to £704 million. By mid-1966 holdings of this group were down to about £200 million; in the mid 1960s these countries were certainly not in the habit of holding more than minimum sterling balances. Much the same applies to the older dominions of Australia, New Zealand and South Africa, which at mid-1966 held about £400 million in sterling.

On the other hand it is likely that the Middle East countries and the colonial and former colonial territories have increased their sterling holdings substantially above those needed for purely trading transactions. At the end of the war the Middle East oil countries had no sterling balances; by 1960 the size of these holdings was substantially greater than of the older dominions combined. The holdings of the colonial territories have also grown rapidly since 1945. The existence of substantial balances, however, does not necessarily mean that the countries concerned hold surplus sterling balances which they could easily dispose of. One leading authority on the sterling area, Mr A. R.

[1] See Bank of England, *Quarterly Bulletin*, September 1966, vol. vi, no. 3, Table 20.

Conan, believes that the large accumulation of sterling in the hands of these countries denotes an under-developed financial system; 'these funds, used for operations connected with currency banking and public finance are held in London because of limited investment facilities in the territories concerned.'[1]

Mr Conan also points out that at one time or another all the leading self-governing dominions have drawn down their sterling holdings to a point where emergency measures were required to prevent further depletion. He concludes that taken as a whole the existing balances in the mid-1960s were for the most part not much more than adequate for the holders' requirements.

3. THE BALANCES AND THE 1967 DEVALUATION

The tendency of overseas sterling holders to run down their holdings and to switch into other currencies was strongly marked in the period leading up to and immediately following devaluation. In some cases, this meant no more than the speeding up of the process of diversification of foreign exchange assets of sterling system countries that had been noticeable over a considerable period of time and that reflected longer term changes in relative economic weights and growth rates of the UK and other industrial countries and with it longer term changes of trade patterns.

The run-down of sterling holdings which for some years had been relative (overseas sterling area countries built up the non-sterling part of their reserves more rapidly than the sterling part) now turned into an absolute reduction in the amount of sterling held. While in the short run this change was clearly connected with the weakness of the pound and of the British balance of payments, the long-term trend suggested that, even with a surplus in UK payments, sterling area countries could not be relied upon to hold as much—or as high a proportion of—sterling in their reserves as they had done in the past.

The Basle Facility

To keep the withdrawal from sterling 'orderly' and to prevent it from leading to renewed crises of confidence, a stand-by credit of $2,000 million (some £830 million) was put at Britain's disposal. It was provided through the Bank for International Settlements in Basle by the Group of Ten countries together with Austria, Denmark and Switzerland. The arrangements were made for an initial three years after the

[1] A. R. Conan, *The Problem of Sterling*, London, Macmillan, 1966, p. 85.

outflow of sterling had become particularly strong in September 1968 and extended for an additional two years in 1971.

Associated with the so-called Basle facility was a series of bilateral agreements between the UK and sterling countries in which the UK guaranteed the dollar value of the greater part of their official sterling reserves in return for an undertaking by these countries not to reduce further the sterling part of their reserves and to keep a so-called Minimum Sterling Proportion.

The agreed minimum proportion was the condition, but not all of it was guaranteed; in the event, the guarantee applied to that part of each country's official sterling reserves which exceeded 10 per cent of its total reserves. Implementation of the guarantee involved a payment—in sterling—of the difference between $2·40 (the sterling parity after the 1967 devaluation) and the sterling-dollar rate whenever this falls 1 per cent below parity and remains at that level for thirty days. By the time the pound was allowed to float in June 1972, and for some months afterwards, no obligation had been incurred[1] on the £2,920 million sterling holdings then under guarantee, but by the end of 1972 payments due were estimated to be of the order of £60 million.[2]

The Basle facility and the associated agreements which it made possible contributed to British and international monetary stability at a time when both were highly vulnerable, but some observers have since concluded that the arrangements have been too successful in the sense of not only halting a rush out of sterling but of encouraging renewed expansion of 'sterling balances', at the very time when the British authorities—and certainly their prospective EEC partners—began to favour an orderly run-down of the reserve role of sterling. It is, however, arguable that the renewed increase in sterling held internationally owes less to the Basle facility than the weakness of the dollar and the strength of the pound in the surplus phase of the UK balance of payments from 1968 to 1971, and that the long-term trends would reassert themselves.

An interesting feature of the Basle arrangements lay in the distinction made between sterling balances owned in sterling area countries—which qualified for guarantees—and those owned in other countries, which did not. Other possible ways of grouping the balances is according to their purpose and/or the degree of their relative stability or volatility. We shall keep this in mind when examining in more detail the fortunes of sterling before and after Basle.

---

[1] Statement by Minister of State at the Treasury, House of Commons, November 9, 1972.

[2] *The Banker*, December 1972, p. 1559.

Reserves and Banking Liabilities

New tables[1] presented by the Bank of England since 1970 and calculated back to 1962 allow us to distinguish more precisely between
holdings of assets that reflect sterling's reserve role[2] and the usually
much more volatile cash or near-cash funds held in the UK by overseas
residents for purposes of trade and investment[3]—sterling in its asset
and trading currency roles. Of these sterling liabilities those held by
residents of non-sterling countries are particularly sensitive to interest
rate differentials and to changes in confidence in sterling; fluctuations of
sterling area holdings by contrast tend to reflect the financing of balance
of payments flows, but even they may at times be affected by interest
rate and confidence factors, for instance expectations concerning parity
changes.

Thus the sterling crisis phase 1964 to 1968 shows a decline of both
types of sterling balances, each by about a fifth. *Reserves* fell from their
end-1964 high of £2,436 million to their end-1968 low of £1,920
million, and *banking liabilities* from £3,049 million to £2,414 million.
Similarly in the recovery phase after the 1967 devaluation *reserves* rose
by two-thirds, reaching £3,209 million, and *banking liabilities* by three-
quarters, reaching £4,180 million in 1971. But it is interesting to note that
in this period both in the overseas sterling area and in the non-sterling
area banking liabilities of the central monetary institutions fluctuated
more sharply than those of 'other', that is private holders.

The changes have—by 1972—established a new pattern. Ignoring the
modest holdings of international organizations like the Bank for International Settlement, sterling area countries hold practically all overseas
reserves and account for two-thirds of *banking liabilities*. While in the
sterling area holdings by central monetary institutions and by other
holders are evenly matched, the latter account for more than three-
quarters in the non-sterling area. Practically all non-sterling area holdings are on deposit with banks, rather than in local authority or government paper, and can be regarded as working balances rather than reserve
assets.

This suggests that sterling continues to be of importance internationally as a short-term asset and trading currency, while its reserve

[1] The *Bank of England Quarterly Bulletin*, December 1970, discusses in some detail
the revised presentation of external liabilities and claims in sterling, which make the
'sterling balances' as shown before that date—and as used earlier in this chapter—not
strictly comparable.
[2] 'Sterling reserves of overseas countries and international organizations'.
[3] 'External banking and money market liabilities in sterling'.

role is now in practice confined to the 'scheduled territories'. But even there it is, as we have seen, losing ground.

As an institution—if indeed it could ever be described as such—the sterling area has become less important in the 1960s than it was in the early post-war years. The increased convertibility of currencies ·has meant that the discriminatory aspects of the sterling system are now less meaningful than hitherto; although it is noteworthy that UK exchange controls discriminate in favour of sterling countries.

These developments reflect a growing feeling among the overseas sterling countries, and to some extent in the UK as well, that there are diminishing advantages to be obtained from the sterling link.[1] As countries become politically independent they often wish to assert their autonomy by holding reserves in currencies other than sterling—usually US dollars, or in gold. It is generally realized that the gains from pooling of reserves no longer exist. We noted above that one of the historical advantages of the sterling area arose from the fact that surpluses in the UK balance of payments were often offset by deficits in the overseas member countries and *vice-versa*. In the 1940s and 1950s, there was a tendency for this to happen and the sterling system therefore performed a valuable function in economizing reserves. But the complementarity no longer applied in the 1960s. Indeed after 1959 the trade balances of the UK and of overseas sterling countries have moved closely parallel.[2] In part this is due to a change in world trade patterns so that the UK now trades relatively less with the overseas sterling area and more with Western Europe. It is also due to the fact that there is less complementarity than hitherto in the export trade of the UK and that of the overseas sterling countries. The latter are becoming increasingly industrialized and indeed their exports often compete directly with those of the UK.

So far as the UK is concerned there has been much debate as to whether the sterling system adds to Britain's external difficulties. It is of course obvious that a country whose short term external liabilities are greater than its short-term assets is in a precarious position once confidence in its immediate external position declines. Accordingly, it is

[1] A. R. Conan, 'Reconstructing the Sterling Area', *The Banker*, London, May 1968.

[2] According to Richard N. Cooper, in the period 1950–9 the simple correlation between movements in the UK and overseas sterling countries trade balances was -0.37. In 1959–66, it was $+0.56$. Moreover, whereas before 1963, changes in Britain's reserves and sterling liabilities partially offset one another, since 1963 they have reinforced one another. 'The Balance of Payments' in R. E. Caves and associates, *Britain's Economic Prospects*, The Brookings Institution, London, Allen and Unwin, 1968, pp. 182 ff.

arguable that the presence of the sterling balances has aggravated the currency crises which have repeatedly smitten the pound since 1945.

Perhaps the most serious difficulty arising from the high level of Britain's short-term indebtedness is the degree of restraint imposed upon domestic growth. On many occasions since the war high interest rates have been necessary to prevent a serious depletion of the sterling balances; the resulting high interest-rate structure, has almost certainly had an adverse effect upon domestic growth as well as imposing a high burden in terms of interest-rate payments.

Since before 1967 the unwritten laws of the sterling system appeared to rule out both sterling exchange controls and a unilateral devaluation as alternative policies, it is arguable that the notorious stop–go policies owe a great deal to the preoccupation of the City and the Treasury with the role of sterling as an international currency. It was widely assumed that the prospects of British financial institutions, and with them some important invisible earnings, depended on the continued existence of the sterling area and the role of sterling as a reserve currency.

The declining share of sterling area earnings and the way in which the City's Euro-currency activities outpaced the City's sterling business permitted a more dispassionate view of the change in the benefit and costs of sterling as an international currency. No doubt the fear of the 'imperial role' of sterling expressed by some of Britain's future EEC partners also played its part. In June 1971 the Prime Minister stated that Britain was prepared to envisage a gradual and orderly run-down of official sterling balances after accession to the EEC.[1] Some economists saw the imposition of exchange controls on capital transactions with overseas sterling countries during the period of the pound float after June 1972 as a step in that direction.

4. AN INVENTORY OF UK EXTERNAL ASSETS AND LIABILITIES

Finally it must be said that the problem of the UK external position is broader than that of the sterling balances. In the 1960s it was more serious as the UK had in those years assumed a considerable number of short- and medium-term obligations not directly concerned with the international role of sterling. But these obligations had been discharged by the middle of 1972,[2] which restored UK 'solvency' and prepared the way for future international borrowings should the need arise again.

If we take a longer view of the UK external capital position, however, the position is not as bad as is sometimes believed. Although Britain

[1] House of Commons, June 10, 1971.
[2] See Chapter 11.

has incurred substantial long-term obligations, perhaps the most notable being the repayment of the post-war US and Canadian credits by the year 2004, it also holds very substantial long-term assets. These assets may not always easily be sold without loss or difficulty but they nevertheless represent substantial national wealth. By their nature the assets involved are not easy to quantify; they consist of securities of foreign Governments and companies owned by Britons, loans to foreign Governments by the British Government, and the value of assets such as mines, plantations, factories and other property owned abroad by UK citizens. The latest inventory of UK external assets and liabilities, compiled by the Bank of England, relates to the end of 1971.[1]

The Bank study shows that external assets of the public sector amounted to £4,880 million and liabilities £5,590 million. External assets of the private sector were *estimated* as £35,000 million, liabilities at £30,055 million. The total of identified external assets of £39,880 million thus outweighed the total of identified external liabilities of £35,645 million, making *net* assets of £4,235 million.

For the reasons outlined in our discussion of the new presentation of the UK balance of payments accounts in Chapter 11, the Bank study does not distinguish between short-term and long-term funds.

It must again be emphasized that these figures are estimates and the authors of the Bank article are most careful to point out the pitfalls of too-casual an acceptance of estimates such as these. But the message is clear; although Britain at times has a serious, even critical, short-run liquidity problem, in the long run it is a wealthy nation possessing substantial overseas assets.

SHORT GUIDE TO THE LITERATURE

There are relatively few books on the working of the sterling system. The most useful are undoubtedly A. R. Conan's book, *The Problem of Sterling*; Susan Strange, *Sterling and British Policy*, Oxford University Press, 1970; and B. J. Cohen, *The Future of Sterling as an International Currency*, Macmillan, 1971. From time to time *The Banker* (London) contains useful articles on various questions relating to sterling.

[1] 'An Inventory of UK External Assets and Liabilities: end 1971', *Bank of England Quarterly Bulletin*, June 1972, vol. 12, no. 2, pp. 213–219.

CHAPTER 20

THE ECONOMICS OF INTEGRATION

In this and the following chapter we examine some of the economic problems involved when a group of countries try to integrate their economies with one another, by establishing some kind of preferential trading arrangement, free trade area, or customs or economic union. Although we shall illustrate the problems by reference to actual integration schemes, we postpone to Chapters 22 and 23 a more detailed discussion of the structure of free trade areas and customs unions at present in operation.

1. TYPES OF INTEGRATION

There are varying degrees of economic integration from loose arrangements such as those of the Commonwealth Preference Area to proposals for tight economic integration as envisaged by the architects of the European Economic Community. Since preferences normally influence trade patterns, which in turn are likely to have repercussions on the domestic economies of the participating countries, it seems reasonable to regard such arrangements as a form—albeit a diluted form—of economic integration.

The best known example of a preferential arrangement is the British Commonwealth Preference Area. Some West European countries, notably France and Belgium, for many years extended preferences to, and enjoyed preferences in, their overseas possessions—arrangements which have been generalized and embodied in the EEC Association Convention.[1] Today exports of the associated countries enjoy tariff free entry into all the metropolitan member countries of the EEC. Since a preference area is a loose form of integration, special institutional arrangements are usually unnecessary and changes in preference margins can be brought about fairly easily. A more formal type of integration is a *free trade area*. Member countries undertake to remove barriers on their mutual trade over a definite period of time, but each country retains the right to determine the level of its tariff and the severity of other trade restrictions *vis-à-vis* non-members. The most significant attempts to form free trade areas since the war are the

---

[1] The Convention arrangements are examined below, p. 316.

European Free Trade Association (EFTA) and the Latin American Free Trade Area (LAFTA).

In contrast to a free trade area, a *customs union* consists of a group of countries which not only establish free trade in goods with one another, but impose a common tariff on imports from non-member countries. A *common market* provides also for the free movement of persons and capital. Members of an *economic union* further undertake to work for a high degree of integration in their domestic policies. The founding fathers of the EEC envisaged the Community as ultimately a single economic area—an economic union. As yet, however, the member countries have a long way to go before they achieve a significant degree of co-ordination in domestic economic policies. Another customs union which might ultimately take on many aspects of an economic union is the Central American Common Market; the Treaties establishing this common market go as far as to make provision for the controlled allocation of new industries between members.

The trading arrangements discussed in this chapter all involve some degree of discrimination. Now the GATT, to which many of the countries participating in these arrangements adhere, is based on the opposite principle of non-discrimination, the kernel of the Agreement being an undertaking by the Contracting Parties to negotiate tariff reductions with one another (or at least refrain from increasing duties), and to extend such reductions to all other Contracting Parties on a non-discriminatory basis. Thus if the United Kingdom agrees with the United States to reduce the import duty on cars the reduction is extended in full to all other Contracting Parties. In accordance with this philosophy of non-discrimination, the GATT is critical of preferential trading arrangements; indeed the Agreement originally forbade the introduction of new preferences or the widening of existing margins, although permitting existing arrangements to continue. More recently, however, the Agreement has been amended to allow both the introduction of new preferences by developed countries in favour of less developed ones, and the establishment of preferences among developing countries.

Although the GATT philosophy is opposed to preferences, it permits the establishment of customs unions or free trade areas (which are of course really 100 per cent preference areas), provided (a) that such arrangements cover the bulk of trade between the participating countries and (b) a definite timetable is set for the eventual removal of the tariff. In the case of a customs union, the Contracting Parties must also be satisfied that the final common tariff is no more restrictive than the average of member countries' pre-union tariffs. The Treaty of Paris establishing the European Coal and Steel Community did not satisfy the first criterion, for it envisaged free trade in only a limited range of products, namely coal, iron and steel. Neither was the criterion satisfied by the Stockholm Convention establishing EFTA, which specifically excludes agricultural goods. In these cases, the council of GATT used its authority to grant a waiver from the full requirements of the agreement, but only after considerable discussion.

2. CUSTOMS UNION THEORY

Twentieth-Century Problems

All forms of international economic integration involve some degree of geographical discrimination. Historically, however, economists have been accustomed to examine the implications of discriminatory arrangements, under the heading of customs union theory, as a kind of umbrella, under which a wide range of related economic issues are discussed. Accordingly, a customs union is taken as a kind of archetype of all forms of economic integration. We shall follow this practice in the present chapter, expecting the student to make the necessary modifications in the analysis when some other type of integration is under consideration.

Several important customs unions were established in the nineteenth century; perhaps the best known was the *Zollverein* formed in 1833 and consisting of almost all the then German states.[1] In many respects the problems arising from the establishment of customs unions in the nineteenth century were less acute (and to the economist less interesting) than those likely to arise today when two or more sovereign countries decide to form a customs union. A century ago trade restrictions almost always took the form of tariffs, which were usually considerably lower than after the Second World War. In the twentieth century, tariffs are in many cases much less important than quantitative restrictions, exchange controls and domestic support programmes as impediments to trade. Thus if free trade is to be established it is often necessary to remove a whole battery of restrictions of various kinds, as well as tariffs. In the nineteenth century, tariffs were used to foster infant industries or raise revenue; but were hardly ever thought of as a means of insulating an economy against external developments or of stimulating domestic employment. Today, as we saw in Chapter 8, tariffs, or more frequently direct trade controls are used both to defend the

---

[1] There is a useful discussion of the *Zollverein* and of several other Customs Unions in J. Viner, *The Customs Union Issue*, New York, Carnegie Endowment for International Peace, 1950.

balance of payments and secure full employment. Thus the removal of trade barriers when a latter-day customs union is being formed can create serious policy problems. If a country maintains balance of payments equilibrium by means of import restrictions rather than domestic financial policies, the removal of those restrictions resulting from participation in a customs union might create a serious payments deficit. In such a case a country might be faced with either the adoption of more stringent domestic monetary and fiscal policies or currency devaluation.[1]

The fact that Governments tend to intervene more extensively in the economic life of a country today than before 1914 creates further problems for union builders. Taxation accounts for a higher proportion of total national expenditure today than even a half century ago. Internal consumption or excise duties, which vary in intensity as between products made or consumed in different member countries of a customs union can cause a distortion of production and trade. If country A heavily subsidizes sugar production but country B, which is relatively efficient in the product, refrains from doing so some special arrangement might be necessary to prevent importers in country B from purchasing their sugar from the relatively high cost but highly subsidized producers in country A. State subsidization of basic industries, for example in the nationalized sector, might also create serious distortions and call for special arrangements. Indeed, problems arising from the building of customs unions illustrate many of the theoretical points made in Chapter 5.

It is convenient to discuss the problems of modern customs unions under two general headings, which we can designate the 'welfare' and 'mechanical' aspects of union building. These are interrelated and few problems fall entirely into one or other category. Under the heading of welfare we ask such questions as what considerations determine whether a given customs union will raise the welfare of its constituent countries or of the world as a whole. Under the mechanics of integration we discuss such questions as the problem of co-ordinating tariff structures or financial policies between countries forming a customs union.

Trade Creation and Trade Diversion

There was virtually no systematic theory of the welfare aspects of customs union before 1950, when Viner's pioneer study, *The Customs*

[1] For an illustration of this point, drawn from the experience of Benelux, see Chapter 21, pp. 293 ff.

Jnion Issue,[1] was published. Until that date, most economists took the
iew that since free trade maximizes world welfare and since the
stablishment of a customs union removes at least some barriers to
rade, a customs union must increase world welfare. Some free trade is
etter than none. But there was next to no literature on the subject and
hose sceptical about the 'partial free trade is better than no free trade'
pproach failed to produce a set of criteria to determine whether a
articular union would have a favourable or unfavourable welfare
ffect.

In his book, Viner showed that a customs union might increase or
ecrease world welfare, establishing a number of criteria which could
e used in deciding whether welfare was likely to increase or decrease
n the case of any specific union. Viner introduced the terms 'trade
reation' and 'trade diversion' to analyse the effects of the change in
rade patterns which might be expected to follow the establishment of
customs union. Trade would be 'created' and the welfare effect would
e positive, when the removal of the tariff barrier inside the customs
nion resulted in a transfer of output from a high to a low cost source of
upply within the union. But if the removal of the internal barrier
esulted in a switch from a low cost *external* source of supply to a high
ost *internal* source, there would be what Viner called 'trade diversion'.

Let us suppose that two countries, A and B decide to form a customs
nion; all barriers on trade between the two countries are removed,
ut barriers on trade with the outside world which we shall call C,
emain. Now suppose that country A is the highest cost producer and
roduces commodity *x* at an opportunity cost equivalent to 5s per
nit. Country B produces commodity *x* at an opportunity cost equiva-
ent to 4s, while costs in country C are equivalent to 3s. Assume that
efore the establishment of a customs union with B country A protects
he industry producing *x* by means of a 100 per cent tariff. This tariff
s sufficient to protect its industry against imports from both B and C.
Now consider what happens when countries A and B form a customs
nion, but continue to impose the 100 per cent duty on imports from C.
nsofar as B's product *x* now sells in country A at a lower price (4s)
han domestic supplies which sell at 5s (omitting all considerations of
ransport and other selling costs), the establishment of a customs union
as resulted in a transfer of demand for the product *x* from country A
o country B. This is a switch from a relatively high to a relatively low
ost source. There is therefore a gain in welfare; using Viner's termino-
ogy, there is trade creation. Country C's sales in A are unaffected since

[1] J. Viner, *The Customs Union Issue*, cited above.

even before the establishment of the customs union they were shut off from this market by the 100 per cent protective duty.

Let us now assume that country A's protective duty had been only 50 per cent—sufficient to protect its producers from imports from country B, which would sell at 6s, but insufficient to afford protection against imports from C, which would sell at 4s 6d. Countries A and B form a customs union, but retain the 50 per cent duty on imports of commodity x from C. Citizens in country A now obtain supplies of commodity x more cheaply from country B than from country C. But whereas consumers previously obtained this commodity from the low cost sources in country C, they now obtain it from relatively high cost sources in country B. The establishment of the customs union has resulted in a switch in supply from a relatively low to a relatively high cost source. There is what Viner called trade diversion; output had been diverted from more to less efficient sources of supply. The formation of a union in these circumstances might be expected to *reduce* total welfare.

Viner's discussion shows that the net effects of the establishment of a customs union might be either trade diverting or trade creating. Are there any criteria by which we can decide whether a particular union is on balance trade creating or trade diverting? Let us look first at the circumstances in which the degree of trade creation is likely to be considerable. Viner himself appeared to argue that the more similar or the more competitive the economies of the countries concerned the more likely is trade creation rather than trade diversion to follow the establishment of a customs union. If member countries produce similar goods the removal of mutual trade impediments is likely to give an advantage to the industry in the country whose costs are lowest. On the other hand, if the countries are making quite distinct types of products, that is if say country A is an industrial one and country B a primary producer, we would expect the gains from the removal of tariffs to be small, since the initial degree of protection in both countries would have been relatively small.

Thus the greatest gains might be expected to arise from customs unions formed by countries whose economies are similar or competitive rather than complementary. Stated in this way, however, the theorem is open to serious criticism, for it suggests that gains are likely to be greatest where the pre-customs union cost ratios of producing a commodity are closest together, and least where they are most dissimilar! Common sense suggests that this cannot possibly be what Viner intended; if true, it would imply that where country A is much more efficient than country B at producing commodity x, the gain from a reallocation of output of x from B to A is less than if A is only a little better!

The whole question was taken up by Dr Helen Makower and Dr G. Morton[1] in an important article a year or so after the publication of Viner's book. These writers argue that if there is any trade creation, the gains will be greater, the more *dissimilar* the cost ratios in the two countries. Thus the greatest gains from the establishment of trade creating customs unions arise when the economies of the countries forming the union are complementary—that is with dissimilar rather than similar cost ratios.

The contradiction between Viner's approach and that of Makower and Morton is apparent rather than real. For what Viner was really telling us is that there is likely to be some trade creation where before the establishment of the union countries produced *similar* goods. If they cannot produce similar products—if there is no 'overlap' in production, it is difficult to see how reallocation can take place. In other words, Viner was stressing the fact that initially some overlap is necessary for *any* welfare gains to accrue. But given this overlap, Makower and Morton showed that the potential gain from establishing the union would be greater, the wider the differences in the cost ratios at which the products *could* be produced in the countries of the union. Professor Meade has expressed the same idea in a slightly different way by suggesting that the formation of a customs union is more likely to lead to a net increase in economic welfare if the economies of the partner countries are actually very competitive or similar but potentially very complementary or dissimilar.[2] Thus from the welfare viewpoint, the best kind of customs union is between countries which are actually competitive, but which *could* produce widely different goods.[3]

The more economically important and the more numerous the countries forming the customs union, the greater is likely to be the scope for a reshuffling of output from high cost to low cost sources of supply. Accordingly, a customs union covering a large number of countries is likely to result in a greater amount of trade creation than a smaller union of countries. Thus the trade creation effects of the formation of the EEC are likely to be greater than that of a Nordic Customs Union of the Scandinavian countries. It is also clear that the higher the initial level

[1] H. Makower and G. Morton, 'A Contribution Towards a Theory of Customs Unions', *Economic Journal*, vol. lxii, no. 249, March 1953, pp. 33–49.

[2] J. E. Meade, *The Theory of Customs Unions*, North-Holland Publishing Company, 1955, p. 107.

[3] This and other related issues are discussed by Professor R. G. Lipsey in an important article, 'The Theory of Customs Unions: A General Survey', *Economic Journal*, September 1960, pp. 496–513.

of the tariff between countries forming a customs union, the greater the welfare gains from its removal.

As for the trade diverting effects of a customs union, much depends upon the height of the union tariff *vis-à-vis* non-member countries. If in some meaningful sense, the union tariff is higher than the previous average of the member countries, then the effect of the establishment of the union is likely to be more 'trade diverting' than if it were lower. Of course, it is arguable that if the establishment of a customs union diverts trade from a low cost source C to a high cost source B, it is still possible that welfare has been raised, if the high cost source B is a relatively poor country, while the low cost country C is a relatively rich one. The transfer of production and income from a rich to a poor country might have favourable welfare effects which offset the unfavourable trade effects. On the other hand, if the establishment of the customs union diverts trade from a low cost poor third country to a high cost rich country, the adverse welfare effects are reinforced. For example, if the UK were to join the EEC and this resulted in a switch of textile imports from low cost developing countries to high cost, high income, West European sources, this could have an adverse effect upon world welfare.

Much of this is self-evident; what we have been discussing, so far, however, is the *production* effect of establishing a customs union. But there are also what we call *consumption* effects, a question not considered by Viner in his book. Welfare changes are likely to arise not only as the result of changes in sources of supply—output substitution— but also from changes in consumption—what is known as consumption substitution. The establishment of the customs union brings about relative price changes; in the absence of market imperfections import prices are lowered, as compared with prices of home-trade products. As the result the consumption pattern of union citizens is likely to change.[1] Other things being equal there is likely to be an increase in imports from the union partner accompanied by a decrease in consumption of home-produced commodities and of imports from non-union countries. Now although the production effects of establishing the union might result in a net trade diversion—that is, a reduction in welfare, there could be an offsetting increase in welfare as the result of the fall in import prices. Thus although there is a switch of import of commodity x from the relatively low cost source in country C to the

[1] As Professor R. G. Lipsey points out in an interesting contribution to this discussion, the consumption effect may operate even if there is *no* production effect. R. G. Lipsey, 'The Theory of Customs Unions: Trade Diversion and Welfare', *Economica*, February 1957, pp. 40–46.

relatively high cost source in country B, the removal of the tariff still results in a lowering of the price of the commodity to the advantage of consumers in country A. There is a positive consumption effect to be weighed against the negative production effect.

It is clearly possible that in the case of a trade diverting customs union favourable consumption effects might more than offset unfavourable production effects. On the other hand, it is by no means certain that the consumption effect will be favourable, for against the welfare gains of (previously taxed) increased imports from the partner country B must be placed welfare losses which might result from decreased imports from outside countries C whose products are still subject to the duty. If there is a net unfavourable consumption effect it reinforces the net unfavourable production effect; in these circumstances a customs union reduces welfare even more than Viner's approach suggests.

Gains from Integration

At this stage the student will be asking whether we can in any meaningful sense measure the gains or losses from integration. In this connection, it is important to distinguish between what we might call the 'real' or welfare gains of an economic union and the effect of the union upon member countries' balances of payments. It is true that an improvement in a country's external position is generally regarded as likely to entail an increase in its welfare and we are in the habit of assessing the advantages or disadvantages of say UK membership of the EEC in terms of balance of payments effects. If it can be shown that entry would mean a likely improvement in the UK balance of payments position, observers are inclined to feel that membership is in some way 'a good thing'. Whereas those who claim that a very serious deterioration in the balance of payments would follow entry are generally regarded as showing that entry would on economic criteria, be 'a bad thing'. In a world in which balance of payments difficulties impose so many constraints upon countries in regard to general economic policy it is perhaps natural to weigh the merits of any integration scheme in terms of its effect upon the balance of payments. But this does not alter the fact that there is a difference between the measurement of the welfare and of trade effects of a given change in tariff levels or structure.

Professor P. J. Verdoorn was one of the first economists to make a quantitative study of both the trade and welfare impact upon member countries of the establishment of a customs union in Western Europe. He estimated the trade and welfare effects of a Union between the present EEC countries, the Scandinavian countries, and the United

Kingdom.[1] He took 1952 as his base year, an elasticity of substitution between imports and domestic production in member countries of -0.05, and an elasticity of substitution for different countries' exports of -2.0. He assumed these elasticities to be uniform in all countries; steel (in which trade between the Six was already free in 1952) and raw materials were eliminated. Using these estimates, Verdoorn shows that the removal of tariffs would have increased intra-Union trade by about $1,000 million or 19 per cent of the 1952 level; he calculated that imports from non-member countries would fall by 6 per cent. Verdoorn then adjusts these estimates to take account of changes in the terms of trade and other secondary effects. After these effects are taken into account, he estimates that the net effect of the changes would have been to increase intra-European trade by $750 million and reduce imports from non-members by $611 million.

Verdoorn translates the trade changes into welfare gains and losses measured respectively by the increase in specialization as the result of increased intra-European trade and the decrease resulting from the loss of imports from non-member countries. The most interesting result of Verdoorn's calculations is the smallness of the welfare gain to the participating countries resulting from increased specialization— less than £70 million—or less than one-twentieth of 1 per cent of the gross product of all the member countries.

A more recent attempt to measure simply the trade effects of various integration arrangements in the North Atlantic area (including Japan) is that of Professor Bela Balassa,[2] and associates. This international team of economists estimated the effect of alternative trade policies upon the trade and production patterns of the countries concerned, but made no attempt to measure welfare gains or losses; they concentrate on the trade effects. The investigators consider for each country or group of countries the trade implications of (a) the establishment of a full North Atlantic free trade area, (b) a European free trade area composing of the present EEC and EFTA countries, (c) an Atlantic free trade area which excludes the EEC, and (d) a general 50 per cent multilateral reduction of tariffs on industrial products by all North Atlantic countries. A uniform import substitution elasticity for all fully manufactured

---

[1] P. J. Verdoorn, 'A Customs Union for Western Europe—Advantages and Feasibility', *World Politics*, vol. vi, July 1954, pp. 482–500.

[2] *Trade Liberalisation among Industrial Countries. Objectives and Alternatives*, for the US Council on Foreign Relations, by the McGraw-Hill Book Company, 1957. Some of the implications of integration for individual countries have been worked out by Balassa and associates in a second volume, *Studies in Trade Liberalisation*, Maryland, USA, The Johns Hopkins Press, 1967.

goods for participating countries is assumed,[1] although alternative estimates of supply elasticities are built in to the model. The first alternative supply elasticity assumes that the expansion of exports within Western Europe would cause a price rise of one third of the tariff reduction—the second assumes infinite supply elasticities, that is no increase in the supply price. In this way calculations are made of the 'static' effects of the trade alternatives. Quantitatively, the results are small. In the case of the UK, for example, participation in a North Atlantic free trade area in industrial products is estimated to cause a rise of between 7·3 per cent and 8·8 per cent in total exports and of between 6·6 per cent and 7·5 per cent in total imports, depending upon the assumption made regarding supply elasticities. These changes are equivalent to less than 1 per cent of the United Kingdom GDP.

Some Simple Geometry

Professor Harry Johnson has devised an interesting expository technique for showing the welfare effects of establishing a customs union. In what follows we outline Professor Harry Johnson's approach to the problem of measuring welfare changes, not only because his contribution is an extremely important one, but also to familiarize the student with some of the elementary geometry of this subject.

Professor Johnson used diagrammatic apparatus similar to that of figure 15 which can be employed both to illustrate and measure the welfare gains resulting from the removal of a tariff.[2] DD is the demand curve for a commodity x in country A. AS is the home supply curve, and BS_1 and BS_2 the supply curves of country B with which A is to form a customs union. Country B can stand for all other member countries of the union. The supply curve BS_1 is B's curve before the customs barrier is removed, BS_2 relates to supply after the establishment of the Union and the removal of the tariff. The fact that these lines are horizontal suggests that elasticity of supply in the rest of the union for commodity x is infinite; a somewhat dubious assumption for a small union like Benelux, but more realistic for, say, a North Atlantic Free Trade area.

Before country A joins the customs union, the total consumption of

[1] Import demand elasticities for finished manufactures are assumed to be as follows: USA—4·12, Canada—2·06, EEC—3·09, UK—2·68, continental EFTA—2·27, Japan—3·09. These estimates are discussed at length by Professor Balassa in the Appendix to Chapter 4, of *Trade Liberalisation among Industrial Countries*, pp. 185 ff.

[2] The following is based upon Professor Johnson's *Money, Trade and Economic Growth*, London, Allen and Unwin, 1962, Chapter III.

x is £OQ_2. Of this total OQ_1 is met from domestic supply, Q_1Q_2 from imports. Now the removal of the tariff between A and B has two effects upon imports into A. Firstly, some of the goods previously produced in country A are now imported from B; this is the production effect. Secondly, imports displace not only identical but also competing goods, for which the now cheaper imports are substitutes; for example,

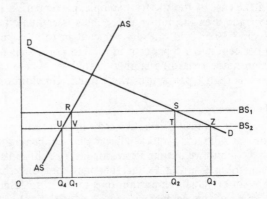

FIGURE 15. Effects of Formation of a Customs Union upon Trade
and Price Showing the Gain from Trade Creation.

the cheapening of imported gramophone records as the result of the removal of the tariff might displace domestic expenditure on cinema-going. This is the consumption effect. There is a welfare gain arising from each of these two effects. Goods previously produced domestically are imported at a lower cost in terms of alternatives foregone, a production gain, and secondly, there is a gain in consumer surplus resulting from the attainment of a given level of *consumption* at lower real cost. Both of these effects can be seen in figure 15.

The elimination of the tariff causes domestic production of good x to fall from OQ_1 to OQ_4. There is therefore a gain in domestic resources saved, represented by the area of the triangle RUV. A little thought shows that the greater the tariff reduction and the greater the reduction in output the more significant will be welfare gains under this head. At the same time, consumer citizens in country A derive a gain from being able to consume more goods than previously. This particular gain is represented by the area of the triangle STZ, which is of course deter-mined by the addition to the supply of good x which consumers now enjoy, and the reduction in the price (ST) following the removal of the tariff. Thus the total welfare gain from trade is equal to the sum of areas of the two triangles RUV and STZ.

In so far as there is a welfare *loss* from the substitution of higher-cost goods from the partner country for low cost goods from non-member countries (the trade diversion effect), this can be measured by the difference in cost between the two sources of imports multiplied by the

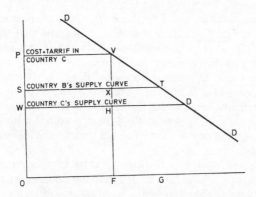

FIGURE 16. Effect of Formation of a Customs Union upon Trade and Price, Showing Loss from Trade Diversion.

amount of trade diverted. Following Professor Harry Johnson again we can show this with the aid of figure 16. The line DD represents demand for a product x in a country A which is about to form a customs union with country B, but not with country C. Country C is however the lower cost producer and its supply curve for x is shown by the line WH. But neither before or after the union do importers in A purchase x from C at the price OW, since a tariff equivalent to WP is levied both before and after the establishment of the Union. Before the Union is formed, however, country A obtains its imports from this country C, since with the tariff applying equally to both possible sources of supply, imports from C are cheaper than those from B. Residents in country A will accordingly import OF from country C at a tariff loaded price of OP. Let us now assume that tariffs between A and B are eliminated, while the tariff between country A and country C remains. Although the opportunity cost of producing x remains lower in C than in B, imports from country C, unlike those from B, are still tariff loaded and are priced at OP as against OS for imports from B. They are therefore displaced by imports from B, which sell at a price of OS, which is of course considerably lower than the price OP at which imports from C are still selling.

Figure 16 helps us to see both the loss from the diversion of output from the low to high cost source of supply and the gain to consumers from increased consumption at a lower cost per unit. As regards the loss of production efficiency, it is apparent from the diagram that whereas before the establishment of the customs union the output OF cost OW per unit when produced in country C, whilst now that the production has been diverted to the higher-cost partner country, the cost per unit is OS. Thus there is a loss on the cost side equivalent to the area WHXS. On the other hand, since after the establishment of the union the price to the consumer is OS, whereas before the trade diversion from country C to country B it was OP, and total consumption is now OG, as against OF before the formation of the union, there is a gain in consumers surplus equivalent to the area of the triangle VXT.

As Professor Johnson points out,[1] further complications follow if we assume that the partner and foreign supply curves are less than perfectly elastic. In this case, the diversion of demand from the foreign to the partner source of supply (from country C to country B) causes non-union marginal costs to fall, and partner country marginal costs to rise. The country therefore gains from improved terms of trade on any trade with non-partner countries surviving the establishment of union. Of course, the steeper the supply curves in both the partner and foreign countries, the more will trade diversionary effects of the union be dampened down. A second consequence of imperfectly elastic supply conditions is that the supply price in the partner rises as trade is diverted. There is accordingly a loss to the country per unit of trade diverted greater than it would be given constant costs.

The conclusion from these studies must surely be that *static* gains and losses from integration whether measured in terms of trade changes or welfare are likely to be small. If there is any dramatic change in the economy of a member country which participates in a customs union it comes from changes in economic growth consequent upon the enlargement of the market through new scope for technological innovation,

[1] *Money, Trade and Economic Growth*, cited above, p. 56.

Professor Johnson made a quantitative estimate of the gains and losses from British participation in a European Free Trade area as early as 1958. His results suggested that the impact of integration was likely to be extremely small, the gain on exports and imports together being about 1 per cent of GNP. The size of this estimate bears out Verdoorn's conclusion that the static effects of integration are likely to be small. 'The Gains from Freer Trade with Europe in An Estimate', *Manchester School of Social Studies*, vol. 26, 1958.

and for improvement in managerial techniques resulting from increased competition. In view of the very substantial growth which has in fact taken place in trade within various customs unions and free trade areas established since the war, it is possible that changes other than those resulting immediately from the reallocation of resources between firms and industries, are quite considerable.[1] So we must examine the 'dynamic' as well as the 'static' effects.

The expansion of the market following the removal of trade restrictions enables many industries to derive economies of larger scale production. There are a number of industries where firms can reach their optimum size and still remain reasonably competitive only if they are supplying a market larger than the home market can provide. There are also external economies of scale to be derived when a whole industry expands as the result of an extension to the market. It is of course true that the international companies establish manufacturing plant and sales organizations behind tariff walls and in this way obtain for themselves a supra-national market. But while tariff and other barriers are significant, manufacturing units tend to be established in a particular country, not because that location is the most desirable economically, but simply because it is necessary to have the plant behind a tariff wall. The removal of tariffs will accordingly enable such companies to site their factories and distributing centres more efficiently, with consequent cost-reduction. Apart from the advantage of sheer size, firms operating in a larger market are likely—because conditions are more competitive —to be much more on their toes in regard to new products and newer methods of production. In a small national market, profit margins are likely to be wide (this is still true of retail margins in West European countries); the opening up of trade provides an incentive for the narrowing of these margins in the attempt to capture the markets of partner countries.

More intensive competition is likely to reduce the number of relatively inefficient (marginal) producers, and by providing both the incentive of the carrot and the fear of the stick is likely to cause not only rationalization within an industry but also better use of managerial ability and capital within the firm. Of course, many of these benefits sometimes described as 'the salutary jolt' argument for freer-trade really derive from increased competition rather than directly from free trade. But free trade is in many cases the only practical catalyst that can trigger off a much-needed shake-up of domestic economies of member

[1] The subject is dealt with by T. Scitovsky, *Economic Theory and Western European Integration*, Allen and Unwin, 1962 edition, and by Bela Balassa, *The Theory of Economic Integration*, Allen and Unwin, 1961.

countries. Some people believe that gains from more intensive competition and from the psychology of freer trade are in practice likely to be more significant than those resulting from the re-allocative effect of integration. But by their very nature, efficiency gains cannot be measured in any meaningful way. One can, of course, say that the economies of some of the EEC countries (France is the one usually mentioned) have become more efficient and achieved a faster rate of growth as the result of the prospect of more intense competition, which faced industrialists in 1958 and 1959. But one cannot be sure of this. Indeed, economists are still at a relatively early stage in their attempt to analyse the *dynamic* gains from establishing customs unions. It is likely that increased import competition would keep management more on its toes and efficient. But by the same token exporters, facing falling tariffs in union partner countries will be able to secure a given income with less effort than previously. They could conceivably react by becoming less cost-conscious or by working less hard. Tariff reductions might have what Dr Corden has called a 'warm sun' effect on exporters.[1] Clearly the whole subject is fraught with difficulties and extreme caution must be exercised in generalizing too hastily on the exciting but analytically elusive *dynamic* aspects of integration.[2]

SHORT GUIDE TO THE LITERATURE

See *Guide* at end of Chapter 21.

[1] Dr Corden has analysed the 'efficiency' aspects of a tariff in a mimeographed study *The Efficiency Effects of Trade and Protection*.

[2] The issue of 'static' versus 'dynamic' effects of integration is discussed with reference to the EEC and to expectations concerning British entry in 'Entry into the EEC: A Comment on Some of the Economic Issues', *National Institute Economic Review*, August 1971. This article examines a number of methods used and results obtained by various authors and has an extremely useful bibliography. The same issue includes M. H. Miller, 'Estimates of the Static Balance of Payments and Welfare Costs of United Kingdom Entry into the Common Market', which brings together comparisons of seven separate studies. See also *NIER*, November 1970, 'Another Look at the Common Market', with an 'erratum' correcting it in February 1971.

CHAPTER 21

SOME FURTHER PROBLEMS IN INTEGRATION

1. CONDITIONS FOR MAXIMIZING BENEFITS

Unfortunately, both for the union-builder and the student, the mere throwing down of customs barriers and the establishment of a common external tariff does not necessarily mean that full advantage will be obtained from integration. In Chapter 9 we saw how theory suggests that the full benefit of a customs union will be derived only if factors as well as goods move freely between member countries. In this section, however, we are concerned more with a different set of problems, namely those arising from the fact that if there are already a number of distortions in the economies of one or more participating countries, it is possible that the removal of one of these—the tariff on products traded between member countries—might not result in an increase in welfare unless the other distortions can at the same time be removed.

This is of course one aspect of the theory of the second best (see p. 74 above). Indeed, when other impediments to perfect competition exist, the theory of the second best indicates that there are circumstances where the removal of the tariff might actually result in a net reduction in economic welfare. Such might be the case if the Government in country A subsidizes its relatively high cost agriculture while the Government in country B refrains from so doing. The removal of A's tariff on agricultural products imported from country B will result in a concentration of production in the relatively high cost source of supply in the union. It would be tedious to detail the many types of situation in which this kind of problem might arise. The student will perhaps be helped most readily by means of simple examples drawn from experience of union building in post-war Western Europe.

Lessons from the ECSC

Our illustrations are taken from Mr H. H. Liesner's account of the difficulties in creating the European Coal and Steel Community,[1] and

[1] The illustrations which follow are taken from *Case Studies in European Economic Union, The Mechanics of Integration*, by J. E. Meade (editor), H. H. Liesner, and S. J. Wells, Oxford University Press, for The Royal Institute of International Affairs, 1962.

from the experience of the early years of the Benelux Union. Liesner points out that when in the early 1950s the countries forming the ECSC agreed to remove restrictions on their mutual trade in coal and steel products there were several ways in which the transport policies, unless modified, would have militated against the free trade objectives of the Community.[1] One of the most obvious arose from the existence of discriminatory freight rates. This discrimination took several forms. A common practice was the levying of differing railway freight rates for the same product as between different countries of origin or destination. For example, in Western Germany there were two general rates for the carrying of coal; the rate on imported coal and on home-produced coal. Over a distance of 400 km foreign coals transported on the Federal railways had to pay 24 per cent more than German coals. Another difficulty arose from attempts by countries to give domestic producers an advantage in third countries by charging a specially low tariff on products intended for export. The Belgian railways accordingly applied higher charges to foreign coal and coke transported through Belgium than on domestically produced coke.

A third device to assist home-producers was that of 'broken freight rates', whereby advantage was taken of the assumption of the railway authorities that the transport of goods across a frontier constitutes not one but two journeys; the first from the point of origin of the product to the frontier; the second from the frontier to the consumer. Accordingly before the establishment of the ECSC a 'terminal fee' was levied at the frontier, theoretically to cover the cost of loading and unloading trucks. In practice this terminal fee was imposed, even when there was no loading or unloading involved. Finally, in all Community countries the freight charge per kilometre fell as distance increased—a practice known as a 'tapering' rate. Now in the case of a trainload of coal passing through two or more countries the rate would cease to 'taper' at the frontier between the first and second countries; at this point the second country's full initial rate would be applied: this rate would in turn taper as the distance over which the load was carried increased until the frontier between the second and third countries was reached. The effect was to make the average freight charge per kilometre of a cargo passing through two or more community countries higher than the rate on a similar cargo carried over the same distance within a single country. Mr Liesner instances the carriage of coal over the German and French Railways at the time of the coming into operation of the common market. The charge for carrying one ton of coal over

---

[1] *Case Studies in European Economic Union*, p. 341.

a distance of 500 km was Bfrs 313 on the German railways and Bfrs 362 on the French railways. But if that ton of coal had been transported half the distance on the German railways and the other half on the French railways, the total cost of transport would have been Bfrs 464—37 per cent more than the average of the two internal rates.

In view of these difficulties it is not surprising that the architects of the Coal and Steel Community decided that free trade was not enough, but that it was also necessary to provide for the ironing out of distortions created by the kind of arrangements we have been describing. The attempt to remove these distortions itself gave rise to many complex problems and although import duties and other trade restrictions on coal, iron and steel products had been removed by 1953, it was not until May 1957 that the introduction of international through rates was achieved by the reduction of terminal fees for international transport of steel and scrap.[1]

Differing Tax Structures

Another case where union builders were forced to consider aspects other than the mere removal of tariffs and frontier trade controls is the Benelux Customs Union at the formation of which in 1948[2] there were substantial differences in rates and patterns of internal taxation. In a customs union benefits are lost although all controls over the movements of goods at the common frontier are removed if marked differences persist in rates of internal indirect taxes. For if the Government in one member country A imposes a substantial excise duty on the production of a commodity x but its union neighbour B refrains from taxing the commodity it may be worthwhile for users and consumers in country A to import the commodity from the untaxed source in country B, even if domestic producers are relatively more efficient at producing the commodity. In such cases some control is necessary at the frontier.

[1] Mr Liesner gives a table which shows a number of illustrative cases of international transport cost reductions resulting from the abolition of discriminatory rates and the introduction of international through tariffs. In the case of the transport of coke from Germany (Gelsenkirchen) to France (Homecourt), total transport charges were reduced by 15 and 20 per cent respectively, as the result of the abolition of discrimination and of broken frontier rates respectively. Since freight rates for coke at the time of the institution of the Community accounted for at least 35 per cent of the final price inclusive of transport charges, the reduction of the distortions discussed in this Section had a considerable effect upon the final price of the products concerned.

[2] See below, p. 293.

It so happens that when the Benelux customs union was established there were significant differences in the relative importance of indirect taxes between the three union partners. In the Netherlands consumption taxes accounted for 38·9 per cent of total tax revenue, in Belgium they contributed 55·8 % of revenue. A good example of the differences in the pattern of consumption taxes in the two countries is the treatment of alcoholic drink. Before the union, Belgians who are beer drinkers, paid relatively light duties on beer, and high duties on spirits; while the Dutch, who seem to prefer spirits, paid heavy duties on beer and low duties on spirits. A raising of the Dutch duty on spirits to the Belgian level would have had an adverse effect (or so it was alleged) upon the rather important distilling industry of the Netherlands, while a lowering of the spirit duty in Belgium would have had an adverse effect upon the consumption of beer in that country. The Dutch did in fact eventually raise their duty on spirits, but it remained well below the Belgian level. As late as 1958 it was Bfrs 157 as against Bfrs 200 in the Belgian-Luxembourg Economic Union.[1] This is but one (and a relatively minor) example of the difficulties faced by the Benelux union in its early days; numerous others could be quoted.

We have so far been concerned with ways in which differences in internal transport rates and indirect taxation limit the advantages derived from the removal of import duties. Unless offset, these differences might reduce the welfare gains from integration. But apart altogether from welfare considerations, a number of difficulties, some of them serious, often arise from the sheer mechanics of integration. Most of these have been exemplified in post-war European customs unions. There is firstly the problem of establishing a common tariff *vis-à-vis* non-member countries. If one member has a specific, while its partner country has an *ad valorem* tariff, some agreement is necessary on the characteristic of the common tariff.

There is also the problem of agreeing the particular height of the new tariff. Should it be simply the unweighted arithmetic average of the previous tariffs of constituent members, great and small, or should more weight be given to the height of the tariff in countries which are major importers or consumers of the various products? How can agreement be reached in the case of certain products, namely agricultural goods, where protection is achieved by means of domestic support programmes rather than import duties?[2]

---

[1] *Case Studies in European Economic Union*, cited above, p. 92.
[2] For a description of ways in which the EEC has attempted to solve these and other problems, see below, pp. 305 ff.

2. THE BALANCE OF PAYMENTS AND THE CO-ORDINATION OF
POLICIES

An even more intractable set of problems arises in regard to the co-
ordination of overall economic policies within a Union. In the nineteenth century domestic financial policies tended to be subservient to
the requirements of countries' balances of payments. If a country ran
into deficit, it safeguarded its reserves by adopting relatively severe
internal financial policies. Countries seldom used tariffs or other import
restrictions to safeguard their balances of payments while pursuing
full employment policies. There was therefore little need for countries
forming a customs union to make special arrangements for co-ordinating
domestic policies. But the situation since the First World War has been
quite different. A country in overall balance of payments deficit can,
and often does, impose direct controls on imports and other payments
and also on outward movement of capital in order to reduce or contain
that deficit.

At the present time in the United Kingdom the authorities restrict
overseas travel expenditure of residents and there are fairly drastic
curbs on the export of capital. Membership of an economic union
means, however, that a country cannot use these restrictions on transactions with its partners. If imports, visible and invisible, from a partner
or group of partners account for a substantial proportion of a country's
total imports, this limitation may be a serious hindrance to such a country
protecting its balance of payments by the use of direct controls. Of
course a union member country is at liberty to impose restrictions on
transactions with third countries, but unless the partner country imposes equally stringent restrictions there is the possibility of goods
entering the country where restrictions on balance of payments grounds
are relatively strict, *via* the country whose restrictions are less severe.
Even the prohibition of such goods of foreign origin from crossing the
frontier between the member countries might be of only limited
usefulness if substitutes for such goods can be produced without too
much difficulty in the territory of the surplus country.

Illustrations from Benelux

The history of the formative years of Benelux well illustrates these
problems. In the early post-war period the overall Dutch deficit was
much greater than that of the Belgium-Luxembourg Economic Union,
where after the middle of 1946 goods from third countries were allowed
to be imported relatively freely. In the Netherlands, on the other hand,

the payments disequilibrium was so serious that extensive dismantlin of import controls both on trade with the Benelux partners and wit the outside world could not take place until the end of 1949. Accordingl considerable difficulty was experienced in liberalizing trade with Benelux and even longer delay occurred in the hammering out of a joint liberal ization programme *vis-à-vis* third countries.

Given that there is a serious overall disequilibrium in the balance of payments of one member of an economic union, and that the countr is resolved at the same time to liberalize trade and capital movement with its partners, three possibilities are open. The first, the acceptanc of successive lines of credit from the surplus partner, we can dismis quickly. Such a course of action might be—as was the case in Benelux— extremely useful as an exceptional crisis measure. It could be of grea importance in giving a debtor country a breathing space in which to adopt more fundamental long-term remedies, but the perpetual issu of doles from one member country of an economic union to anothe is clearly quite unthinkable.

A second and more fundamental basis for policy might be the adop tion of a fluctuating exchange rate between the partners as a regulato of the balance of payments. When in 1948 the establishment of a custom union between the Benelux countries, and France and Italy, the so called Fritalux or Finebel Union was under discussion, it was suggeste that payments equilibrium between the partner countries might be achieved by means of fluctuation in the rates of exchange of thei several currencies. But nothing came of the Fritalux proposals and i neither the Benelux Union nor the European Economic Community were special provisions made for exchange rate adjustment betweer currencies. In this connection it must be said that whatever the ad vantages of a general system of fluctuating exchange rates—and they are considerable, in the case of a customs union where it is desired to attain the maximum freedom of factor movements and integration of economic policies there are serious practical difficulties in departing from a regime of fixed exchange rates. It is, for example, difficult to see how the full integration of capital markets and of rights of establish ment of firms in other member countries of an economic union can be secured if there are frequent exchange rate variations.[1] In the case of the European Economic Community, the Agricultural Fund[2] would

---

[1] This is fully discussed by T. Scitovsky in *Economic Theory and Western European Integration*, Unwin University Books, Allen and Unwin, 1958. See especially Chapter II.

[2] See below, p. 307.

be extremely difficult, but not impossible, to administer if exchange rates between members were constantly changing.

A third alternative means of reconciling free trade with equilibrium in balances of payments is by the adoption within each member country of policies appropriate to its balance of payments position. Each member country must ensure that its monetary, budgetary and incomes policies are such as to secure overall balance of payments equilibrium without the need for controls on transactions with its union partners. It was largely because the Governments of the Netherlands and the Belgium-Luxembourg Economic Union were unwilling to make domestic policies subservient to the requirements of payments equilibrium with their respective Benelux partners, that so many years passed before the final consummation of the Union took place. During the early years of the customs union, the Netherlands was in serious overall balance of payments deficit, while the Belgium-Luxembourg Economic Union was in a reasonably strong position. Accordingly import restrictions and exchange controls on dealings with third countries were much more stringent in the Netherlands than in the Belgium-Luxembourg Economic Union. There was therefore difficulty in co-ordinating policies *vis-à-vis* non-member countries.

The problem was exacerbated by divergences in the domestic policies followed in the member countries. At an early stage after the Liberation the authorities of the Belgium-Luxembourg Economic Union felt able to lift internal price controls and most restrictions in imports, but this policy was matched with fairly stringent monetary and budgetary policies. In and after 1946 Belgium had one of the highest bank rates in Western Europe. In the Netherlands, on the other hand, monetary and budgetary policies were much less stringent, but detailed price and import controls were retained long after they had been abandoned in the Belgium-Luxembourg Economic Union. In part due to the differences in the impact of war on the two economies and in part due to differing economic policies for internal balance, the removal of quantitative and other controls in 1947 and 1948 would have caused a marked upsurge of imports into the Netherlands where goods were cheap but scarce from the Belgium-Luxembourg Economic Union where they were dear, but relatively plentiful.

Thus the Benelux Union, in its formative years from 1944 to 1949–50, forms a fascinating case study of the two union partners, in widely divergent balance of payments positions, experiencing great difficulty in progressing towards free trade, and in adopting a common import policy *vis-à-vis* the outside world, largely on account of their reluctance to adopt financial policies consistent with these ends. It was only after

1948 that a distinct change of emphasis appeared in Dutch policy.[1] From that year price controls were relaxed, subsidies reduced, and budgetary policies tightened. Accordingly it was possible gradually to liberalize trade between the partner countries and to co-ordinate policies *vis-à-vis* the outside world.

One of the worries of the Benelux situation was that during the years of physical shortage in the Netherlands, the Belgium-Luxembourg Economic Union refused to import freely virtually the only goods of which the Netherlands at that time had an exportable surplus—namely agricultural products. The authorities in the Belgium-Luxembourg Economic Union regarded the protection of their high cost farming community as of greater importance than progress towards the economic union.

Capital Movements

Now even if all the partners in an economic union eschew policies of direct price and incomes control as the means of containing domestic inflation and put their trust in policies of overall financial control, serious difficulties in regard to liberalizing capital movements might be encountered if some partners emphasize monetary and others budgetary policies for internal balance. This again can be illustrated from the experience of Benelux. Up to the middle of 1954 little progress had been made in the liberalization of capital movements within Benelux.

By 1951, both the Netherlands and the Belgium-Luxembourg Economic Union had forsaken direct controls (although a modified wages policy was still in operation in the Netherlands), relying upon broad financial policies for balance of payments equilibrium. But whereas after 1949 the Netherlands had more or less balanced budgets and low interest rates, in Belgium there were substantial budget deficits, but rates of interest were high. If capital movements had been free, there would have been an outflow of capital from the Netherlands, where interest rates were low, to the Belgium-Luxembourg Economic Union, where they were high. Accordingly, the Netherlands government was unwilling to allow the loosening of capital movements until interest rates had grown closer together.

Many of the problems which bedevilled Benelux were much less serious in the case of the European Economic Community. By that time post-war recovery was complete; virtually all domestic price controls had been removed; all the participants were using the interest

[1] Problems arising from differences in financial policies in the member countries of the Benelux Union are discussed in the Benelux section in *Case Studies in European Economic Union*, cited above.

rate as an important means of maintaining both domestic and balance of payments equilibrium. As the result of the OEEC liberalization programme, almost all quantitative restrictions on members' mutual trade in non-agricultural products, had been abandoned. Moreover, except for Italy in 1964, and France in late 1968, all the member countries of the EEC have enjoyed relatively favourable balances of payments. In part this has been due to the favourable world economic climate in which the EEC was established, and to the fact that domestic rates of growth have been such that the occasional clamping down of domestic demand in the interest of external equilibrium has been possible without undue domestic strain. Serious problems arose, however, in the later 1960s and early 1970s, some of which we examine in the following chapter.

SHORT GUIDE TO THE LITERATURE

The relevant works have been cited in the footnotes of the last two chapters. In particular I would commend Professor Meade's books, *The Theory of Customs Unions* and *Problems of Economic Union*, cited in footnotes. Professor Lipsey's 1960 *Economic Journal* article 'The Theory of Customs Unions' is an extremely valuable survey. Many of the problems of integration are discussed by Professor Bela Balassa, *The Theory of Economic Integration*, London, Allen and Unwin, 1962, and in a very useful symposium, *Economic Integration in Europe*, ed. G. R. Denton, Weidenfeld and Nicolson, 1969. The first chapter by N. Lundgren includes a survey of empirical work on customs unions and free trade areas.

CHAPTER 22

INTEGRATION IN THE POST-WAR WORLD: A

In this chapter we shall examine the structure of some of the post-war integration schemes, paying especial attention to the economic problems facing union builders in Western Europe, where most progress has been made in economic integration, although we shall also consider briefly attempts to build unions in other parts of the world. As we have already noted, the GATT is somewhat ambivalent in its attitude towards geographical discrimination. Until recently the GATT[1] set its face against the extension of preferential trading arrangements, but in spite of this it has always permitted the establishment of customs unions—largely for political reasons.[2]

The political arguments in favour of integration were particularly strong in post-war Western Europe; they largely reflected the cold-war situation and the desire to ensure some measure of international control over the revival of German military power. Many people concerned with the German question were convinced that only by the integration of Germany into some fairly tight-knit community would further European conflict be impossible. It was also realized in Western Europe itself that the military and economic might of the United States of America and the USSR was such that no single nation in Western Europe was capable of a truly independent policy *vis-a-vis* these giants. Whilst the political and strategic arguments for integration carried most weight, there were also strong economic reasons for the growing together of the states of Western Europe. In particular, the advancing technology of the war years had demonstrated that European nations were no longer big enough for any one of them alone to derive the full advantage from the economies of large scale production.

In Western Europe the integration movement resulted in attempts to establish economic, political and military institutions. In the early post-war years some success seemed likely in achieving military co-ordination, and at one time it seemed possible that NATO might develop into

[1] The GATT now accepts the extension of new preferences by developed to less developed countries and the establishment of preferences within the latter group of countries. See below, p. 346.

[2] In 1947 the state of customs union theory was such that some free trade was widely believed to be better than none and customs unions were accordingly welcomed on economic grounds.

institution for sharing the economic burden of defence—perhaps
en becoming the precursor of some kind of Atlantic Confederation.[1]
the event, however, only limited progress has been made towards
ilitary or political integration.[2] Such success as integration has
hieved in Western Europe is largely in the economic field.

In regard to the demand for economic integration there have been
arked differences of emphasis. Some people, especially in the Scan-
navian countries and in the UK envisage the movement as a programme
joint action by sovereign states on specific issues; others advocate
e establishment of supra-national bodies capable of a federal approach
economic and political programmes. The former attitude, sometimes
scribed as 'functionalist' coloured the creation of the OEEC (later the
CD); the more closely integrated approach lay behind the establish-
ent of the European Coal and Steel Community (ECSC) and the
uropean Economic Community (EEC). In addition there were many
ho favoured a purely sectoral approach, as for example through the
ortive 'Green Plan' which promised the establishment of a common
ntrolled market in agriculture in Western Europe. In the following
ctions we examine in a little more detail some of the differing economic
tegration schemes of Western Europe, using integration in a wide
nse to include 'functional' as well as institutional types of integration.

1. THE OEEC

ade Liberalization

estern Europe's relatively rapid recovery from Second World War
ved much to massive aid from the United States under the European
ecovery Programme. In proposing aid, however, the US Government
ade it quite clear that the US would help the countries of Europe only
they would help themselves. A first step towards this self-help was a
oser economic co-operation than before among the erstwhile warring
tions of Europe. The Governments of Western Europe responded

1 These ideas were developed by Professor J. E. Meade in an article in *Lloyds
ank Review*, October 1951, reprinted as the Appendix 'Some Economic Problems
Atlantic Union Re-armament', in *Problems of Economic Union*, Allen and Unwin,
53.
2 The attempt to establish a truly Western European Army of some forty divisions,
earing a common uniform and subject to European control, failed when Great
ritain failed to participate and when (in 1954) the French Parliament refused to
tify the Treaty setting up the European Defence Community (EDC). In the political
here, the Council of Europe (meeting in Strasbourg), which was to have been the
olitical counterpart to the OEEC (see below), has been primarily a debating chamber
ith little impact upon foreign or other policies of member countries.

with alacrity to this challenge, and in April 1948 a Convention for th
establishment of the Organization for European Economic Co
operation was signed by the representatives of sixteen European
countries and the allied Commander-in-Chief in Germany.[1]

The OEEC was the body responsible for the distribution of American
aid and for furthering co-operation in trade and payments among
recipient countries. One of the notable achievements of the OEEC in it
early years was the acceptance by member Governments of the OEEC
Code of Liberalization. The object of the Code, adopted by the OEEC
Council in August 1950, was the dismantling in accordance with a pre
arranged time-table of quantitative restrictions on members' mutua
trade. The time-table laid down the target of a 60 per cent liberalizatio
of the 1948 level of private imports by the autumn of 1950. Largely
owing to the outbreak of the Korean war in 1950 and the consequen
serious balance of payments disequilibria in many countries, thi
target was not achieved until much later. In fact, in November 1951
the British Government reimposed import controls on a number o
products previously liberalized. This retrograde step resulted in a reduc
tion in the percentage liberalized of UK private imports from OEEC
countries to 46 per cent by the end of 1952. These cuts were not full
restored until 1955. In spite of such set backs the OEEC Code was usefu
in setting up the liberalization targets, and enabling the Organizatio
to follow closely members' progress towards abolishing restrictions.

The EPU

In moving toward more liberal trade, countries of Western Europe
were assisted by the establishment in July 1950 of the European Pay
ments Union, itself an offshoot of the OEEC. Up to this date many
countries felt unable to relax trade restrictions for fear of balance o
payments repercussions. Few countries were in a sufficiently strong
external position to risk removal of restrictions without some kind o
'cushion' to protect their reserves. Such a cushion was provided by the
European Payments Union. The EPU had two main functions. Firstly
it established a clearing mechanism so that member countries needed
to concern themselves only with their payments positions *vis-a-vis*
their union partners as a group and not with individual member
countries. Secondly, it also provided temporary—but automatic—help
to countries in deficit with other Union members. A country in defici

[1] The founding members of the OEEC were Austria Belgium, Luxembourg
Denmark, France, Greece, Iceland Eire, Italy, Netherlands, Norway, Portugal
Spain, Sweden, Switzerland, Turkey and the United Kingdom. Canada and the
USA had associate status.

with its EPU partners was required to settle in gold only to a limited proportion, but a proportion which increased as its cumulative deficit mounted. In this way deficit members were provided with an incentive to correct disequilibrium.

Each member was allotted a quota, which determined its 'drawing rights'. Within 20 per cent of its quota, a country was not required to make any settlement of its cumulative deficit with its fellow EPU members in gold. But if at the monthly notification its cumulative deficit was between 20 per cent and 40 per cent of its quota, 20 per cent of the deficit was to be settled in gold; the remainder took the form of an increase in its debit with the Union. If the cumulative deficit was between 40 per cent and 60 per cent, 40 per cent of it would be settled in gold, and so on for successive 20 per cent *tranches* until the cumulative deficit reached 100 per cent of a country's quota, when settlement was required entirely in gold. Each member county had an account with the EPU at the Bank for International Settlements (BIS) at Basle.

In the case of a surplus member, as its cumulative surplus increased the first *tranches* of its quota would be met largely by the accumulation of credit with the EPU; a relatively small proportion of the surplus being settled in gold. But as a surplus country approached the limit of its quota, settlement was increasingly in gold, until the cumulative surplus equalled the member's quota, from which point settlement was entirely in gold.[1] The EPU commenced operations in July 1950; as with the Code of Liberalization, there were setbacks in the early years, Germany and France rapidly exhausting their quotas.[2] But for several years the EPU performed a valuable function in lubricating the machinery of intra-European trade; undoubtedly it gave OEEC member countries confidence in liberalizing trade with their European partners. As time passed, however, the EPU was progressively 'hardened', that is members were required to settle an increasingly high proportion of their deficits in gold. Finally, as part of the general move towards convertible currencies, the EPU was wound up in 1958 being replaced by the European Monetary Agreement (EMA); the new arrangement does not provide for the automatic extension of credit.[3]

[1] The fullest account of the early post-war payments mechanisms and of the EPU is in Professor Graham L. Rees' book, *Britain and the Post-War European Payments System*, University of Wales Press, 1963.
[2] For a detailed description of the difficulties of these years see W. Diebold (Jnr), *Trade and Payments in Western Europe* Harper Bros. N-York, 1952.
[3] Although it has provided limited payments assistance to Greece and Turkey the EMA has been of small significance.

A considerable amount of the work done by the OEEC (and the OECD) consists of fact-finding and exchange of information. Many standard sources of statistical material on the economy of Western Europe are provided by the secretariat; the OEEC studies of various European industries and of the economies of member countries are rightly re garded as authoritative surveys. The published recommendations of OEEC/OECD country studies have considerable weight; they provide information enabling observers to assess more intelligently the economic implications of policy decisions currently taken by member Govern ments. There are numerous other fields in which members co-operate notably the co-ordination of aid programmes through the Develop ment Assistance Committee. There is also a European Productivity Agency administered by the OECD.

By 1959, the dollar shortage was over; most European currencies were convertible into dollars and post-war recovery could be regarded as complete. Henceforth emphasis was less on the removal of bottle-necks and shortages within Western Europe and more on economic development in a world context. Accordingly the OEEC was replaced in 1961 by the Organization for European Co-operation and Develop-ment with the US, Canada (and from 1964 Japan and 1971 Australia) as full members.[2] Technical co-operation, and the examination and confrontation of national policies continue, but increasing stress is now upon the place of member countries in the world rather than the European economy. Neither the OEEC nor the OECD have been much concerned with tariff questions. It is true that in the early post-war years a European Customs Union Study Group was set up under the aegis of the OEEC, but at that time tariffs were far less important than quantitative controls as restraints on trade. In any case, tariff questions were widely regarded as being the prerogative of the GATT, which of course was based on the principle of multilateral rather than regional tariff reductions. Although Article 9 of the OEEC Convention laid down that it was part of the Organization's task to study customs unions and free trade areas, the impetus towards customs unions came from outside the OEEC.

---

[1] Notably OECD (previously OEEC) *General Statistics* (monthly) and the detailed *Foreign Trade Statistics*. The latter are especially useful for students of international trade anxious to obtain details of trade among industrialized countries. The January-December volume of series C, giving a country/commodity trade breakdown of all member countries is invaluable.

[2] The establishment and work of the OECD is described by Henry G. Aubrey in *Atlantic Economic Co-operation*, F. A. Praeger, 1967.

2. TOWARDS CLOSER INTEGRATION IN WESTERN EUROPE

he first post-war customs union in Western Europe was the Benelux
Union, consisting of the Belgium-Luxembourg Economic Union[1] and
he Netherlands. Although discussed by the Governments in exile
uring the war, the Benelux Customs Union came into operation only
n January 1, 1948. As we noted in Chapter 20, the experience of
Benelux is interesting since it illustrates so many of the varied diffi-
ulties faced by union builders in the modern world. Although tariffs
etween the member countries were removed and the Benelux tariffs
is-à-vis outside countries established as early as 1948, it was several
ears before quantitative trade controls and exchange restrictions
ere removed on trade between members. Apart from difficulties
rising from the harmonization of tax and other legislation, the delay
n removing all restrictions was caused by the unwillingness of the
artner countries to subordinate domestic economic policies to the
equirements of the union. For example, until 1949, the Netherlands
ollowed a *dirigiste* policy of low interest rates accompanied by fairly
tringent direct economic controls—including a vigorously enforced
vages policy, whilst Belgium adopted a fairly liberal economic regime,
ndeavouring to contain price and wage increases by high interest
ates and balanced budgets.[2]

The European Coal and Steel Community

One of the serious political difficulties facing Western Europe in
he early post-war years was the German problem—how to integrate
Germany into the European Community without giving opportunity
or the resurgence of nationalism which had, twice in a generation,
lunged Europe into war. In its economic aspect this was the problem
f allowing the recovery of heavy industry in Germany, notably in
ron and steel, while making it impossible for these resources to be
sed for aggression. The Schuman Plan envisaged the solution of this
question in the close integration of the coal, iron and steel industries
f Western Germany with those of the rest of Western Europe. The
Treaty of Paris, which resulted from the Schuman Plan, provided not
nly for free-trade in these products, but established a supra-national
ody—the High Authority—to ensure that integration went further
han the mere removal of tariffs and other trade barriers. As noted in

[1] The building of the Belgium-Luxembourg Economic Union in the inter-war
ears is described by Professor Meade in *Case Studies in European Economic Union*,
ited above, pp. 13–58.
[2] p. 293 above.

the previous chapter[1] the Treaty of Paris provides for free trade through
out the ECSC in coal, iron ore, steel, and for effective competitio
by the elimination of discrimination in price, subsidy and transpor
policies.[2] In a textbook of this nature it would be inappropriate t
discuss in detail the purely institutional aspects of the Coal and Stee
Community[3] but the supra-national features of the powers of the Hig
Authority had important consequences for the economies of th
member countries. The Treaty of Paris gave to the High Authorit
powers greater than those normally enjoyed by executive bodies o
international economic institutions. Provided it acted within th
framework of the Treaty of Paris, the High Authority had genera
oversight of the operation of the free market in coal, iron and steel. I
could impose maximum and minimum prices for both domestic an
export products; it could impose production quotas upon membe
countries' coal and steel industries. The Treaty also gave the Hig
Authority the right to impose levies when output exceeded a give
level, and to hand over the proceeds to enterprises producing less tha
a certain quota. In time of shortage the High Authority could alloca
supplies among member states. The Treaty of Paris also gave the Hig
Authority considerable fact-finding powers, in particular the right t
be given details of investment programmes of individual enterprises.

There were a number of built-in checks to the powers of the Hig
Authority. For example, it was required to confer with a Consultative
Committee representing producers, consumers and dealers. In certai
matters, the High Authority shared power with the Council of th
Community whose members, representing the viewpoints of thei
several Governments, acted as liaison between the Governments and
the High Authority. The European Parliament was given power to
pass a vote of non-confidence in the High Authority and to require
its resignation; but in practice the influence of the Parliament on day-
to-day decision taking was never great. Perhaps more significant is
the influence exercised by the Court of Justice not only over the High
Authority, but also over the whole operation of the Community.

In spite of the supra-national powers given to the High Authority

[1] See above, p. 289.

[2] Signed by the Benelux countries, France, Italy and Western Germany in 1951.
Britain refused to join the Community as a full member, but later became an associate, sending observers to Luxembourg.

[3] There are several good surveys of the ECSC in its early days, notably W. Diebold
Jnr, *The Schuman Plan*, New York, 1959, and L. Lister, *Europe's Coal and Steel
Community*, New York, 1960. There is detailed information on the question of the
operation of the Community in *CECA 1952–62. Resultats, Limites, Perspectives*,
ECSC, Luxembourg, 1963, and in the Annual General Reports of the Community.

nd the Course of Justice the achievements of the ECSC can be of only ualified satisfaction to its founding fathers. Difficulties have been xperienced when national interests and those of the Community lash; indeed at times domestic pressures led to the virtual suspension f the free market. For example, for several years the Belgian coal elds were allowed to receive special and substantial protection. Frequently it has seemed that the ECSC is a fair-weather integration scheme. But the Community has substantial achievements to its credit. Investment policy has been co-ordinated more closely than would have been he case in the absence of the Community. A particularly valuable iece of pioneer work has been the implementation of the resettlement nd retraining provisions of the Treaty. Originally re-adaption assisance was provided only for firms and workers directly affected by the Common Market, but in 1960, the High Authority resolved to assist lso interests affected by longer-term structural changes.

As time passed, a number of the functions of the Coal and Steel Community tended to become merged with those of the other European Communities—the EEC and Euratom. Indeed the executive organs of he three Communities were merged in 1967. As a separate body the Authority has now disappeared, although the three Communities, as pposed to the three executives, continued to exist. The work of the High Authority has now been taken over by the enlarged Commission f the Communities. There is now one Commission, one Court of ustice and one European Parliament, for the ECSC, Euratom and EEC. As with the High Authority, the first loyalty of the members of the Commission is to the Community rather than to their own countries. The Commission has substantial powers to initiate Community action. Although members have individual responsibilities the Commission cts as a collective group in its relatious with the Council, other Community bodies, and outside member countries. In the last resort, owever, important decisions are taken by the Council, members of which, of course, represent their own national Governments to which hey are answerable. In fact, in the later 1960s and early 1970s, more nd more issues were decided by the Council and its Committee of Permanent Representatives rather than by the Commission.

3. THE EEC IN THE TRANSITION PERIOD

The EEC countries together account for one-third of world trade, more than twice the share of the United States. Over 50 per cent of mports into the Community countries are from other member counries; for the Benelux countries, the proportion is three-quarters. The

EEC is economically one of the fastest-growing areas of the world; trade between member countries expanded five times in value between 195? and 1971 and gross national product nearly doubled.

The enlarged Community of Nine accounts for one-fifth of the world's combined national product and for four-tenths of world trade.

The Transition Period

In many respects the establishment of the EEC, like that of the ECS? was the result of political rather than economic causes. The failure of the French National Assembly to ratify the European Defence Community Treaty in 1954 brought about a switch in emphasis among integrationists from political to economic methods of achieving their goal. Not long before, the European Coal and Steel Community had been brought to a successful birth. Why not proceed further along these lines, extending the common market in coal and steel to other products? Why not develop the supra-national aspects of the Treaty of Paris to cover integration over a wider area of the member countries economies? When in June 1955 the Foreign Ministers of the Six met at Messina, they issued a declaration proclaiming their desire to see a common market covering all goods moving between their countries. A committee under the chairmanship of M. Spaak was quickly established reporting back to the Ministers within a year. As the result of their Report, two Treaties were drawn up and signed at Rome in March 1957. One set up the European Economic Community (EEC), the other the European Atomic Energy Community—Euratom.

The object of the EEC is set out in Article 2 of the Rome Treaty as follows:

The mission of the Community shall be, by establishing a common market and gradually removing differences between the economic policies of member states to promote throughout the Community the harmonious development of economic activities, continuous and balanced expansion, increased stability, a rapid improvement in the standard of living and closer relations between its member states.

It is clear that the Treaty envisages much more than the establishment of a common market; there is also to be a steady growing together of the economies of the member states, until the Community eventually becomes an economic union.

The more immediate objective of the Treaty, the creation of a common market was achieved relatively easily. In fact the time-table was accelerated and free trade in industrial products established by July 1, 1968—two years earlier than laid down in the Treaty. There were no serious difficulties either in removing tariffs on intra-Community trade or in agreeing the shape of the common external tariff. The latter is in general the arithmetic average of the tariffs of member countries; for most products this has meant the raising of Benelux duties—and to a less extent those of Western Germany, with a corresponding lowering of French and Italian ones.[1]

In agriculture, the architects of the Community envisaged an organized rather than a free market. At the institution of the EEC all the member states protected their agriculture by means of both tariffs and domestic support arrangements; it was accordingly necessary for them not only to remove tariffs on agricultural products but to substitute a common policy for the various national support programmes. The need to establish a common policy in agriculture was recognized from the early days of the Community, especially since agriculture plays a more important role in the economies of member countries than it does in the United Kingdom. Agricultural output accounts for between 6 and 14·6 per cent of the national incomes of the EEC member countries. More than one sixth of the total working force of the Community is directly engaged in agriculture, while many more are engaged in dependent industries and trades. Agricultural products account for some 10 per cent of the total exports of community countries; the proportion is highest in the Netherlands (nearly one quarter). There are some serious structural problems in European agriculture; more than two-thirds of all Community farms are less than twenty-five acres; costs tend to be high, and productivity low. In the absence of Government support, farm incomes would lag even further behind those of workers in other industries.

The EEC deals with the agricultural problem by means of an agreed common policy, the outlines of which were agreed after much difficulty on January 14, 1962. Since that date details have been filled in and by 1968 the main guidelines of policy in regard to the various products had become clear. The most important decision in 1962 was to set up a European Agricultural Guidance and Guarantee Fund (EAGGF). This Fund is in two sections (a) the Guarantee Section, which takes over the finance of domestic price support from member Governments and is also responsible for financing subsidies on exports to non-member

[1] The official common external tariff is to be found in *Tariff Douanier des Communautés Européennes*, Service des Publications des Communautés Européennes, modified in subsequent additions. A ready comparison of the pre-Community tariffs of members countries with the common external tariff for industrial products on a three-digit SITC basis is in *Atlantic Tariffs and Trade*, Political and Economic Planning, Allen and Unwin.

countries, and (b) the Guidance Section, which finances structural improvements in member countries.[1]

The second keystone of Community agricultural policy is the establishment of Community prices for the various products. Whereas in the case of industrial products it was felt that forces of competition would ensure a more or less uniform price for similar products throughout the Community, in agriculture, domestic support policies were such that positive steps had to be taken to ensure uniformity of prices. Given the wide price divergencies between member countries, free trade would have created unbearable strains in certain member countries. Notably, the price of wheat in Western Germany, Italy and Luxemburg was much higher than in France. Accordingly the policy of the Community is to move towards a common price for a wide range of farm products, notably grain, milk and milk products; beef and veal, rice, sugar, oilseeds and olive oil.

The common price for grains came into operation July 1, 1967; it represented a significant drop in prices received by German, Italian and Luxembourg farmers, who were, however, compensated by payment from the Agricultural Fund of three annual lump sums of decreasing size. A basic community *target price* is determined for each grain, the actual target prices for various areas (not countries) of the Community being derived from it, account being taken of differing transport costs. In addition to the target prices there are *intervention prices*—at which the authorities are obliged to buy grain offered to them. An intervention price is in fact a guaranteed producer price and is lower than the target price. For each product too there is a *threshold price*, the basis for calculating the import levy. This price is

---

[1] Methods of financing the Fund have varied considerably over the years. In 1969, it was decided to include payments in respect of agriculture in the Community budget which as from 1975 would be financed as follows: Governments would hand over to the Community the proceeds of all agricultural levies and customs duties collected (less 10 per cent to cover collection costs) and supplement this to the extent necessary with contributions amounting to at the most a 1 per cent rate of the common value added tax. Between 1971 and 1974 levies on agricultural imports would be handed over together with an increasing proportion of customs duties on other goods. Any balance of expenditure would be met by members from national budgets according to a fixed key: Belgium to pay 6·8%, France 32·6%, Germany 32·9%, Italy 20·2%, Luxembourg 0·2%, Netherlands 7·3%. In 1968–9, the last year for which full figures were available, the percentages of the member countries' receipts from the Guarantee Section of the Fund were: Belgium 7·2%, France 40·6%, Germany 18·5%, Italy 15·0%, Luxembourg 0·1%, Netherlands 18·6%. During that year, the total contributions made to the Fund were: Belgium and Luxembourg 9·0%, France 24·4%, Germany 29·7%, Italy 25·4%, Netherlands 11·5%. In 1972, the Community budget amounted to $4,000 million of which $3,500 was earmarked for the Fund.

fixed to equate the price of the imported commodity to the target price, account being taken of transport costs. The levy itself is a variable import charge, designed to bring the price of imported products to the target price. In the case of grains the levy is adjusted daily in accordance with the changing world price.

In formulating a common farm policy it is clearly necessary to advance on a wide front more or less simultaneously. Otherwise some members will be unduly favoured at the expense of others. For example, France, a grain producer, clearly stands to gain as the result of unification of the market in grains. Dutch farmers, on the other hand, are most interested in a wider market for dairy produce; Belgian farmers are anxious to see a common market in sugar, while Italian agriculturists are primarily interested in horticulture. Accordingly, following the establishment of a common grain policy, a number of decisions have been taken in regard to other products. In July 1966, common prices for milk and milk products, beef and veal, sugar, rice, rapeseed, and olive oil were agreed. These came into force at various dates in 1967 and 1968. There are differences in detail in the way in which the common price and policy is implemented in each of these products. For example for pigmeat, there are no target prices, and the market intervention system is not as automatic as in the case of grains. A basic pigmeat price is fixed annually by the Council and this is taken as a guide by the authorities in deciding whether or to what extent to intervene in the market of a member country. There are, however, minimum Community import prices, known as *sluice-gate prices* adjusted at quarterly intervals. Sluice-gate prices apply also to eggs and poultry.

In fats and oils, Community protection against imports from non-member countries is provided by the common external tariff, but for olive oil (of particular importance to Italy), a system of import levies operates and there is substantial Community financial support for domestic producers. A complicated system operates for sugar. Each sugar beet factory in the Community is allocated a quota based on its previous five years output; up to the limit of this quota a factory receives a minimum price guarantee. Sugar produced above the quota, however, must be exported. Such exports sold at world prices, are not eligible for refunds. Special arrangements have been made for trade in fruit, vegetables, and wines. Intra-Community trade in these products is now liberalized, and community quality standards are in operation. There is, however, a rarely-used escape clause which can be invoked in times of glut, in accordance with a carefully laid-down community procedure. By the end of the transitional period, the single market stage had been achieved for well over nine-tenths of national output, leaving the rest to be brought in by the middle of 1970.

In 1964–5 the total expenditure of the Fund amounted to $234·3 million; by 1971, it had risen to nearly $2,000 million, of which the guarantee section accounted for $1,800 million, thus nine-tenths of the Fund's expenditure has been devoted to the finance of support policies of various kinds rather than to the fostering of agricultural improvement. Some 50 per cent of the guarantee expenditure was devoted to subsidizing exports, most of the remainder being taken up by price support for cereals and dairy produce in the internal market. In so far as the subsidization of home consumption and exports causes a resource misallocation by encouraging the continued employment of labour and capital in agriculture when these resources could more profitably be employed in other activities, the effect of the guarantee arrangements of the Fund is economically undesirable. On the other hand it is argued that substantial social costs would be incurred by the sudden exposure of the agricultural economies of community states to low cost imports. Throughout the Community there has been a substantial drift away from the land, of about 550,000 workers a year.

It has become increasingly clear that the almost exclusive reliance on price policy has been extremely costly and has not been successful in regulating supplies: at times serious surpluses were developing in some products. Nor has it been efficient in improving farm incomes. The Mansholt plan (called after the then Commissioner in charge of agriculture) of 1968 and subsequent versions attempted to shift the emphasis towards structural improvement and inducements to farmers to leave the land. But Governments have been slow to accept the political and social implications and it took until 1972 for some of the proposals to become operative. By then two further important changes of emphasis were under preliminary consideration: the possibility of direct income subsidies supplementing support policies and a stronger link with regional development through the provision of alternative employment for the modernization and improvement of agrarian structures.

The Unification of Taxes

We have examined the agricultural provisions of the EEC in some detail, partly on account of the importance of this sector of trade to the Community, and partly because a number of difficulties in building the Community have arisen in the agricultural sector. Agriculture in the EEC also provides an interesting case study of the forms taken by farm protectionism in the modern world. Incidentally it also illustrates the point made in Chapter 6, namely that tariff, trade and exchange controls are by no means the only, or in some products even the most important, weapons of protection. There are, however, a number of other areas in which the Community countries have attempted to come closer together but where serious difficulties have been encountered. We can perhaps illustrate these difficulties by looking at some of the more important provisions of the Treaty of Rome. One such provision is contained in Article 99 which lays down that the Commission shall 'consider in what way the law of the various member states concerning turnover taxes, excise duties, and other forms of indirect taxation . . . can be harmonized in the interest of the Common Market'.

In Chapter 21 we drew attention to the necessity of harmonizing indirect taxes within a customs union. So far in the EEC, virtually no progress has been made in unifying direct tax rates, but at least a start has been made in unifying indirect tax systems, by the decision of the member Governments to adopt by 1970 the French value added tax system in place of the various sales tax systems previously in operation. It has been agreed that within the Union such taxes should be levied on the 'origin' rather than the 'destination' principle. The origin principle means that goods are taxed according to the rates imposed in the country of origin. Under the destination principle, on the other hand, duties imposed in the country of origin are rebated to the exporter at the border: such goods then enter the partner country duty free and are then subject to internal taxes in exactly the same way as domestically produced goods. The EEC countries have agreed to move over to the origin principle in regard to intra-Community trade, while the destination principle will be retained for exports to non-Union countries.[1]

There are four major types of indirect tax: (*a*) single stage turnover taxes, levied at *either* the manufacturing, wholesale or retail stage; (*b*) gross multi-stage turnover taxes, which are cumulative and are levied on the *transactions* value at each stage of the production and distribution process; these are sometimes known as 'cascade' type taxes; (*c*) net multi-stage turnover taxes, levied on value *added* at each stage of production and distribution-these are known as 'turnover value added' (TVA) taxes; (*d*) excise duties which are single stage taxes on single products, usually varying with the product. The cascade type of tax predominates in Belgium (rate 6 per cent), the Netherlands (5 per cent), Germany (4 per cent), Italy (3·3 per cent), Luxembourg (2 per

---

[1] EEC Commission *Report of the Fiscal and Financial Committee* (Neumark Report), Brussels, 1963.

cent). France alone applies the 20 per cent value added duty.[1] The decision to accept the French TVA system was taken by the Council of Ministers in April 1967; but as we have noted, harmonization relates to tax methods rather than rates; tax equalization at the frontiers will still be necessary. The Council, however, issued a directive requiring the Commission to submit by the end of 1968 proposals for removing the tax frontier. Virtually no progress has been made in unifying direct taxation. Amost certainly, the first step will be the harmonization of systems of corporate taxation, but it will be several years at least before personal taxation is harmonized.

The Co-ordination of overall Economic Policy

An area in which progress has been made is in the freeing of movements of labour and the harmonizing of social conditions. The Treaty provides for the free movement of capital and the right of establishment to business enterprises of all kinds throughout the Community. By 1967 capital movements, both short and long-term were virtually free, although the conditions under which new issues could be raised differed from country to country. Perhaps the most serious difficulty in this respect arises from divergences in company law and practice in the various member countries.[2] Such differences have, for example, rendered almost impossible the merging of companies across frontiers. When the Agfa-Gaevert merger was negotiated in the 1960s, years of complex legal discussions were necessary. Steps have now been taken to bring about a harmonization of company law but progress so far is extremely slow. In 1967 a group of Community lawyers, led by Professor Pieter Sanders of the Faculty of Law at Rotterdam University, produced a draft European Company Structure which is likely to become the basis for future policy. The Statute envisages that, alongside present national enterprises, there will be established European Companies, formed from amalgamation of existing ones and subject to detailed community requirements as to articles of incorporation, voting rights of shareholders and responsibilities of directors. It is not yet clear whether legislation establishing such companies will be introduced on a supranational Community basis, as favoured by the Commission, or whether it will be enacted by each member country separately, as advocated

---

[1] The implications of tax harmonization within the EEC and within an Atlantic free trade area are discussed by Professor Douglas Dosser in his contribution, 'Fiscal and Social Barriers to Economic Integration in the Atlantic Area', in *Studies in Trade Liberalization*, ed. Balassa, cited above.

[2] One important practical difference is that whereas in Italy—as in the UK—shares are virtually all registered, in other EEC countries bearer shares predominate.

by the French. One aspect in which legal difficulties have prevented fuller integration is in the field of direct investment, that is the setting up by companies of branches or subsidiaries in other member countries. Many enterprises established within the Community were by non-member countries, particularly by the US.

An important element in ensuring free mobility of capital movements within the EEC is the co-ordination of interest rate policies. Interest rates are still determined by individual member countries, although the central bankers, together with the Finance Ministers, meet at almost monthly intervals in the Monetary Committee of the Community. The Monetary Committee was established to implement Article 104 of the Treaty which requires each of the member states to pursue 'the economic policy necessary to ensure the equilibrium of its overall balance of payments and to maintain confidence in its currency, while ensuring a high level of employment and the stability of the level of prices'. Clearly, the more freely capital moves between members, the greater the need to harmonize monetary policies. With this consideration in mind, the Monetary Committee regularly examines the financial policies of member countries. For example, when in Western Germany overall demand slackened at the end of 1967, the Committee recommended the Federal Republic to adopt an easier and more flexible monetary policy. The German authorities responded to this recommendation by reducing the discount rate from 5 to 4 per cent, and introducing measures to increase the liquidity of the banking system. On the other hand, when in 1966 there was a substantial inflow of foreign exchange into Italy, the Committee was more concerned about the prospect of a superfluity rather than a shortage of liquidity.

The Monetary Committee also concerns itself with the methods of monetary control used by the authorities in member countries. As early in community history as 1962 a study was made of the instruments of monetary policy.[1] There has been a growing together of the machinery of monetary control; but substantial differences still exist. For example, open market operations by the Bank of France are on a more modest scale than in other community countries, while the Treasury plays a more direct role in monetary affairs.

Monetary policies form only one part of overall economic policy, and are closely linked with budgetary policies. In 1962 excess demand built up in France and especially in Italy; as the result of integration already achieved this quickly spilled over to affect first the Netherlands

---

[1] *The Instrument of Monetary Policy in the Countries of the European Economic Community*, EEC Commission, Brussels, 1962.

and later Belgium. There was need for a co-ordinated and anti-inflationary policy throughout the Community, but especially in Italy. Faced with this situation, the Council adopted in April 1964 a Recommendation calling on member Governments to take action to restore equilibrium within the Community, giving priority to price stabilization. The Recommendation laid down that in each country, the expansion of Government expenditure should not exceed 5 per cent a year; this was a clear step forward towards integration.

Co-ordination in budgetary matters has been improved by the establishment in 1964 of the Budget Policy Committee and the Medium-Term Economic Policy Committee.[1] As yet these Committees have no legal powers within the Community, but they make recommendations to the Council, and (perhaps as important) provide a means for the informal interchange of opinion and information as does the Committee of Governors of Central Banks.

One of the stated objectives of the Rome Treaty is the freeing of movements of persons as well as of capital. This involves more than a simple decision to allow workers to move freely from one part of the Community to another; it requires also some harmonization of working and living conditions, and of social security arrangements.

By 1967 labour could move freely to take on jobs in different parts of the Community. To make this possible, social security rights have been guaranteed to migrant workers from as early as 1959; it is estimated that by 1964, the total value of the benefits received by Community citizens working member countries other than their own was about $80 million.[2] The percentages of national income allotted to social security in 1970 in the member countries range between 17·2 and 20·6 per cent—a considerable narrowing of the range of 13·4 to 18·1 per cent in 1958.

There has been a growing together in real wage rates throughout the Community; wages have risen fastest in Italy, Germany and the Netherlands, whose wage rates were at the lower end of the Community scale in 1958. An interesting feature of the EEC is the establishment of the European Social Fund, which provides finance for the re-employment and retraining of workers whose livelihood is adversely affected by freer trade within the Community. Member countries contribute to the Fund in accordance with a scale laid down in the Rome Treaty (France and Germany together contribute about two-thirds the total).

[1] See G. Denton, 'Planning in the EEC', in *The Medium Term Policy Programme in the EEC*, London, Royal Institute of International Affairs, 1967.

[2] Lionello Levi Sandri, 'Social Policy in the Common Market 1958–65', *Community Topics* No. 22, European Community Information Service.

Up to 1967, Italy had benefited most; but the Netherlands had also on balance gained from the Fund's operation. In all other member countries outgoings exceeded receipts. Between 1960 and 1970 over 1,300,000 workers (800,000 of them Italian) benefited from the Fund's activities.

Attempts have been made to co-ordinate regional policies within the EEC. Clearly, the need to pay special attention to the requirements of a given region could be used as a device for giving an unfair advantage to the industry of a particular member country. This could also create difficulties for industries in closely neighbouring regions of partner countries. In connection with the plans for economic and monetary union, there has been a change of emphasis in regional policy. In adopting the Third Medium-Term Programme, the Council recognized that balanced development of the Community requires the Community to supplement national measures in some areas of common interest: in the case of certain large peripheral or frontier regions of considerable backwardness; where the common agricultural policy has important regional impact; where economic change strongly affects the potential of regions, in particular as a result of the decline of a dominant local economic activity. Several Community institutions, the European Investment Bank, the European Social Fund and the Agricultural Fund now contribute to regional development programmes, in particular in the south of Italy but also in the western and south-western areas of France, the northern Netherlands and parts of Germany along the eastern frontier. A new plan involves the establishment of a Community investment corporation to take a stake in private companies in such regions.

There are two sectors where progress towards integration has been notoriously slow. The one is in competition policy, the other in co-ordinating transport policies. In competition policy, the object of the Community is to eliminate distortions arising from monopoly and other forms of market restrictions which, if unchecked, would prevent full advantage being reaped from the freeing of trade. Article 86 forbids the abuse by a firm of its 'dominant' position; but such abuse is difficult to define and detect, and in any case the legal difficulties of interpreting the relevant articles are considerable. As regards rules on restrictive practices, article 85 prohibits a wide range of collusive agreements, but also established 'gateways' which permit specific arrangements—for example, an arrangement promoting technical or economic progress, the fruits of which are passed on to consumers. To implement articles 85 and 86 the Commission has set up administrative machinery whereby firms are required to notify the Commission of cartels and restrictive agreements. The Commission then examines the agreement either giving a clearance or declaring it to be against the Treaty of Rome. By 1970, the Commission had received about 37,000 notifications, although only 556 involved more than two enterprises. It is in fact widely believed that a very large number of firms have failed to register agreements, the response rate being anything between 5 and 50 per cent.[1]

In transport, in spite of much paper work, little progress has been made towards an integrated policy. Freight rates in various countries differ; licensing arrangements for long distance road transport have not been co-ordinated, although a limited number of bilateral agreements have been made relating to road haulage. Indeed, changes in the German system proposed in 1967 are likely to take the Federal Republic further away from, rather than closer to, the systems of the other Community members.

The Association

This brief review of some of the difficulties encountered in building the EEC is little more than a thumb-nail sketch of selected problems facing the Community. All we can hope to do is to exemplify some of the points made in Chapters 20 and 21. Before leaving the EEC however, some mention must be made of the special position of certain overseas countries (virtually all in Africa) which by tradition have strong political and economic ties with the Metropolitan European countries. They are what are known as the Associated Countries. When in 1957 France threw in her lot with her ECSC partners to establish the EEC, part of the price she exacted was special treatment for exports from her colonies to the whole Community, together with the acceptance of a colonial development programme for her colonies financed by all the Six. Although, when the Rome Treaty was signed, Belgium and Italy also had economic and political interests in Africa, France was overwhelmingly more interested than the other members in maintaining the favoured status of her colonies. By the end of the 1950s the prices of many materials and foodstuffs produced in French territories were substantially above world prices, and as the market of metropolitan France for these products was becoming saturated the colonies were looking for wider outlets. Why not in the markets of France's new community partners? Hence the Agreement generalized preferential

---

[1] For a discussion of the whole question of EEC policy regarding monopolies and restrictive practices, see . Swan and D. L. McLachlan, *Concentration or Competition: A European Dilemn* Royal Institute of International Affairs and PEP, London, 1967. This is one of a seri. of very useful Chatham House-PEP booklets on various integration problems in Europe.

entry arrangements enjoyed by colonies and associated territories in their respective metropolitan countries to all the community countries. The associated countries were permitted to impose restrictions on imports from metropolitan countries to protect infant industries, although such restrictions had to be non-discriminatory as between EEC countries. In 1964, an agreement known as the Yaoundé Association Convention between the European Community and eighteen African countries replaced the original provisions. In 1969 a second Yaoundé Convention brought an extension which came into force two years later.

In principle there is free trade between the African countries and the Community with the exception of agricultural products subject to the Common Agricultural Policy and processed agricultural products for which the Community grants more favourable access than to third countries. Between 1958 and 1971 imports into the Community from the associates nearly doubled to $1,600 million while exports doubled to $1,400 million. This compares with Community imports from less developed countries as a whole, which very nearly trebled over the period.

Financial assistance is an important part of the Convention. Grants to the value of $800 million are provided over a period of five years by the European Development Fund and the Fund, together with the European Investment Bank, offers $200 million in loans. The latter are, however, only available for potentially profitable projects. Financial assistance is directed to projects of inter-African regional co-operation, the promotion of productive sectors of the economy and trade promotion.

Industrialization and diversification have been a prime objective for the Association. In the earlier years, most of the available funds went into the encouragement of local import-competing production of consumer goods. For the 1970s, the period of the second Yaoundé Convention, the development of export-oriented industries that could stimulate the economy by foreign exchange earnings is seen as a complementary path to development. At present, exports originating in the Eighteen constitute no more than 6 per cent of total manufacturing exports of all less developed countries. Almost all of it goes to the Community. A report by the Commission seeks to identify those products which give the African states a comparative advantage in European markets and would enable them to utilize the available local mineral and vegetable resources.

In the early days of the Community, the Association arrangements were attacked by many non-associated countries as a device to perpetuate colonialism and the division of Africa. When Britain first negotiated entry in 1961, many Commonwealth countries refused even to consider association. But in 1971 an association agreement with Kenya, Uganda and Tanzania came into effect. Trade arrangements are similar to those of the Yaoundé Convention but no financial assistance provisions are included. In connection with UK entry, an offer to negotiate association agreements was made to twenty Commonwealth countries, mostly in Africa; in 1972, Mauritius availed itself of the offer and joined the Yaoundé Convention. The East Caribbean Common Market, which groups seven British associated states and one colony, and CARIFTA (the Caribbean Free Trade Area), took a similar decision in principle later in the same year.

To conclude this section, a passing mention at least should be made of the ever-widening circle of trade relations and trade agreements of the Community. Apart from Africa, there are two major areas of special concentration: the Mediterranean, where by mid-1972 association agreements had been negotiated with Greece, Turkey, Morocco, Tunisia and Malta and trade agreements with Algeria, Spain, Israel and Cyprus; and secondly, Latin America.

4. ECONOMIC AND MONETARY UNION

In the preceding section, we have discussed some of the problems the Community faced in the 'transitional period' provided for in the Treaty of Rome. As one would expect, most of these continue into the 'definitive' stage which began in 1970. In fact, the very progress achieved in dismantling barriers between member economies highlights the problems and even aggravates them. Economic interpenetration facilitates the transmission of national disequilibria and the elimination of the 'internal frontier' reduces the effectiveness of the traditional means of adjustment. This makes parallel and compatible economic development of members essential: in actual fact, the late 1960s and early 1970s have been conspicuous for the divergence in member countries' economic performance and policy, in particular as regards prices. This showed up the manifest disparity between completion of the Common Market stage and limited progress achieved towards the adoption of common policies. The experience of these later years may serve as an example of the disintegrating effect of this discrepancy.[1]

[1] The trend to disintegration resulting from price and parity divergencies is discussed in the introductory sections of the third medium-term programme examined in this chapter; difficulties arising in the period of independently floating Community currencies in 1971 are listed in *Consequences for the Community of the Present Situation*, Brussels, September 1971, both for the agricultural policy and for the accounts of a number of Community funds and other institutions.

In the period 1965–8, average annual growth rates had ranged from over 3 per cent in Germany to over 6 per cent in Italy. Inflation had been low in Germany and Italy (2 per cent a year) but high (3·5 per cent and 4·5 per cent a year) in France and the Netherlands. This led to trade and balance of payments surpluses in the low, and deficits in the high, inflation countries. Speculation against the franc and the guilder and in favour of the mark and the lira ensued and led to a massive outflow of francs, particularly into Germany in 1968 and 1969 in the expectation of a devaluation in France and a revaluation in Germany. More than $2,500 million, four-tenths of the accumulated French gold and convertible currency reserves, were lost and the swelling German reserves threatened inflation in that country. In August 1969, the French Government that followed de Gaulle devalued by 11 per cent and, after allowing the mark to float for several weeks, a new German Government upvalued by 9·3 per cent in October. In the preceding twelve months, a system of border tax adjustments, in effect a customs levy on exports and a customs subsidy on imports, both at the rate of 4 per cent, had been in operation. The common agricultural policy was upset both by the period of the float and by the parity changes.

Community market prices are expressed in units of account (u.a.) which are equal to the gold content of a pre-1971 US dollar. So French farmers would have received more of their now cheaper francs for their produce, surpluses would have grown and high food prices would have led to inflation. The German farmers stood to lose as they would have received fewer of the now dearer marks. In order not to overturn the system of uniform Community farm prices or to bring about sudden changes in farmers' incomes, France was allowed to subsidize farm imports and tax farm exports for a period of two years. German farmers were compensated for their losses: the two largest members of the Community had insulated their farm sectors from the Community agricultural market, and the Community had been obliged to sanction the type of barriers to the free flow of trade that it had progressively dismantled over the preceding ten years. The need for common or at least more closely co-ordinated economic policies was once more underlined by the disintegrating consequences of disequilibria of prices, external payments and exchange rates.

Under the impact of the 1968–9 experience, the EEC heads of state, at a conference held at The Hague in December 1969, set as their next target the establishment of full economic and monetary union[1] by the late

1 The preceding summary of the economic crisis of the EEC is based on E. W. Brassloff's account in the entry 'European Integration' to the 1972 edition of Collier's *Encyclopaedia*. This also deals with the associated political crisis. Both were resolved

1970s for the existing Community and the enlarged Community of Nine, an aim that was later endorsed by the three new member countries, Britain, Denmark and Ireland. It was to be achieved in stages that would coincide with the transitional period for enlargement and for the formation of a free trade area in industrial goods throughout most of Western Europe as consequence of a series of special relations agreements with the six EFTA countries that had not applied for membership.

According to subsequent resolutions by the Council of Ministers, the Community would by 1980 constitute a single market in which persons, goods, services and capital would move freely without distorting competition or creating structural and regional imbalances; form a single monetary entity within the international system on the basis of firmly fixed exchange rates for the currencies of the Six and later a single currency backed by a Community-level central banking system; have provided for the harmonization and unification of the most important general economic and monetary policy decisions at Community level.

The proposals are in the main based on a series of Commission memoranda[1] and the Werner Report[2] (worked out by a group of experts headed by the Luxembourg Prime Minister) which sketched the measures necessary in a three-stage process. Member countries are gradually to co-ordinate their economic and monetary policies, harmonize their taxes, narrow exchange rate margins, establish a Community capital market and a mutual balance of payments assistance mechanism.

Institutionally, the final stage presupposes the existence of two Community bodies to take over or complement the role of national authorities—a decision-taking centre for economic policy, which could influence national budgets, deal with changes of parity of the single currency or the Community currencies as a whole, and be responsible for the other sectors of economic and social policies to be handled on a Community level. Secondly, a central banking system empowered to deal with internal monetary policy on money supply, interest rates, and external policy on exchange markets and the management of the Community's monetary reserves.

at The Hague in December 1969 and the drift to disintegration was checked by the adoption in principle of a complex package of policies for the 1970s, completing the Common Market stage, enlarging the Community and providing for progress towards economic and monetary union.

[1] For instance: memorandum from the Commission to the Council on 'A Plan for the Phased Establishment of an Economic and Monetary Union', Brussels, March 4, 1970.

[2] 'Report to the Council and to the Commission on the Realization by Stages of Economic and Monetary Union in the Community', Luxembourg, October 8, 1970.

While it is generally agreed that the measures in pursuit of monetary and economic union must be complementary and mutually reinforcing, there are different schools of thought among individuals and national Governments with regard to priorities. France is seen to favour the promptest establishment and maintenance of fixed exchange rates between members with a narrow or zero margin of permissible fluctuations, partly because the proper functioning of the agricultural policy demands it. She also supports the establishment of machinery for the support of such stable parities in cases of balance of payments difficulties or speculative pressures. On the other hand, France is not over-anxious to delegate general economic decision-making powers to Community-level institutions. Germany and the Netherlands are credited with the fear of the development and spread throughout the Community of inflation by countries which have a less strong traditional commitment to price stability and the conviction that this and balance of payments problems are inevitable unless strong measures for joint control and compatibility of general economic policies are established. Italy, Belgium and the UK and the other new members of the Community are believed to insist that structural and regional policies, financed at least in part at Community level, are an indispensable priority because, in the early stages, monetary unification is bound to aggravate already existing regional and structural imbalances.

The overall strategy adopted represents a compromise in the traditional Community manner. The narrowing of exchange rate margins decided upon in 1971 and again in 1972 expresses the wishes of the 'monetarists', as they have come to be called; the strengthening of the existing network of consultative policy bodies and the establishment of a 'steering committee' for short-term policy at Community level corresponds to the demands of the 'economists'. Similarly, a complex set of interlocking plans for increasing the efficiency of structural adaptation and regional development and reducing the human costs and social stresses inherent in such change is believed to go some way towards the requirements of what we might call the 'structuralists'.

A series of complementary decisions was taken in 1971 to co-ordinate more effectively various aspects of economic policy and to establish or strengthen appropriate policy centres for the first phase of the three-stage plans. In respect of monetary and credit policies, the Council agreed that prior and obligatory consultations should be intensified through the Monetary Committee and the Committee of Governors of Central Banks within the terms of the Council's guidelines for short-term economic policies. The member states also adopted the Community's Third Medium-Term Economic Policy Programme for 1971–

1975.[1] It contained for the first time compatible quantitative guidelines as well as overall economic and structural policy guidelines which were to be carried out at both national and Community levels. It concentrated on the compatibility of trend as shown by four key economic indicators: movement of prices, level of unemployment, rates of growth and the balance of payments. Over the period the Community should not exceed average annual price increases of 2·5 to 3 per cent (a measured by the GNP deflator) or between 2·3 and 2·8 per cent (a measured by the consumer price index). Unemployment projection ranged from 0·8 per cent for Germany to 3 per cent for Italy. The target for the growth of real GNP was set at 5 to 5·5 per cent a year. The external balance was forecast to average 1 per cent of the Community's gross national product over the five years while the surplus on current account was put at 0·3 per cent. Germany was expected to have a surplus Italy and the Netherlands a deficit and the other countries to come close to breaking even.

The significance of these figures lies in the fact that they do not represent an averaging out of individual country projects; they have been arrived at after national forecasts had been examined for their internal plausibility and consistency and for their compatibility on a Community level and suitably adapted. The programme also provides for the necessary structural and general economic measures to be taken in each country to permit the balanced realization of the projections, for current examination of progress and periodic revision of projections. The programme was later adapted to the changed economic climate, the results of the currency crisis of 1971 and the new structure of exchange rates.

It was recognized that medium-term policy had to be supplemented by closer co-ordination of national short-term policies through the establishment of mutually compatible guidelines for the main elements of national economic programmes and the institution of guide figures for national budgets. In view of the inflationary climate of 1971, restrictive monetary and credit policy was suggested and member countries were advised to balance their budgets or at least to reduce deficits in 1971 and to keep public expenditure in line with changes in gross national product in 1972; permissible increases would range from 7·5 to 8·5 per cent in the case of (inflationary) Germany to the (exceptional) 11 to 12 per cent in the case of (stagnating) Italy. The targets were set so as to restrict price rises to a range of 3–3·5 per cent and wage rises to 6–7 per cent by the end of 1972.

---

[1] 'Third Medium-Term Economic Policy Programme', February 9, 1971, published in the *Official Gazette*, no. 149, March 1, 1971.

As it was understood that the first stages towards economic and monetary union were bound to involve the emergence of balance of payments disequilibria, mechanisms for short-term and medium-term monetary assistance were established. For each of these, the central banks made available $2,000 million.

As a first practical step towards monetary unification, the Community had decided on the narrowing of exchange rate margins between Community currencies. At the time, maximum IMF margins amounted to 1 per cent, those within the European Payments Agreement to 0·7 per cent. The EEC foresaw a further contraction to 0·6 per cent either side of parity. This was intended to come into operation in mid-1971 but by then the dollar crisis had begun and some Community currencies no longer maintained official par values. Then, as again in 1972 when the floating of the pound called into question the Smithsonian realignment of currencies and the renewed Community scheme for narrowing of margins, there were two alternatives available that would have maintained fixed parities between Community currencies for the purpose of the Common Agricultural Policy and of monetary unification. One was for the whole Community to adopt exchange controls, for instance the (French) two-market system in which 'commercial' or current account transactions are conducted in fixed rates, while 'financial' or capital movements are kept under control by having to be financed by way of a freely floating rate; the other alternative was to let all Community currencies float *en bloc* as was suggested by Germany. In the event, no agreement was reached in 1971 and the first step towards narrower fluctuating margins was postponed for a year. Negative effects similar to those of 1969 resulted for the Common Agricultural Policy and the working of some of its institutions.[1]

It prompted certain member states to introduce measures to compensate for the influence of parity changes on agricultural prices. Germany and the Netherlands were authorized to levy appropriate 'amounts' on imports and grant subsidies on exports of farm produce to avoid import prices falling below their old levels and causing serious disruption. The relevant regulations were extended to Belgium and Luxembourg when these countries also decided to widen the margin of fluctuation but no 'compensatory amounts' were fixed for Italy because the lira did not float far enough from parity. After the currency realignment of December 1971, the German Government sought a revaluation of the unit of account to balance the revalued mark. At first the Community favoured as a compromise the revaluation of the unit of account up to the lower degree of Benelux devaluation. As this would, however,

[1] Details may be found in the General Report on the Activities of the Communities of 1971 and 1972.

have split the market into three areas corresponding to the differential revaluations of Germany, Benelux and France/Italy the proposal finally involved maintaining the value of the unit of account, granting compensatory amounts of 2·76 per cent to the Benelux countries and special rebates on value added tax to compensate German farmers for their additional revaluation to the order of 1·85 per cent. Farmers in Italy, which devalued by 1 per cent, were to receive this additional increase on official farm prices. This still left the agricultural market divided into two regions and, most significantly of all, the system of rebates and levies was to apply without a stated time limit.

The Smithsonian agreement brought with it a further difficulty for Community trade patterns and for agricultural prices: the widening of margins to 2¼ per cent either side of parity allows a total of 4½ per cent fluctuation against the intervention currency. As long as this is a non-Community currency (the dollar), two Community currencies could conceivably fluctuate by as much as 9 per cent against each other if each moved across the whole permissible range in opposite directions. This situation no doubt contributed towards the decision to return to the idea of narrower Community margins in April 1972, this time to half the IMF margin. Intervention to keep Community currencies within this narrower band (in the current jargon: the snake) is by means of Community currencies; intervention to keep the narrower Community band within the wider IMF band (the tunnel) continues in dollars. In connection with using Community currency reserves for intervention, the formation of a Community Reserve Fund was proposed as a condition for the scheme's survival should the international monetary crisis erupt again. This raised once more the key choice facing Community countries—and new members—as regards their objective of full economic and monetary union:

> They can either recognize that a move towards monetary union is only sustainable if it is accompanied by far-reaching measures of economic integration, covering broad areas such as regional policy, monetary and credit policy, which have hitherto been regarded as the preserves of national governments. Alternatively, an attempt to continue on the present path must lead to a multiplicity of controls and exceptions which is bound in anything but the very short term to negate the objectives which the members of the enlarged Community have set themselves.[1]

One may add: it is not so much a question of economics but of political will.

[1] *Financial Times*, July 4, 1972.

Books and articles on European Integration have proliferated in recent years, but surprisingly few deal with the specifically economic aspects. For a general short survey of the EEC I recommend Uwe Kitzinger's stimulating paperback *The Challenge of the Common Market*, Oxford, 1961 (subsequently revised). A useful but to my mind slightly mis-named study is Randall Hinshaw's *The American Community and American Trade*, London, F. A. Praeger, 1964. This book in fact deals with EEC trade relations with less developed countries as well as with the USA. A dated but still valuable book is I. Frank, *The European Common Market: An Analysis of Commercial Policy*, Stevens and Son, 1961. The fascinating question of why economic growth in the EEC countries has been faster than in the UK is the subject of A. Lamfalussy's book *The UK and the Six. An Essay on Economic Growth in Western Europe*, Macmillan, London, 1963.

As to specific issues, we recommend M. Maclennan, M. Forsyth, G. Denton, *Economic Planning and Policies in Britain, France and Germany*, Allen and Unwin, 1968, which deals not only with these countries but also with the background to and early stages of the EEC's medium-term policy; E. Kirschen, *Financial Integration in Western Europe*, Columbia U.P., 1969; and P. Coffey and J. R. Presley, *European Monetary Integration*, Macmillan, 1971. As to agriculture, the 'Man-sholt Plan' was published as *Agriculture 1980*, Brussels, 1968; a critical account of the Common Agricultural Policy can be found in M. Butterwick and E. Neville-Rolfe, *Food, Farming and the Common Market*, Hutchinson, 1969.

There exists by now an extensive literature concerning the UK and the European Communities. We refer students to the NIESR studies quoted in Chapter 20 (and to the attached bibliographies); also to the sym-posium *The Economics of Europe*, edited by J. Pinder, Federal Trust for Education and Research, 1971. The official assessment is given in two White Papers, *Britain and the European Communities, an Economic Assessment*, HMSO, Cmnd. 4289, February 1970, and *The United Kingdom and the European Communities*, HMSO, Cmnd. 4715, July 1971.

The student who wishes to keep abreast of developments in the EEC is advised to consult the Community's quarterly *Bulletin*, where most major policy decisions are recorded. There is also an extremely interest-ing glossy monthly *European Community*, published in New York and London, as well as within the Community.

CHAPTER 23

INTEGRATION IN THE POST-WAR WORLD: B

1. THE EUROPEAN FREE TRADE ASSOCIATION

The founders of EFTA were Austria, Denmark, Norway, Portugal, Sweden, Switzerland and the UK, while in 1961 Finland became associated; Iceland joined in 1970. Unlike the EEC, EFTA has no common external tariff; neither has it ever aspired to develop into a customs union, even less an economic union. The Stockholm Convention, under which EFTA was established, makes no provision for the freedom of factor movements, for close co-ordination of monetary and budgetary policies, or for a common policy in agricultural products. The Convention does, however, envisage the expansion of agricultural trade between members by the negotiation of bilateral agreements, providing favoured treatment for specific agricultural products. By 1967 eight such bilateral agreements were in operation. The EFTA countries have a population of just over 100 million, that is, 3 per cent of the world's total; EFTA does 16 per cent of the world's trade. The UK accounted for half the total population of EFTA, but under half its total industrial output, under half its trade with the outside world and for only a quarter of trade within EFTA.

In the discussions in the 1950s on future trade arrangements for Western Europe, the UK, the Scandinavian countries and Switzerland favoured the establishment of a wide free trade area rather than a tight customs union. Sweden, Switzerland Denmark and Norway were substantial importers of raw materials and semi-manufactured goods; as such they wished to retain low import duties. As political neutrals, Sweden and Switzerland had an added reason for not binding themselves too closely into a full economic union of the west. Austria, although a high tariff country, with the bulk of its trade with EEC countries, was for reasons of her neutrality hardly in a position to become a member of the Community.

When the discussions on the formation of a Western European free trade area failed at the end of 1958, the establishment of EFTA did not follow immediately. Indeed the British Government was at first reluctant to encourage the formation of EFTA, but partly due to the pressure of British and Swedish business interests, the future EFTA member

Governments came together in 1959, and in January 1960, signed what was to become known as the Stockholm Convention. The Convention provided for the gradual reduction of tariffs on industrial products traded between member countries by 1970; the first cuts (of 20 per cent) were made in 1960. In fact the tariff reduction programme was accelerated, and by January 1967, virtually all tariffs on industrial goods were reduced to zero. The Stockholm Convention requires the elimination of all protective elements in the internal duty structures. Although this was supposed to have been achieved in 1964, a number of complaints about the effect of such duties were subsequently made by member Governments.

EFTA was established with the minimum of administrative machinery. The chief executive body is the Council, consisting of representatives from each country at ministerial or senior official levels. The Council is advised by a Consultative Committee, consisting of representatives from the main sectors of economic life in the member countries; trade union, employers and other groups. In May 1963 the Economic Development Committee was set up to examine the role of planning in member countries, and also problems of specific industries, e.g. the tourist industry in Finland. Later an Economic Committee was established to provide a regular forum for discussion of general problems affecting members and to consider specific problems referred to it.

In 1959, the last full year before the Association came into being, EFTA countries exported goods to the value of $18 billion; in 1971, the comparable figure was $45 billion; intra-trade increased from $3·7 billion to $13 billion.[1] In the first ten years, trade between member countries had more than doubled and had thus grown faster than world trade. Exports to third countries had risen by the lower annual average of nearly 7 per cent and imports from third countries of nearly 6 per cent. During that period world exports expanded by nearly 7·5 per cent. On this basis, it has been stated that 'there is no convincing reason to conclude' that the somewhat larger increase in intra-EFTA trade was the result of trade diversion.[2] At least for the early years of EFTA's existence (1959–65), however, a study of trade flows attributed a quarter of the total increase in intra-trade to the creation of EFTA but saw that increase more or less evenly divided between trade creation and trade diversion.

In the Nordic countries, the share of trade creation in the total import effects is generally above average, which suggests that they have made

1 EFTA Bulletin, March 1972.
2 Sir Eric Wyndham White, former Director-General of GATT, in 'Ten Years of EFTA 1960–1970', EFTA Bulletin, May 1970.

full use of the opportunities EFTA has offered to increased specialization. On the other hand, for Portugal, Switzerland, Austria and the UK, little trade creation is shown. The UK has gained considerably in exports, particularly in textiles and clothing, Portugal also benefited greatly in this product group, while for paper and pulp, a sector in which trade creation was very noticeable, most export gains were made by the Scandinavians. During the early years of the EEC and EFTA, there appears to have been a shift in UK demand away from EEC and towards EFTA sources of supply, and this was especially marked in the case of products upon which tariffs were relatively high. This suggests that tariffs do influence trade patterns, but much more detailed research is necessary to confirm this. Such evidence as the EFTA secretariat has been able to collect for the first three years of EFTA sheds some doubt on whether really significant relative changes in consumer prices followed tariff reductions.[1]

The above-mentioned study also found definite evidence that the changes in the pattern of *trade* induced by the creation of EFTA had had the expected effects on the pattern of *production*, by increasing specialization and productivity. Adding dynamic effects on trade and investment to the static effects—which, as we have seen, show a good deal of trade diversion—the study concluded that the creation of EFTA had affected positively gross national products of all member countries.[2] There remains the important question of whether EFTA's contribution to an increased national product is a once-and-for-all or a continuing effect.[3]

Great Britain and Denmark became members of the European Community as from 1973. This brings them behind the common external tariff of the Community. In order to avoid a break in the existing free trade arrangements with the remaining EFTA countries, the EEC has been negotiating a series of *special relations agreements* which will, over a period of five years, timed to coincide with the transitional period of the new EEC members, establish a free trade area for industrial goods covering most of Western Europe. This will allow the remaining EFTA countries continuing access to 'traditionally' EFTA markets. Access to 'traditionally' EEC markets will be curtailed in the case of 'sensitive items' such as paper, aluminium, fibres and special steel, which are however particularly important export items for the remaining EFTA countries.

[1] There is an EFTA Report on this subject entitled *The Effect on Prices of Tariff Dismantling in EFTA*, European Free Trade Association, Geneva.
The changing pattern of Western European trade between 1955 and 1965 is examined at length in *International Trade, 1966*, GATT, Geneva, 1967.
[2] *The Effects of EFTA on the Economies of Member States*, EFTA, Geneva, 1969.
[3] EFTA Bulletin, March 1972.

A later, rather more comprehensive, study based on sophisticated new statistical techniques provides *quantitative* estimates of the trade effects of the creation of both EFTA and the EEC and *qualitative* assessments of effects on production, productivity and economic growth. The study concludes that both trading groups were successful in creating new trade though at a relatively high cost in terms of trade diverted. These costs were highest in EFTA countries which are more 'complementary' in production than the EEC.

To establish the effects of the formation of two separate trading groups in Western Europe the study calculates a figure for 'export impedance' (the reduced export opportunities suffered by EFTA and EEC as a consequence of the existence of the other). This figure is found by dividing the sum of reciprocal trade diversion by the value of combined trade creation. For 1967 the study puts combined trade creation at $3,580 million, trade diversion at $1,838 million and thus the 'trade creation surplus' at $1,742 million. 'European export impedance loss' is given as 29.1 per cent.

No attempt is made to quantify *dynamic* effects, but they are shown to be positive, leading to increased economic growth and productivity of member countries' economies.[1]

2. CMEA

In Eastern Europe there are no economic groupings which correspond to the EEC or EFTA. Moreover, while market criteria are now much more important than in 1960, trade between Communist countries still does not depend to any extent on the interplay of market forces; thus an analysis in terms of tariffs and the co-ordination of commercial policies is not meaningful. The nearest approach to a comparable economic grouping in the East is Comecon (from its initial letters in Russian), or the Council for Mutual Economic Aid (CMEA). Comecon was founded in 1949 and consisted of the USSR, Poland, Czechoslovakia, Hungary, Rumania and Bulgaria. These countries were later joined by the German Democratic Republic (Eastern Germany) and Albania, Outer Mongolia also becoming a full member in June 1962. Comecon countries contain about one-tenth of the world's total population and account for a similar proportion of total world trade.

---

[1] Only the barest hint of the scope and interest of this study is possible here. Students are referred to the original: *The Trade Effects of EFTA and the EEC, 1959–1967*, Economic Department of EFTA, Geneva, 1972. A summary may be found in the EFTA *Bulletin* of June 1972, pp. 6–21.

Comecon has an executive organ, which watches over the co-ordination of national economic plans, investment programmes and trade policies. One interesting feature of Comecon has been the setting up of-Standing Commissions, each of which specializes in a branch of economic activity; they are located permanently in one of the countries with an interest in the economic sector for which each is responsible. Thus the Commission for Oil and Gas is at Bucharest and for Agriculture at Sofia. Joint ventures in these branches by CMEA countries also further 'socialist division of labour' and specialization of production.

Within Comecon there seems to be virtually no surrender of national sovereignity. Each member has one vote and decisions are not binding until ratified by national Governments. One difficulty within Comecon is the unequal status of the various members. Both in economic and political strength, the USSR towers above the others, but even among the non-Russian groups there are substantial differences. The German Democratic Republic and Czechoslovakia, well ahead of the other members in industrial development are not particularly anxious to see industrialization spreading among the agricultural group. On the other hand, less industrialized members like Rumania are determined to lift themselves out of dependence upon primary products. Until 1962 payments agreements between members were normally bilateral; but in recent years there have been partially successful attempts to multilateralize trade. In 1964 the International Bank for Economic Cooperation was established, at which members hold transferable accounts. Balances arising from trade within the block can be credited to these accounts at the Bank.

A new impetus was expected in 1971 to result from the formation of the CMEA Investment Bank. It will not only finance projects that are part of the co-ordinated national Five Year Plans (1970–5) but also assist 'co-production' and co-export agreements between CMEA institutions and Western firms. The Bank is intended to provide supplementary foreign exchange to member countries wishing to acquire high technology from outside the area and raises loans on the Euro-dollar and Euro-bond markets.[1]

3. INTEGRATION IN DEVELOPING COUNTRIES

LAFTA

Outside Europe the most established developments in integration are in Central and South America. The Latin American Free Trade Area

[1] Accounts of the earlier years of CMEA are: Dr M. Kaser, *Comecon*, OUP for RIIA, 1960; J. P. D. Wiles, *Communist International Economics*, Blackwell, 1969; and CMEA, *A Survey of 20 Years*, Moscow, 1969.

(LAFTA) established by the Treaty of Montevideo, came into operation in June 1961. It includes the relatively powerful countries Argentine, Brazil and Mexico, the medium-influence nations Chile, Peru and Uruguay, and less developed Paraguay. Colombia and Ecuador joined later. The aim of the Treaty is the elimination of all customs duties and other restrictions on mutual trade of member countries. Free trade is being achieved by annual tariff negotiations, at which each participating country undertakes to reduce by one-twelfth the average level of its tariff on imports from other members. A country may use discretion as to which particular tariffs to remove at each annual round. Accordingly, tariffs which least affected domestic producers were removed in the early years, leaving hard core ones until towards the end of the Union-building period. This tendency created serious difficulties before the free trade area was finally established. Problems also arise from the substantial imbalance in degree of industrialization and in balance of payments strength, between Mexico on the one hand and the less developed countries on the other—especially Paraguay, one of the poorest nations in the world. Since the war the stronger partners have been actively engaged in industrialization leaving other members a long way behind. Weaker countries accordingly find difficulty in establishing industries in the face of competition from the economically more advanced stronger members.

Central American Common Market

Another integration scheme of Latin America, the Central American Common Market (CACM) is, as its title suggests, based on a customs union, not a free trade area. The CACM includes Guatemala, Honduras, Nicaragua, Costa Rica, and El Salvador. After a somewhat slow start the Common Market appeared well on the way to being firmly established. Since most member countries are at a relatively early stage of industrialization, resistance by vested interests is less strong than in LAFTA. An interesting feature of the Treaty establishing the Common Market is the arrangement whereby new manufacturing enterprises are established by prior agreement in designated parts of the Union. For example it was agreed that a tyre factory should be established in Guatemala and an insecticides plant in Nicaragua. A fairly detailed blue print has been produced for the allocation of future investment projects. These proposals are based on rational criteria; for example Costa Rica, which has a relatively abundant supply of reasonably skilled manpower is destined to develop assembly industries while El Salvador, which already has a developed textile area, will increase its activities in this field. Guatemala, with its natural resources will have a chemical industry.

In many respects early progress towards integration in the Central American Market had been remarkable. As early as the end of 1964, a common external tariff applying to some 98 per cent of all imports had been agreed; it was expected that all external tariffs would be equalized within two or three years of that date. Between 1960 and 1964 intra-trade trebled; manufactures accounting for some 70 per cent of members' mutual trade. But as in the case of LAFTA, internal trade accounts for only a small proportion of the total trade of members. The member countries have established a Council of Ministers meeting every three months; they have also given attention to the co-ordination of labour and social policies and they hope eventually to have a common currency. The relatively rapid progress in the early years gave rise to high hopes, but later the scarcity of overall resources for development made it increasingly difficult to overcome the problem of equitable allocation. Both CACM and·LAFTA faltered, and the achievement of the still more ambitious scheme of a Latin American Common Market, to be completed by 1985, became more and more unrealistic.

The Andean Common Market

In 1966, Bolivia, Ecuador, Chile, Colombia, Peru—later to be joined by Venezuela—formed a regional sub-group. They planned to revitalize LAFTA by grouping more closely the smaller and more vulnerable member countries but, after a successful agreement in 1968 to develop a regionally specialized chemical industry by allotting the output of specific products to particular countries, decided to form a union of their own, while continuing inside LAFTA. The Cartagena agreement of 1969 established the Andean Group which got off to a very successful start to its more far-reaching plans of harmonizing economic and social policies as well as eliminating internal tariffs and establishing a joint external tariff. An Andean Development Bank is to encourage joint industrial development projects, and institutional instruments have been fashioned that should allow a maximum of progress.

The Andean Group is establishing close direct ties with the EEC for the purpose of economic and technical co-operation, against a background of a doubling of Latin American exports to the Community between 1960 and 1970 and the fact that by 1969 Europe had replaced the US as the leading customer for Latin American exports.

In 1971, the Andean Group drafted a common policy for regulating trade marks, patents, licences and royalties and, most important of all, for the treatment of foreign capital. This excludes specifically the

ning and petroleum industries, leaves member countries free to decide
their own attitudes towards other basic industries and generally prohibits further foreign investment in banking, insurance, transport and
communications industries. The key provisions encourage foreign firms
to turn themselves into joint foreign ventures with ownership and
control in Latin American hands should they wish to avail themselves
of the opportunities of the free movement of goods offered by the
Andean Common Market.

The investment policy reflects Latin American moves towards greater
active control of the vital and expanding manufacturing sector as a
guarantee of economic independence; at the same time, it provides
safeguards for foreign investment as to the free transfer of profits up to
14 per cent and as to adequate compensation in the case of expropriation.

Africa

We have already noted that some eighteen African countries have
special relations with the EEC. A number of African countries, some of
which are included in the eighteen associates have also tried to form a
customs union among themselves. Since 1959, the former French
colonies in Central Africa have been working towards an Equatorial
Customs Union. These are the countries of Chad, Gabon, the Central
African Republic and the former French Congo. They have tried to
retain the advantages of free mutual trade which they enjoyed when
under French rule. They appear to have been fairly successful in doing
this since goods and capital move freely within the Union and a common
tariff is in the process of establishment. Another group of ex-French
colonies have been attempting to form the West African Customs
Union. This consists of Dahomey, Mali, Mauretania, Niger, Senegal,
Ivory Coast and Upper Volta. A serious difficulty, however, is the
collection and division of customs revenue. Since some of these countries are landlocked and internal communications are poor, the greater
part of the Union's customs revenue has to be collected at the ports, a
practice giving rise to endless arguments and disputes.

The Maghreb

The North African countries Algeria, Morocco and Tunisia have
since 1964 collaborated in the Permanent Consultative Committee on
the Maghreb (PCCM). It studies the feasibility of common development
projects in such fields as energy, road, rail and air transport, and—
with some initial success—an export price and promotion policy for
agricultural products such as wine, olives and esparto grass. However,

the difficulties of reaching the proclaimed objective of a Maghreb Common Market for manufactures appear forbidding in view of conflicting industrialization policies; current national development plans as well as those for the early 1970s are being drawn up independently and unrelated to each other.

It should be clear from the above, that Europe is not the only area where integration is proceeding apace; on the other hand it is much too early to be sure that the many free trade areas and customs unions now in being established in the developing world will in fact come to full fruition. There are clearly a number of difficulties wholly or partially absent in Europe. For example, in developing countries there is a tendency for Governments to rely more heavily upon indirect than direct taxation; the loss of revenue consequent upon the abolition of tariffs can be quite considerable. There is also the very serious problem of inequalities between member countries. A country just on the threshold of industrialization might well find its hopes doomed for a generation if its industries have to face tariff free competition from low cost neighbouring countries. There is moreover often an important difference in motive. Whereas integration between developed industrialized countries has as its primary objective a better allocation of resources among the participants, as between less developed countries the aim is to encourage growth and industrialization. Certainly unions of developing countries are likely to be judged more for their effects upon growth than upon the reallocation of already existing resources.

SHORT GUIDE TO THE LITERATURE

A number of authors have recently reconsidered integration theory with special reference to less developed regions. In *A Theory of Economic Integration for Developing Countries*, F. Andic, S. Andic and D. Dosser illustrate their approach with special reference to the Caribbean. F. Kahnert, P. Richards, E. Stoutjesdijk, P. Thomopoulos, *Economic Integration among Developing Countries*, Development Centre, OECD Paris, 1969, contains a discussion of the theory in its special relevance to less developed countries and an account of the performance of existing schemes.

The entry on 'European Integration' in Collier's *Encyclopaedia* has been referred to (Chapter 22) in connection with the EEC. It deals also with EFTA and CMEA. The earlier entry is by S. J. Wells, the 1972 entry by E. W. Brassloff. Annual volumes keep the statistics up to date.

CHAPTER 24

THE LESS DEVELOPED COUNTRIES

Perhaps the most significant single development in applied international economics since the early 1950s is a growing awareness of the special problem of the less developed countries. In this chapter we deal with some of the special external economic problems of these countries, sometimes referred to as 'developing', sometimes as 'less developed' or even 'underdeveloped' countries. I have chosen the description 'less developed' rather than the more fashionable 'developing', since many relatively rich countries are in fact developing faster than the countries with whose problems we are concerned. By less developed countries we generally mean those where incomes per head are relatively low, where only limited supplies of capital are available, and where a high proportion of the labour force is engaged in primary production. The most important feature of these countries, however, is their poverty.

There can be no hard and fast dividing line between rich and poor; neither is there a universally accepted list of countries classified as less developed. Perhaps the most widely used list is that of the United Nations. This comprises (a) all countries in Africa, except South Africa, (b) North and South America, except the USA and Canada, (c) Asia, with the exception of Japan, but including Cyprus, (d) Oceana, with the exception of Australia and New Zealand. The OECD list covers the same countries as the UN, but also includes Greece, Spain, Yugoslavia, Malta, Gibraltar and Turkey; it omits in Asia, China, North Korea, North Vietnam and Mongolia.

The Overseas Development Institute in its very useful handbook, *World III*, classifies as developing countries the OECD list plus China, North Korea, North Vietnam and Mongolia.[1] In general we use the ODI classification in this Chapter.

1. THE PROBLEM

Some two-thirds of the world's population live in countries whose income per head is below £100 a year; together these countries account for less than 13 per cent of world income. At the other extreme, 7 per

---

[1] Adrian Moyes and Theresa Hayter, Overseas Development Institute, *World III, A Handbook on Developing Countries*, London, Pergamon Press, 1964.

cent of the world's population, living in countries where income p
head is over £500 a year, enjoy no less than 36 per cent of world incom
Differences in *per capita* income are very marked indeed as betwee
different countries. Income per head in the USA in 1971 was over £2,0C
per year, and in the UK £900, but in 100 countries less than £160 and i
25 lower than £40. Of course these estimates must be treated with reserv
The methods of collecting statistics, even of population, let alone (
income, are often very unsatisfactory. Moreover, less develope
countries usually have large subsistence farming sectors whose outp
is notoriously difficult to measure. It is of course also true that physic
needs, for example of clothing and shelter, are usually rather less i
such countries than in developed ones. But when all allowance has bee
made, the fact remains that people whose lot it is to live in the le
developed world are usually desperately poor, ill-fed, ill-housed an
ill-educated.

There are a number of reasons for the poverty in which the great
part of mankind lives. Firstly, there is the population problem. I
1850 the population of the whole world was 1,200 million; in 1900
was still only 1,550 million. Between these years Malthusian check
prevented more than a moderate population increase. By 1950, howeve
largely as the result of the decline in the death rate, world populatio
reached 2,500 million. In each of the two following decades, th
population increase was greater than in the whole of the first half c
the twentieth century. Thus by 1970, world population had grown t
over 3,500 million, the greater part of this increase having taken plac
in the less developed countries. At present the populations of thes
countries are growing at about 2·6 per cent a year, as compared wit
1·3 per cent in the developed countries. Most—but not all—les
developed countries have probably passed their 'optimum' populatio
levels for their present capital and natural resource endowments.

A second reason for the poverty of these countries is their relativel
low levels of productivity. In part this is due to enervating climate
widespread malnutrition, and general geographical disadvantages
Political and social factors, such as inefficient methods of land tenur
and the class system in its various forms, also add to their difficulties
But one of the most serious handicaps under which less develope
countries work is the grave shortage of capital. Because incomes ar
low, savings are low, and because savings are low, investment is low
Hence such countries persist in primitive methods of cultivation; thei
manufacturing industries tend to be technologically backward an
their transport systems inadequate. There is a kind of vicious circl
of poverty from which developing countries can hope to break ou

nly by massive development programmes financed from wealthier
ountries.[1]

Fourthly—and this is our immediate concern in the present book—
evelopments in the world economy have caused in recent years a
eterioration in the position of the less developed countries *vis-a-vis*
he more developed ones. No longer does it seem that the growth in
he high-income industrialized countries is automatically transmitted
o less developed ones. Whereas in the nineteenth century it was reason-
ble to infer that expansion in the then developed countries (notably
Britain and Western Europe) automatically created expanding demand
or the products of the developing countries of the New World, this is
o longer the case. In the twentieth century foreign trade has failed to
e the engine of growth that it was in the nineteenth century. As the
ndustrialized countries grow, they trade increasingly with one another,
ather than with the poorer countries. Thus we are witnessing an
ncreasing segmentation of trade, rich countries becoming progressively
nore self-sufficient in the kind of goods (foodstuffs and raw materials)
raditionally imported from less developed countries. Thus whereas in
953, the less developed countries (excluding those with centrally
lanned economies), accounted for 27 per cent of world trade, by 1971
heir share had fallen to 19·6 per cent. Over the same period the share of
eveloped industrial countries rose from 58·7 per cent to 65·5 per cent.

There are a number of reasons for the declining share of less developed
ountries in world trade. To some extent the fall has been due to techno-
ogical and commercial factors (for example, the substitution of synthe-
ics for certain raw materials). But there is no doubt that policies
dopted in the developed countries, notably the deliberate fostering
f domestic agriculture, have contributed to the difficulties. In practice
t is often difficult to disentangle the purely commercial factors from
he policy ones. For example, it is a matter of discussion whether
ndia's failure to capture a larger share of the UK import market in
otton textiles is due to poor salesmanship by the Indian exporters,
r to the restrictions placed on imports of these goods by the British
Government.

The less developed countries as a group are still heavily dependent
pon exports of primary products, about 24 per cent of their exports
onsisting of foodstuffs, 32 per cent of fuels, and 20 per cent of crude
aw materials. Exports of manufactures which consist widely of base
metals, account for only 24 per cent of the aggregate value of their

---

[1] A full discussion of the 'vicious circle of poverty' in less developed countries
s in Gunnar Myrdal's book, *An International Economy Problems and Prospects*,
London, Routledge and Kegan Paul, 1956.

exports. This export pattern puts them at a disadvantage, for, over the last fifteen or twenty years, demand for foodstuffs and for many raw materials produced by less developed countries has grown less fast than demand for manufactures. The value of world trade in primary products did not quite double between 1953 and 1971 while trade in manu factured goods more than quadrupled. And by 1971 the value of industrial countries' exports of *non-manufactures* was of the same order of magnitude as that of the less developed countries!

2. PRIMARY PRODUCTS

In recent years demand for foodstuffs has grown less rapidly than demand for manufactured goods, or raw materials. Industrialized nations of the west are, in many case, now at a point where their citizens wish to spend only a relatively small part of their increased incomes upon foodstuffs, especially basic foodstuffs of the type exported by developing countries. Moreover present-day food consumption often takes on a more sophisticated form than in the past. Foodstuff are elaborately processed and packaged; they are often consumed in restaurants or hotels. This means that although in some cases consumers total expenditure on foodstuffs is rising, expenditure on the raw material element of the foodstuffs is growing only relatively slowly But more important is the increased self-sufficiency of the industrialized nations in basic foodstuffs. Crop yields in industrialized countries of the west have risen very much more rapidly than in the traditional less developed primary producing countries. This trend is partly the result of purely technical factors, for example the use of fertilizers, more efficient methods of agriculture and the consolidation of farm holdings it is doubtless also in part the result of deliberate protectionist policies

Virtually all industrialized countries protect their agriculture. As regards temperate farm products, the effect of protectionism on exports of less developed countries should not be exaggerated. Their exports of dairy products, eggs and poultry are relatively small, re presenting only marginal additions to domestic supplies in industrialized countries. The less developed countries most affected in this sector are the Latin American Republics, notably Argentina and Uruguay. But the effect of increased self sufficiency in temperate foodstuffs will clearly have the effect of increasing rather than decreasing the magnitude of the problems faced by less developed countries as they try to expand exports of these products. The most serious difficulties of the less developed countries are in those foodstuffs which compete closely with those produced in industrialized countries. The most important of these are sugar, oils and oilseeds.

Closely Competing Foodstuffs

Since the war the developed countries have become much more self-sufficient in sugar. This is especially true of Western Europe, which in 1951–4 produced 64 per cent but by 1971–2 produced nearly all of its requirements. In 1951–3 the EEC was 88 per cent self-sufficient in sugar; by 1971–2 it had reached a structural surplus of one million tons. World trade in sugar is considerably affected by preferential arrangements, less than one-tenth of total sugar exports being traded at the world price. The remainder is bought and sold under special arrangements at prices well above those in the free market; for example, under the Commonwealth Sugar Agreement, the UK agrees to purchase pre-determined tonnages; the US grants quotas to certain suppliers as does the Soviet Union to Cuba. Producers of other countries suffer discrimination and in spite of the revival of a general International Sugar Agreement in 1968, are very much at the mercy of often violent fluctuations in world prices. The difficulties of non-sheltered producer countries are intensified by the assistance given to beet sugar production in industrialized countries. Some two-thirds of world sugar imports are subject to quantitative restrictions; 32 per cent to deficiency payments, and 26 per cent to import levies. The GATT has estimated that only 4 per cent of imports are not subject to non-tariff measures. In many cases the guaranteed minimum price for domestic sugar production in industrialized countries is three or four times as high as the free market price.

In the near future a very real problem is likely to arise for cane sugar producers. For the world as a whole (excluding mainland China and the USSR) there has been a slowing down in the rates of increase in consumption. Between 1952 and 1956 the annual compound rate of increase of sugar consumption was 5·3 per cent; for the later period of the 1960s it was estimated at about 6·3 per cent. Indeed in recent years the level of consumption has actually declined in some high income countries, notably Sweden and Denmark. Unless some radical change is made in domestic sugar-beet policies, the outlook for developing countries which depend largely upon cane sugar for their export proceeds is extremely gloomy.

A similar but less acute problem arises in oils and oil seeds. These are produced by developing countries in tropical regions (exports of tropical oils and seeds account for 40 per cent of total world trade in oil seeds, fats and oils) but these exports compete directly with other edible oil seeds, notably cotton seeds, soya beans and linseed, which are produced in temperate industrial countries, especially the USA. In some countries there has been a considerable substitution of soya beans (mainly from the United States) for imports of tropical oil seeds from the developing countries. Soya beans have a relatively high protein content and are in great demand for cattle cake. Tropical oils also have to compete against animal fats, produced as a by-product of the domestic livestock industry in industrialized countries. The continuation of these trends is almost certain to mean a general stagnation in world demand for tropical oil seeds. But the policies followed in developed countries seem likely to make matters worse rather than better for developing countries. Although the common market external tariff on oil seeds is zero, France and Western Germany continue to restrict imports of these goods by means of quantitative restrictions. Moreover the EEC operates a system of levies, threshold and intervention prices on oils, designed to protect Italy's oil producers. Further, recent shortfalls of world supplies and higher producer prices for oils and oil seeds have given fresh impetus to the growing production and use of synthetic protein substitutes.

Non-Competing Foodstuffs and Basic Materials

Coffee, cocoa, tea and bananas are the most important foodstuff exports of developing countries which do not compete directly with those of high income industrialized countries. In the case of such products there is no question of domestic support policies in developed countries, and in general actual tariff barriers are low—with the possible exception of the EEC 20 per cent common external tariff on banana imports. In the US, import duties on coffee, cocoa beans, and tea, are zero. One of the most serious barriers limiting entry of tropical beverages into developed countries arises from high fiscal charges, which have the effect of damping down internal demand. These internal revenue charges often result in substantial price increases to the consumer. For example, the internal duty on coffee consumed in Western Germany is equivalent to 98 per cent of the import price; for Italy the percentage is 128 per cent, and for Sweden 80 per cent (excluding general turnover taxes).

Many developing countries depend heavily on exports of raw materials. The problem here is not so much one of overcoming import restrictions and domestic support policies in industrialized countries as of eliminating price fluctuations and of maintaining a steady flow of imports into the major industrial countries. As we noted above, the slow growth of world trade in raw materials has been caused in part by the progressive substitution of synthetic materials for natural products. Another factor has been the slow growth in consumption of natural and synthetic fibres in some industrialized countries, especially in North America. Almost all apparel fibres enter industrial countries free of import restrictions, but in the case of the US, cotton imports are limited by quota; in recent years such imports have been equivalent to about only 2 per cent of domestic consumption. Since domestic prices are well above world market prices, the US provides export subsidies for raw cotton.

Generally trade in raw wool is free of import restrictions, but in the US the domestic wool producers are supported. Few countries impose restrictions on imports of natural rubber or hides and skins, but in almost all major industrial countries domestic livestock support policies reduce the scope for the import of these products. Imports of metal ores and metals are, in general free, but there are some import restrictions on copper, lead and zinc which have adverse effects upon developing countries' trade. Petroleum is in rather a different position from that of most other primary products. It has an assured and very rapidly growing market. This has lately enabled the oil-producing countries to avoid competing against each other. Acting through the Organization of Petroleum Exporting Countries (OPEC) they have in 1971 and 1972 renegotiated and considerably increased crude oil prices. In addition gulf producers receive an extra $8\frac{1}{2}$ per cent to compensate them for the fall in the value of the dollar in which prices are expressed. Tariff barriers on crude oil are few and easy to scale, but most industrialized countries impose substantial duties on petroleum products.

Processed Materials

Although import restrictions on raw materials are relatively moderate, this is by no means true of barriers to trade in processed and semi-processed materials. In the case of almost all metals exported in a processed state, developed countries impose higher tariffs or more stringent restrictions than on the original basic metals. The United States, for example, imposes a duty equivalent of 7–8 per cent on unwrought copper; but on copper alloys the duty ranges as high as 22 per cent. The United States duty on iron ore is zero; on pig-iron it is 9 per cent. On wood the United States duty is again zero, but on boards and veneers is 11 per cent. Similar differentials apply in the case of the EEC and the United Kingdom. It is this 'escalation' of the tariff structure that frequently makes the 'effective protection' rate for processing industries in these developed countries considerably higher than the rate of the 'nominal' duty and thus hinders the growth of similar industries in less developed countries.[1]

Commodity Agreements

In recent years there has been a great deal of discussion of alternative solutions to the problem of commodity trade. Where the products are produced almost entirely in the less developed countries and where no immediate substitutes are available, there is much to be said for establishing commodity agreements. Such agreements can have the somewhat limited objective of ironing out fluctuations in prices or producers' incomes; or they can aim at maintaining prices or incomes at a level higher than would prevail on a free market. In the latter case they become a means of transferring resources from consuming to producing countries. Even if an Agreement does no more than stabilize prices it can have a useful function; for especially where countries[2] depend upon a relatively few export commodities, price fluctuations can have a serious effect upon their balance of payments, national incomes and development plans. Commodity agreements can operate on the *quota, buffer stock* or the *multilateral contract* principle. In the first case they seek to maintain price by allocating export 'quotas' to the producing countries. In the case of buffer stocks, a manager or agency is appointed to purchase stocks when world prices are low, and sell when prices are high. Under the contract principle, importing countries undertake to buy agreed quantities from producing countries when the price falls to an agreed minimum; on the other hand, exporting countries undertake to sell agreed quantities when the price rises to an agreed maximum.

Since the war, the most important commodity agreements have been in wheat, sugar, coffee and tin. The Wheat Agreement operates on the multilateral contract principle but since it concerns few less developed countries we shall not discuss it here. The coffee and sugar agreements have operated on the 'quota' principle, while the tin agreement has been implemented by means of a buffer stock. The quota method involves the difficulty of agreeing an equitable method of allocating quotas and of revising them to take account of changing cost structures. The International Sugar Agreement was only renegotiated in 1968 after being in abeyance, but the International Coffee

---

[1] The concept of 'effective protection' is discussed in Chapter 6.

[2] For example, Ghana, 66 per cent of whose exports consist of cocoa; Ceylon, 66 per cent of exports tea, Malaya, 75 per cent rubber and tin, and Mauritius, 99 per cent of whose exports consist of sugar.

Agreement illustrates some of the achievements and difficulties of this kind of arrangement. In the 1960s there was substantial over-production of coffee[1] but since 1962 the fall in world prices has undoubtedly been arrested by the existence of the Agreement. The Agreement covers 98 per cent of world trade. Each producing country is allotted an export quota, but the quota is subject to selective adjustment during the year in the light of changes in the price of the type of coffee exported.

The dominant members are Brazil and the US who have 40 per cent of the producers' and consumers' votes respectively. The whole structure of the ICA could be expected to change when it comes up for renegotiation in time for the coffee year 1974. It is under pressure from the African producers of *robusta*-type coffee, who are gaining increasing market shares. This is at the expense of the traditional (Latin American) coffee suppliers, who produce *arabica* types which are milder and more expensive, but no better suited to the purposes of the increasingly important *soluble* coffee industry.

In the meantime, frustrated by a refusal of the US to agree to an increase in coffee prices in compensation for the fall in the value of the dollar in which coffee prices are quoted, the major coffee producers took a leaf out of the oil-producing countries' book. They attempted to bridge their own competitive conflicts by agreeing in the 'Geneva Document' of April 1972 to hold back supplies from the market through a buffer-stock arrangement of their own and thus maintain prices independently of the consumer panel of the ICA.

So far, attempts to negotiate quota buffer-stock arrangements for cocoa have failed, but in 1972 a conference of forty countries held in anticipation of UNCTAD II established a possible framework for a future agreement, even if no compromise on prices could be found between producer and consumer countries. No progress has been made in negotiating a tea agreement.

An international buffer stock agreement involves the purchase and sale of the commodity when its price moves outside agreed limits. Clearly the arrangement is suitable only where the product can be stored at relatively low cost and without danger of deterioration. Moreover initially large resources of finance and stocks are necessary if the scheme is to function. In addition, care is required in fixing maximum and minimum prices. If the range is too low, stocks will quickly be exhausted. If it is too high, the financial resources of the manager or agency are likely to be depleted. The best-known example of a buffer stock arrangement is in tin; for which there were three

[1] See M. Z. Cutajar and Alison Franks, *The Less Developed Countries In World Trade*, ODI cited above, pp. 65 ff.

successive agreements after 1956 which collapsed under the pressure of persistent high prices and the consequent exhaustion of the buffer stock. The Fourth International Tin Agreement came into force in September 1971. It has the advantage of a higher price range, namely £1,350–£1,650 per metric ton, and of the fact that its twenty-seven member countries are more representative of both major producers and consumers, including as they do for the first time both West Germany and the USSR.

Although the less developed countries are still very much in favour of extending commodity agreements, post-war experience has shown the limitations of such arrangements as a mechanism for helping the less developed world. In fact the number of commodities to which the types of agreement we have outlined could be applied is fairly restricted.

There are clearly limits on the effectiveness of agreements to raise prices and hence returns to producing countries if fairly close substitutes for the products in question are available. Price raising agreements in respect of raw cotton, natural rubber, raw wool, hides and skins and jute are likely only to speed up the pace of substitution. In fact products which in this way face serious competition from substitutes are said to account for about one-fifth of the value of all primary product exports from developing countries. Another group consists of products which are produced in substantial quantities in both developed and less developed countries; this group includes iron ore, copper, zinc, and manganese ore. Finally there is group of primary products which are not only produced also in a number of industrialized countries but which face serious import restrictions in those countries. Obvious examples are sugar, vegetable oils and oilseeds, rice, tobacco and citrus fruits. All in all, it seems unlikely that price raising agreements could cover more than about a quarter of the exports of less developed countries. Such products are coffee, tea, bananas, cocoa, spices and tin.

3. MANUFACTURES AND SEMI-MANUFACTURES

Although manufactures and semi-manufactured goods still account for a very small proportion of total exports of less developed world, it is a rapidly growing share. Moreover, for certain less developed countries, the share of such products in total exports is very large indeed. Virtually all Hong-Kong's exports consist of manufactured goods. In the case of India and Pakistan the proportion is by no means negligible.

There are several reasons, however, why the young manufacturing

TABLE 13. TARIFFS ON SELECTED MANUFACTURES OF INTEREST TO DEVELOPING
COUNTRIES
Pre-Kennedy Round
Per cent *ad valorem* m.f.n.

	EEC	UK	USA
Sports goods	19	10–25	14
Bicycles	17	20	21
Diesel engines up to 50 h.p.	15–19	16–24	9
Electric motors up to 50 h.p.	10–12	17·5	12
Electric fans (domestic)	15	17·5	18
Steel furniture	12–17	15–20	11·5
Sewing machines	12	15	9
Leather footwear	18–20	10–20	9
Coir manufactures	19	17	18
Cotton fabrics	15–18	17·5–25	21
Cotton clothing	20–21	17·5–25	24
Jute manufactures	23	20	9
Arithmetic average of items comprising above groups	16	18	15

SOURCE: GATT.

industries of the less developed countries find it difficult to increase
exports of manufactures sufficiently to compensate them for short-falls
in earnings from primary products. For most manufacturing processes,
a large market is essential; this many countries lack. Incomes per head
are so low as severely to limit the size of the home market and as we
saw in Chapter 23 attempts to establish customs unions in less developed
countries have not so far been conspicuously successful. Unit costs are
accordingly high and this problem is made more difficult by technological deficiencies, poor economic infra-structure and scarcity of
managers. Even where a less developed country successfully establishes
a low cost domestic industry, its prospects of exporting are often
marred by import restrictions in both developed and less developed
countries.

There is evidence that in most industrialized countries tariffs on
products of especial interest to less developed countries are rather
higher than on manufactures generally. A calculation based on GATT
sources, shows EEC, UK and USA, tariffs on a number of products in
which the less developed countries appear to have some comparative

cost advantage. The arithmetic average of these duties is substantially higher than the average for all manufactures. Of course it would be unwise to argue that the reduction or removal of these tariffs would automatically ensure a substantial expansion of manufactured exports from developing countries. After all, India has for years enjoyed duty free entry in the UK for virtually all her manufactured exports, but apart from textiles, the volume of such exports is very small indeed. Supply and marketing problems might well prevent advantage being taken of freer access.

The General System of Preferences

Faced with the difficulties of increasing their exports of manufactures to the industrialized countries, at the first United Nations Conference on Trade and Development (UNCTAD) in 1964 a number of less developed countries proposed a scheme, whereby all less developed countries would enjoy tariff preferences on their exports to industrialized countries. At the 1964 UNCTAD this proposal met with a great deal of opposition from some of the developed countries, notably the USA, but between the 1964 and 1968 Conferences a marked change in attitude occurred. Indeed, at the second Conference the delegates of both groups, developed and less developed voted unanimously in favour of adopting a general system of preferences (GSP). They accordingly agreed to set up a Special Committee on Preferences charged with the task of preparing a scheme which could be brought into operation in 1970.

But by that date it had become clear that the eighteen industrial countries that had undertaken to offer such preferences could not agree on the scope and modalities of a single system. Accordingly, separate schemes were gradually brought into operation; the EEC offer came into effect on July 1, 1971, the Japanese on August 1, the British on January 1, 1972. By that time, the US was the only major industrial country not offering such preferences. The individual schemes differ considerably; some offer a straight elimination of tariffs on LDC's manufactures, the EEC operates a complex country and commodity quota system for such duty-free imports. Most schemes have in common the exclusion or restriction of some 'sensitive' commodities. Among the most important of the latter, and on which restrictions are most resented by the LDCs, are various kinds of textiles and processed foods.

Even so, some important opportunities are created by the GSP; the EEC scheme, for instance, is estimated to cover around $1,000 million worth of trade on the full preferences and $350 million on the limited preferences and to involve a loss to the Community of around $100 ·

million in tariff revenue. The Yaoundé countries have not concealed the fact that they consider the EEC offer to the rest of the 91 LDCs too generous. This brings out a problem associated with such preferential schemes; it involves comparative discrimination against, or a loss of comparative preference to, those countries that had preferential access to major markets before, as had Commonwealth countries with the UK or the Yaoundé and Arusha countries with the EEC. Not all of them will gain sufficiently from new access to compensate for the loss of previously existing preferences.

The full effect of the preferences must be measured not so much against 'nominal' tariff rates but the degree of 'effective' protection taken from industrial country producers.[1] The scheme may in this way be of real benefit to LDCs in establishing processing industries. On the other hand, the benefits are likely to be uneven as some less developed countries are in a very much better position to do so than others. As tariffs on trade between the developed countries are progressively reduced, the value of a general system of preferences to the less developed countries is steadily eroded. The implementation of the Kennedy Round tariff reductions, for example, has made the prefereuce margin less by 1972, than when the proposal was discussed at the 1964 UNCTAD.

4. THE PROBLEM OF AID

The Flow of Aid

We have so far considered primarily the trade problems of the less developed countries. But their economic difficulties are unlikely to be solved by freer or even preferential access, desirable though this may be. A more fundamental problem is to secure the transfer of resources from relatively rich to relatively poor countries. Some transfer of resources from rich to poor countries can be secured by commodity agreements, the liberalization of cotton textiles quotas and generalized preferences. But if living standards are to be raised in the foreseeable future, a much more massive transfer is necessary. Only then will the less developed countries be able to implement their capital investment programmes so essential for economic growth. Accordingly the direct transfer of resources from rich to poor countries by means of grants and loans is necessary—and looks like being so for a long time to come. In a book of this nature we cannot consider the details of the post-war international aid programme. All we can hope to do is to give some idea

---

[1] We have discussed the concept of 'effective' protection in Chapter 6.

of the form that the transfer of resources through aid is taking and to outline some of the problems involved.[1]

In the post-war world, aid takes several forms. It may take the form of outright grants, loans, assistance in kind[2] and technical aid. The flow of resources may be in the form of private investment or Government ('official') aid. Government aid in its turn is subdivided into

TABLE 14. NEW FLOW OF RESOURCES TO DEVELOPING COUNTRIES

($ million)

	Official development assistance	Other flows	Total flows	As percentage of donor countries' GNP at market prices
1960	4,700	3,200	7,900	0·83
1961	5,200	3,900	9,100	0·87
1962	5,500	2,900	8,400	0·76
1963	5,700	2,800	8,500	0·70
1964	5,900	3,200	9,100	0·75
1965	5,800	4,500	10,300	0·78
1966	6,100	3,700	9,800	0·71
1967	6,600	4,700	11,300	0·73
1968	6,400	6,800	13,200	0·79
1969	6,600	7,000	13,600	0·75
1970	6,800	7,900	14,700[1]	0·74

[1] Grants by private voluntary agencies amounted to an additional $840 million. No comparable figures are available for previous years.

SOURCE: Compiled from data of Development Assistance Committee of OECD.

bilateral, that is Government to Government aid, and multilateral aid, made available to the recipient country through one of the international agencies. In all these cases a direct transfer of resources occurs—although if the aid consists of loans, repayment eventually involves a transfer in the reverse direction. Table 14 shows that the annual net flow of

[1] The reader is again referred to the Overseas Development Institute study *World III*, cited above.

[2] The best-known example of aid in kind is the shipment of grain (mostly wheat) from the USA, under the Public Law 480 passed in 1954, whereby US agricultural surpluses are made available to less developed countries. In times of famine these are often sent free, but more usually they are paid for in local currency by the recipient Government, which then disposes of them either by sale or distribution to needy persons and areas. India has been by far the largest beneficiary.

resources from the main donor countries (these are the members of the Development Assistance Committee of the OECD) has risen fairly rapidly since 1960 in absolute terms but has fallen as a percentage of donor countries' Gross National Products at market prices. These percentages should be compared with the target set at the first UNCTAD, where a resolution was adopted recommending that 'each economically advanced country should endeavour to supply financial resources to the developing countries of a minimum net amount approaching as nearly as possible to 1 per cent of its national income'. It was made clear that the 1 per cent target related to official and private capital flows, net of loan repayments and capital repatriation but there has been some dispute as to the definition of national income.[1]

Inter-Government Aid

Inter-Government aid is either bilateral, when country A makes a specific loan or grant to country B, or multilateral, when aid is provided *via* one of the international agencies. By far the greater part of aid (about 90 per cent) is in the form of bilateral country to country assistance, but the International Bank for Reconstruction and Development (IBRD) and its affiliates are increasingly active in the field. Bilateral assistance by a group of donor countries is often co-ordinated, as for example, through the Aid India Consortium set up in 1956, the Aid Turkey Consortium of 1962 or the Colombo Plan which co-ordinates aid to South and South-East Asia. But such aid is still essentially on a Government to Government basis; each donor country determines its contribution and the recipient country is aware of the source of the aid —and of any strings which go with it.

The most important multilateral agency in the aid field is of course the IBRD, set up at the same time as the IMF, and administered on similar lines.[2] The IBRD, sometimes known as the World Bank, finances its activities from its own resources, that is from member countries' subscriptions, and from the sale of bonds on the open market. In its early years the IBRD was concerned primarily with post-war reconstruction in Western Europe; it was not until 1948 that the first loan was made to a less developed country—Chile.[3] Up to 1965, over a third of

---

[1] The less developed countries claimed that national income should be taken to mean gross national product at market prices, whilst the developed donor countries argued that it should be taken at factor cost. For the developed countries as a group, GNP at market prices is about 25 per cent greater than net national product at factor cost. In 1968, the developing countries' claim was accepted.

[2] One of the best factual surveys of the Bank and its affiliates is in M. A. G. Van Meerhaeghe, *International Economic Institutions*, London, Longmans, 1966.

[3] Ibid. p. 130.

IBRD loans were made to Asia and the Middle East, a quarter to the Western Hemisphere and one-eighth to Africa. One-third of the loans financed electrical development, and one-third transport undertakings. Although agriculture and forestry have claimed only 7 per cent of the Bank's loans, much of the expenditure on power and transport has led directly to improvements in the agricultural sector. A feature of the Bank's work is the support given to local development corporations, which are able to assist numerous enterprises, too small for direct Bank financing.[1]

The Bank grants loans for periods of seven to twenty-five years at commercial rates of interest. Before making a loan the Bank satisfies itself as to the credit-worthiness of the country concerned; indeed some of the studies of the IBRD missions provide extremely valuable analysis of economic conditions and prospects in recipient countries. The IBRD finances only the foreign exchange component of a given project.

IDA and IFC

Since the Bank adopts somewhat stringent criteria for the assistance grants, by the 1950s there was a general feeling that its activities should be supplemented by other forms of multilateral assistance. Accordingly, the International Development Association (IDA) was established in 1960 as an affiliate of the IBRD. The IDA is financed separately from the IBRD, with subscriptions from both developed and less developed countries.[2] The object of IDA is to grant assistance on much more liberal terms than the IBRD. Loans are free of interest (although a service charge of 0·75 per cent is imposed), and the repayment period may be up to fifty years, with ten years of grace before repayment need commence. IDA finances a much wider range of economic activity than the IBRD; although most of its credits so far have been for transport, irrigation and power schemes, it also devotes considerable capital to broader educational and social objects. There is no doubt that IDA has fulfilled a useful role; the main difficulty from the middle 1960s has been to find sufficient finance to meet the many urgent claims on its resources.

A quite different function is performed by the World Bank's other affiliate, the International Finance Corporation. Thus was set up in

---

[1] Details of the Bank's current activities are to be found in its *Annual Report*, published in Washington DC. Informative articles also appear in the Fund and Bank Review, *Finance and Development*, published quarterly.

[2] The former must pay their subscription entirely in gold and convertible exchange, while the latter are required to contribute only 10 per cent in this way, the remainder being in national currency.

1956, to invest in private undertakings without Government guarantee. It operates on a commercial basis investing mainly in industrial enterprises; but it never provides more than half the finance required by a particular project. Interest is at commercial rates and repayments are usually between seven and fifteen years. While the IBRD and IDA are lending agencies; the IFC can provide finance also in the form of risk-bearing equity; thus in contrast to both the IBRD 'conventional' lending rate, and the soft terms of IDA credit, IFC financing is as far as possible in line with the expectations of private investors—and is intended to attract their participation. In some instances IFC participation may be needed to provide 'first money' to get a project off the ground. In others it may be required as 'last money' to fill the gap left by private enterprises. By far the biggest commitment of the IFC is in Latin America, but after 1964, the Corporation widened its interests in Africa and Asia. The IFC has its own capital, subscribed by member countries, but from 1966 on, the Corporation has been allowed to supplement its own share capital and reserve by borrowing from the Bank.[1]

Altogether, considerable strides have been taken in establishing aid channels in the last two decades. But a large number of problems remain. Perhaps the most serious is that of servicing past debt.

The burden of past debt has strengthened the demands of the less developed countries for 'softer' loans than they have in the past received. At the 1968 UNCTAD this took the form of the demand that development loans should be based on the very soft IDA model as regards interest rates. At the 1972 UNCTAD in Santiago, demands for dealing with the current repayments burdens were passed but without success. There still remains also, in spite of some assurances given earlier, the unfulfilled demand of the less developed countries that aid should no longer be 'tied' to the exports of a particular donor country.

Theoretically there is much to be said for the untying of aid. When a donor country specifies that aid should be spent upon its own products it not only restricts the number of import choices open to a recipient country, but often forces the recipient to pay a higher price for equipment than would otherwise be necessary. On the other hand, in terms of practical politics, the fact that aid can be tied to its own exports probably encourages Governments to make their aid programmes larger than would otherwise be the case. The serious US balance of payments position would certainly seem to preclude any substantial liberalizing of the present fairly stiff US policy in regard to tying. Moreover, all the

---

[1] There is a most useful article by David Grenier on the work of the IFC in the Fund and Bank Review, *Finance and Development*, vol. iv, no. 2, June 1967.

time that a substantial donor like the US ties its aid, other countries are
likely to follow suit, for fear of losing export opportunities.

In one respect the less developed countries secured an important
concession at the 1968 New Delhi UNCTAD. It was there agreed that
the 1 per cent of national income target for the net flow of resources
from developed to less developed countries should be 1 per cent of
gross national product at market prices (rather than at factor cost). To
this was later added the further demand that official development
assistance should be at least 0·7 per cent of donors' gross national
product. However, at the third UNCTAD in 1972, *total* transfers were
about 0·7 per cent, while *official* assistance accounted for less than half
of even that modest total.

If there was little progress on aid, it was no greater on trade. No concessions were offered by the industrial countries on the central issue of
improved access to their markets for non-competing primary products
(through extended and improved commodity agreements), for competing primary products (through moderation of agricultural support
schemes) or for manufactures (through improvement of the tariff
preference schemes).

Less developed countries were similarly frustrated by the lack of
response to their proposal for 'the link' between the issue of SDRs and
development assistance by way of making future allocations to less
developed countries either directly or through multilateral agencies and
aid schemes. In the event, the industrial countries committed themselves
only to the study and consideration of such schemes.

Perhaps the only tangible progress made at the 1972 UNCTAD had
been the undertaking of special measures for the twenty-five 'least
developed countries' identified as such by the United Nations. Criteria
for inclusion in this category, which covers about a tenth of total Third
World population are gross national product per head of less than £40
as well as a lack of educational and other facilities for development.

5. THE SECOND UN DEVELOPMENT DECADE

The modest achievements of the 1972 UNCTAD were in sharp contrast
with the size of the problem. This can be gauged by the briefest review
of the outcome of the first UN development decade (DD) in the 1960s and
the objectives agreed for the second DD which started in January 1971.
There had been some expectation that the Santiago UNCTAD would
decide the practical measures to implement the policies.

The economic growth for the first DD—5 per cent of GNP a year—

exceeded the target. This result was, however, largely due to the high growth rates obtained by a very small number of countries. On a per capita basis the gains were even smaller for most of the LDCs because of population increases of the order of 2½ per cent a year.

The Strategy for the Seventies gives an overall target of at least 6 per cent growth per year but supplements it with a per capita target of at least 3½ per cent, and includes in its statement of aims a more equitable distribution of income and wealth, higher employment, greater income security and improved facilities for education, health, nutrition, housing and social welfare and the safeguarding of the environment.[1]

The lack of progress at UNCTAD also highlights the two key issues that seem likely to dominate the 1970s: the problem of indebtedness and the problem of unemployment.

External Public Debt

Since the late 1950s, there has been a series of debt crises that could only be overcome by the rescheduling of countries' obligations. In the 1960s, the external public debt of less developed countries rose by about 14 per cent per year and by the end of the decade reached a total of $50 billion. The reverse flow of debt service payments on *official* accounts amounted to $4·7 billion in 1967; this is quite distinct from dividend payments on *private* foreign investments. For 1965–7, debt services equalled 87 per cent of new public loan disbursements in Latin America, 73 per cent in Africa and between 40 per cent and 50 per cent in Asia. On present assumptions, debt services could equal or exceed new lending by 1977.[2]

Unemployment

The annual growth rate of more than 5 per cent throughout the 1960s did nothing to avoid a progressive worsening of the unemployment situation. On the contrary, developing countries sometimes find themselves in a situation where industrial growth leads to a fall in employment as production passes from the handicraft to a capital-intensive industrial stage. A recent report[3] puts unemployment, where statistics exist, at between 8 per cent and 12 per cent. This is visible unemployment and ignores low-productivity employment and underemployment. The report points out that industrial development in the Third World

[1] The reports on the OECD Strategy for Development can be found in the quarterly issues of the OECD *Observer*, particularly after 1970.

[2] *Partners in Development* (the Pearson Report), 1969, pp. 72 ff.

[3] UN Committee for Development Planning, report of Working Party on Unemployment, June 1972.

has tended to overlook the plentiful supply of labour in favour of needlessly high technology production techniques and suggests that this has resulted frequently in a widened gap between a country's rich and poor sectors.

It is estimated that industry will absorb no more than 10 per cent of people seeking employment and that for many years most new employment will have to be found in agriculture. In this connection the introduction of land reforms is recommended, as a disproportionate share of the gains of the Green Revolution, which more than doubled Third World agricultural output in the first DD, tends to go to comparative well-to-do farmers rather than to landless labourers and needy sharecroppers. But even with additional employment on the land, the number of unemployed in the developing countries is expected to reach 200 million within the next two years and rise to 300 million by 1980.

The extent of the problem makes the amount of development assistance provided at present and promised for the future by the richer nations pitifully small. Clearly mankind has a long way to go before it does more than touch the fringe of the problem of world poverty. But the student of international economics has at least the satisfaction of knowing that he is working on problems the solution of which will go some way towards eradicating the poverty and physical misery in which many of his fellow men are at present doomed to live.

SHORT GUIDE TO THE LITERATURE

The number of articles and books in this field is truly enormous and I list below only general studies. Many of these, however, contain references to more specialized works which many students will wish to consult.

As introductory texts I can do little better than suggest, on trade, the Overseas Development Institute handbook by M. Cutajar and Allison Franks, *The Less Developed Countries in World Trade*, London, 1967, and, on aid, the ODI handbook by A. Moyes and Teresa Hayter, *World III*. Bigger and more detailed books are J. Pincus, *Trade, Aid and Development*, New York, McGraw-Hill, 1967, and H. G. Johnson, *Economic Policies Towards Less Developed Countries*, London, 1967. The specialist student should also consult the International Economic Association symposium (ed. R. F. Harrod and D. C. Hague), *International Trade Theory in a Developing World*, London, 1963. A very scholarly study from Hal B. Lary is *Imports of Manufactures from Less Developed Countries*, New York, National Bureau of Economic

Research, 1968. A few libraries possess some of the voluminous documentation prepared for the 1964, 1968 and 1972 UNCTAD. Much of the strategy for the Second Development Decade is based on the wide-ranging Report of the Commission on International Development: *Partners in Development* (called the 'Pearson Report' after its Chairman), 1969. Most up-to-date and detailed information is provided in the *Handbook of International Trade and Development Statistics*, UN, New York, 1972, prepared in connection with the third UNCTAD.

SUBJECT INDEX

absorption approach (incomes) 187–90
accommodating transactions 143–4
Africa 61, 79, 318, 333, 335; South, 61, 241, 263, 266, 335
Agfa-Gaevert merger 312
agricultural policy of EEC 307–10
Albania 329
Algeria 318, 333
American Stabilization Fund 196
Andean Common Market 332–3
Argentine 263, 330, 338
asymmetry in the international monetary system 236, 255
Australia 45–6, 61, 105, 116, 204, 263, 266, 335
Austria 258, 267, 300, 326, 328
autonomous transactions 143–4

balance of payments 140–65; and income changes 166–75; and integration 293–7; and protection 120–1
balancing item 160ff
barter terms of trade 59–62, 64, 66
Basle facility 267–8
Belgium 204, 234n, 273, 292–5, 300, 303, 308
Bolivia 186, 332
Brazil 186, 330
Bretton Woods 223, 224, 226
British Commonwealth Preference Area 273
British Exchange Equalization Account 196
Bulgaria 329
Burma 52
Burundi 233

CACM (Central American Common Market) 274, 331–2
Canada 53, 121, 229, 248, 258, 263, 271, 300n, 302, 335; experiment in fluctuating exchange rates 197–200

CARIFTA (Caribbean Free Trade Area) 318
Cartagena agreement see Andean Common Market
Central African Republic 333
Central American Common Market see CACM
Ceylon 266, 342n
Chad 167, 333
Chile 330, 332, 349
China 335, 339
CMEA (Council for Mutual Economic Aid) (Comecon) 329–30
Code of Liberalization 87
Colombia 330, 332
Comecon see CMEA
common agricultural policy 307ff, 324
Commonwealth Sugar Agreement 339
Community indifference curve 72–4
consumption effects 138, 139
Costa Rica 331
Council for Mutual Economic Aid (Comecon) see CMEA
Cuba 339
currency adjustment 179–87; systems 16, 17
customs union 274–88
Cyprus 318, 335
Czechoslovakia 329

Dahomey 333
demand elasticities 183, 184
Denmark 69–71, 105, 267, 300, 326, 339
devaluation 21, 266–71
Development Assistance Committee 348ff
dollar standard 257–9; dollar surplus 132–4

Ecuador 330, 332
EEC (European Economic Community) 59, 121, 274, 279, 281, 282, 292–7 passim, 299, 305–25, 328, 340, 346–7

357

NAME INDEX

Alexander, S. S. 187n, 190
Andic: F. 334; S. 334
Artus, R. E. 199n
Aubrey, H. G. 302n
Aufricht, H. 228n

Balacs, P. D. 161n
Balassa, Bela 48-9, 81, 94, 185n, 282, 287n, 312n
Baldwin, R. E. 165n
Ball, R. J. 185
Barker, T. S. 80n
Bastable, C. 31
Beckerman, W. 33n
Benham 115n
Bernstein 244n
Beveridge, W. 115n
Bhagwati, J. 28n, 47n, 55, 67, 75n
Bharadwaj, R. 52
Black, S. W. 255n
Bloomfield, A. 211
Bowley 115n
Branson, W. H. 254n, 255n
Brassloff, E. W. 319, 334
Brodsky, G. 378, 387
Brown: A. J. 51; W. A., Jr 84n; W. R., Jr 211
Buchanan, N. S. 50
Burton, F. N. 151n
Butterwick, M. 325

Cairncross, Sir Alec 186n
Cairnes, J. E. 30-2
Cary, John 23n
Caves, Richard E. 23n, 34n, 44n, 45n, 48n, 55, 74n, 93n, 95, 108, 124n, 131, 135n, 190, 201, 215n
Chamberlain, Neville 83
Churchill, Winston 223
Clarke, W. M. 153n
Clement, M. O. 23n
Cobden, Richard 83

Coffey, P. 325
Cohen, B. J. 256n, 272
Conan, A. R. 267, 270n, 272
Cooper, Richard N. 260, 270
Corden, W. M. 23n, 53n, 55, 80n, 94, 95, 135n, 139, 215, 221, 288
Cutajar, M. 343n, 354
Cutler, D. S. 246

Dell, Sidney 334
Denton, G. 314n, 325
Devons, Ely 64, 148n
Diebold, W., Jr 84n, 301n, 304n
Dorrance, G. S. 65-6
Dosser, Douglas 312n, 334
Dunn, R. M., Jr 201
Dunning, J. H. 155

Edgeworth, F. Y. 33, 109
Ellis, H. S. 67
Ellsworth, P. T. 51, 52

Fleming, J. M. 93, 94
Ford, A. G. 211
Forsyth, M. 325
Frank, I. 325
Franks, A. 343n, 354
Frisch, Ragnar 93

Galambos, P. 151n
Galbraith, V. L. 85n
Gardner, Walter 164, 165
Graham, F. D. 34-6
Grenier, D. 351n
Grubel, H. G. 80n, 244n, 256n

Haberler, Gottfried 15, 20, 23n, 38, 39, 41, 43, 46, 55, 65-7, 74n, 76, 96, 107, 108, 125, 195n, 248, 249n, 257n, 258n
Hague, D. C. 354
Halm, G. N. 250n
Hamilton, Alexander 99n